NUCLEAR INC.

NUCLEAR INC.

The Men and
Money Behind Nuclear Energy

Mark Hertsgaard

Pantheon Books, New York

To Mom,

and to Dad

*Grateful acknowledgment is made to the following for
permission to reprint previously published material:*

Business Week: Excerpt from article "The Petro-Crash
of the 1980's," quoted from November 19, 1979 issue of
Business Week by special permission. Copyright © 1979
by McGraw-Hill Book Co., Inc. All rights reserved.
Forbes Magazine: Excerpt from article in *Forbes*, June
1, 1966. Reprinted by permission of *Forbes* Magazine.
Fortune Magazine: Excerpt from article by John
McKitterick. Reproduced from *Fortune*, October 1970,
by permission of *Fortune* Magazine.
Monthly Review Press: Excerpt from *Monopoly Capital*
by Paul A. Baran and Paul M. Sweezy. Copyright ©
1966 by Paul M. Sweezy. Reprinted by permission of
Monthly Review Press.
Washington Post: Excerpt from article by Joanne
Omang, *Washington Post*, March 28, 1980. Copyright ©
1980 by the *Washington Post*. Reprinted by permission
of the *Washington Post*.

Library of Congress Cataloging in Publication Data

Hertsgaard, Mark, 1956-
Nuclear inc.
Includes bibliographical references and index.
1. Atomic energy industries—United States.
I. Title.
HD9698.U52H47   1983   338.4'762147'0973   82-
48952
ISBN 0-394-53040-3

Manufactured in the United States of America

First American Edition

Contents

Acknowledgments

The Institute for Policy Studies is literally the only place in the United States where I could have written this book. Nowhere else would a young and unproven writer have found the financial support and especially the intellectual freedom to pursue this complex and controversial subject. Everyone at the Institute has helped me in one way or another over the years, often without knowing it, but I am particularly grateful to Robert Borosage, the director, who let me talk my way into writing this book. I hope the finished product lives up to his implicit vote of confidence. Special thanks also to my friend and colleague Michael Moffitt, who first brought me to the Institute in 1976 and from whom I have since learned much. Richard Barnet and Howard Wachtel were important mentors to me. Basker Vashee was a comrade in the fullest sense of the word. Doug Ireland arranged the right introduction at the right time.

Financial support was provided by Pro Bono Publico, the Funding Exchange, the Youth Project, David Hunter and the Stern Fund, the Musicians United For Safety Energy, and Stanley Weiss.

Others who helped in innumerable, important ways were Patrice Gallagher, Lynn Kitzmiller, Michael Rossiter, San Lepper, Robert Engler, Louis Clark, Carol Benke, Susan Coyle, Ken Barr, Jill Bullitt, David Fenton, Denis Hayes, Jeff Stein, Bereket Selassie, Ann Wilcox, Harvey Wasserman, Diana De Vegh, John Berger, Alyce Wiley, Alice Mayhew, Kim Newton, Rachel Fershko, Charlotte Jackson, Deirdre English, Mark Dowie, Norman Levy, James Cox, Doris Porter, and Nancy Lewis.

Peter Hertsgaard, Joshua Klein, Molly Andrews, Albert Staats, John Gunn, and Boyd Gilman searched, copied, filed and searched again; I hope they learned as much from our brief associations as I did. Todd Anderson did thorough research, offered provocative comments, and responded to the final emergency. John Alves kept me from straying and gave me a title. Ric Pfeffer helped show me the path. The memories of Orlando Letelier and Ronni Karpen Moffitt keep me moving along it.

André Schiffrin, managing director of Pantheon Books, was the first person in the publishing business who didn't need to be told what made this different from other nuclear books. Wendy Goldwyn was a marvelous editor: committed, insightful, hard-working, and possessed not only of an understanding of my vision but also a willingness to let me take risks in pursuing it. LynNell Hancock's rare gift of indefatigable cheerfulness made the last mile much easier.

David, Anna, Mary, Betsy, Denny, Dick, Patrice, Gareth, Mark, Andy, Peter, Marc, Tom, Susan, and all my family freely gave love and support when I needed it most. To each of them, a special thanks.

MARK HERTSGAARD
December, 1982
Paris

Author's Note

I began the investigation that resulted in this book in 1978, while working at the Institute for Policy Studies, an independent research institute in Washington, D.C. My goal in writing the book was to tell the story of America's nuclear establishment with the thoroughness, critical analysis, and historical sweep of scholarship and the pace, human insight, and immediacy of journalism.

Surveying the many written histories of atomic energy in the United States, I quickly found that none of them focused specifically on the industry that grew up around the technology. Important pieces of the story had been told, especially in the remarkable volumes that Atomic Energy Commission official historian Richard G. Hewlett and others had written about the AEC's activities through the mid-1950s; for any student of atomic history, *The New World*, *The Atomic Shield*, and *The Nuclear Navy* are the necessary starting points. *The Nuclear Barons*, Peter Pringle and James J. Spigelman's superbly written and comprehensive account of global nuclear development, proved an invaluable source of anecdotes and information regarding the early years of nuclear power and the government officials who promoted it. The RAND Corporation's study *The Development and Commercialization of the Light Water Reactor* and Irvin C. Bupp and Jean-Claude Derian's *Light Water* described how and why the light water reactor came to be the dominant U.S. design, and the enormous and troubling consequences of that choice for global nuclear power development. *The Atomic Establishment*, by H. Peter Metzger, exposed the corruption of oversight responsibility and other misdeeds on the part of the AEC and the Joint Committee on Atomic Energy that led to the abolishment of both bodies in the mid-1970s. And Warren H. Donnelly of the U.S. Library of Congress had written extensively and insightfully on the relationship between the development of the commercial nuclear industry and U.S. foreign policy measures such as Atoms for Peace.

The many hearings the Joint Committee on Atomic Energy held and the reports the AEC issued concerning the industry's development were also important sources of information, but the histor-

ical narrative that comprises chapters 2 through 4 of this book could
not have been written had I not had access to the industry's own
historical records and its executives' personal recollections. The
Atomic Industrial Forum kindly allowed me to visit the library in
its Bethesda, Maryland office, where I spent weeks poring over all
available issues of *Forum Memo*, the monthly newsletter the trade
association began publishing in 1953, and of *Nucleonics*, the predecessor of *Nucleonics Week*. To assess nuclear power's performance and reception within the business world, I reviewed all
nuclear-related articles that appeared from 1960 onward in *Business Week, Fortune, Forbes, Barron's*, and other business-oriented
publications.

The executives themselves were my richest source of information about not only the industry's history but also its structure, day-
to-day operations, ideology, and strategy for the future—topics explored in chapters 5 through 8. I conducted over one hundred
hours of formal, tape-recorded interviews with forty key executives
from twelve top companies that represented each of the industry's
main sectors: reactor and component manufacturing, power plant
construction, uranium production, and electricity generation; a full
list of names, titles, and company affiliations is included in appendix 1. The companies, the public relations officials who scheduled
my interviews, and the executives themselves were with few exceptions gracious, cooperative, and eager to tell their story. (One
firm, reactor manufacturer Combustion Engineering, allowed me
to speak with its executives only on the condition that material
resulting from the interviews be reviewed by the company for
accuracy prior to publication.)

The reason I was made so welcome, I think, was that the companies realized I took them seriously and hence was likely to give
their views a fair presentation at a time when they were increasingly coming under public attack. I had written each of them three-
page, single-spaced letters describing the Institute for Policy Studies and the book I hoped to write. I explained that I intended, not
to "prove" the case about nuclear energy one way or the other, but
to analyze the industry behind it—its history, its strengths and
weaknesses, and especially its future prospects. I identified eight
separate types of individuals whom I wished to interview—including an engineer, domestic and international sales representatives,
a lawyer, and the most senior executive in charge of nuclear affairs—and listed the questions I wished to ask of each. In almost
every case, my requests were granted. Later in the investigation,

I also managed to interview the chief executive officer (a corporation's number one official) at eight of the industry's leading firms.

Scores of interviews were also conducted with sources throughout official Washington—in Congress, the White House, the Departments of State and Energy, and the Nuclear Regulatory Commission. To balance the industry perspective, I spoke with financial analysts at such prominent Wall Street investment banks as Drexel Burnham, Brown Brothers Harriman, and Moseley, Hallgarten and Estabrook, and with antinuclear activists and researchers.

Many of my formal corporate interviews took place in early 1979, before the Three Mile Island accident of March 28, but I do not believe that my portrayal of the industry is thereby rendered inaccurate. Since the accident, I have continued to meet and to talk with executives often, over the telephone and at industry conferences and social gatherings, and to follow their activities closely in the trade press. Moreover, the industry's history, composition, and internal dynamics and its executives' backgrounds and personal beliefs—all topics explored at length in the formal interviews—did not change after the accident, and neither did the basic problems threatening the industry's survival.

Citations for the quoted material and facts that inform the text, as well as additional documentation and suggestions for further reading, can be found in the Notes at the end of the book. Tables listing the industry's top twenty-four firms and detailing their size and nuclear involvement are to be found in appendix 2. The information on the corporations' debt, stock ownership, and relationships with financial institutions was compiled by the Corporate Data Exchange, a nonprofit organization in New York City.

NUCLEAR INC.

Energy: The
Struggle for Tomorrow

Knowledge will forever govern ignorance; and a
people who mean to be their own governors must
arm themselves with the power which knowledge
gives.

JAMES MADISON

Great turning points in human history are always times of opportunity and struggle, and the global energy revolution now under
way is no exception. Although decades remain before the Earth
surrenders its last drop of oil to humanity, the signs are unmistakable that the Age of Petroleum is passing; human civilization in
the twenty-first century will rest upon a radically different energy
foundation.

The struggle over what that foundation shall be, and how we
will navigate the transition from here to there, has already reached
a fierce intensity. How it is resolved will have a profound influence
on everything the people of the world do, from the feeding and
employment of every individual to the preservation of a livable
environment and the prevention of thermonuclear war. Energy is
central to all organized human activity, and it is the absolute life-
blood of an advanced industrial society like the United States.
Without it, factories and offices fall silent, food cannot get to market, transportation and communication become impossible, chaos
and misery soon reign. What we do about energy will shape our
society and our daily lives for decades to come.

For more than thirty years, atomic fission has been proclaimed
by government and business leaders throughout the industrial
world as the solution to the challenge posed by the eventual ex-
haustion of fossil fuels. In the United States and the Soviet Union,
in Europe and Japan, billions of dollars have been spent grooming
nuclear energy as petroleum's successor. Nuclear power: the ulti-

mate technical fix. Nuclear fast breeder reactors promised to produce virtually limitless energy for centuries; man had finally created the perpetual-motion machine that could free him from
scarcity forever; he had become master of the natural world around
him. Humanity had gained, in the words of one early atomic proponent, "a chance to enter a new Eden . . . abolishing disease and
poverty, anxiety and fear." Throughout the 1950s and 1960s, nation
after nation tied its energy future to the magic of the atom. Even
countries that still derived much of their energy from burning wood
bought nuclear reactors.

Such exuberance has inevitably faded in recent years as yesterday's glorious visions gave way to a disappointing reality. The story
is essentially the same in every country with an advanced nuclear
program. Questions about safety precautions were raised repeatedly during the 1970s and answers, when they were given at all,
were not very reassuring. Economics, which had always been advanced as nuclear power's strongest selling point, became an increasingly embarrassing subject for atomic proponents as nuclear
power plants suffered frequent shutdowns for repairs and threefold
and fourfold cost overruns. By the end of the decade critics in the
United States were pointing to the slowing growth in the nation's
demand for electricity and to the feasibility of such alternatives as
solar energy as evidence that nuclear power was unnecessary and
could be gradually phased out altogether. Increasing numbers of
their fellow citizens were agreeing; opposition to nuclear power
rose slowly but steadily throughout the decade, not just in the
United States but also in Japan and Western Europe, even though
those countries lacked America's vast domestic energy resources.
Officialdom by and large dismissed the doubters either as misin-
formed or as troublemakers, and continued to promote nuclear
power. But the March 1979 accident at the Three Mile Island plant
in Pennsylvania gave new credibility to those who had been warning that splitting atoms was an unacceptably dangerous way to
obtain electricity. Israel's pre-emptive bombing raid in June 1981
against a nuclear reactor in Iraq that Israel claimed was being used
to prepare nuclear weapons further reminded the world that the
line between the civilian and the military atom was easily crossed.
Then, just as opposition to nuclear power seemed to be cresting,
it was joined by a spontaneous, unprecedented international out-
burst of mass opposition to nuclear weapons. Two-million-plus
people marched in the capitals of Western Europe in the fall of

1981, and another three-quarters of a million took over the streets of New York the following June to demand an end to the nuclear arms race.

Today the nuclear enterprise faces the gravest crisis in its history. The 1980s were supposed to be a time of triumph and vindication for the politicians and businessmen who joined together in the 1950s to show the world there was also a peaceful, benevolent side to the energy force that had destroyed Hiroshima and Nagasaki; instead they find themselves struggling for their very survival. The four giant companies that are the mainspring of the U.S. commercial nuclear industry—reactor manufacturers Westinghouse, General Electric, Combustion Engineering, and the Babcock and Wilcox subsidiary of McDermott—have not received a domestic nuclear power plant order since 1977. Electricity-demand growth plunged after 1973 from its traditional 7 percent annual rate to an average of 3.5 percent for the rest of the decade. U.S. electric utility companies, the reactor manufacturers' main customers, were consequently left with trickling cash flows and many more power plants operating than they could possibly use. In response, they not only stopped buying new nuclear plants but eventually canceled eight previous orders. The Big Four reactor manufacturers hoped that foreign sales might make up for the domestic market slump, but there too they were stymied. The markets of Western Europe and Japan were for all practical purposes closed in the early 1970s to protect domestic nuclear industries suffering from the same problems as their American counterpart. And stiff competition from the French and the West Germans, combined with mounting foreign-debt burdens of once potentially major customers such as Brazil and Mexico, meant sales to Third World countries were few and far between.

It was not supposed to work out this way. Building nuclear power plants was supposed to have been as sure a path to immense riches as drilling oil was. Almost a dozen giant companies fought in the bloody corporate battle waged in the late 1950s and early 1960s for control of the American nuclear industry, and each shared the assumption that nuclear power would be one of the world's largest and most profitable businesses for decades to come. But these hopes were frustrated even for the Big Four manufacturers that managed to survive the shake-out battle when the nuclear market collapsed in the mid-1970s. At the time, the Four were just about to recover their huge initial investments and begin reaping the substantial profits they had long anticipated. But now, according to General Electric's nuclear vice-president Bertram Wolfe, "It's questionable whether we will ever be cumulatively profitable, whether the returns on the business will ever make up for our losses plus the interest they would be accruing."

Yet contrary to the conventional wisdom in energy circles, nuclear power is not dead in the United States. Despite the many setbacks, the men who run America's leading nuclear corporations are not giving up. High-level executives from each of the Big Four told a 1982 conference on the industry's future that their firms were committed to staying in the nuclear business indefinitely. John West, nuclear vice-president at Combustion Engineering, said his company had not yet shut down any of its nuclear facilities because it wanted to be ready "for when [the business] revives—not if, but when." Philip Bray of General Electric said that GE also was "preparing for the future resurgence of nuclear projects in America," and explained, "We were the first. We aren't going to stop now."

At the heart of the executives' determination to press on is an absolutely unshakable faith in the inevitability of nuclear power. The Three Mile Island accident did not cause industry leaders to reconsider this basic assumption. "I just don't understand this talk about nuclear being dead," complained Leo Yochum, Westinghouse's top financial officer, barely forty-eight hours after the accident began. "There's a nuclear imperative in this country. We know it, Wall Street knows it, and we're prepared to meet it."

Three Mile Island was actually a blessing in disguise for the nuclear executives. Not only did it shock them into realizing that their nuclear imperative was not necessarily a self-fulfilling one, it also spurred them into action while there was still time to win the nuclear fight. Two weeks after the accident, industry officials were already planning a massive public relations campaign designed to convince Americans that the United States cannot survive as a free and prosperous nation without nuclear power. Robert Kirby, chief executive officer of industry leader Westinghouse, told his industry colleagues at the Atomic Industrial Forum's 1979 annual conference, "The public must be told that it will have to choose ... between nuclear energy and some tough alternatives. Alternatives like inflation, higher unemployment, no economic growth, and national insecurity." By the spring of 1982 the industry's newly formed Committee for Energy Awareness had communicated that message to millions of Americans and was requesting an increase in its annual budget to between $25 and $40 million so that it might spread the word even more effectively through a nationwide campaign of pronuclear television commercials. A public opinion poll *CBS News* conducted in April 1979, while the Three Mile Island accident was still fresh in people's minds, indicated that Americans may well be swayed by the industry's message. For although the poll found that opposition to nuclear power had grown sharply in the previous two years, it also showed that, when given a choice between further nuclear development and paying higher prices for foreign oil, Americans favored nuclear two to one.

The industry's comeback effort has gone virtually unremarked in the mass media, perhaps because most discussion of nuclear power there tends to focus on issues of safety and costs and to neglect broader questions of economic interest and power. For all the reports, pro and con, about the economic and health effects of nuclear power plants, there has been surprisingly little investigation of the corporations that actually produce them. Americans wishing to participate in the national political debate that must ultimately settle the fate of nuclear power are thus deprived of information essential to an informed opinion. The widespread belief that nuclear power is all but finished in the United States, for example, reflects a profound underestimation of the power and determination of the economic interests behind nuclear power as well as a naïveté about what exactly is at stake in the nuclear struggle.

The twenty-four giant transnational corporations that dominate the nuclear power industry constitute what may be the single largest and most powerful business enterprise in history. They sold a staggering $400 billion worth of products in 1981, and all but five of them rank among the one hundred fifty biggest companies in America. Their enormous influence over the U.S. economy is amplified still further by close associations with eight of the nation's nine biggest banks, its seven largest insurance companies, and many of its top investment and law firms. Along with their allies in the electric utility industry, they have invested countless billions of dollars in the nuclear business. Understandably, they are committed to recovering a profit on that investment. But it is a cynical and condescending analysis that ascribes the industry's calls for a nuclear revival to simple corporate greed. In fact, most nuclear executives deeply believe that theirs is a moral and just cause. They regard nuclear power as the very embodiment of progress and feel privileged to help bring it into being. In their minds, what is at stake in the struggle over nuclear power is not just their own corporations' profitability but the future of American capitalism, technological society, and indeed Western civilization. As Bertram Wolfe of General Electric declares, "A large percentage of the people involved go through the frustrations of this business because they fundamentally believe that what is at risk is American society."

The 1980 election of Ronald Reagan gave a powerful boost to the industry's counteroffensive. The President himself has been a vocal nuclear advocate since his days as public spokesman for General Electric in the 1950s, and the men he appointed as his chief nuclear power advisers were either drawn directly from the industry or were very sympathetic to its plight. Reviving commercial nuclear power is a top priority for the Reagan administration. Nuclear power was the only major nonentitlements program, besides the military, that Reagan completely spared during his first year of federal budget cuts. Besides increasing federal subsidies to nuclear power, the Reagan administration also reversed much of the previous Carter policy to contain the global spread of nuclear weapons by lifting the ban Carter had placed on nuclear fuel reprocessing and by easing restrictions against U.S. nuclear exports. In its first major nuclear-power policy statement, the administration delivered what industry executives had long said they needed more than anything else: a strong presidential endorsement of the safety and necessity of nuclear power, and a commitment to slash the "morass of [government safety] regulations that do not enhance safety but that do cause . . . economic uncertainty."

Ronald Reagan's bold actions seemed to re-establish a unity of approach between the government and the industry that had not existed since the days of the Nixon presidency and the old Atomic Energy Commission. In fact, Washington has always been a more than equal partner to the corporations in developing nuclear power. The United States' experience in this regard is not unique: the state plays, if anything, an even more active role in other countries' nuclear programs, for a simple reason. The very nature of nuclear fission technology makes close and permanent state involvement inevitable. The enormous expense and risk involved in harnessing the power of the atom are simply beyond the capability of private enterprise. Moreover, as U.S. policymakers have recognized since the end of World War II, there is no firm line dividing the military and nonmilitary uses of atomic energy; national security therefore demands that the state maintain an effective veto over commercial power development. And because the production processes of nuclear power and nuclear weapons are, in the words of a key 1946 government report, "in much of their course interchangeable and interdependent," the same private corporations and government agencies that produce one often produce the other as well.

It is to convey this interconnection between the nuclear corporations and their government sponsors that I have chosen to call the entire conglomeration America's Atomic Brotherhood. But there is a second reason for the name as well, for this interconnection is not just financial and organizational but also profoundly ideological. A striking characteristic of leading figures throughout America's Atomic Brotherhood is an almost religious devotion to atomic energy and all for which it stands. These men share a deep faith in the essential goodness and above all the historical inevitability of atomic energy. They are proud of their past accomplishments and they look forward to building a nuclear future. Through their fascination with and loyalty to atomic energy, they are bonded together like members of the same religious order or fraternal society. To be sure, this has not prevented frequent and sometimes bitter quarrels within the Brotherhood. As we shall see, there have been numerous instances in the Brotherhood's forty-year history where the wishes of the corporate executives clashed with those of the national security managers and politicians. But the disputes were usually over means, not ends, and, as with real brothers, were consistently put aside when one or the other faced attack from an outsider. The importance of this solidarity to the future struggle over nuclear power can scarcely be overestimated. It unifies and strengthens the men of the Brotherhood against adversity and motivates them to keep fighting in full expectation of victory.

This book tells the story of America's Atomic Brotherhood and its determination to make ours a nuclear nation and world. It is still too early to do more than speculate about the likelihood of their success. All that can be said with certainty is that the struggle over nuclear power is far from ended.

2

The Birth of
the Atomic Brotherhood

> We managed to build the bomb. Then, with a bril-
> liant sense of public relations, we called the power
> production by the same name—*nuclear* power. It
> was crazy. It's like if Edison had invented the elec-
> tric chair and then tried to market light bulbs.* We'd
> probably still be reading by candlelight.
>
> EDWARD SCHERER,
> *Director of Licensing,*
> *Nuclear Power Systems Division,*
> *Combustion Engineering, Inc.*

What went wrong with nuclear power? How did it come to verge
on collapse in this country? In the 1950s Americans welcomed it
as a technological panacea and hailed its discoverers as heroes.
But although some still hold that view, the intervening years have
witnessed an unmistakable change in attitudes. According to an
NBC News/Associated Press poll released in November 1981, 56
percent of the American public now opposes the construction of
more nuclear plants—up from 25 percent in a similar poll conducted in 1977.

---

* Edison did invent the electric chair, but for a different reason. Contrary to popular
mythology, he was as much a hard-driving, clever businessman as he was a talented
inventor. Back when electricity was still a novelty, Edison began to promote centrally located, privately owned power stations as a way of creating a market for
electricity. His plan was based on the use of "direct" current; his main competitor
relied on "alternating" current. Edison invented the electric chair, which ran on
"alternating" current, and then persuaded the state of New York to adopt it for use
against criminals. He hoped that demonstrations of his new invention would turn
public opinion against his competitor's product, which Edison named "killer" current. What makes this tale particularly relevant here is that Edison's competitor
was George Westinghouse, father of the Westinghouse Electric Company that is
now the world's leading nuclear power company. Just to make the story complete,
Edison himself was later bought out by J. P. Morgan, the great American financier,
whose Thompson-Hudson Company later became General Electric. Westinghouse
and GE have been rivals ever since in many fields, including nuclear power.

Today, barely a generation after its birth, America's nuclear power industry is at a crossroads. Is it, as many observers suspect, headed for extinction? Or will it, as industry executives steadfastly maintain, rebound from its current troubles and eventually become a major supplier of energy for the United States?

Questions about the industry's future cannot be answered without first understanding its past. Many of the basic strengths and weaknesses that today characterize the industry can be traced to their beginnings in the formative years of the 1940s and 1950s and to the contradictory relationship which then took shape between the industry and the federal government. The primary impetus for nuclear power development came, not from private entrepreneurs seeking a profitable new line of business, but from top officials within the government's national security apparatus who viewed nuclear power in much the same way they viewed nuclear weapons: as an instrument for achieving their postwar goal of expanding and consolidating American power around the world. America's development of nuclear power was organized from the start by a partnership of private corporations and the national security apparatus of the federal government—a fact that has dominated the industry's entire history.

The story begins during World War II with the Manhattan Project. "The Manhattan Project"* was the code name for the top-secret $2 billion effort sponsored by the U.S. government to produce the world's first nuclear weapons. It was there that the corporations, universities, and government agencies that later came to dominate the nation's nuclear energy program first collaborated. Out of that collaboration emerged the Atomic Brotherhood that has set the course of American nuclear development ever since.

The Manhattan Project began in August 1942 when President Roosevelt, advised (mistakenly, as it turned out) that Hitler's Germany was well on the way to building an atomic bomb, secretly ordered the U.S. Army to get there first. Roosevelt chose Colonel (soon to be General) Leslie R. Groves to direct what has been called "the greatest single achievement of organized effort in history."

The President and his national security advisers were for obvious reasons anxious that word about the Project not leak out. The first stage of U.S. government–sponsored atomic research had begun in

---

* The actual code name was "The Manhattan Engineering District," but here I use the popularly recognized identification.

June 1940 after Roosevelt unilaterally established the National Defense Research Committee, a group of top scientists from such leading American universities as Harvard and the Massachusetts Institute of Technology. In the fall of 1941, when Roosevelt endorsed full interchange between the American and the more advanced British atomic research programs, he ordered that budget, schedule, and other major policy considerations be restricted to a small group composed of himself, Vice-President Henry Wallace, Secretary of War Henry Stimson, Army Chief of Staff General George C. Marshall, Office of Scientific Research and Development Director Vannevar Bush, and National Defense Research Committee member and Harvard University president James B. Conant. The President deliberately concealed the program's existence from Congress by burying it within the Office of Scientific Research and Development budget, which he controlled directly.

"Three months' delay might be fatal," Harvard president Conant warned the rest of the group in the summer of 1942. Given Conant's conclusion, based on Allied intelligence reports, that the Germans were perhaps as much as a year ahead of the Allies in the race for the atomic bomb, the six men directing the Manhattan Project agreed that there was no time to inform Congress fully about the top-secret program. In 1944, when steeply rising costs made direct congressional appropriations unavoidable, Stimson, Marshall, and Bush clandestinely met with the top congressional leadership and described the broad outline of the Project; the necessary funds were approved without floor debate. Fear of Nazi spies led to extraordinary security precautions within the Project as well. Among the 150,000 people employed in the Manhattan Project, very few knew the actual purpose of their work. General Groves prohibited communication among scientists working in different laboratories (a precaution that scientist Leo Szilard, among others, later complained slowed progress considerably); security police censored mail and listened in on telephone conversations.

Although it was Groves, Bush, Stimson, and the other top officials who set its basic direction, the actual work on the Manhattan Project was done by men and women drawn from America's leading universities and private corporations. The construction and operation of the sophisticated equipment that eventually produced the enriched uranium and plutonium used in the Hiroshima and Nagasaki bombs required the industrial expertise of large corporations like Du Pont and Union Carbide. And without the brilliant scientists from such elite universities as Columbia, Chicago, and California, solutions to the countless theoretical and practical problems of creating atomic bombs would not have been found. With the federal treasury behind him, General Groves had little trouble acquiring topnotch scientific talent. For the industrial expertise he needed, he called on traditional War Department contractors such as Westinghouse and Dow Chemical. Because these giant companies had done military work in the past, Groves could easily and without delay approach their top executives about the Project. Equally important, he could trust them to keep quiet about his offer. A third obvious attraction of corporations like General Electric and Union Carbide was their immense size and sophistication, which allowed them to mobilize vast amounts of resources overnight.

Both the universities and the companies were attracted to the Manhattan Project for a mixture of idealistic and pragmatic reasons. Patriotism was of course a powerful motivation. "During the war, the importance of the effort drew many of the country's best people into the nuclear work," recalls Joseph Dietrich, formerly the top nuclear scientist at reactor manufacturer Combustion Engineering. But for the corporations, the benefits of getting in on the ground floor of a technology that one day might revolutionize human civilization were also obvious, especially to the high-technology firms Groves had approached about the Project. Groves made it still easier for companies to accept his invitation by offering something the U.S. government had never before provided: "cost-plus" contracts. By pledging to absorb all costs and pay the company an additional fixed fee, such contracts guaranteed profits in advance at no risk to the company.

Centralization of authority, strict secrecy, and fantastic government subsidies were unavoidable if America was to win the nuclear bomb race. The only hitch was that these tactics for coping with the wartime emergency did not fade away after the race was won. Rather, it became clear that they were directly linked to the nature of nuclear technology. Too expensive for private firms to develop alone and too dangerous for the government not to control absolutely, nuclear energy in its postwar development was destined to reflect its wartime upbringing.

In his memoirs Harry Truman wrote that he was morally opposed to hunting, on the ground that one should not shoot at creatures that can't shoot back. Had Truman applied this same code of ethics to human beings, he might not have given the orders in August

1945 that led to the mass execution of thousands of Japanese civilians. Although he had assumed the vice-presidency in January
1945, Truman was told nothing about the Manhattan Project until
he became President upon Roosevelt's death on April 12. From
the moment he learned an atomic bomb could be built, however,
he was determined it would be used. He made no effort to block
the considerable bureaucratic momentum towards dropping a
bomb that had accumulated during the Project's three years of full-
speed effort; as General Groves later assessed it, Truman's decision
to use the bomb "was one of noninterference—basically, a decision
not to upset the existing plans." Along with his top advisers, Truman ignored considerable evidence, primarily intercepted cable
traffic, indicating that the Japanese were eager to agree to surrender
terms, and clung to the belief that dropping the bomb was necessary to shorten the war and save American lives. Fifteen years later
James Byrnes, Secretary of State at the time of the Hiroshima and
Nagasaki bombings, revealed that global power politics was an
equally important motivation when he admitted that the attacks
were intended to limit Soviet postwar influence in Asia as much
as to precipitate an unconditional Japanese surrender. The sudden
obliteration of two major population centers did give the Soviet
Union, as well as the rest of the world, a clear warning that the
United States was not to be crossed in the postwar era. As British
historian P. M. S. Blackett has written, "The dropping of the atomic
bombs was not so much the last military act of the second world
war as [it was] one of the first major operations of the cold diplomatic war with Russia. . . ."

When the new Congress convened in early 1946, there was no
question that the United States would continue its atomic energy
program. The strongest pressure for building more atomic bombs
came from top national security officials, who insisted that the
United States be ready and able to wage atomic warfare against
the Soviet Union in the postwar era. To retreat from atomic superiority would be perceived by the Kremlin as a sign of American
weakness, argued Presidential Counsel Clark Clifford in a secret
1946 memo to President Truman. Clifford advised that the United
States "should entertain no proposal for disarmament or limitation
of armament as long as the possibility of Soviet aggression exists."
National security officials believed the secret of atomic weapons
had to be protected at all costs, for two reasons. The first was an
understandable determination to protect the physical security of
the United States; a country that somehow obtained atomic secrets

could make bombs that it could then drop on the United States. The second was the enormous political leverage the atom would give over other nations, especially the Soviet Union. Truman and his advisers thought that by hoarding their secrets they could maintain the American atomic monopoly for perhaps another twenty years. During that time American dominance of world affairs would be beyond challenge. And even if other countries did eventually discover the secret on their own, the United States by then would have attained an insurmountable advantage in atomic technology.

The American aspirations to an enduring atomic monopoly turned out to be, as Chester Barnard, then a Bell Telephone executive and top nuclear adviser to the Truman administration, later admitted, "a most deadly illusion." Robert Oppenheimer and other Manhattan Project scientists had warned the President and his top advisers that other countries would probably be able to build their own bombs within four to five years. After all, the British and the Canadians knew the basic secrets from their participation in the wartime project; and the French, Germans, and Soviets were able to make fairly educated guesses. These countries were hardly blind to the atom's revolutionary implications for global power politics, and they were determined not to be left behind the Americans. Stalin, for example, soon after Hiroshima summoned his top physicists and engineers to the Kremlin and addressed them: "A single demand of you, comrades: Provide the bomb—it will remove a great danger from us." British leaders too were determined to assert themselves, even though their empire was a shambles and their country nearly bankrupt after the war. "[The Americans] were rather apt to think they were the big boys and we were the small boys," sniffed Prime Minister Clement Atlee. "We'd just got to show they didn't know everything."

The corporations, scientists, and military leaders involved in the Manhattan Project had their own personal, bureaucratic, and financial reasons for wanting atomic work to continue: these reasons generated conflicting ideas about the appropriate focus of the program. In general, the military wanted to build more bombs and perhaps explore naval applications of nuclear energy. The corporations went along with that idea, but also pushed strongly for permission to develop the commercial applications. At that early date nobody knew how far off competitively priced nuclear electricity was, but the corporations were confident that American know-how was equal to the challenge. The universities were also eager to resume their weapons development work; the sizable infusions of federal funds would enable them to attract top scientists and enhance their influence and prestige.

The only note of serious discord came from some of the Project's scientists, led by the Hungarian immigrant Leo Szilard. In the summer of 1945, after Germany's surrender had negated the original rationale for the Manhattan Project, Szilard had organized many of the leading physicists and biologists at the atomic laboratory in Chicago to petition President Truman not to drop the bomb on Japan. This group was joined after the bombings by colleagues from the Oak Ridge, Tennessee laboratory who were equally appalled at the use to which their creativity and toil had been put. Fearful of a postwar nuclear arms race between the United States and the Soviet Union, the scientists lobbied Congress and drafted statements calling for international agreements barring further atomic weapons development, but to no avail. And when it came to the "peaceful atom," even many of the dissidents endorsed the corporate position. They strongly supported the idea of a government research program that would seek to discover nonmilitary applications of atomic energy, especially in the apparently promising fields of medicine and electricity production. How much the scientists' enthusiasm stemmed from simple intellectual curiosity and how much from a desire to atone for the "original sin" that Robert Oppenheimer said he and all Manhattan Project physicists shared in after Hiroshima and Nagasaki is impossible to say. Years later David Lilienthal, the first chairman of the Atomic Energy Commission, wrote that not only the scientists but many who shaped America's postwar atomic program had been motivated by a grim determination that "the discovery that had produced so terrible a weapon simply *had* to have an important use."

Despite the general agreement that the United States should move forward with atomic energy after the war, there were some nasty congressional fights over who would control that program and what purposes it would serve. Even before the Hiroshima bombing, the Army had drafted a bill to create within the executive branch an extraordinary new agency called the Atomic Energy Commission. The generals had definite ideas about who could be trusted with the awesome new powers of the atom: four of the nine members of their proposed agency would be active military officers, and the agency's actions would be subject to a military veto but not to congressional oversight. According to the official Atomic Energy Commission history, in late October 1945 impatient Army lobbyists pushed for a vote in the House of Representatives' Military Affairs Committee after just five hours of hearings, and then tried to hurry the bill through the Senate without "unnecessary discussions." But the legislation faltered beneath a wave of suspicion that the military would use atomic energy for its own greedy and dangerous purposes.

Such suspicion was widespread right after the war. Senator Brien McMahon, a freshman Democrat from Connecticut who within two years would be promoting himself as Mr. Atom, capitalized upon that sentiment, drafting an alternative bill whose key feature was a guarantee that the Atomic Energy Commission's top five officials would all be civilians. The War Department blasted McMahon's bill when he introduced it in December, but it actually outlined an AEC whose powers and mandate did not differ significantly from the military's earlier proposal. Both bills envisioned a commission with complete control over nuclear power *and* nuclear weapons, and over all nuclear materials, plant, and equipment; one that would fund and carry out its own research and retain patent rights (although McMahon's proposal allowed the AEC to give private firms patents for processes and equipment unrelated to weapons or fissionable material). And despite McMahon's proud rhetoric about his bill releasing basic scientific information into the public domain, it would still be the AEC commissioners who would decide, on the basis of national security, what was basic information that could be released and what was sensitive information that could not. These commissioners would be appointed by the President. The Pentagon would retain considerable influence over the AEC's actions, thanks to an amendment by Republican Senator Arthur Vandenberg that gave the AEC's Board of Military Advisors (an advisory body of top Pentagon officials appointed by the President to serve as liaison between the AEC and the War Department) a tacit veto over all AEC decisions.

Legislators were so absorbed in safeguarding America's atomic secret that they forgot until the last minute a basic tenet of American democracy: the idea of checks and balances. The McMahon bill would centralize all authority over nuclear matters within a single secretive agency located in the executive branch and heavily influenced by the military. The potential for abusing that power seems, in retrospect, obvious. Yet it was not until the final draft of what was to become the Atomic Energy Act of 1946 that full-scale congressional oversight of the AEC was written into the law. The Joint Committee on Atomic Energy was created to serve as the public's watchdog over the nation's atomic program.

The decision to grant the AEC total control of nuclear affairs greatly disappointed the corporations. The act as first drafted had certainly favored industrial exploitation of atomic energy; its preamble identified one of the bill's purposes as "the strengthening of free competition among private enterprise as far as practicable." That phase, argued such business associations as the National Association of Manufacturers and the electrical utilities' Association of Edison Illuminating Companies, implied that corporations should be granted unfettered access to the government's atomic secrets.

But Washington's overriding concern at the time was to prevent other countries from learning and harnessing the secrets of atomic fission. Achieving that goal would be impossible if corporate investigation and development of the atom were allowed. American policymakers appreciated, as historian Ronald W. Clark has written concerning the Baruch Plan, the 1946 U.S. proposal for the international control of nuclear weapons, "that there was no firm line dividing military and non-military uses and that once a country had embarked on a programme for the industrial use of nuclear energy it became virtually impracticable to prevent the secret manufacture of nuclear weapons." The national security managers' view that nothing was more important than maintaining the United States' atomic monopoly took precedence over the corporations' desire to get on with the production and sale of atomic energy. It was the first of many instances where the interests of the Atomic Brotherhood's corporate and government wings would diverge from one another.

The ostensible purpose of the 1946 Atomic Energy Act was to bring the atomic bureaucracy, which had secretly created itself during World War II, under legal, public control. Now a civilian commission, rather than an Army general, was in charge of the nation's atomic program. That commission in turn reported to a "watchdog" commmittee on Capitol Hill, whose job it was to make sure that the AEC did not abuse its public trust. The nation's atomic program would be a classic example of American democracy in action.

But as it turned out, these reforms did not significantly alter the patterns that had formed during the Manhattan Project. The government would still pay large corporations billions of dollars to produce atomic weapons. Americans—and indeed, most of their elected representatives in Congress—would still be kept ignorant about nearly everything the Atomic Brotherhood did. Although it was now five civilians who made the critical decisions about atomic energy, those decisions were still made behind closed doors; and while behind those doors, the AEC commissioners could still classify as secret anything they wished. And since it was the President's responsibility to nominate the AEC commissioners, his key national security advisers retained indirect control over the management of the program.

The men who became AEC commissioners generally exhibited a healthy respect for, in the words of the AEC official history, "the military significance of atomic energy and importance of cooperation between the civilian and military authorities." Two of the first five commissioners, Lewis Strauss and Sumner T. Pike, were former investment bankers who had retired from Wall Street after making their fortunes in the 1920s. Strauss had also achieved the rank of rear admiral during his wartime service as personal assistant to Navy Secretary James Forrestal, an old Wall Street friend. Robert Bacher, another commissioner, was a leading nuclear scientist who had worked during the Manhattan Project at the Massachusetts Institute of Technology and at the Los Alamos weapons laboratory. During his confirmation hearings, Bacher made sure, according to the official AEC history, to tell the Joint Committee "that he appreciated the need for close liaison with the military services and that he was not among the scientists who had protested the adoption of the Vandenberg amendment in 1946."

The Joint Committee on Atomic Energy was supposed to keep the AEC on the straight and narrow, but as H. Peter Metzger documents in *The Atomic Establishment,* the two groups over the years "changed from healthy adversaries into pals . . . the committee was transformed from a critic into an apologist, from an attacker of the AEC into its defender." The corruption of atomic oversight might have been foreseen, given Washington's overwhelming commitment to atomic energy and the contradictory responsibilities outlined for the atomic bureaucracy in the 1946 Atomic Energy Act. Instead of giving the AEC the job of promoting atomic energy and the Joint Committee the job of regulating it, the act charged both agencies with *both* jobs. The tremendous access of corporate interests and national security officials to the levers of government power, facilitated by the veil of secrecy surrounding atomic energy, would over time stimulate a bias within the agencies towards their promotional rather than their regulatory functions. This predisposition led to a series of goverment cover-ups, lies, suppression of information, and other wrongdoing whose eventual cumulative effect was to compromise severely the Atomic Brotherhood's credibility with the American people.

Hindsight shows that the 1946 Atomic Energy Act did not make the atomic bureaucracy significantly more open or publicly accountable than it had been. Rather, a democratic façade was dropped over what remained a secretive subsidy program run according to the wishes of America's national security managers. The 1946 act transformed the secrecy, centralization of authority, and generous corporate subsidies that were previously justified only by the wartime emergency into permanent features of the nation's atomic energy program. In so doing, it legitimized the Atomic Brotherhood born during the Manhattan Project and enshrined it as the permanent, dominant influence over America's future atomic program.

THE QUIET CORPORATE ADVANCE

American postwar military and foreign policy rested on the assumption that a clear-cut superiority in nuclear weapons would deter all challenges to the United States and guarantee U.S. policymakers freedom to manage the world as they saw fit. As Clark Clifford wrote in the previously mentioned secret 1946 memo to President Truman:

> The language of military power is the only language which disciples of power politics [meaning the Soviets] understand. . . . In order to maintain our strength at a level which will be effective in restraining the Soviet Union, the United States must be prepared to wage atomic and biological warfare. . . .

Yet immediately after the war the United States was prepared to do no such thing. On the afternoon of April 3, 1947, the new AEC chairman, David Lilienthal, privately reported to President Truman the embarrassing truth that there was not a single operable bomb in the U.S. atomic arsenal. Moreover, U.S. supplies of plutonium and uranium-235 were nearly depleted, and a shortage of uranium loomed ahead. To rectify the situation, Truman and the AEC that summer ordered that the plutonium production plant at Hanford, Washington, increase output and that another uranium enrichment plant be built at Oak Ridge, Tennessee. These expansions would provide enough fissionable materials for four hundred bombs—the number the Air Force had said would be necessary to ensure that the United States possessed "the most effective atomic striking force possible."

For the next five years, the AEC spent most of its time and money atomically fortifying what was already the most deadly military machine the world had ever known. Private corporate contractors involved in nuclear weapons production were guaranteed ample profits by cost-plus contracts, while the weapons program's political invulnerability guaranteed a steadily expanding market. Nevertheless, private companies remained eager to explore nuclear energy's commercial applications as well and impatiently pressured Washington for permission to do so. Their view—that the AEC should accelerate power reactor development in order to increase public acceptance of nuclear energy—had lost out during a crucial January 1947 meeting of the directors of the AEC's nuclear laboratories to the hard-line military argument that the Cold War international climate made more and bigger bombs the top priority. The companies did not give up, however, and the more resourceful ones saw and exploited the opportunity to use their work on weapons as a backdoor entrance to the nuclear electicity business, despite the fact that the 1946 Atomic Energy Act had outlawed commercial nuclear activity. General Electric and Westinghouse, in particular, gained invaluable practical experience through building and operating plutonium production reactors for the AEC and designing nuclear submarines for the U.S. Navy.

Charles Weaver, who started with Westinghouse in 1936 as an engineer and has since risen to become executive vice-president for corporate world relations, credits his company's early leadership of the nuclear power business to the work that Westinghouse did on the Navy's nuclear submarine project. "Our perception of nuclear energy's commercial potential certainly accounted for a large part of our interest in the Navy work," Weaver recalled. Captain (now Admiral) Hyman Rickover, the chief proponent of the Navy nuclear program, convinced Gwilym Price, Westinghouse's chief executive officer in 1947, that nuclear energy had many industrial applications other than its obvious military uses, and that Westinghouse should devote a major chunk of corporate resources to establish itself in the nuclear field. The best way to do that, according to Rickover, was to help build nuclear submarines for the Navy.

Price agreed, and in 1948 he picked Weaver to coordinate the formation of Westinghouse's Atomic Power Division. Weaver located the division at the government-owned Bettis nuclear labo-

ratory, not far from Westinghouse's corporate headquarters in Pittsburgh. He took as his core nuclear cadre six Westinghouse
scientists who had worked in Oak Ridge, Tennessee, on the Navy's
Daniels Pile Project in 1946.* Then Weaver added support staff by
getting Price to transfer research specialists, engineers, and managers from other Westinghouse divisions into his Atomic Power
Division. In early 1949—barely a year later—Weaver's division
landed some Navy contracts for reactor coolant systems, and later
it got an AEC contract to develop the reactor for what became the
Nautilus submarine.

The specific advantage of the Navy work was its obvious applicability to commercial nuclear power. The basic goal in building
atomic bombs was to unleash the maximum explosive force from
the fission process. The Navy's goal, however, was almost precisely
the opposite; it wanted to *control* the fission process and apply the
fantastic amounts of energy it released to the propulsion of ships
and submarines—a process broadly similar to what power stations
would do. In the process of its work for the Navy, Westinghouse
acquired, largely at government expense, the three main factors
that accounted for its early domination of the nuclear power business: trained engineers and scientists; the technical information,
raw materials, sophisticated equipment, and working space needed
for researching and developing nuclear technology's practical applications; and a customer that bought the finished products at a
profitable price.

General Electric's military work also camouflaged its growing
interest and involvement in civilian nuclear power in the late
1940s. In fact, according to Weaver, GE at the time was even further
advanced than Westinghouse. Soon after the war, Manhattan Project Director Leslie Groves (who remained in charge of the U.S.
atomic program until the Senate confirmed the new AEC commissioners in April 1947) had asked GE if it would take over from the
Du Pont corporation the operation of the government's plutonium
production plant in Hanford, Washington. GE's wartime performance had impressed Groves, and he hoped that "the possibilities
of future power applications might be an inducement" for the giant
company. GE agreed to help Groves, but demanded that in return
it be given its own nuclear laboratory where it could pursue basic

* One of the six was Nunzio Palladino, who worked for Westinghouse for twenty
years, designed the reactor core for the *Nautilus* submarine and the Shippingport
reactor, and in 1981 became chairman of the Nuclear Regulatory Commission under
the Reagan administration.

atomic research and development. Groves allocated $10 million of his fiscal year 1947 budget for construction of the GE facility, the Knolls atomic laboratory in Schenectady, New York. Two broader advantages that GE enjoyed over Westinghouse were that GE was a much larger corporation and that it possessed the reputation of being a technically excellent company that was willing to gamble on the future.

There is evidence of strong nuclear competition between GE and Westinghouse as early as 1948. AEC Chairman David Lilienthal had created the Industrial Advisory Panel in October 1947 to make sure that the AEC's civilian reactor research was sharply and practically focused. Before another twelve months passed, Dr. Walter Zinn, director of the government's prestigious Argonne National Laboratory in Chicago, was complaining that the focus was getting too sharp. Zinn claimed that the GE-Westinghouse rivalry, along with pressure from Captain Hyman Rickover of the Navy, was forcing reactor development to proceed at an imprudently hasty pace.

At the time GE had just put its scientists at the Knolls laboratory to work on developing liquid-metal fast breeder reactors—which could, in theory, produce, or "breed," more fuel that they consumed—with the aim of getting the United States around its crippling shortage of uranium. GE also saw two other commercial advantages of breeders. First, they figured to compete well in the marketplace, since, once perfected, they could produce almost infinite amounts of electricity. Second, GE could probably get an AEC subsidy to develop breeders because of their immediate relevance to the weapons program. In the Cold War climate of the late 1940s, projects with no military applicability stood almost no chance of receiving AEC money; GE had therefore to use the same strategy that Westinghouse had followed with its Navy work: find a project that had commercial relevance while also having enough immediate military applicability that the government would fund it. Breeders fit those requirements perfectly.

The AEC did fund GE's fast breeder project, but not for long. The support was contingent on the breeder's producing adequate amounts of plutonium. But when GE scientists adjusted their design accordingly, their reactor was no longer efficient as a source of power. GE finally gave up the idea and, like Westinghouse, signed onto the Navy's submarine program.

It was then 1950, five years after the Hiroshima bombing, and already two corporations—GE and Westinghouse—were laying the groundwork to dominate the future nuclear power industry. "Because the military work was all secret," says official AEC historian Richard Hewlett, "nobody else knew how close GE and Westinghouse were to producing a decent reactor." But it was clear that GE and Westinghouse were, at any rate, further along than any other company.

Other would-be nuclear corporations were by no means blind to what GE and Westinghouse were doing. But what could they do about it? The AEC gave no sign that it was ready to let them in on the secrets of atomic energy or to begin a full-scale commercialization program. And in 1950, President Truman reinforced the AEC's military orientation with his directive ordering a drastic acceleration of nuclear weapons production and the development of the next generation of "superweapons"—hydrogen bombs. Truman's directive came in response to the 1949 detonation of the Soviet Union's first nuclear weapon; it touched off the one-sided arms race that continued throughout the 1950s.

But the Cold War dimmed the prospects of a civilian nuclear energy program only temporarily. Other Cold War diplomatic maneuvers—the 1949 formation of the North Atlantic Treaty Organization (NATO) and the desire over the next few years to shore up military alliances in Europe—forced Washington to begin sharing more of its atomic information with European allies. That gave American corporations like Monsanto and Dow Chemical the opening they needed. How, they asked, could the AEC give foreigners information that it withheld from its own companies? Wasn't that just inviting those countries to take the lead in nuclear power away from America?

That logic, combined with steady political pressure, liberated the classified information that the companies had wanted for so long. Finally, they would be able to judge the feasibility of nuclear electricity for themselves. Their studies began in 1951 under what the AEC called its Industrial Participation Program. Ashton O'Donnell, now vice-president for nuclear fuel and operations at the Bechtel Corporation, remembers that at least eight industrial study teams, some including as many as twenty companies, lined up for the security clearances needed to survey the previously secret data. "The Congress and the AEC encouraged us," says O'Donnell, "but we had to spend our own money evaluating and studying. So it was actually a risk for us."

The risk was evidently worth it. Dow Chemical and the Detroit

Edison electric utility company were so excited by what they learned from the AEC's files that they immediately began to make plans to build and operate their own nuclear power plant. The importance of government subsidies and nuclear power's link to nuclear weapons—two central and recurring themes in the nuclear industry's future development—were both evident in the Dow–Detroit Edison proposal. It called for the AEC to pay for and run the reactor and to recover the plutonium it produced for use in building nuclear weapons. The utility would own the plant and would sell the electricity it produced. Other companies made similar overtures. The only hitch was money: the studies all said that civilian nuclear power was technically feasible, but too expensive. If nuclear power was to go beyond the drawing-board stage, the government would have to help pay for it.

As the 1950s wore on, the AEC and the rest of the government's atomic-policy makers re-evaluated their previous position and grew increasingly disposed towards private exploitation of civilian nuclear power. In September 1952 the AEC catapulted civilian nuclear-reactor development from the bottom of its priorities list to the very top. Later that same year the Joint Committee on Atomic Energy began extensive hearings on atomic energy and private enterprise.

Pressure from private corporations helped bring about these shifts, but an even deeper and more powerful motivation was, oddly, the protection of U.S. national security. True, it was national security considerations that had frustrated would-be nuclear power companies since 1946, but the world had changed much in the meantime. Most important, the U.S. atomic weapons monopoly was a thing of the past. The Soviet Union in 1949 and Great Britain in 1952 had each exploded a nuclear bomb. And there was news that both those countries had also begun investigating nuclear energy's industrial potential. U.S. national security managers quickly came to believe they could no longer afford to hoard atomic information. If the United States did not begin to develop nuclear power itself and reassert its nuclear superiority, it would forfeit the global influence that it brought. AEC Commissioner Thomas Murray declared in 1953 that if the Soviet Union were to produce the world's first industrial nuclear power plant, more damage would be done to U.S. interests than even the Soviet's successful hydrogen bomb explosion had done, because the industrial atom could be parlayed into real foreign policy gains with the world's underdeveloped countries. "Once we become fully conscious of the possibility that power-hungry nations will gravitate towards the USSR if it wins the nuclear power race," Murray warned, "it will be quite clear that this power race is no Everest-climbing, kudos-providing contest."

In a stunning reversal of previous policy, the National Security Council decided in early 1953 that the United States must initiate a strong industrial atomic program. The council's secret memo said that "the early development of nuclear power was a prerequisite in maintaining the U.S. lead in the atomic field." Alvin Weinberg, director of the government's Oak Ridge National Laboratory, elaborated on this theme in testimony before the Joint Committee later that year. The government was "vitally interested" in nuclear power, Weinberg explained, primarily "because our potential in military nuclear explosives and, ultimately, in general economic strength, would be greatly increased if we had a large-scale economic central nuclear power industry."

The Security Council's decision came soon after the inauguration of new President Dwight Eisenhower and set the tone of his administration's atomic policy over the next eight years. Lewis Strauss, the financier, retired admiral, and former AEC commissioner whom Eisenhower picked to chair the Atomic Energy Commission, lost little time in getting a civilian reactor project under way. In the process he crossed paths with Captain Hyman Rickover, the man who spearheaded the Navy's nuclear program and first drew Westinghouse and General Electric into nuclear reactor work.

Rickover was a talented, persistent, single-minded perfectionist who drove himself and his subordinates mercilessly in pursuit of his goals. He was also a bold man who possessed tremendous powers of persuasion. In the fall of 1951 Rickover faced an AEC bureaucracy that was unenthusiastic about his new idea to develop nuclear reactors for aircraft carriers. So he went over the AEC's head to the Joint Chiefs of Staff. Soon after Rickover's presentation, the Joint Chiefs made the development of a carrier reactor a military requirement, leaving the AEC with little choice but to fund the project.

It was this project that Strauss later seized upon to initiate the commercial power-reactor development program. It had not taken Rickover long to choose the design for his carrier reactor: the light water design had been his favorite since the nuclear submarine project, and by applying it to the carrier, he could save both time and money. (In another carry-over from the submarine work, Rickover selected Westinghouse as his main contractor. It would turn

out to be one of Westinghouse's most important contracts ever.)
This design seemed to offer an additional benefit: since it was
capable of producing significant amounts of power, choosing it for
the carrier project allowed Rickover to placate those in the government's atomic bureaucracy who were pressing for faster progress
on civilian reactor development. But the tactic backfired. It was
precisely the light water design's power applications that led
Strauss's AEC to decide simply to arrange to reorient Rickover's
carrier project to produce a commercial rather than a naval reactor.
In a letter to Joint Committee Chairman Sterling Cole explaining
the decision, Strauss wrote that the Eisenhower administration
believed the United States could not afford to wait for the "last
word" in an economical power reactor: "Only by moving into the
construction phase can we fulfill the requirement of the National
Security Council which recently held that 'the early development
of nuclear power by the United States is a prerequisite to maintaining our lead in the atomic field.' " Cole did not need much
convincing. Like his colleagues on the Joint Committee, he was
strongly committed to rapid development of commercial nuclear power and welcomed the reorientation of Rickover's carrier
project.

What Strauss, Cole, and the rest of the atomic establishment
cared most about was finding a reactor design that was sure to
work. Reliability, not economics, was the criterion. The idea was
to prove American nuclear superiority, not to lower electricity costs.
It was this need for early completion of a reliable power reactor,
Strauss wrote to Cole, that led the administration to conclude that
Rickover's light water reactor project should be continued and that
Westinghouse, which by that time was quite advanced on the project, should remain the prime contractor and Rickover the government supervisor. Soon thereafter the AEC chose the Duquesne
Light Company of Pittsburgh to operate the new reactor. Construc-
tion began at Shippingport, Pennsylvania, in September 1954, and
three years later Duquesne Light began operating the United
States' first civilian nuclear reactor.

President Eisenhower demonstrated the government's commitment to nuclear power by initiating the construction of the Shippingport plant himself. Television audiences across the nation
watched the balding former general stride across a control room
carrying in his right hand what young children could have mistaken
for a magic wand. Grinning broadly, the President passed his metal
rod over the shiny transformer in front of him, and the first bull-

dozer at the distant construction site snorted to a start. It appeared that Americans would soon enjoy the electricity "too cheap to meter" that their government had promised them.

Shippingport, and the 1953 National Security Council decision that brought it about, were the first major steps towards nuclear power in the United States. But it is worth remembering that Shippingport was not the result of a stupendous technical break-through nor of a willingness on private industry's part to take a risk, but of a national security decision to reassert American atomic superiority during the Cold War. In their hurry to get a reactor, any reactor, pumping out electricity, the government's atomic bureau-crats seized upon the handiest reactor design available, Rickover's light water reactor. Their choice gave the light water model a head start and momentum that others were never able to match and led the industry to base its commercial future on a reactor design that some experts have subsequently suggested was economically and technically inferior.

The Shippingport decision had a second, far more important effect on the nuclear industry's long-term development: it marked the end, if temporarily, of the Atomic Brotherhood's internal dis-pute over what to do about commercial nuclear power. The national security officials who had previously vetoed nuclear power devel-opment now demanded it. They saw nuclear power as a Cold War weapon, a way of "proving" America's superiority to the rest of the world. But because, in the words of Richard J. Barnet, "Staying number one is a struggle for permanent victory," the United States could not stop with Shippingport. Since the decision had been made that American national security depended upon staying ahead of other countries in nuclear power, nuclear power devel-opment had to be extended. And precisely because of nuclear power's national security ramifications, that development had to take place within the same institutional framework as nuclear weapons production. The same centralization of authority within the same government atomic bureaucracy, the same secrecy, the same corporate subsidies—in short, the same rules and ideology that characterized the weapons program—would shape the power program.

America's nuclear power industry had reached a critical point. Before, it had been the corporations pushing for private nuclear power; now, the shoe was on the other foot. The industry benefitted heavily from the government's new commitment to nuclear power throughout the 1950s, receiving hundreds of millions of dollars in federal subsidies and transferring to the government many of the risks ordinarily associated with initiating a new business. National security, a curse during the 1940s and early 1950s, had become a blessing.

Now that the National Security Council had changed its position on nuclear power, the Atomic Brotherhood unanimously supported immediate commercialization. But this necessitated amending federal law, which still prevented private ownership of nuclear materials.

It was in anticipation of that opportunity that the Joint Committee on Atomic Energy had begun to hold hearings in 1952 on atomic energy and private enterprise. One of the more trenchant comments was in testimony from Dr. Alvin Weinberg, director of the government's Oak Ridge atomic laboratories, who pointed out, "It is taking a Cold War to give motivation to the development of nuclear reactors for power in much the same way it took a hot war to give motivation to the development of the original nuclear bomb." Throughout the hearings pro-industry witnesses argued that a strong nuclear power program was critical to protecting the Free World against communist aggression. But, they charged, a strong program was impossible so long as the government monopoly continued. AEC Commissioner Keith Glennan's statement is typical of the pro-industry forces' backhanded attacks on the government's atomic monopoly: "This nation needs its best brains and skill at work on these problems [of developing peaceful atomic energy] as the Free World struggles to combat foreign ideologies . . . but let us accomplish that purpose without resorting to the methods of the aggressors—the totalitarianism we abhor."

The hearings raised anew the central issue of corporate versus public control of the atom. Scattered throughout the government and the trade unions were populists and other critics of big business who feared private monopolization of this important new energy source and called for vigilant government oversight to ensure free competition. Benjamin Sigal of the Congress of Industrial Organizations (CIO) went further, calling for public operation and ownership of the atomic energy industry. In his testimony Sigal cynically asked:

What sweeter arrangement, from the point of view of private industry, could have been provided, within the barest limits of common decency, than for the federal government to take all the risk, spend fantastic sums of money, and at the same time give private industry the benefit of all the knowhow that has been acquired . . . ?

Sigal continued:

[A] few corporations desire to get in on the ground floor before atomic power on a competitive basis has actually been produced, so as to prepare the way for the creation of a huge private monopoly to substitute for the present public monopoly.

Lewis Strauss offered a more genteel interpretation of the corporate viewpoint:

For their part, executives in private industry believed that there ought to be assurances that the government was willing to allow a private atomic energy industry to develop, that risk-taking would be compensated by profits for success and financial allowances made for failures; and that regulations would be established with progress and profit in mind as well as safety and security.

The executives got their wish with the 1954 Atomic Energy Act. The new law allowed corporations to build and own nuclear plants and equipment, carry out nuclear research, and use nuclear fuel (over which the government retained control). To encourage industrial research and development, the new law outlined a more liberal patent policy and ordered the Atomic Energy Commission to cooperate with private industry by supplying them more information about nuclear technology. Cries of "creeping socialism" during the 1953 hearings led to the inclusion of a clause in the new law that prohibited the AEC from constructing its own nuclear plants to generate electricity. The act also boosted the corporate cause in the halls of Congress by granting astonishing new powers to the procommercialization Joint Committee. The Joint Committee became the only body in Congress that could draft and submit its own legislation and then act as a joint House and Senate "conference committee" to prepare the legislation for final vote. The Joint Committee on Atomic Energy thus was able to practice a take-it-or-leave-it attitude towards the Congress as a whole regarding nuclear legislation.

The overhauling of federal atomic law set off a flurry of corporate activity. In late 1954 General Electric established its first corporate department concerned solely with nuclear power. Thanks to its Shippingport work, Westinghouse was even further along. In 1955 it broke ground for its first nuclear manufacturing facility, the atomic equipment division in Cheswick, Pennsylvania. Westinghouse also inaugurated a Commercial Atomic Power Activities program in which it worked with utilities to analyze possible applications of nuclear power. Babcock and Wilcox, a heavy electrical equipment manufacturer that had been marginally involved in the Manhattan Project and the Shippingport project, set up its first nuclear facilities in 1956 in Lynchburg, Virginia. A year later, Babcock and Wilcox signed a contract to design and build the power plant for the world's first nuclear-powered merchant ship, the N.S. *Savannah*. Combustion Engineering, the last of the Big Four reactor suppliers that would come to dominate the industry, had begun building submarine reactors in the mid-1950s and entered the commercial business in 1959 when it bought General Nuclear Engineering, a small firm headed by leading Manhattan Project scientist Walter Zinn.

After the Joint Committee had pushed the 1954 Atomic Energy Act through Congress, it pressured the AEC for still faster action on industrial nuclear energy. The AEC resisted at first, arguing that many technical questions remained unanswered. But finally the Joint Committee prevailed, and in January 1955 the AEC announced its new Power Reactor Demonstration Program. The idea was that it would cooperate with private industry to build prototype plants that could deliver hard data and information on costs, engineering, and the other practical questions that needed answering before utilities would order nuclear power plants. By shouldering much of the financial burden, the AEC hoped to encourage wider participation by industry, partly so that competition would be maintained but primarily to keep the United States ahead in the global race for commercial nuclear superiority.

The man ultimately responsible for the program was the AEC chairman, Lewis Strauss. Strauss, a die-hard conservative with an ideological devotion to pure private enterprise, had no quarrel with the Power Reactor Demonstration Program's main purpose: building demonstration reactors that would provide the "real-life" information private firms needed in order to decide which reactor designs worked. But according to the former investment banker's strict interpretation of the canons of private enterprise, the government's responsibility ended once a reactor's technical feasibility had been demonstrated. Anything beyond that was investment for marketing purposes, for which corporations themselves should pay.

Both private industry and the Joint Committee responded to this idea of limited federal participation with vicious attacks against Strauss. They complained that the AEC's financing terms were too stingy to entice the private investment needed to create an industry. The conflict was a new version of the struggle over corporate versus public control that had plagued the Atomic Brotherhood since World War II. Knowing of Strauss's Wall Street background, Joint Committee liberals accused him of deliberately holding back nuclear power development until private industry was financially ready to take it over. In fact, Strauss was moving slowly because he too was against a government giveaway program. But he opposed even more strongly the option favored by some Joint Committee liberals—a nationalized nuclear program. According to AEC historian Hewlett, "Strauss was obsessed with keeping nuclear power private. He would have let the program go down the drain rather than getting the government in there. He knew the game those business guys played, just like Ike knew about the dangers of the military. Strauss wanted nuclear power, but he didn't think government should subsidize its development, because once you start down that road industry expects you to fund everything, take all the risks and they get all the profits."

By 1956 it was clear that the Power Reactor Demonstration Program was going nowhere. Unenthusiastic about accepting so much of the risk and cost themselves, private firms had tendered barely a dozen proposals to the AEC for constructing prototype reactors. The Joint Committee cited the corporate response as evidence of Strauss's failure. Two members, Senator Albert Gore and Congressman Chester Holifield, drafted a bill to rectify the situation. The Gore-Holifield bill would have given the AEC hundreds of millions of dollars to construct, own, and operate six full-scale demonstration plants. Raising as it did the public power issue directly, the Gore-Holifield bill provoked one of the bloodiest clashes ever over federal nuclear policy. Although passed in the Senate, it was finally defeated in the House of Representatives by a coalition of House conservatives, the Eisenhower administration, the electric utilities, and other parts of the evolving nuclear power industry, which rallied around the cause of defeating "socialism" in nuclear policy.

This struggle over corporate versus public control of the atom was yet another instance of confusion and conflict within the Brotherhood that slowed nuclear development. The AEC under Lewis Strauss wanted a pure private-enterprise solution and was willing to outwait the industry to get it. The Joint Committee wanted the nationalization of the nuclear power business. The industry wanted neither of these two extremes; rather, it preferred an arrangement whereby the government would help cover the costs of commercialization but still allow the corporations to control and profit from it.

The defeat of the Gore-Holifield bill in 1956 decided the issue in the corporations' favor. With the threat of nationalization now rendered empty, the industry grew bolder in demanding more subsidies. Nervy industry representatives began to use the very same national security arguments that Gore and Holifield had used to press for nationalization to secure instead even bigger favors from Congress. That tactic produced one of the most extraordinary subsidies in congressional history: the Price-Anderson Act of 1957. Fear of reactor accidents was one major reason why the electric utilities hesitated in the 1950s to buy nuclear power plants. Private insurance companies had refused to accept the risk of the thousands of deaths and injuries and the billions of dollars in property damage that government studies said might result from a nuclear power plant accident. The nuclear industry was also unwilling to accept liability. Although the industry and the AEC at the time were assuring the public that nuclear power was safe, Charles Weaver of Westinghouse now admits that his company was actually uncertain about reactor safety: "We knew at that time that all questions weren't answered. That's why we fully supported the Price-Anderson liability legislation. When I testified before Congress, I made it perfectly clear that we could not proceed as a private company without that kind of government backing." Faced with either absolving the industry from risk or not having a strong civilian nuclear program, Congress passed the Price-Anderson Act, which limited corporate liability in case of a reactor accident to $60 million and total liability to $560 million. Arbitrarily chosen, both figures were pittances in light of the government's own projections that an accident could cause over $7 billion worth of damage.

To obtain the Price-Anderson Act and other subsidies, the corporations had to display an ambivalent attitude about nuclear power; if they looked too anxious to get into the business it would weaken their bargaining power vis-à-vis the government. But while the corporations in the late 1950s publicly were professing doubts about the viability of nuclear power without generous federal subsidies, privately they were already engaged in vicious competition for leadership of an industry they assumed would be a big moneymaker in the future.

"Everybody was in there cutting each other's throats," reminisces Thomas Ayers, the former chairman and chief executive officer of the Commonwealth Edison Company, a Chicago utility that has built more nuclear power plants than any other utility in the country. Commonwealth's first nuclear plant, Dresden One, was one of the few successes of the Power Reactor Demonstration Program. "The people in the business were anxious to be up front in this new technology, so they were willing to offer plants or equipment at more favorable prices than otherwise," says Ayers. "In the big capital goods businesses, the thing you don't want to be is left behind. It wasn't just GE and Westinghouse—they made the reactors—but it was people who made pumps, reactor vessels, and fuel."

Nevertheless, it would still be a few years before a market for nuclear power plants developed in the United States. The Joint Committee–sponsored McKinney Panel had foreseen that likelihood back in 1955 when it reported that, owing to the relatively low electricity costs in the United States, "A gap may occur for the power equipment manufacturing industry between present domestic interest in atomic power reactors and actual sales." How to sustain the industry while it waited for the U.S. market to take off? The panel suggested using foreign aid to foster a market for nuclear reactors in Europe, where energy costs were higher. In fact, such a program was just then getting under way.

ATOMS FOR PEACE AND PROFIT

While there are numerous cases of conflict within the Atomic Brotherhood, two examples of nearly perfect harmony stood out during the 1950s: the Atoms for Peace program inaugurated by the Eisenhower administration in 1953, and the Euratom program that came along later in the decade. Like the Shippingport reactor, the Atoms for Peace program stemmed from the national security decision to take all necessary measures to maintain U.S. nuclear superiority. Shippingport would demonstrate America's competence at building nuclear power plants, but America also had to share that skill with other nations, or else risk having them obtain the information from the Soviet Union, Great Britain, or others.

It was too late to stem the flow of atomic information around the world, Secretary of State John Foster Dulles lectured the Joint Committee: "If we try to do it, we will only dam our own influence, and others will move into the field with the bargaining power that that involves." That being the case, the next best policy for the United States was to provide the information itself. That way other countries' nuclear programs would at least remain dependent upon the United States. According to President Eisenhower, the original intent of the Atoms for Peace program was not that sinister. The man who later would warn Americans of the dangers of the rise of "the military-industrial complex" wrote in his memoirs that he hoped to promote global disarmament with his plan to share the "peaceful atom" with the rest of the world. Foreign nations reacted very favorably to Eisenhower's December 1953 speech at the United Nations, with diplomatic statements welcoming both the halt to the superpowers' arms race and the chance to use the atom to spark economic growth. The President's speech called for both the United States and the Soviet Union to contribute nuclear materials from their own stockpile to a newly established International Atomic Energy Agency (IAEA). That agency would then allocate the donated materials to countries around the world "to serve the peaceful pursuits of mankind. . . . A special purpose would be to provide abundant electrical energy in the power-starved areas of the world."

But in official Washington, the disarmament features of the President's proposal were quickly dismissed or forgotten, while Cold Warriors on Capitol Hill hammered away at the plan's offers to give other countries research reactors and other assistance, calling it a giveaway of U.S. secrets. Secretary of State Dulles attempted to quiet these critics by emphasizing the potentially disastrous national security consequences of *not* offering more atomic information:

> There is a growing tendency for certain raw-materials-supplying nations, which are not industrially well advanced, to turn to other countries for nuclear power information, because they have been disappointed by our inability to give them significant help. . . . There is no need here to emphasize how important it is for us to stay ahead of the USSR in providing knowledge of how to put atomic energy to peaceful uses.

Congress tacitly endorsed the peaceful-exchange features of Atoms for Peace when it overhauled atomic energy legislation in

1954. The 1954 Atomic Energy Act greatly expanded the possibilities for international exchange of nuclear information by authorizing the executive branch to negotiate bilateral nuclear power agreements with foreign countries. President Eisenhower quickly followed up by offering friendly nations millions of dollars in foreign aid to purchase experimental research reactors and to educate and train their own cadre of nuclear experts. The catch was that all technology and equipment had to be supplied by U.S. firms. Eisenhower ordered the Export-Import Bank, a taxpayer-supported agency charged with facilitating U.S. exports by granting low-cost loans to recipient countries, to help finance the deals.

Twenty-two nations signed the obligatory bilateral agreements in 1955, and by April 1958, a total of thirty-nine nations had linked their nuclear futures with the United States. For obvious reasons, the United States was determined to prevent the recipient nations from using their new knowledge and materials to make atomic bombs. The agreements stipulated that the recipients not construct their own uranium enrichment facilities (thereby making the recipients totally dependent upon U.S. fuel and preserving the American uranium enrichment near-monopoly) and that U.S. officials have uninhibited inspection privileges of all nuclear laboratories and plants to make sure no weapons were being produced.

Atoms for Peace gave the United States effective control over the atomic programs of many foreign nations. But in addition to meeting that national security objective, Atoms for Peace also handsomely benefitted America's awakening nuclear power industry. The worldwide adoption of U.S. nuclear technology gave American firms a leadership position in the international market that would stand up for many years. The research and power reactors ordered by foreign nations during the late 1950s and early 1960s stimulated the U.S. industry with millions of dollars of business and invaluable practical experience at a time when the domestic program was still getting untracked.

America's atomic partnership scored another victory later in the 1950s with the Euratom program. Following the oil embargo induced by the Suez Canal crisis of 1956, Europe's capitalist nations began to explore ways to increase their energy independence. Nuclear power was an obvious choice, and the United States was an obvious place to get it. Louis Armand, the French president of the new European Atomic Energy Community (Euratom), told the European Parliament in 1958: "The U.S. does not immediately need atomic energy, since it has abundant and cheap conventional

energy. . . . In this case, why not set up in Europe a large complex
of industrial nuclear power stations, making use of the experience
already acquired in the U.S.?"

American business and political officials jumped at the suggestion. The Joint Committee said, "Perhaps of greatest interest to the
U.S. is the opportunity in the Euratom program to demonstrate
U.S. leadership in atomic energy development, an objective which
the Committee considers to be of the highest importance." In debate in the Senate, Senator John Pastore remarked "The proposed
program is important both in terms of strengthening the move
toward European integration and in terms of fostering an attractive
new market for sale of American atomic power equipment abroad."
And AEC Chairman Strauss was pleased that the program would
"provide industry in the United States and Europe with important
engineering experience and data on capital and operating costs."

In other words, Strauss hoped that the Euratom program would
succeed where his Power Reactor Demonstration Program had
failed. American companies had shunned the Demonstration Program because of Strauss's tight-fisted spending policies and his
demand that they share all risks of cost overruns with the AEC.
But Euratom looked far more inviting to private industry. With the
United States *and* the governments of Western Europe underwrit-
ing all expenses, subsidies flowed freely. Better yet, the European
electric utility companies pledged to absorb all cost overruns. Another advantage of the Euratom program was that it was, as the
Babcock and Wilcox Company wrote to the Joint Committee, "a
means of securing a good and early foothold in Euratom countries
for American pressurized water and boiling water reactor types."

The irony of Euratom, as Senator Henry Dworshak pointed out
during the Senate debate, was that the United States was preparing
to spend up to $475 million to develop in Europe something that,
just the year before, the Eisenhower administration and the nuclear
power industry had denounced as sinful for the United States:
publicly owned nuclear power stations. But that flirtation with
public enterprise was perhaps balanced out by the red-blooded
American negotiation tactics used to secure the Euratom contract.
To be blunt, the United States bought the contract. The prevailing
consensus in Europe was that the gas-graphite reactor design being
developed independently by the French and British was the best
in the world. But when Euratom President Louis Armand and two
other Euratom officials toured America, they were dazzled by the
size of its nuclear facilities, the many different kinds of reactors

being developed, and the obviously huge sums of money the United States was spending on nuclear power. Four AEC officials accompanied the Europeans throughout their visit, charming them with rosy predictions of the economics of American-made reactors. The *coup de grâce* came when Washington offered to contribute up to $475 million to aid Euratom's research and construction program; the British, who were also negotiating with Euratom, simply could not match the American bid.

Representatives from the United States and Euratom signed the treaty in November 1958. Its modest aim was to construct the equivalent of 1,000 megawatts of nuclear capacity (by way of comparison, the Dresden One plant was 209 megawatts) over the next five years. The Europeans paid for the American reactors and know-how with subsidies from the U.S. government; in effect, Euratom played the middleman for U.S. government subsidies to U.S. corporations that built nuclear plants in Europe. The U.S. Export-Import Bank provided low-interest loans, and the Atomic Energy Commission leased enriched uranium fuel to Euratom and helped to fund a joint research-and-development program.

After all the fanfare, Euratom produced only three nuclear reactors in Europe (all supplied by General Electric and Westinghouse). Technical problems developed that drastically limited the cost reductions and other expected U.S. domestic benefits. But that was a short-term disappointment. "The Euratom program didn't really stimulate the U.S. nuclear program," admits Charles Weaver of Westinghouse, "but it did stimulate the European dialogue about nuclear power."

With Euratom the United States became the world's acknowledged leader in industrial nuclear energy. The American light water reactor design became the most sought-after in the world, and American companies, especialy GE and Westinghouse, found many European firms eager to establish commercial ties so they could market the light water technology. Competition from the British and French gas-graphite technology was quashed as the most important potential reactor manufacturers in the rest of Europe switched development priorities to light water reactor systems. Here was almost perfect harmony within the American Atomic Brotherhood. The government's interest in maintaining world leadership in civilian nuclear power motivated it to outspend the British and snatch the Euratom contract from them, and that bold maneuver in turn helped install Westinghouse and General

Electric as the all-powerful godfathers of the evolving world nuclear power industry.

Many of the men who now run the nuclear power industry first started the long climb up the corporate ladder in the 1950s. One top General Electric official remembers being told during his job interview, "You shouldn't pass up this chance. You know, in ten or twenty years, our nuclear power business is going to be bigger than the entire company is today. A young man like you could go far." Nuclear executives had good reason for such high hopes. Although they had yet to sell their first commercial nuclear power station by the end of the 1950s, they had nevertheless come a long, long way from 1946.

Now, instead of being illegal, it was positively patriotic to build nuclear power plants. It was in fact so patriotic that the government decided that every American should help pay for them, even if they were constructed in a foreign country. The government naturally had its own reasons for making that decision, but so what? The effect was the same. Industry executives had a clear opportunity to gain control over the entire world nuclear power market, with a minimum of cost and risk to themselves, and they were eager to seize it.

But, as the economists like to say, there is no such thing as a free lunch. Along with the billions of dollars of research-and-development funding, insurance subsidies, and the like came a dependence upon the federal government that years later would come back to haunt the industry. It was easy for executives with visions of nuclear megaprofits to forget that they were but half of a partnership, and that there had been no nuclear power business at all until the national security managers decided in 1953 that the United States needed one. In the long run the industry would pay a price for the massive support it received during the 1950s. Two decades later the industry's inevitable dependence upon the federal government would come back to haunt and nearly destroy it.

3

The
Corporate Nuclear War

The enthusiasm for nuclear power grew a lot faster
than I expected. Maybe it built just a little too fast.
Maybe we didn't adequately foresee within the industry, the Congress, and the AEC all the factors
that were involved. . . . Maybe if it had moved a
little slower, we'd be better off today.

CHARLES WEAVER
*Executive Vice-President for Corporate World
Relations, Westinghouse Electric Corporation*

The language of warfare pervades the business world. The chief
executive officer of a company is often referred to as its "general";
the employees are "troops." Together they plot and carry out "strategies" to "invade" a competitor's market. The "enemy" company,
in turn, moves to "defend" its "territory" and perhaps to "retaliate"
with a flashy new marketing "campaign" that "attacks" what corporate "intelligence" identifies as the opponent's weak points. As
in real wars, "casualties" result, and there are the vanquished and
the victors.

Such military terminology can be justly applied to the events of
the 1960s and early 1970s within America's nuclear industry. During these years nuclear corporations, especially General Electric
and Westinghouse, took over leadership of the Atomic Brotherhood
from the Atomic Energy Commission and began an aggressive
campaign to spread nuclear power stations across America and the
world. Where no market for nuclear-generated electricity existed,
they created one, using cost statistics based on hope instead of
reality. GE and Westinghouse were the foremost propagators of this
nuclear propaganda, but the AEC was most willing to go along. Its
claim in a 1962 report to President Kennedy that nuclear power

was "on the threshold of competitiveness" was rather wildly optimistic; it revealed the degree to which the federal atomic bureaucrats were willing to sacrifice objectivity to bring into being the technology they held so dear.

Although the government had pumped billions of dollars into nuclear power by the early 1960s,* additional subsidies were required before electric utilities ordered their first nuclear power stations in the mid-1960s. These subsidies took the form of falsely low pricing of the power plants by General Electric and Westinghouse, and represented the first salvo in Westinghouse's and GE's invasion of that part of the electric utility market which traditionally had enriched Babcock and Wilcox, Combustion Engineering, and the coal and railroad industries. The aggrieved industries fought back with price cuts and other defensive measures. Before long, oil companies such as Exxon and Gulf joined the nuclear fray. Meanwhile, the Westinghouse-GE competition spilled over into the European and Third World electrical markets, where the Big Two sold nearly half as many reactors as they did at home during the 1960s. To protect against inevitable future tariff barriers, the Two raced to establish networks of affiliated foreign companies that stretched from Tokyo to Paris.

These events were among the high points of the corporate nuclear war that raged quietly across the United States and the world during the 1960s and early 1970s. Most accounts term these the glory years of nuclear power, a time when business was booming, the industry rapidly maturing, and the public still believed in the product and its promoters. Industry forecasters gleefully anticipated $800 *billion* worth of business in the United States alone through the end of the century, and an equivalent sum in foreign markets.

But the battles for markets and industry leadership would take their toll. Struggling first to make nuclear competitive with coal and later to expand their respective market shares, the Big Four reactor vendors—General Electric, Westinghouse, Babcock and Wilcox, and Combustion Engineering—pushed each other into a mutually destructive style of competition that propelled nuclear's

---

* The AEC estimated in 1962 that it had spent $1.275 billion researching and developing nuclear power reactors—about twice as much money as would-be nuclear companies had invested to date. This was but a small fraction of what the AEC was spending on nuclear weapons work. Yet it understated the total government subsidy to nuclear power, for it excluded monies spent on those parts of the nuclear fuel cycle common to both weapons *and* power production, such as uranium exploration, price supports, and enrichment services.

costs onto an irreversibly upward course. The AEC and the Joint Committee on Atomic Energy were so determined that nothing should prevent nuclear power from taking its rightful place as a major U.S. energy source that they blatantly defaulted on their regulatory responsibilities. By regarding those who challenged their version of reality as "kooks" or troublemakers, these federal atomic bureaucrats in fact damaged—perhaps irreparably—the credibility so necessary for the commercial survival of nuclear power. The AEC downgraded reactor safety research and suppressed from public knowledge its own studies about nuclear health hazards. In so doing, it unwittingly set in motion the political forces that now threaten to destroy nuclear power.

THE BIG TWO

In the early 1960s nuclear power remained uncompetitive with coal as a source of electricity. The reactor manufacturers understandably felt frustrated. Nuclear energy was being stymied by a Catch-22 situation: so long as nuclear was more expensive than coal, no utility would order a nuclear power plant. Yet nuclear's costs would not fall until the manufacturers gained more experience building reactors.

It appeared that Westinghouse had found a way out of the dilemma in 1962 when, with the help of AEC subsidies, it garnered orders for two commercial-size reactors. Alarmed officials at General Electric feared that Westinghouse might take an insurmountable lead in the race for technological superiority if GE did not begin selling reactors immediately. They were also worried about the global market and competition from the heavy water and gas-cooled reactors then being developed in foreign countries. "We had a problem like a lump of butter sitting in the sun," said John McKitterick, GE's vice-president for corporate planning. "If we couldn't get orders out of the utility industry, with every tick of the clock it became progressively more likely that some competing technology would be developed that would supersede the economic viability of our own. Our people understood this was a game of massive stakes, and that if we didn't force the utility industry to put those stations on line, we'd end up with nothing."

GE chairman Fred Borch then decided to "ram this thing right on through" by employing a creative but daring marketing strategy that made investing in nuclear power plants a no-risk proposition for utilities. Normally, a utility ordering a power plant dealt with a whole range of subcontracting firms and regulatory agencies, and assumed all risks of material shortages, labor strikes, construction delays, and the countless other snags that can lead to cost overruns. But now GE guaranteed delivery of a complete facility, ready for operation, by a specified future date and for a firm price that was competitive with coal-fired plants. Because all the utility had to do was turn the key, walk in the door, and start the generating equipment, GE referred to these as "turnkey" contracts.

By subsidizing the price of nuclear power to falsely low levels, General Electric hoped to persuade U.S. utilities to buy enough plants to make costs eventually fall. "The turnkeys made the light water reactor a viable product," explains GE nuclear vice-president Bertram Wolfe. "They got enough volume in the business that we could build an engineering staff, standardize our product, and put up facilities to mass-produce things so that the cost went down. That way we got over this tailor-made, one-of-a-kind, high-cost plant."

GE sold its first turnkey plant in December 1963 to the Jersey Central Power and Light Company. Westinghouse flinched at the idea of taking such mammoth risks itself, but it realized that leadership of the industry was at stake, and so moved to neutralize GE's bold maneuver by offering its own turnkey deals. "The competition was rather desperate in those days," recalls Westinghouse executive vice-president Charles Weaver. "To meet it, we had to go a route we didn't necessarily feel was desirable but that we could stand up under. The turnkeys were a very unfortunate perturbation away from the normal way to construct power plants. The construction costs went haywire, and we all suffered. GE," he adds, "suffered a lot more than Westinghouse."

GE officials admit that turnkeys were "a financial disaster." Final costs turned out to be almost 100 percent higher than initial estimates. A study by the RAND Corporation concludes that GE and Westinghouse together lost almost $1 billion on the thirteen turnkey plants they constructed during the mid-1960s, or about $75 million per plant. Nevertheless, the turnkeys served their primary purpose of creating a market for nuclear power plants. They also signaled an important leadership shift within the Atomic Brotherhood. After a decade of government encouragement of commercial nuclear power, the corporations had finally moved aggressively to help themselves.

Some competing company officials chuckle about the financial soaking that GE and Westinghouse took with the turnkeys, but the more sophisticated executives are in fact grateful for the giants' actions. "Both GE and Westinghouse recognized the necessity of taking the leadership role and financial risk in order to get utility acceptance of nuclear power," concedes Babcock and Wilcox nuclear vice-president John McMillan. "They relieved the utilities of substantial risk, allowing them to get familiar with nuclear power, and then going back to the traditional way of business."

The corporate subsidies of the mid-1960s tremendously boosted electric utility companies' interest and confidence in nuclear power. Domestic orders jumped from seven in 1965 to twenty in 1966 and surged to a record high of thirty in 1967. These were aptly christened the "Great Bandwagon" years by Philip Sporn, then president of the American Electric Power Company. Despite a complete lack of data on actual operating costs for reactors (only eight were even operating by 1967), nuclear sales continued at a brisk pace through the late 1960s. With the reactor vendors and the AEC confidently proclaiming the profitability of nuclear power, the utilities saw each additional sale as further proof of the commercial viability of light water reactors. Business analysts began to predict that nuclear energy would account for half of all future power plant orders.

Once they had broken through the utilities' resistance with the low turnkey prices, Westinghouse and General Electric reverted to normal contractual procedures and slowly but deliberately began raising their prices. The utilities did not protest the increases, because they knew that costs of new products are often underestimated. They were also placated by the manufacturers' continual promises that reactor costs would soon stabilize, as the vendors climbed the "learning curve" of this new technology and realized more economies of scale.

But nuclear plant costs did not stabilize; they rose higher and higher. "On the average, the cost of all light water plants ordered in the mid- and late 1960s was underestimated by more than a factor of two in constant dollars," according to an analysis by Harvard economist Irvin Bupp and French nuclear expert Jean-Claude Derian. In other words, nuclear power plants cost utilities (and ultimately ratepayers) twice as much as the reactor vendors claimed. "Claimed" is the key word. The prices the reactor vendors quoted for nuclear plants were mere estimates; there was not one shred of evidence to back up their optimistic assessments. How could there be until one of the plants had been built and operated? The first turnkey plants would not come on line until 1969. And even so, the reactors being sold during the middle to late 1960s were so much larger and more complexly designed than the turnkeys that any cost comparisons would be almost worthless. The Big Four reactor vendors nevertheless persisted in promising ultracheap nuclear electricity. The AEC repeatedly endorsed the industry's estimates. Both parties were guilty, in Bupp and Derian's words, of "blurring the distinction between empirically supported fact and expectation—often quite obviously self-interested expectation."

Hindsight makes it clear that the reactor manufacturers underestimated the prices for nuclear power plants not just during the turnkey era but throughout the 1960s. The crucial difference between the two time periods, however, was who paid for these mistaken estimates. Because the turnkey contracts stipulated that the plant would cost the utility a fixed amount, it was General Electric and Westinghouse that had to swallow the first round of cost overruns. But after the turnkeys, any cost overruns became the responsibility of the utilities and therefore of the ratepayers. Thus freed from financial liability, nuclear manufacturers apparently shaded their cost estimates in an optimistic direction in an attempt to garner more orders and solidify their new position in the electric utility market.

The General Electric–Westinghouse nuclear invasion badly wounded would-be competitors. Babcock and Wilcox and Combustion Engineering, the two heavy-equipment manufacturers that had been masters of the boiler supply business for decades, were two prime examples. "You have to realize that GE and Westinghouse were actually integrating backwards in the utility market," explains William Connolly, Combustion Engineering's senior executive vice-president for corporate and investor relations. Westinghouse and GE had long supplied nearly all of the huge turbine generators that U.S. utilities used to transform steam energy into electricity, but they had never tried to make the heavy-pressure vessels that actually boiled water into steam in the first place. That business was dominated by Babcock and Wilcox and Combustion Engineering, and it would have been virtually impossible to overcome the cost advantages they possessed after years of experience.

But the invention of nuclear reactors—which were, after all, only machines that boiled water in a different way—offered GE and Westinghouse the chance to attack the Babcock-Combustion stronghold. By selling nuclear reactors, GE and Westinghouse could not only increase overall sales but, more important, expand their control over the entire utility supply business. That, in turn, would allow them greater freedom to raise prices for all utility equipment. (The utilities themselves had worried about that likelihood back in the mid-1950s, and strongly urged Combustion Engineering to enter the nuclear reactor business to maintain at least the semblance of competition, according to nuclear division spokesperson Fitzgerald D. Acker.)

In carrying out their invasion, Westinghouse and GE had the distinct advantage of being especially large, wealthy companies. Although both ranked in the *Fortune* 500, neither Combustion nor Babcock had the immense financial resources needed to match the turnkey offers made by the two giants. "The turnkey era was a real threat to us," admits Babcock and Wilcox vice-president John McMillan. "But we made a conscious decision to stay out of it, because our experience told us we couldn't afford it. We did bid for the nuclear steam supply systems during the turnkey years, but we couldn't compete with GE's and Westinghouse's prices." As a result, GE and Westinghouse captured every nuclear reactor order placed by U.S. utilities from 1962 to year-end 1965. Babcock and Wilcox and Combustion Engineering had to content themselves with merely supplying components until January 1966, when Combustion won the contract to supply the reactor for Consumers Power's Palisades plant. Although Combustion notched a second order and Babcock picked up three of its own later in the year, there was no question that market control rested with the Big Two. Westinghouse and General Electric together boasted an 80 percent cumulative market share by the end of 1966. (For a full record of reactor sales, see appendixes.)

The decision by Babcock and Wilcox and Combustion Engineering to enter the nuclear reactor business was thus more a defensive maneuver to protect their industrial "turf" than an aggressive stab at a lucrative new business. "We went in at a time when the projections were that half of the additional installed capacity for the rest of the century would be nuclear," explains Connolly of Combustion. "That meant that the market for our most fundamental product, namely steam supply systems, would be literally cut in half if we stayed in only coal. So in order to protect our birthright as a company, we had to go in."

Other companies did not fare so well. In the 1950s, a dozen or so companies (including such formidable competitors as Manhattan Project veterans Dow Chemical and Union Carbide) were planning to manufacture nuclear reactors, but by the mid-1960s most of them had given up. "The shake-out period for the nuclear industry took place in the early 1960s," recollects Bertram Wolfe of General Electric. "There was some drop-out in the late 1950s, but it was the turnkey years that really did it. A lot of companies ran into technical problems. And they found out it was a long-term endeavor and that profits were way in the future." Explaining why General Electric, Westinghouse, Combustion Engineering, and Babcock and Wilcox were the ones who persevered, Wolfe says, "You either had to be a big firm or one that was inherently tied to the utility industry, so that you looked at your welfare as being tied to them."

Meanwhile, still other companies were struggling to gain control over the other parts of the evolving nuclear energy business. The Bechtel Corporation, the gigantic family-owned construction company headquartered in San Francisco, quickly grabbed a commanding lead in the construction of nuclear power plants. United Engineers and Constructors, a subsidiary of U.S. military contractor Raytheon, and Stone and Webster, an old New England firm, were next in line. The surge of plant orders in 1966 had perked up the uranium-mining business, which had atrophied following the AEC's 1957 decision to curtail orders of uranium ore. Since the AEC was the industry's only important customer, the cutback had caused many mines and mills to close and some smaller companies to go out of business. But when Congress rescued the industry in 1964 by amending the Atomic Energy Act to allow private ownership of nuclear fuel and encourage private competition among miners and producers, the industry began to regain its feet and competition ensued. By 1967 uranium demand had risen to the point where such producers as Anaconda, Utah Construction, Kerr-McGee, and the rest of the industry's firms had nearly tripled their estimates of drilling activity for the next three years. The industry's ranks swelled further in the late 1960s as oil companies Exxon, Gulf, Continental, and Phillips began acquiring vast tracts of land as a hedge against the future day when fuels other than petroleum would energize industrial society.

The fresh burst of exploration and drilling came for the industry just in the nick of time. Uranium was then selling for between $5 and $6 a pound, just cheap enough to make nuclear competitive with coal as an electricity source. But if more uranium reserves were not soon located, the growth in demand induced by the Great Bandwagon sales would nudge uranium fuel prices up to where nuclear could not compete. The fact, however, that most observers expected nuclear to claim half of all future power plant orders gave miners plenty of incentive to find more uranium.

This expectation also spurred Westinghouse and General Electric to secure positions in what promised to be a booming market for processed nuclear fuel. GE predicted in January 1966 that within fifteen years the business of supplying utilities with uranium fuel rods would be worth more on an annual basis than the nuclear reactor business. "It was like razors and razor blades," explained one investment analyst. "Gillette didn't make its money on the razors—it basically sold them so it could sell the blades, which get used up and need to be replaced. The nuclear fuel business was based on the same principle." GE analysts believed that reactor sales would provide the bulk of sales in the industry's early years and grow from a $200 million market in 1965 to a $1.3 billion market in 1980 (in 1965 dollars). Well over one hundred 700-megawatt plants would be operating by then, and each of these would consume $6 million worth of fuel a year. The two markets together would amount to $2.5 billion per year by 1980, plus another $500 million in overseas sales. GE's total sales in 1965 had been $6.2 billion.

The back end of the fuel cycle also seemed to offer lucrative investment opportunities. In 1968 GE broke ground for a $64 million spent-fuel reprocessing plant in Morris, Illinois. Nuclear Fuel Services, a subsidiary of Getty Oil, already had in service a smaller reprocessing plant in West Valley, New York. Allied Chemical announced its intention to have a reprocessing facility with a capacity of five tons a day ready by 1973. National Lead and Atlantic Richfield also expressed strong interest in reprocessing.

In the years of the Great Bandwagon market the reactor vendors reaffirmed their faith in the future of the nuclear power business in the strongest way they could—by investing hundreds of millions of their own dollars in it. General Electric's $60 million fuel fabrication plant opened for business in Wilmington, Delaware, in 1967. The same year, GE announced a major expansion of its turbine generator plant in Schenectady, New York. Combustion Engineering poured $45 million into a pressure vessel production plant in Chattanooga, Tennessee, and Babcock and Wilcox brought a similar plant on line in Mount Vernon, Indiana, for $25 million. It added a components plant in Barberton, Ohio, in 1966 and a fuel fabrication facility at the company's Lynchburg, Virginia headquarters in 1967. Westinghouse exhibited the most ambitious capital investment program: in the spring of 1967 it announced a $285 million expansion of its general manufacturing capacity and admitted that the bulk of the money was going into nuclear equipment and fuel facilities. By late 1968, Westinghouse management felt so confident of the future of nuclear power that it upgraded the capital investment program another $165 million to $450 million.

Shortly after that bold maneuver Gulf Oil, the eleventh largest U.S. corporation, announced its plans to enter the nuclear equipment business. Gulf had recently purchased the atomic energy subsidiary of General Dynamics, whose management had by 1967 finally admitted that the company could not afford to keep pumping millions of dollars into a business that would not pay off for another decade. Gulf renamed its new acquisition Gulf General Atomics and announced that it planned to make a serious run at the Big Four reactor vendors. The high-temperature gas-cooled reactor, which is similar to the light water reactor except that a gas replaces water as the primary coolant, was the centerpiece upon which the oil giant's plans for overtaking the leaders rested.

The hundreds of millions of dollars invested in the nuclear equipment and fuels businesses during the 1960s went a long way towards accomplishing what had long been a primary goal of the Atomic Energy Commission: the private sector's takeover of the nuclear power business from government stewardship. The massive investments in permanent manufacturing facilities signaled, even more clearly than had the earlier turnkey subsidies and Great Bandwagon sales, private capital's confidence in the tremendous long-run profit potential of nuclear power.

The AEC now gladly surrendered leadership of the light water reactor business to the corporations and devoted itself to protecting the industry's flanks. During the 1960s numerous challenges arose to the economic competitiveness and the public acceptability of nuclear power. None knew better than the AEC how critical federal subsidies were to nuclear's supposed competitiveness with coal. That the nuclear industry had had to resort to such desperate measures as the turnkey deals illustrated just how tenuous nuclear's grip on the utility market was; overly stringent regulation on the AEC's part might kill nuclear power before it emerged from commercial childhood. These realities defined the AEC's attitude towards nuclear power regulation until its dissolution in 1975. If the nuclear national security imperative was to be fulfilled, if the federal atomic bureaucracy was to perpetuate itself, if the nuclear corporations were to reap the tremendous profits they anticipated, in short, if nuclear power was to make it in America, then the AEC had to carry out its regulatory responsibilities, in the words of its former chairman Lewis Strauss, "with progress and profit in mind, as well as safety and security."

The incompatibility of nuclear power's economic survival with stringent safety regulation became obvious when it came to licensing the nuclear power plants. It was the job of AEC staffers to check all plants for safe design and sound construction before they were allowed to operate. But no objective criteria and procedures were drawn for the task. Rather, according to a study by the RAND Corporation, the AEC throughout the 1960s conducted only "informal, subjective reviews" of utilities' applications for operating licenses, and *not once* did it refuse to grant such a license. This effective rubber-stamping resulted partly from pressure exerted by the electric utilities, for which every month of delay caused by too careful a scrutiny of plant design translated into tens of millions of dollars in extra interest charges and inflation penalties. But equally if not more important was the determination of reactor vendors and the AEC itself that nuclear power not backslide into uncompetitiveness. As RAND expert Elizabeth Rolph writes, "since the competitive margin for a nuclear plant was exceedingly narrow (if it existed at all), every cost posed a serious threat to marketability."

When the Joint Committee on Atomic Energy held hearings in the spring of 1967 on the licensing of nuclear plants, industry representatives proposed that the AEC adopt more lenient regulations concerning the siting of the plants. One specific industry request was that they be allowed to build nuclear plants closer to the people who would use them, so that transmission costs could be reduced to a level comparable to that of coal-fired plants. Westinghouse's top nuclear executive, Joseph Rengel, earnestly informed the Joint Committee that "plants can now be designed, built, and operated safely in metropolitan areas." Corporate spokesmen also urged that the AEC's licensing process be kept as short and as free of unexpected delays as possible, and offered to help the AEC staff draw up the very licensing criteria their companies would have to meet—a wish that was later granted. Industry officials further requested that, in order to prevent expensive reworking of existing reactors or those already being constructed, newly issued safety regulations apply only to plants not yet under construction.

Critics have pointed out that this request ignored the fact that nuclear power was not yet close to being a mature technology. The size and technical complexity of reactor designs was increasing rapidly during the 1960s, while operating experience was revealing ever greater numbers of safety deficiencies. Under the circumstances, the industry's proposed freeze on safety regulations can only be explained by assuming executives were absolutely convinced that light water reactors were immune from serious accidents. That conviction was perhaps also why industry representatives felt comfortable pushing the AEC to de-emphasize basic accident research. Instead, the industry wanted the AEC to devote its light water reactor research budget to developing and testing new components, designs, and operating standards—in other words, to subsidize reactor improvements that the industry already planned to make for commercial reasons. The industry's presumed confidence in nuclear safety did not, however, preclude its demanding in 1967 that Congress renew the Price-Anderson Act, which relieved the industry of nearly all liability for any major nuclear accident.

The low priority that the AEC placed on nuclear safety is readily apparent from the relatively insignificant amounts of money it budgeted for safety research during the 1960s and early 1970s. While it was spending hundreds of millions of dollars trying to make nuclear power commercially viable, the government's atomic regulatory agency budgeted on an average a mere $35 million a year for safety research and development. And in some years the AEC did not even spend the entire allocation.

This period of benign neglect coincided with the emergence of numerous serious health and safety issues, including the lack of sufficient protection against a "meltdown" of the reactor's fuel core, an accident that might kill and injure thousands; the effect of earthquakes on nuclear reactors; and the health effects of the low-level radiation emitted by nuclear reactors. Nor had the AEC yet taken action on what was probably the most serious problem associated with nuclear fission: how to dispose of radioactive waste products that would remain deadly poisonous for thousands of years.

In addition, the AEC continued the practice begun in the early 1950s of concealing from the public any bad news about nuclear energy. Brookhaven National Laboratory, in a 1963 update of a previous study for the AEC, concluded that a core meltdown in a large commercial power plant would result in 45,000 fatalities and devastate an area equal to that of the state of Pennsylvania. The AEC kept the revised study secret, so as not to alarm citizens. In 1971 the AEC tested the reliability of the emergency core-cooling system, a new safety feature added to provide a second line of defense against a core meltdown. The AEC tried (unsuccessfully) to downplay the disquieting fact that the cooling system had failed to function properly; later, its top researcher on such cooling systems charged that the AEC was censoring reports from his laboratory to prevent Congress from raising embarrassing questions about nuclear reactor safety.

In 1963 the AEC commissioned two of its top scientists, Drs. Arthur Tamplin and John Gofman, to study the health effects of low-level radiation. Tamplin and Gofman examined the data for six years before issuing conclusions that shocked all proponents of nuclear power, especially their AEC bosses in Washington. According to their findings, "If the average exposure of the U.S. population were to reach the allowable 0.17 rads a year average [a rad is a unit of radiation exposure], there would, in time, be an excess of 32,000 cases of fatal cancer plus leukemia per year, and this would occur every year." The two experts recommended that the AEC reduce by a factor of 10 the maximum dose of radiation that nuclear power plants could release onto the general population. Even more chilling was their judgment that "the hazard to this generation of humans from cancer and leukemia is twenty times as great as had been thought previously. The hazard to all future generations, in the form of genetic damage and deaths, has been underestimated even more seriously." Although these findings would be supported by a National Academy of Science study in 1972, the AEC considered them nothing short of heresy. Dr. Tamplin was stripped of his budget and research staff, and Dr. Gofman later resigned, claiming harassment from his AEC superiors. The AEC denied taking retribution against the scientists.

Internal AEC documents leaked in 1974 by dissident staffers to *New York Times* reporter David Burnham provided evidence of other incidents where the AEC had suppressed damaging information. The documents showed, according to Burnham's report, that "on at least two important matters the commission consulted with the industry it was supposed to be regulating before deciding not to publish a study critical of its safety procedures." The internal memos showed that AEC officials consistently "were apparently more concerned about the possible public relations impact of safety studies than the actual safety of reactors."

The AEC had so little money to expend on light water reactor safety during the 1960s partly because it was spending hundreds of millions of dollars helping the industry develop the next generation of nuclear technology: the breeder reactor. The breeder had captured the imagination of nuclear officials back in the 1940s because of its dual capabilities: it simultaneously yielded electricity for industry and plutonium for the military's atomic bombs. Furthermore, since it produced more plutonium over the long run than it consumed, the breeder appeared to offer virtually inexhaustible amounts of low-cost energy. Nuclear scientists, excited by the thought of building a perpetual-motion machine, dreamed of putting an end to scarcity and want. The breeder was more than the next logical development in nuclear technology; it would be the enabling instrument of the next industrial revolution, making possible such feats as the air-conditioning of Africa and the heating of the Subarctic. The scientists realized that such reliance on breeder reactors would have the unavoidable consequence of producing many tons of plutonium, but considered that a manageable problem.

General Electric, with AEC funding, had begun exploring the breeder concept as early as 1948. Although technical difficulties and military imperatives forced the scuttling of that project, the AEC continued breeder research and development throughout the 1950s. Meanwhile, Washington's determination that the United States become and remain the number one nuclear nation had forced the hasty commercialization of the Navy's light water reactor, a design grossly inferior (in theory) to the breeder in thermal and economic efficiency. Having gambled the preservation of America's commercial and diplomatic nuclear hegemony on the light water reactor, the industry and the government had good reason to follow through with its full-scale commercialization. But officials on both sides of the Brotherhood agreed that the light water design was a stopgap measure, to be employed only until the breeder was ready for commercial operation.

By the mid-1960s, each of the major reactor manufacturers was working earnestly on breeders. The laboratory competition was as intense and important as the real-world struggle for reactor sales. Companies such as North American Aviation and General Dynamics, which had been left behind by the GE-Westinghouse turnkey rush, realized that they had to compete successfully in breeders if they were to remain in the nuclear power business. According to Willard Rockwell, then its chief executive officer, North American

Aviation was spending over $20 million annually on research and development in the race for technical leadership of breeder technology. But GE and Westinghouse were equally determined not to relinquish their hard-won control of the nuclear industry. Both had active breeder programs, and GE had even begun building an experimental reactor in Arkansas with financial help from the AEC, the West German government, Euratom, and a group of American utilities.

The AEC was anxious to subsidize the industry's campaign to commercialize breeder technology, especially after the surge of reactor orders by American utilities in 1966 and 1967. It was worried that the United States might exhaust its uranium reserves before the year 2000 unless steps were taken immediately to develop breeders and other types of more fuel-efficient reactors. A partial meltdown on October 5, 1966, at the Enrico Fermi demonstration breeder reactor located just outside Detroit did nothing to change this view.*

Milton Shaw, a protégé of the Navy's nuclear czar, Hyman Rickover, and the man who directed the AEC's breeder development program during the 1960s, claims that the government spent even more to develop breeder reactors than it did on light water technology. "The industry was relatively low-funded for the development of light water reactors," says the former top official. "The government didn't set up the industrial base for light water reactors the way it did for the breeders."

Westinghouse got the jump on its competitors in 1967 by capturing the AEC's contract to design and operate the Fast Flux Test Facility, the government's research plant for breeder work. The next step was to demonstrate the technical feasibility of a commercial-size breeder reactor. The reactor manufacturers were indignant when Milton Shaw insisted that the AEC play an active role not just in the demonstration project's financing but also in the day-to-day technical decisions. Late in 1969, the AEC awarded contracts for the reactor's conceptual design to GE, North American Aviation, and Westinghouse. By 1972, Shaw had pulled together a consortium of some seven hundred utilities into a Project Management Corporation, which would help manage the project and pay a fraction of its cost. In April 1972, the reactor manufacturers, anxious after the three years of delay, submitted bids to design and

* For the full story of the Fermi accident, see John Fuller's *We Almost Lost Detroit* (New York: Reader's Digest Press, 1975).

build the demonstration breeder. "By the time the bids were made, Westinghouse, GE, and Rockwell International [North American's new name after its 1970 merger with Atomics International] all had sizable organizations already in place, ready to pursue the breeder work," recalls Dr. Arthur Randol, a former breeder expert for the American Nuclear Energy Council.

When Westinghouse was awarded the all-important contract to build the nation's first commercial-size breeder reactor, Joseph Rengel, the company's executive vice-president for nuclear energy, told *Business Week* he saw the selection "as reinforcing our number one position in the reactor business." So did GE and Rockwell. The AEC placated the runners-up by naming them junior contractors, which ensured that each would get about a third of the work passed down by Westinghouse. Babcock and Wilcox also got a slice of the project when it was chosen to supply the pressure vessel for the reactor, which would be located at Clinch River, Tennessee, near the government's Oak Ridge atomic complex. The project's $700 million cost was shared among the utility consortium ($257 million), the reactor vendors ($20 to $40 million), and the taxpayers (the remainder), who were also responsible for any cost overruns. There have been many. As of 1982, estimates are that the final cost of the Clinch River breeder reactor project will be more than $6 billion, a nearly tenfold increase over initial projections.

THE GLOBAL MARKET

The extension and consolidation of U.S. control over the nonsocialist world's development of nuclear power was another of the Atomic Brotherhood's great achievements in the 1960s. Continuing the atomic foreign policy evidenced first in the Atoms for Peace program and later in the Euratom treaty, the U.S. government locked foreign countries into dependence on U.S.-supplied nuclear fuel and equipment by offering it to them at massively subsidized prices. Washington's subsidies helped Westinghouse and General Electric become the unquestioned leaders of the world nuclear power industry. According to an analysis by the Pacific Studies Center, the U.S. government's Export-Import Bank had by 1974 supported the sale of nuclear plants and fuel to foreign countries with loans and financial guarantees of approximately $2.4 billion. Exports accounted for nearly one-third of all reactors the Big Two sold between 1956 and 1974. Royalty payments from foreign cor-

porate purchasers of Westinghouse's and General Electric's nuclear know-how were another source of revenue.

The Big Two's overseas sales not only cushioned them against
the ups and downs of the domestic market but also further widened
the gap between them and their smaller, nonexporting competitors,
Babcock and Wilcox and Combustion Engineering. Exports were
especially important to Westinghouse and GE in the years before
U.S. utilities fully accepted nuclear power: of the seventeen large
reactors sold by the Big Two before 1965, eleven went to foreign
customers. And when domestic sales slumped for two years beginning in 1969, the Big Two managed to keep their business volume
up by landing contracts for nine reactor exports. These later exports
were doubly important since revenues were needed to help pay
off the massive capital investment program then under way. In
contrast, Babcock and Wilcox and—to a lesser extent—Combustion
Engineering were hurt badly when sales slumped right after the
investment surge. According to a source inside the company, Babcock and Wilcox lost approximately $30 million a year on its nuclear
business during the late 1960s.

The Big Two's nuclear export superiority was due not only to
their greater size and international business experience but also to
their early mastery of light water reactor technology. William Fleming, the head of Combustion Engineering's International Division,
admits, "We lost out to GE and Westinghouse in Europe because
we were late in developing nuclear power in the United States."
But it was not so much that Combustion Engineering and Babcock
and Wilcox were late as it was that GE and Westinghouse were
early. The Big Two's work for the Manhattan Project and their
consequent involvement in the Navy's nuclear program gave them
a crucial head start on light water reactor technology, which in turn
enabled them to sell nuclear reactors sooner and cheaper than their
competitors. With capital-intensive products like nuclear reactors,
more sales volume meant lower production costs, lower prices for
the buyer, and therefore still greater sales in the future. Technological superiority was a self-reinforcing advantage that simultaneously translated into market leadership.

By 1968 General Electric had exported twelve nuclear reactors
and Westinghouse eight, mostly to advanced capitalist nations such
as Japan, West Germany, Spain, and Italy. These twenty sales gave
the two American multinationals a 25 percent share of the nonsocialist world's nuclear equipment market. To further their goal of
global nuclear superiority, each of the Big Two strung together

networks of foreign licensee companies during the 1960s. The corporation executives were savvy enough to realize that Japan and the advanced capitalist nations of Europe would not long allow foreign domination of a commodity with such obvious economic and national security ramifications as nuclear power; as soon as possible, they would use federal subsidies to create their own nuclear power industries, just as the United States had. Indeed, the nuclear establishments of France, Canada, and Great Britain (each of which had begun developing nuclear power during or shortly after World War II) were already quite advanced on their own nuclear programs and hence did not permit the import of U.S.-supplied reactors.* GE nuclear vice-president Bertram Wolfe explains how his company responded to the situation: "When we were planning our export markets in the 1960s, we realized that our markets would be limited by the fact that the Europeans would develop their own nuclear capability. That was part of the reason we chose to push for licensing agreements, rather than saturate them with reactor components."

These agreements called for the foreign licensee company to pay a certain annual fee to its American partner for the privilege of copying and marketing the American's already developed technology. The American partner also received royalties from each sale by the licensee; these usually amounted to 3 or 4 percent of the sale's total value. In some cases, Westinghouse and GE would license a foreign company in which they owned a substantial portion of the outstanding stock, thereby profiting in three separate ways.

For example, in 1964 GE signed a multi-year technology-exchange agreement with Allgemeine Elektricitats Gesellschaft AG Telefunken (AEG), a leading West German multinational corporation in which GE had a 12 percent ownership share. AEG shared a dominance of West Germany's electrical equipment business with the Siemens corporation that was similar to the control GE and Westinghouse exercised over the American market. Not surprisingly, Westinghouse soon thereafter signed a licensing agreement with Siemens in order to compete against the General Electric–AEG team. Siemens reportedly paid $2 million for Westinghouse's nuclear technology.

The licensing agreements allowed the Big Two to continue to

---

* The one exception was France's importation in 1960 of a 309-megawatt pressurized water reactor from Westinghouse.

profit from markets ostensibly closed to them. "The reason to establish a licensee agreement in the first place is because in the
long run you assume that market may be closed to you," says John
Kreuthmeier of Westinghouse's international nuclear division. "So
you are not likely to serve that country unless you link up with
somebody inside the tariff wall."

GE's and Westinghouse's licensing strategies were in most instances closely related to their success in exporting plants to a
country. GE's first nuclear exports were to West Germany in 1958,
to Italy in 1959, and to Japan in 1960. Their first licensing agreements followed the same pattern, beginning with the 1964 link
with AEG. In 1967 GE added Italy and Japan to its licensee empire
by signing with Ansaldo of Italy and with Hitachi and Toshiba, its
traditional business partners in Japan. Westinghouse's first two
nuclear exports were to Belgium and Italy in 1956. The following
year, Westinghouse signed licensing agreements with Belgium's
Ateliers des Constructions Electriques de Charleroi (ACEC) and
with two Italian companies, Fiat and Breda. In 1958 Westinghouse
broke the pattern when it squeezed into the French market via a
licensing agreement with Framatome, a newly created nuclear subsidiary of Creusot-Loire, a leading French manufacturer. Westinghouse also added licensees in Spain and in Japan during the 1960s;
the entry into Japan was accomplished through an expansion of
its traditional relationship with the Japanese giant corporation,
Mitsubishi Heavy Industries.

"Westinghouse thinks in terms, not of a U.S. market versus a
foreign market, but of a world market," declared Frank Delzio, the
company's top official in Europe during the early 1970s. In that
time period the European component of that world market took on
special significance, because Westinghouse and GE were running
neck and neck in nuclear reactor orders back in the United States.
Nuclear power was just then beginning to come into its own in
Japan and Europe, and a number of underdeveloped countries also
tied their energy futures to the power of the atom. In the six years
between 1969 and 1974, GE and Westinghouse amassed between
them an outstanding export record, selling thirty-six reactors overseas—almost double the twenty exported during the previous
twelve years. Westinghouse exported twenty-one of the thirty-six
reactors, which catapulted it into a slight lead over GE in cumulative exports.

In an important new development, more than a third of the Big

Two's exports were to underdeveloped countries such as Taiwan, South Korea, Brazil, and the Philippines. (Previously, the only exports to a Third World nation had been two reactors GE sold to India in 1962.) Nuclear power was marketed as a kind of technological magic wand that would help transform these nations from economic backwardness to modern industrial prosperity. The selling was made easier by the fact that most of these countries had been U.S. client states for years.

But the main foreign challenge facing the Big Two in the early 1970s was finding a way to infiltrate the increasingly resistant European market. The strong attraction was the projection that $30 billion worth of nuclear equipment and fuel would be bought and sold there during the coming decade. Although much of this business figured to be transacted in the continent's industrial heartland of France, West Germany, and Great Britain—countries that by now had their own nuclear equipment manufacturers—the rest of Europe remained open to American exports. Italy bought three reactors from GE. Spain purchased eight U.S.–supplied reactors, and Switzerland, Sweden, and Belgium bought two each. Westinghouse clearly got the better of GE in each of these national markets except for Italy; it swept the Swiss, Swedish, and Belgian orders and allowed GE only two of the eight Spanish sales.

The key to Westinghouse's greater success at penetrating these markets in the face of intense economic nationalism was its chameleonlike ability to assume the form and appearance of a domestic company. The European governments were demanding local participation in nuclear plant orders; Westinghouse responded sooner than GE did, and began prominently featuring its licensee firms in all its contract bids. GE's lack of a licensee company in either Belgium or Sweden was cited by all concerned as a major reason why it lost those countries' orders to Westinghouse. And while GE ran its international nuclear sales operation from the United States, Westinghouse in 1970 established in Brussels a nuclear subsidiary known as WENESE (short for Westinghouse Electric Nuclear Energy Systems Europe), which served as the linchpin of Westinghouse's European empire.

When France finally admitted in 1969 that the gas-cooled nuclear reactor technology it had been developing since the 1950s was a failure, Westinghouse tried to get in on the ground floor of France's reinvigorated nuclear program via an ambitious attempt to purchase a controlling share in Jeumont-Schneider, a leading French nuclear equipment firm. Although the French government rebuffed that effort, after long negotiations it did allow Westinghouse to purchase 45 percent ownership in Framatome, the firm with which it had held a licensing agreement since 1958. Meanwhile, Westinghouse was buying up 70 percent of the equity in its Belgian and Spanish licensees, ACEC and Westinghouse, SA. It also established a licensee relationship with the Swedish firm SGAB, and with the Nuclear Power Company of Great Britain, in anticipation of future British dissatisfaction with its gas-graphite reactor technology.

Thus, Westinghouse by the end of 1971 possessed a strong commercial base in every major electrical equipment market in Europe except for West Germany, where it was searching for a suitable replacement for the renegade Siemens, which had terminated its agreement with Westinghouse in 1969. Unlike GE, which regarded its licensees as individual appendages to the parent company, Westinghouse molded them into a multinational manufacturing unit. In explaining the Westinghouse strategy in December 1970, the company's European nuclear boss, Frank Baker, said, "I hope someday we'll build a plant in, say, Finland, with a pressure vessel from our partner Creusot-Loire [Framatome] in France, pumps from ACEC in Belgium, and pipes from Italy." An extra advantage Westinghouse derived from teaming up with its European licensees was its consequent qualification for the low-interest loans that European governments gladly gave to spur exports.

The building of a nuclear empire in Europe was in keeping with Westinghouse chairman Donald Burnham's goal of making 30 percent of total sales to overseas customers, an accomplishment that Burnham believed would help Westinghouse in its constant struggle to catch up with arch-rival General Electric. And Westinghouse did best GE in the European nuclear sweepstakes. With its licensees acting as the point men in their respective countries, Westinghouse nuclear products found their way into markets that probably would have been inaccessible had the sales operation been conducted directly from Pittsburgh headquarters. Although GE attempted to imitate the Westinghouse strategy in 1974 by launching its own European nuclear subsidiary, Rotterdam Nuclear, the move came too late for GE to regain the ground it had already lost.

THE GOLDEN YEARS

The early 1970s were a time of euphoria within the American nuclear power industry, when all the grand visions of the past appeared to be on the verge of realization. U.S. utility companies began ordering nuclear power plants like never before—140 reactors were bought between 1970 and 1974, an average of 28 a year. But even that blistering pace would have to quicken if the industry was to fulfill President Nixon's wish to have 1,000 nuclear plants in use by the year 2000.

Despite the drastic increase in reactor orders, the already bitter competition between the Big Four grew sharper. The battle still centered around General Electric and Westinghouse, each of which was prepared to do whatever was necessary to be number one in nuclear energy. Westinghouse management believed it had finally found in nuclear power a business where it would not have to play its usual role of second fiddle to GE. But its larger rival would hear none of it. "As far as GE is concerned," declared Thomas Paine, vice-president of GE's Power Generation Group, "it is absolutely necessary to be first in nuclear energy, and that includes the nuclear fuel business." More than competitive pride was at stake: nuclear power was expected to be the main source of energy in the approaching postpetroleum era. Industry officials predicted $800 billion worth of nuclear fuel and equipment would be bought and sold by the year 2000, making nuclear energy one of the largest industries in the world economy. It also figured to be one of the most profitable. It enjoyed almost unlimited financial and political support from the federal government and, owing to the advanced, highly capital-intensive technology it employed, was destined to be controlled by a small number of large corporations.

The Big Two spared no effort in their battle to be number one. Westinghouse invested $60 million a year—the equivalent of its Power Systems Company's entire earnings in 1973—to expand its nuclear production capacity. Exact comparable figures for GE are not publicly available, but industry insiders reckoned it was spending at least as much as Westinghouse, if not more. GE's Thomas Paine did admit to *Business Week* in 1973 that his company was investing more in nuclear energy than in any other business, and that it had "laid plans for expansion and consolidation in all phases of the nuclear business until the turn of the century."

But by the end of 1974 it was clear that Westinghouse was getting the better of GE. It had won both the battle for Europe and the AEC contract for the Clinch River breeder reactor, and had opened a significant lead over GE in the race for reactor orders from U.S. utilities. Westinghouse landed fifty-two orders during the domestic sales surge of the early 1970s, giving it a 37 percent share of the market. GE fell to a 26 percent share in those years, while Combustion Engineering climbed to 18 percent and Babcock and Wilcox registered 12 percent. As a result of the sales blitz, industry observers stopped looking with skepticism upon Westinghouse's claims that its nuclear business was turning a profit. GE and Babcock and Wilcox also announced that their nuclear operations were finally in the black on an annual basis. It appeared to be only a matter of time before the Big Four completely recovered their huge initial investments in nuclear energy and began reaping the fantastic profits they had been waiting for.

One worry the Big Four did have was Gulf Oil's successful penetration of the nuclear business. Its General Atomic nuclear subsidiary had slipped past the Big Four to sell eight nuclear plants during the early 1970s, and the oil giant quickly made it clear it was not content to stop there. In late 1973 Gulf announced that it planned to spend $500 million to improve its high-temperature gas-cooled reactor and make a strong bid for an increased share of the nuclear market. This massive capital investment was made easier by a $200 million infusion of cash from another oil company, Royal Dutch/Shell. Shell's purchase of half of Gulf's General Atomic subsidiary was the cheapest entry into the nuclear business available to it. A Shell official told *Business Week* the company's studies "showed that we could not expect at this stage to develop our own nuclear technology on a reasonable time scale and on a competitive basis."

In a related development, Gulf and Shell officials announced plans to join with Allied Chemical in a company called Allied General Nuclear Services, which planned to build and operate a reprocessing facility in Barnwell, South Carolina. This was good news for the entire nuclear industry, since previous efforts at reprocessing were turning out to be dismal failures. Getty Oil had closed its West Valley, New York plant in 1972 after six years of unprofitable operations, and left the state of New York with the job of disposing of more than 600,000 gallons of radioactive waste products. Severe technical and safety problems had rendered GE's Morris, Illinois reprocessing facility inoperable and eventually caused GE to close the plant.

But the most pressing problem on the minds of nuclear industry executives in the early 1970s was the ever-rising cost of nuclear power plants. The price stabilization so often and confidently promised by reactor vendors in the 1960s never occurred. Measured in real, noninflated dollars, the plants that began to produce electricity in the early 1970s were about twice as costly as the turnkey-era plants; those that came on line in 1975 were three times as expensive.

Industry executives blamed nuclear's spiraling costs on environmentalists; their protests and lawsuits postponed the construction and licensing of power plants and forced the government to mandate what seemed to nuclear proponents an endless series of arbitrary, overly strict, retroactive regulations that hindered nuclear progress. This view was in fact contradicted by a study by the RAND Corporation, which concluded that it was not environmentalists or government regulations that were the problem, but rather industry mismanagement and the immaturity of commercial nuclear technology. By insisting on rapid commercialization of light water reactors (instead of a gradual program of development, testing, and then commercial deployment) and regarding safety regulations as mere perfunctory annoyances, the industry brought on its own problems. The RAND study argued that the rapid pace of evolution in nuclear plant design prevented the Atomic Energy Commission from developing sensible, objective regulations and forced lengthy and costly reviews of each individual license application.

Yet even RAND's analysis fails to reach the root of the problem, which was the intense rivalry between the Big Four reactor vendors for market leadership. Two basic assumptions defined the nature of that competition. The first was that a mutually reinforcing relationship existed between technical leadership and market leadership: technical and cost advantages led to increased sales, which made possible the additional research and development and the economies of scale needed to drive reactor costs down still further. The second assumption was based on the capital-intensiveness of nuclear-generated electricity. It held that the larger the reactor was, the cheaper its electricity would be. Thus, the fight for market leadership seesawed back and forth, depending on which vendor had the largest, most sophisticated reactor on the market. Richard Van Hollen, Combustion Engineering's sales manager for its Nuclear Power Systems Division, summarizes the industry's leapfrogging pattern of competition through 1974 this way: "A reactor vendor would come out with a new design, and in response to challenges from other people, he would make it about 5 to 7 percent larger to justify it to the utilities. And that reactor would sell like hot cakes for about a year, and then the vendor on the bottom of the heap would come out with a new design that was another 5 percent larger, and he'd sell for the next year and a half."

This frenzied style of competition had four separate but related inflationary effects on the cost of nuclear power plants. First, the extra money spent redesigning and enlarging the reactor had to be recovered upon sale. Second, the constant changes in reactor size and design meant that vendors did not stick with any one design long enough to learn to produce it in the cheapest, most efficient manner; in other words, it was harder for vendors to climb the learning curve of nuclear technology. Nor could vendors fully enjoy the economies of scale available through mass production of the same piece of equipment. Finally, the shifts in reactor design forced the AEC to perform a custom review of each license application, a time-consuming process that cost electric utilities millions of extra dollars in interest payments and inflation penalties.

The constant upgrading of nuclear power reactors also posed potentially great risks to public safety. James Deddens, manager of Babcock and Wilcox's Project Management Department, explains that in response to the competition, vendors would sometimes have to "go out on a technical limb" and promise things that could not always be delivered. "When you get into that kind of competitive situation," says Deddens, "you may sell something that hasn't been tested as thoroughly as it would be today." According to Deddens, this was especially true of firms such as Babcock and Wilcox and Combustion Engineering, which lacked the lavish research and development budgets of the Big Two. The danger posed by nuclear reactors designed hastily and under intense competitive pressure was apparent to at least one major utility industry figure as early as 1968. Philip Sporn, president of the American Electric Power Company, approached the threat in a cautious but businesslike manner, warning, "We're going to have some accidents with atomic plants. . . . Let's get our experience and have our accidents now before we take more chances with more plants."

The AEC put an end to this cycle when it set a 1,300-megawatt ceiling on reactor size in March 1973. Deddens of Babcock and Wilcox sees the AEC's move as a blessing. "It stopped the horsepower race," he says. "We were extrapolating plants further and further out [in size] without the benefit of operating experience." Deddens concedes that no vendor could have unilaterally taken such a decision, because "the competition would not have allowed it." The AEC further encouraged standardized reactor designs as a means of reducing the time of AEC staff needed to review and approve plants for construction and operation.

Nevertheless, nuclear's costs continued to escalate much faster than the inflation rate. Luckily for the nuclear industry, the price of coal also rose steadily in the early 1970s. A remark made in 1971 by an AEC official was, if anything, even more accurate three years later: "Nuclear power remains highly competitive only because increases in fossil-fuel plants' investment costs and fuel costs have permitted it to do so."

But since nuclear's cost did not seem to have any negative impact on sales during the early 1970s (U.S. utilities ordered a record forty-one reactors in 1973), industry executives felt secure in dismissing it as an annoying but temporary problem that would disappear once opposition to nuclear power was overcome. But in fact antinuclear sentiment appeared to be growing, and largely because of the Atomic Brotherhood's own arrogance. In 1969 the Congress passed the National Environmental Policy Act (NEPA), which, in H. Peter Metzger's words, "imposed a specific responsibility on federal officials to *reorder their priorities* [his emphasis] so that the environmental costs and benefits will assume their proper place along with other considerations." Later that year, citizens worried about thermal pollution of Chesapeake Bay intervened at the construction hearings for two nuclear plants that the Baltimore Gas and Electric Company wanted to build at Calvert Cliffs, Maryland. When the AEC refused to consider the plants' environmental effects, the citizens sued to force it to comply with NEPA requirements. In July 1971, the U.S. Court of Appeals in Washington, D.C., ruled in the citizens' favor and excoriated the AEC for interpreting NEPA so narrowly as to make "a mockery of the Act." Unfazed, the nuclear industry pressured the AEC to appeal or otherwise resist the ruling of the court (and therefore Congress). But James Schlesinger, then a young bureaucrat President Nixon had plucked from the Office of Management and Budget and appointed as the new chairman of the AEC in an attempt to shore up the commission's public credibility, refused to yield to the industry's entreaties. In October 1971 Schlesinger admonished the American Nuclear Society that "it is not the AEC responsibility to ignore on your behalf an indication of Congressional intent, or to ignore the courts."

In 1972 the White House tried to remove the NEPA thorn from the nuclear industry's paw by asking Congress to gut the act of its power. Nixon asked Congress for special legislation that, among other things, would have relieved utilities planning nuclear power plants from preparing environmental-impact statements and submitting to public hearings.

The dangers posed by such obvious prejudice compelled *Business Week* to suggest in a June 1973 editorial that the AEC be broken up in order to contain the erosion of public confidence in nuclear power. But the nuclear industry, blinded by commercial success and visions of future grandeur to the swelling public resentment and resistance about to engulf it, obstinately refused to heed such good-intentioned and intelligent warnings.

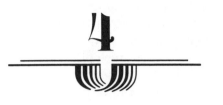

The Fall from Glory

Just when they least expected it, the men who ran America's nuclear power industry suffered one of the most stunning reversals of fortune in the history of American capitalism. It seemed impossible that their industry—composed of some of the world's most powerful global corporations, backed to the hilt by the world's mightiest government, and possessing a technology that seemed the very embodiment of progress—might not fulfill the triumphant destiny they had so long envisioned. But once confident of the inevitability of their victory, these men were forced by a series of setbacks during the second half of the 1970s to adjust to an entirely different vision of the future.

Many of these setbacks came, surprisingly, at the hands of the industry's long-time partner in Washington, which in the interest of preventing nuclear plant accidents at home and blocking the spread of nuclear weapons abroad began marginally to reduce its support of the industry. The change of heart came at a bad time: owing to their own deep-seated financial problems and to reduced growth in America's demand for electricity, U.S. utilities ordered scarcely a dozen nuclear plants after 1974. Foreign sales also dried up as Washington tried to stanch the dangerous flow of nuclear materials around the world by restricting U.S. exports. Industry officials felt their federal partners had betrayed them in their hour of direst need, and relations within the Atomic Brotherhood deteriorated to an all-time low.

What made the United States' turn away from nuclear power during these years doubly bewildering to industry officials was their conviction that, thanks to the Organization of Petroleum Exporting Countries, the nation needed nuclear power more than ever before. OPEC's September 1973 oil embargo and the subsequent skyrocketing prices heralded a dramatic shift in the international economic balance of power; suddenly the United States and the other advanced industrial nations were subjected to the same frightening vulnerability to the decisions of foreign nations that the world's colonies and neo-colonies had endured for centuries. The obvious threat this posed to national security motivated governments in the advanced industrial nations to accelerate their already ambitious nuclear programs.

In the United States, President Nixon requested the elimination of public participation in the licensing of nuclear plants and increased government subsidies to private energy companies. Project Independence, the plan Nixon claimed would free the United States from dependence upon foreign energy sources by the year 1980, placed major emphasis on nuclear power and especially on breeder reactors. The President's goal of having nuclear power supply over half of America's electricity by the twenty-first century would, according to the AEC, require that four hundred plutonium-fueled breeders dot the countryside by then. In the meantime, utilities would have to order between forty and forty-five light water reactors per year. Wall Street approved these strategies. Security analysts there enthusiastically received a November speech by General Electric's chief executive officer, Reginald H. Jones, in which Jones touted nuclear energy as the solution, achievable "in this century," to the energy crisis paralyzing the economies of the capitalist world.

It appeared that America's energy crisis would turn out to be the nuclear industry's gain. The same looked to be true in Europe, which lacked the United States' domestic energy resources. American reactor manufacturers expected European utilities to begin ordering $40 billion worth of nuclear fuel and equipment *every year*. As one GE official noted happily, "Several large countries—France, Italy, and Spain—have said as a matter of national policy that all new electrical capacity additions will be nuclear." Western Europe's economic policy body, the Organization for Economic Cooperation and Development (OECD), pledged that nuclear would supply half of its total energy by the year 2000. And in Japan, which had even fewer domestic energy resources than Europe, an all-out effort to increase nuclear reliance was announced. The government envisioned sixty-six operating nuclear plants by 1985—an elevenfold increase—and began discussions with General Electric and Exxon about building an enrichment plant in Japan. U.S. nuclear companies anticipated that OPEC's actions would also force underdeveloped nations to buy more nuclear power plants.

No sooner had these grand plans been articulated than they began to unravel. Although U.S. utilities tendered twenty-six orders for nuclear power plants in 1974, the more important and ominous news was that they had to back out of eight previous orders. The Consolidated Edison Company's inability to pay its quarterly dividend in April 1974 was a stark symbol of the financial difficulties that forced the cancellations.

In addition to the eight nuclear plants canceled in 1974, the construction schedules of scores more were deferred by utilities with neither the money nor the customer demand to justify them. In contrast, orders for coal-fired plants, which were less capital-intensive and hence cheaper to finance, increased, outnumbering nuclear sales for the first time since 1969. Desperate utilities quickly demanded from their public regulatory commissions massive rate increases, which boosted revenues more than 30 percent in 1975. Nevertheless, the nuclear decline continued. Utilities canceled eleven plants that year—almost three times as many as they ordered.

Nuclear officials wasted no time in blaming the stall on environmentalists and overly stringent government regulations. William R. Gould, chairman of the Atomic Industrial Forum, told the Joint Committee on Atomic Energy it had to speed up the licensing and construction process before utilities could resume ordering nuclear plants in the amounts necessary to solve the nation's long-term energy problems. Only by cutting government red tape, he argued, could the Joint Committee alleviate the financial problems that were discouraging utilities from purchasing nuclear power plants. Gould suggested the elimination of the public hearing at the operating-license stage and an end to expensive equipment retrofits. "When the AEC insists on a design change after a construction permit has been issued, it may well mean replacing a piece of equipment or a system that requires so long a lead time for delivery that it prolongs the construction schedule," he explained. The longer the project drags on, the greater the impact of interest charges and rising price inflation on the plant's total capital cost. Gould denied that such a speed-up would compromise the plant's safety.

Both President Nixon and, later, President Ford endorsed the industry's approach, but the implementing legislation they sent to

Congress did not pass. The defeat of these measures reflected the nuclear industry's trouble on the political as well as the economic front. Public criticism of the Atomic Energy Commission's past deceits, arrogance, and pro-industry bias forced the government to abolish the AEC in an attempt to regain public support for commercial nuclear power. Effective January 1, 1975, the AEC's promotional tasks, including weapons production, were assigned to the newly created Energy Research and Development Administration (ERDA), which later became the Department of Energy. Licensing and regulatory responsibilities were placed under the new Nuclear Regulatory Commission (NRC). Although the changes were basically cosmetic (84 percent of ERDA's new nuclear staff were former AEC employees), they signaled that the atomic establishment was no longer immune to public pressure.

This pressure had grown in the early 1970s as the isolated nuclear critics and citizen interveners of the 1960s were joined by national environmental and consumer representatives such as Friends of the Earth, the Union of Concerned Scientists, and Ralph Nader. Public hearings on the emergency core-cooling system (ECCS), which the Union of Concerned Scientists and citizen interveners had forced the AEC to convene in 1972, were an important catalyst for bringing together these groups. Through cross-examination and the introduction of interoffice memoranda, the nuclear critics demonstrated that, contrary to the AEC's soothing public pronouncements, there was considerable doubt within the AEC about whether the emergency core-cooling system would actually work. Thus, the ECCS hearings also revealed two important facts about the federal atomic bureaucracy: not all of its scientists were confident about nuclear safety, and the AEC leadership was willing to lie to prevent knowledge of that fact from reaching the public.

Meanwhile, Dr. Henry Kendall, an MIT scientist who had had a change of heart after years of designing nuclear weapons for the government, had involved Ralph Nader in the nuclear issue. Nader's Critical Mass '74, the first national antinuclear conference, brought together 1,200 dedicated but rather dejected activists who had been fighting what appeared to be hopeless, isolated battles in their local communities against proposed nuclear power plants. Their major resistance tactic, legal intervention in the licensing process, was not working. Looking at the extremely limited role for public participation in the process and the AEC's blatant pro-industry bias, nuclear opponents began to believe that the system was rigged against them.

Their solution was to take their case to the public. In films, leaflets, and public forums, local activists spread the word about nuclear power's dangers to public health and safety. They pointed to the revelations of the ECCS hearings and the low-level radiation and cancer study conducted by AEC scientists Gofman and Tamplin as evidence that some expert scientists disagreed with the nuclear establishment about nuclear power. The scientific community provided activists further ammunition on August 6, 1975, when the Union of Concerned Scientists sent to the President and the Congress a petition signed by over 2,300 scientists, including numerous Nobel Prize winners, which called the dangers of nuclear power "altogether too great" and urged a non-nuclear energy future for the United States. The Atomic Brotherhood's own past misdeeds also provided nuclear opponents with compelling arguments. The list of AEC deceptions, cover-ups, and favors to industry had grown embarrassingly long by 1975 and had been verified in front-page reports in the *New York Times*. Confronted with an issue whose technical details were intimidating and about which the experts seemed to disagree anyway, and now with evidence that their government had been suppressing the full truth for years, many average citizens were persuaded to oppose nuclear power.

The nuclear industry responded by initiating its own public relations offensive. The *New York Times* reported on January 17, 1975, that "the atomic energy industry has decided to almost double the funds it devotes to influencing the views of key Government officials, newsmen and such organizations as labor unions and women's groups." In a secret memo obtained by *Times* reporter David Burnham, Atomic Industrial Forum president Carl Walske explained to his board of directors that a major reason for the increase of the annual budget to nearly $1.4 million was the abolition of the Atomic Energy Commission, which meant that instead of the "countless AEC features, speeches, media relations, booklets, films, and background papers about the benefits of nuclear power, there will soon be only a vacuum." Part of the extra funds would be used to produce similar materials, Walske wrote. Another major component of the AIF's new public relations strategy would be "the generation of positive news events." This was to include the ghost-writing and direct placement of articles in order "to minimize the filtration factor of the reporters and editors." Such steps were necessary, explained the memo, because the national media "cannot be relied upon to publish a full and balanced account of nuclear power."

The AIF also decided to move its main office from New York to Washington, with the aim of exerting a stronger influence on Washington policymakers at a time when Congress was considering such crucial issues as an extension of the Price-Anderson Act's nuclear-accident insurance coverage and whether the Clinch River breeder reactor project should be continued. Because the AIF's trade-association status precluded direct lobbying, the nuclear industry founded the American Nuclear Energy Council for that purpose in 1975; Craig Hosmer, a California Republican who until his 1974 retirement had been a long-standing, active member of the Joint Committee on Atomic Energy, was chosen to head the new organization.

Nuclear corporations in 1976 drew upon their trememdous financial resources to beat back legislative challenges to continued nuclear development in California and six other states. Industry press releases gloated over the 2 to 1 margin by which voters supported nuclear power, but were understandably silent about the millions of dollars of corporate money that delivered the victories. Industry forces spent from ten to one hundred times as much as nuclear opponents on the various public referenda. In California alone, utilities, reactor vendors, and other corporations contributed $3.5 million.

The Atomic Brotherhood's public image took another pounding in 1976 when four nuclear engineers—three from General Electric and one from the new Nuclear Regulatory Commission—resigned, charging that nuclear power was not nearly as safe as their superiors were claiming. The GE Three, as they came to be called, testified to the Joint Committee on Atomic Energy that "the *cumulative* effect of all design defects and deficiencies in the design, construction and operation of nuclear power plants *makes a nuclear power plant accident, in our opinion, a certain event*. The only question is when, and where."

The nuclear establishment also began employing extralegal measures against nuclear critics in the mid-1970s. The most famous example is the case of Karen Silkwood, a young worker and union activist who was protesting health and safety practices at Kerr-McGee's nuclear fuel plant in Oklahoma. Company agents harassed and spied on her, and may have tapped her telephone. On the evening of November 13, 1974, Silkwood died in a mysterious car accident while on her way to deliver documentation of the hazards at the plant to a reporter and an official of the Oil, Chemical, and Atomic Workers Union. The state police said she fell asleep at the wheel. A private investigator with eighteen years of experience in reconstructing auto accidents concluded that Silkwood's car had been forced off the road from behind. The allegedly incriminating documents had vanished. However, in May 1979, a jury found Kerr-McGee guilty of negligence leading to plutonium contamination of Silkwood prior to her death; it ordered the company to pay $10.5 million in punitive damages for the willful disregard of her safety and for the harassment to which she was subjected while trying to protect her fellow workers.

Most of the surveillance, harassment, and infiltration of antinuclear groups was carried out by private utilities, often working in conjunction with local police officials. The Georgia Power Company in 1973 hired nine private investigators and began budgeting $750,000 a year to spy on activists. The Virginia Electric Power Company in 1975 asked the state legislature for the power to arrest suspicious persons around its nuclear plants and for access to confidential state and local police records. The Atomic Industrial Forum assisted these and other sleuthing activities by compiling profiles of leading nuclear critics, including the Union of Concerned Scientists, Friends of the Earth, the Environmental Policy Center, and Ralph Nader.

The increased pressure did not dissuade antinuclear activists from adopting more direct and militant tactics themselves. Civil disobedience was introduced into the antinuclear movement on February 22, 1974, when organic farmer and local activist Sam Lovejoy of Montague, Massachusetts, knocked down a weather-monitoring tower that Northeast Utilities had erected in preparation for building a nuclear plant on that spot. Lovejoy turned himself in to the police and admitted full responsibility for the action, which he claimed was justified by the ruling authorities' refusal to protect the populace from the grave dangers posed by the plant. Lovejoy was acquitted on a technicality. A year later, 28,000 nuclear opponents halted construction of a nuclear reactor at Wyhl, West Germany, by physically occupying the site. Antinuclear activist Anna Gyorgy wrote in her book, NO NUKES: "The [Wyhl] action inspired nuclear opponents around the world. It seemed that by force of numbers, non-violent, direct action might succeed as a 'last resort' against nuclear power where intervention and referenda had failed."

The first American site occupation came on August 1, 1976, when eighteen members of the newly formed antinuclear Clamshell Alliance marched onto the Seabrook, New Hampshire site. A second occupation three weeks later resulted in 179 arrests and gave impetus to further Clamshell organizing. Over the winter the loose coalition grew to include approximately thirty-five local antinuclear groups throughout New England; activists began to lay plans for a third site occupation on May 1, 1977. The arrest that day of 1,414 demonstrators attracted the attention of both the national media and other antinuclear activists. The Clamshell Alliance became the political and organizational model and inspiration for numerous similar groups that quickly sprouted up wherever nuclear plants were being built or operated.

These types of direct action, along with massive public education, continuing legal and legislative challenges to nuclear power, and the growing environmental consciousness of the American people, significantly changed the political environment in which the Atomic Brotherhood operated. To be sure, federal policymakers in both the Nixon and the Ford administrations remained devoted to a strong domestic nuclear program. And while the national growth of antinuclear sentiment during the 1970s hardly immobilized the federal atomic bureaucracy, it nevertheless did check its ingrained tendency to implement whatever policies industry executives demanded. To a business that was as thoroughly dependent upon government support as the nuclear industry, that was a heavy blow.

PROLIFERATION: THE GHOST OF ATOMS PAST

Utility financial problems, a growing antinuclear movement, and the continuing slump in America's electricity demand had brought domestic nuclear reactor sales to a virtual halt by 1976. To make things worse, global business prospects had been soured by the re-emergence in the mid-1970s of an age-old dilemma of the Atomic Brotherhood—the unavoidable connection between nuclear power exports and the global proliferation of nuclear weapons.

The trouble could be traced back directly to the Atoms for Peace program begun in 1953. President Eisenhower, Secretary of State John Foster Dulles, and the other leading national security officials who conceived of and implemented Atoms for Peace were quite aware of its security risks. A precondition for any foreign country seeking research reactors and enriched uranium from the United States was a pledge not to try to produce nuclear explosives. The United States enforced this pledge by demanding that the recipient country's nuclear facilities be constantly open to inspection by the U.S.-controlled International Atomic Energy Agency. Confident that these safeguards, combined with its overwhelming superiority in nuclear (and all other) affairs, gave the United States sufficient influence to prevent any country from attaining nuclear weapons, every administration from Eisenhower's to Nixon's vigorously promoted U.S. nuclear exports.

The day of reckoning for that policy and others like it came in the early 1970s. Although nuclear proliferation was rooted in the Atoms for Peace program, the proximate cause of its re-emergence in the 1970s was the Nixon administration's attempt to turn the enrichment stage of the nuclear fuel cycle over to private corporations.

Nuclear industry giants like General Electric had always seen the government's monopoly over the uranium enrichment process as temporary. Eventually, like the rest of the nuclear fuel cycle and the reactor business, uranium enrichment would be transferred to private ownership. GE began preparing for that day back in the late 1950s; although the enrichment process remained a closely guarded government secret, GE scientists struck out on their own to discover and develop a commercially viable enrichment method.

All went well until 1967. But then, just as GE's scientists were about to unlock the enrichment mystery, the AEC, in the name of national security, confiscated all of the company's research materials on enrichment. This proved to be but a temporary setback, however, since Richard Nixon announced soon after his January 1969 inauguration that he planned to invite private industry into the enrichment business.

According to energy economist Vince Taylor, whose study of Nixon's attempts to foster a private enrichment industry is the basis for much of what follows here, Nixon's first impulse was simply to sell the AEC's three enrichment plants to the highest private bidders. That plan was bitterly attacked by the utility industry, which realized that no matter how accomplished, privatization would produce a "homogeneous oligopoly" (translation: monopoly by a handful of similarly motivated companies), which would jack up nuclear fuel prices. The utility protest became a moot point when the interested purchasers let it be known that *they* were not interested in buying until the long-run profit picture for the uranium fuel business brightened considerably. The situation was reminiscent of the Eisenhower administration's repeated attempts during the mid-1950s to coax private companies into building nuclear plants; though corporations liked the idea in principle, they nevertheless held back until the price was right. Back in the fifties, the Price-Anderson Act was passed as a way of coping with the situation. Now, the price of uranium fuel was forced up.

This was easily done, since the AEC enjoyed virtual monopoly control over the noncommunist world's supply of enriched uranium. Any monopolist knows that to raise prices he need only limit supply; this Nixon endeavored to do. First he refused to expand the production capabilities of the government-owned enrichment plants, despite the AEC's projection, based on the early 1970s orders blitz, that such an expansion was urgently needed if a nuclear fuel shortage was to be avoided a decade hence. (The AEC's projections were made before the collapse of the domestic nuclear reactor market in late 1974.) This brought the administration into conflict with the Joint Committee, which was more committed to preventing a fuel shortage than to easing the private takeover of the enrichment business. Some committee members also questioned Nixon's plan on national security grounds. The Joint Committee's coolness to the idea stemmed partly from "turf" considerations: with private companies making the decisions about enrichment, the committee would have that much less control over the U.S. nuclear program. To placate the Joint Committee and persuade it not to establish a government corporation to manage uranium enrichment, Nixon ordered the AEC in 1971 to expand its stockpile of enriched uranium. This the AEC accomplished through a neat technical fix: lowering its enrichment plants' utilization rate of uranium-235. This step, combined with an upgrading of the plants' equipment, delayed the date when additional enrichment capacity would be needed until fiscal year 1982, thus giving the administration more time to entice private corporations into the enrichment business without risking a fuel shortage.

The administration's next maneuvers came in early 1973 when the AEC announced a new, tougher policy on enrichment supply contracts. No longer would U.S. and foreign utilities be able to get as much enriched uranium as they wanted on a mere six months' notice. Beginning in September, utilities had to contract with the AEC for ten years of enriched uranium supplies, and they had to do so eight years before they actually needed the first fuel shipment. In other words, utilities had to commit themselves to buying fuel nine to eighteen years before they might actually need it. And if they later tried to change the terms of their contracts, the AEC would assess a penalty charge of 50 to 75 percent of the contract's total worth. Utilities balked: there were too many uncertainties involved in building power plants for them to lock themselves into such a long-term agreement. But the AEC stood firm. Under the circumstances, business prudence dictated that utilities order the maximum amount of fuel they might need. The risk of not having fuel for a reactor easily outweighed the cost of having too much of it too soon.

Having thus demonstrated his intention to force up uranium prices, Nixon in June 1973 gave seven select corporations special clearance to study the government's classified uranium enrichment technology. The list included the biggest names in the nuclear industry: Bechtel, General Electric, Westinghouse, Exxon, Union Carbide, and Goodyear. Over the next twelve months, these giant corporations laid their plans for taking over the enrichment business. The administration's actions had nicely prepared the way. The AEC's new contracting procedures had lined up specific future customers for private enrichers and, more important, had so concentrated demand that the companies entering the enrichment business would have little trouble maintaining high prices in the future.

Utility executives realized this was their last chance to secure a guaranteed supply of fuel for future nuclear reactors, so they scrambled to place their orders before the AEC closed its order books in June 1974. Because the AEC's new contract also stipulated that the customer deliver the necessary amount of raw uranium to the AEC's enrichment facilities promptly, utilities immediately bought up all the existing uranium reserves and began searching frantically for more. This sudden surge in demand pushed uranium ore prices way up, thereby fulfilling another of the Nixon administration's privatization-related goals.

When the AEC stopped taking enrichment orders, it had received many more than it had the capacity to fill. U.S. utilities had ordered a record forty-one nuclear plants in 1973, and especially in the months directly following the October 1973 oil embargo, there seemed every reason to believe that nuclear power would be called upon to provide a large and expanding share of future U.S. energy needs. Most important, the restrictive criteria of the AEC's new enrichment contracts had caused utilities to exaggerate the amount of nuclear fuel they would actually need.

On July 1, 1974, Alabama Governor George Wallace announced
that Uranium Enrichment Associates (UEA), a consortium of private companies including Bechtel, Union Carbide, and Westinghouse, had chosen Alabama as the site where they would construct
the nation's first private uranium enrichment plant. It appeared
that one month before he resigned from the presidency, Richard
Nixon's wish for private participation in the uranium enrichment
business had been fulfilled. But barely two weeks later, the Edison
Electric Institute, the trade association of privately owned utilities,
and the Tennessee Valley Authority complained to the Joint Committee that the Uranium Enrichment Associates were offering utility customers "unbusinesslike" terms and effectively forcing them
to assume all risks for building the UEA's $2.75 billion plant in
Alabama. The utilities suggested that future enrichment needs be
met by expanding government capacity, an idea that appealed to
the Joint Committee. By September, the UEA's Alabama project
had been delayed and Westinghouse had dropped out of the consortium. General Electric, which had been considering a joint enrichment venture with Exxon, also announced its withdrawal in
September, citing the very large investments required and the
political uncertainties surrounding the issue.

Despite the counterattack from the utility industry and the Joint
Committee and the ensuing desertion of two corporate allies,
Bechtel refused to give up on the enrichment idea. On May 30,
1975, Bechtel made an unsolicited proposal to the Ford administration, requesting billions of government dollars to make the takeover of the enrichment business by private companies like Bechtel
a no-risk proposition. Less than a month later, President Ford sent
Congress the Nuclear Fuel Assurance Act, which mimicked the
Bechtel proposal by calling for $8 billion in government guarantees
to companies that entered the enrichment business. The administration's legislation was attacked from many sides (conservatives
disliked its government giveaway features, and liberals feared the
effects it might have on nuclear proliferation), but the White House
refused to back down. On July 30, 1976, opponents of the Bechtel-
Ford proposal scored a dramatic 170 to 168 victory on an amendment gutting the Nuclear Fuel Assurance Act. Five days later, the
act's sponsors used a parliamentary procedure to force a second
vote. This time, the amendment was *defeated* 193 to 192. The Ford
administration's victory came only because the top three Democratic leaders in the House at the last minute voted to support the
White House.

The administration and the Joint Committee then tried to push the act through the Senate right before its October adjournment. But opposition from liberals and a threat from Democratic Senator James Abourezk of South Dakota to filibuster the bill caused the measure to go down to a narrow, 33 to 30 defeat. Instead the Senate approved the building of the additional enrichment facility in Portsmouth, Ohio, a policy that the Carter administration would reaffirm the following year.

Meanwhile, Nixon's deliberate limitation of the AEC's supply of enriched uranium had greatly accelerated the decline of U.S. control over global nuclear commerce. The supply had been so severely limited that the AEC had been unable to fulfill the nonsocialist world's demand for enriched uranium in 1974, the year it planned to leave the business to make way for private enrichment corporations. After closing its order books in June 1974, the AEC kept its customers in suspense for two months while deciding which utilities would receive guaranteed contracts for enriched fuel and which conditional contracts. Because the AEC could hardly favor foreign over domestic companies, it happened that many European, Japanese, and Third World utilities were awarded only conditional contracts. Although President Nixon quickly issued a statement that the United States would in fact honor these contracts as well, the damage had been done. The humiliated and outraged foreigners began to make their own arrangements to secure fuel.

Nixon apparently had assumed that since the United States held a monopoly over enriched uranium, other countries had no choice but to accept his new enrichment policy. That was a costly miscalculation based on a reality that no longer existed; the days when the United States could order its allies around were over. It was true that in the past the United States' enrichment monopoly had given it nearly complete control over other capitalist countries' nuclear power programs: countries could not go nuclear without U.S. approval in the form of enriched uranium exports, and the United States could stall any country's nuclear development merely by withholding the enriched fuel. But this was no longer the case.

In his single-minded campaign to privatize the enrichment business, Nixon undermined his own power base when he cut off foreign nations' enriched uranium supplies, for this forced an end to their dependency on the United States. This was not so important in the case of the advanced capitalist nations, which were already heading in that direction. The Western European countries had long resented being vulnerable to the whims of Washington and had begun building their own enrichment facilities in the late 1960s for completion late in the 1970s. In the meantime, they managed by obtaining enriched uranium from the Soviet Union. Rather, where Nixon's actions mattered most was with Third World nations intent on nuclear development. With the U.S. enrichment facilities undergoing a change in ownership, nations like Iran, Brazil, Pakistan, and South Africa began looking to cut nuclear deals with whoever could fulfill their wishes.

Here, finally, was the chance European nuclear companies had been waiting for to break the GE-Westinghouse stranglehold on the Third World nuclear export market. During the early 1970s, a combination of intentional government policies and inevitable industrial shake-out had "rationalized" Western European nuclear industries, particularly in France and West Germany, to the point where only one large firm remained in each country. Kraftwerk Union monopolized the supply of nuclear reactors in West Germany, and Framatome, a subsidiary of Creusot-Loire, did likewise in France. Yet despite their monopoly status at home, neither company's nuclear business could survive and prosper without selling substantial numbers of reactors on the global market. Nuclear technology was so expensive and so capital-intensive that in order to recover their tremendous investments and begin reaping the profits they expected, both Kraftwerk Union and Framatome had to sell more reactors than their domestic electricity markets alone could absorb. Since most other advanced industrial nations had prohibited nuclear imports by the early 1970s in order to protect their own developing nuclear industries, the only market left to Kraftwerk Union and Framatome was the Third World.

Nixon's enrichment privatization campaign gave them the entrée they needed. Thanks to their decision to construct their own enrichment facilities, European nuclear exporters could and did offer Third World customers guaranteed nuclear fuel. In 1974, that new marketing technique rewarded Kraftwerk Union and Framatome with two reactor orders each from Iran, orders that GE and Westinghouse believed were rightfully theirs.

But the deal that really upset the Americans came in 1975, when West Germany announced that Kraftwerk Union was exporting eight power reactors to Brazil. What made that news especially hard to take was that Brazil had first tried to make the same deal with the American companies Westinghouse and Bechtel, only to be frustrated by actions in Washington. Gordon Hurlbert, the hard-driving president of Westinghouse's Power Systems Company, blames his company's loss of the Brazilian order partly on the fight over public versus private enrichment: "Brazil came with an order for six plants to Dixy Lee Ray [then AEC chair], and she had to say the U.S. couldn't accept any more orders for enriched uranium and that the matter was hung up in our Congress over whether it will be private or public enrichment." Bechtel had even gone so far as to offer to build Brazil its own uranium enrichment facilities. Determined to prevent Brazil from obtaining nuclear weapons capability, the State Department forced Bechtel to withdraw the offer.*

Ten—or even five—years earlier, that would have decided the matter for Brazil. But nuclear exports were no longer the sole province of GE, Westinghouse, and the Atomic Energy Commission. Now the Germans and French, who also could offer enriched uranium and American-style reactors, were determined to break the American monopoly on Third World nuclear exports. The intense competition made nuclear power a buyer's market. The State Department's veto of Bechtel's offer came in April 1975. Its non-proliferation intent was thwarted less than a month later when the West German government announced that it planned to provide Brazil not just with power reactors but with uranium enrichment and reprocessing facilities.

Washington was in shock. West Germany had just broken the unwritten nuclear export rule and agreed to give Brazil keys to the nuclear weapons club. Had the Germans gone completely out of their minds? Hadn't the dangers of allowing poor countries access to fissionable materials been made terrifyingly clear a year earlier by India's nuclear explosion? And there was further concern over intelligence and media reports that Pakistan, Israel, South Africa, and perhaps other countries had or were developing nuclear weapons.

---

* There are a number of ironies to the Westinghouse-Bechtel loss in Brazil. These two companies, along with Union Carbide, made up the Uranium Enrichment Associates, the private consortium formed to exploit the opportunity made available by President Nixon to enter the uranium enrichment business. It was Nixon's actions in creating that business opportunity that helped encourage the Brazilians to approach the West German government and Kraftwerk Union in the first place. Furthermore, it was Westinghouse that originally gave Kraftwerk Union its start in the nuclear business by signing a technology licensing agreement with the German firm. (Westinghouse had done the same, of course, with the French nuclear company, Framatome.)

An intense policy debate broke out within the Ford administration and the Congress over how the United States should respond. On one side stood the nuclear industry and such allies as AEC Chair Dixy Lee Ray, who immediately after the announcement of the West German–Brazilian deal criticized U.S. policy on export safeguards as "self-defeating." Nuclear proliferation was inevitable, this group argued. The days of U.S. atomic monopoly were over; what the United States accomplished by refusing to sell fuel cycle technology to countries like Brazil was the deprivation of its own nuclear corporations of billions of dollars' worth of export sales and the relinquishing of any influence it might have had over foreign nuclear programs. Better some influence than no influence. Instead of trying to stop proliferation, the United States should strengthen its technical leadership and thereby give foreign nations incentives to buy American, rather than French or German, nuclear technology.

Opponents of this viewpoint charged it with being concerned more with the commercial well-being of the nuclear industry than with the national security of the United States. Liberal senators such as Abraham Ribicoff and Charles Percy argued that short-term profit considerations could not be allowed to blind decision makers to long-term global necessities. If a stable, peaceful international economic order advantageous to West Germany, the United States, and the rest of the advanced nations was to be maintained, then they had to cooperate on preventing nuclear weapons proliferation. Somehow they had to restrain themselves from the kind of bitter nuclear export competition that had led West Germany to sell enrichment technology to Brazil and led France to sell reprocessing facilities to Pakistan. Senator John Pastore best articulated this viewpoint when he urged the world's nuclear supplier nations to adopt common export rules, "rather than [allow the] competitive degradation of safeguards in pursuit of profit."

It soon became clear that this second viewpoint had carried the day; Western European diplomats leaked news to reporters that the United States had scheduled a secret conference of nuclear supplier nations to begin in London on June 18, 1975. The United States had invited Canada, Great Britain, the Soviet Union, France, West Germany, Italy, and Japan to discuss how they could harmonize nuclear export policies. But the conference participants found it difficult to rise above mutual suspicion and forge a meaningful agreement. The Europeans charged that the American concern over weapons proliferation was a sham; the United States just wanted to regain and consolidate its dominance of the nuclear export market. The meeting ended on June 26 with delegates claiming to have made "some progress." Almost as if to mock the insignificance of the achievement, the West Germans and the Brazilians signed their nuclear trade agreement in a formal ceremony in Bonn the very next day.

A Two-Billion-Dollar Mistake

The price of uranium rose an astonishing 300 percent between 1972 and September 1975, owing primarily to President Nixon's policies. This increase naturally raised operating costs for nuclear utilities and electric bills for their ratepayers. But ironically, it was Westinghouse—one of the companies most interested in taking over the enrichment business—that suffered most from the jump in uranium prices. In fact, the giant nuclear company was nearly bankrupted.

Westinghouse's troubles resulted from some risky reactor deals it made during the early 1970s. Locked in a desperate struggle with General Electric for the nuclear industry's number one position, Westinghouse began trying to win reactor orders by adding "sweetener" clauses to its sales contracts. The sweetener that came back to haunt Westinghouse was its promise to supply the uranium fuel for its reactors at a guaranteed, fixed price of around $10 a pound. Many utilities jumped at the offer, which effectively insulated them from the ups and downs of the uranium market. Westinghouse, for its part, was gambling that the long-term price of uranium would not go much higher than $10 a pound.

As Westinghouse gradually opened a lead over GE in overall reactor sales, the gamble appeared to have paid off. GE nuclear vice-president Bertram Wolfe concedes, "The reason Westinghouse sold so many reactors is because it sold so much uranium." Herbert Sprague, a nuclear fuel salesman for GE, adds, "We realized what Westinghouse was doing, but we consciously decided not to speculate in uranium in that manner." To be sure, GE was also offering to supply nuclear fuel to utilities, but under far less risky conditions. Unlike Westinghouse, GE promised to provide only as much uranium as it already held in company stockpiles. Westinghouse, on the other hand, was selling uranium it did not have but assumed it could buy in the future.

GE's caution doubtless cost it a few reactor sales, but it just as certainly saved the company from the financial disaster that soon struck Westinghouse. As short-term demand for uranium shot up in response to the AEC's new enrichment policies, the price of uranium jumped to $26 a pound by September 1975. Westinghouse was trapped. It was legally obligated to deliver over 70 million pounds of uranium it did not have. Buying the stuff on the open market would mean nearly $2 billion in losses for the company— unthinkable. Company lawyers ordered to find a way out of the mess came up with the arcane doctrine of "commercial impracticality," a legal device that excuses companies from financial liability for circumstances beyond their control. Westinghouse announced to the world its embarrassing predicament and informed the utilities that, owing to the extraordinary rise in price, it would not be able to honor its uranium commitments.

The utilities were outraged. Nixon's enrichment policy had put them through the wringer once, and now Westinghouse was trying it again. Ignoring Westinghouse's claims that fulfilling the contracts would cripple the company, twenty-seven utilities responded by suing the giant for the uranium it owed them. Meanwhile, in the words of one uranium industry executive, "utilities really had no choice but to go into exploration [for more uranium], since the existing suppliers had nothing more to sell them, and couldn't risk promising future supplies that might not materialize. So the utilities put a lot of inexperienced money into the business, which raised production costs for everyone else." The sudden jump in demand boosted prices still higher; by the end of 1975, uranium cost $35 a pound.

Westinghouse officials could only hang their heads in shame when an outside consultant blasted the company's uranium dealings as "the most stupid performance in the history of American commercial life." But in 1976, help came to beleaguered Westinghouse from a most unlikely source. The Australian chapter of the environmental organization Friends of the Earth released to the press confidential documents showing that an international cartel had been secretly manipulating the price of uranium since 1972. Here was the blameworthy villain Westinghouse needed to make its commercial-impracticality defense plausible. Westinghouse immediately blamed its inability to fulfill its uranium contracts on the cartel's actions. It then filed antitrust suits for triple damages against nearly every major uranium producer in the world, including fellow nuclear industry titan Gulf Oil. Gulf angrily countersued, charging Westinghouse with conspiring to monopolize the nuclear reactor, fuel fabrication, and uranium markets.

The lawsuits caused one federal judge to christen this "The Lawyers' Full-Employment Case." For lawyers, it was a wonderfully convoluted case "from whose bounty will flow legal fees to educate the children and grandchildren of a generation of antitrust lawyers." Indeed, Westinghouse alone spent $25 million in uranium-related legal fees in 1976, and again in 1977.

The dispute was finally settled out of court in early 1981, with neither side conceding guilt. Westinghouse nevertheless extracted nearly $100 million in compensation from Gulf and other members of the uranium cartel. However, as June Taylor and Michael Yokell document in *Yellowcake: The International Uranium Cartel,* Westinghouse's predicament in fact could not be blamed on the cartel's price fixing, which had only a minimal impact on the U.S. uranium market. Taylor and Yokell show that the real cause of the uranium price jump was the Nixon administration's private enrichment campaign—something that Westinghouse had welcomed, supported, and planned to profit from.

On November 4, 1976, the people of the United States elected as their President a peanut farmer from Georgia who promised them in his campaign speeches that he would deploy nuclear power "only as a last resort." To an industry that had heard every president since Harry Truman wholeheartedly endorse nuclear power, it was a chilling phrase. And although Jimmy Carter soon demonstrated that he intended not to halt nuclear power but only to manage it more astutely, the subtlety was lost on incredulous nuclear executives. To them, Carter was antinuclear and not to be trusted.

The executives' perception led them to identify Carter as the source of their troubles. But while it is true that relations within the Atomic Brotherhood deteriorated to an all-time low during his presidency, Carter himself cannot be held more than marginally accountable for it. The disease afflicting the Brotherhood had been spreading for a long time by the late 1970s, and there were limits to what any president—Republican or Democrat—could have done to arrest it. Those limits were set not just by the aftereffects of past atomic policies but also by the fundamental reality that U.S. global power was declining. And some of the steps needed to restore that power—limiting nuclear proliferation most especially—were, at least in the short term, directly at odds with the needs of the nuclear industry. It was the same contradiction that had plagued the Brotherhood ever since Washington refused to allow the cor-

porations to develop the industrial atom in 1946: the industry could
not function well without the government's full support, but the
government's strong commitment to nuclear power was occasionally superseded by its broader responsibilities and loyalties. Jimmy
Carter favored the expansion of nuclear power, but only if it could
be done in a way that did not further weaken U.S. control over the
world order or completely alienate his domestic political support.

To withstand the threat to its survival, the industry needed more
than qualified, selective support from Washington. Industry representatives informed the Carter administration of this twice within
its first two months in office. On March 10, 1977, top General
Electric officials George Stathakis and Edward Hood met with
James Schlesinger, President Carter's top energy official, and explained that GE might have to leave the nuclear business if federal
nuclear policy was not brought into line with industry demands.*
The GE men came away from the meeting convinced that Schlesinger was strongly committed to their sort of changes, but with
questions about his influence over Carter. Less than two weeks
later, Schlesinger met with another group of nuclear industry representatives, who told him that unless the government took action
soon to end the hiatus in nuclear plant orders, the industry would
fold and not be able to deliver the reactors the country would
certainly need in the 1980s. Craig Hosmer, the former senior member of the Joint Committee who was operating in his newly assumed capacity as head of the industry's American Nuclear Energy
Council, asked Schlesinger, "How many times can you take this
horse [meaning the nuclear industry] and beat it . . . and still have
it there when you need it?"

In April, President Carter made two major announcements that
revealed his strategy for reconciling the needs of the nuclear industry with the imperatives of American foreign policy. First, he
announced on April 7 that he wanted to cancel the Clinch River
breeder reactor project and defer indefinitely the reprocessing of
spent nuclear fuel. These were opening moves in what would be
a major continuing effort by his administration to curb the global
production and trade of plutonium, the material with which foreign

---

* Some of the specific changes GE suggested were a limitation on public participation in nuclear plant licensing in order to avoid "legal pollution," a better accounting of the trade-offs between energy needs and environmental purity in the
implementation of the National Environmental Policy Act, and "more responsible"
federal policies concerning the back end of the nuclear fuel cycle and U.S. nuclear
exports.

countries or terrorist groups could fashion atomic explosives. Then on April 18, the President unveiled his response to the energy crisis, a problem he solemnly called "the moral equivalent of war." Apparently the time of "last resort" Carter referred to in his campaign speeches had suddenly arrived, for his National Energy Plan called for a sharp increase in the construction of conventional nuclear power plants. A detailed analysis by energy expert and nuclear critic Barry Commoner illustrated that, contrary to the President's claims that conservation was the cornerstone of his program, "the Plan relied more on nuclear power (23 percent) than on conservation (17 percent) to meet new demand for energy." Furthermore, the President was not opposed in principle to breeder reactors, as his previous Clinch River announcement had led both environmentalists and industry officials to believe. A careful look at the fine print towards the back of his plan revealed that Carter planned to use the money saved by scrapping Clinch River to develop alternative types of breeders that would not produce weapons-grade, proliferation-prone plutonium. Carter's nuclear policy did not repudiate but merely amended the industry's central assumption regarding the long-term future of the nuclear business: that breeders would replace light water reactors sometime after the turn of the century and would then continue to be a major U.S. (and world) energy source for centuries to come.

There was little President Carter could do immediately about the main obstacle to his goal of building more light water nuclear power plants; the post-OPEC stagnation in America's demand for electricity made new power plants of any sort unnecessary for the time being. But he and his administration did try to create the kind of political environment in which a nuclear comeback could occur, once the nation's utilities had worked off their overcapacity a couple of years hence. In October 1977, the newly formed Department of Energy announced that it was taking over from private industry the legal responsibility for the ultimate disposal of the high-level radioactive waste produced by nuclear power plants. To assuage the growing public anxiety about the still unsolved waste problem, the department intensified its efforts to devise a comprehensive disposal plan. In order to relieve the battered electric utility industry of some of the financial expense and risk of building nuclear plants, the administration attempted to reduce the length and unpredictability of the nuclear construction process. President Carter himself presided over the White House meeting where leaders of the building trades union agreed to a no-strike rule on all nuclear construction sites, an agreement that was expected to cut building schedules by eighteen to twenty-four months. The administration in the same month also introduced a bill in Congress to speed up the licensing process for nuclear plants. Energy Secretary James Schlesinger made the familiar claim that future energy shortages were inevitable unless the administration's bill, which he claimed would cut licensing time in half without sacrificing safety, was passed.

President Carter also did his best to make his campaign to halt nuclear weapons proliferation as painless for the industry as possible. Carter's nonproliferation strategy amounted to a clever mixture of the two opposing viewpoints that had surfaced in Washington immediately after the West German–Brazilian nuclear deal in 1975. The United States would curb proliferation by renouncing the use of plutonium and steadily pressuring other nuclear supplier nations for tougher export restrictions and safeguards; simultaneously, it would strengthen the global competitiveness of U.S. nuclear companies through larger export subsidies, quicker approval for export licenses, and an expansion of American uranium enrichment capacity. By the end of 1977, U.S. diplomats had persuaded West Germany and France not to export nuclear reprocessing technology. In addition, the United States had forced both South Korea and Pakistan to back out of previous deals to buy reprocessing plants from the French. The Carter administration also got forty other countries to join in a two-year study called the International Nuclear Fuel Cycle Evaluation (INFCE). The study would not only buy time for Carter's diplomatic maneuvers to work but would also focus the world's attention on the gravity of the proliferation problem and perhaps develop "proliferation-resistant" fuel cycle technologies similar to the kind that Carter hoped to develop in the United States.

The U.S. Senate and House of Representatives endorsed the core of the Carter administration's nonproliferation policy when they passed (almost unanimously) the Nuclear Non-Proliferation Act of 1978. Diligent lobbying by the administration and the nuclear industry had stripped the act of originally drafted provisions that would have prohibited U.S. nuclear exports to any country engaged in uranium enrichment or reprocessing. The final, milder version of the bill required foreign countries wishing to buy U.S. nuclear materials to accept marginally tougher safeguards on their nuclear facilities and to agree not to re-export purchased materials or to use them to make nuclear weapons. Gloria Duffy and Gordon

Adams, senior researchers at the Council on Economic Priorities, a nonprofit research institute, pointed out in a 1978 report that the intent of the act was to encourage both nonproliferation and U.S. nuclear exports at the same time. The act contained strong antiproliferation statutes (such as the one sanctioning U.S. storage of foreign nuclear wastes in order to deter foreign reprocessing) side by side with obvious export promotion measures (such as the direction given the Nuclear Regulatory Commission to provide export licenses quickly to prove that the United States was a reliable nuclear supplier). Commenting on the act nearly a year after the President signed it into law on March 10, 1978, Westinghouse's Power Systems Company president Gordon Hurlbert said, "Carter and the administration promised us that the purpose of it [the Nuclear Non-Proliferation Act] was to help us with exports, and so far we've been very pleased. They gave us the export licenses for Kori 5 and 6 [two plants Westinghouse exported to South Korea] in four to five months, and that's very good performance."

Nevertheless, there was a growing resentment among nuclear industry officials that Carter was not doing more to help them. Their industry was in deep trouble, desperately in need of strong federal support, and the man in the White House continued to equivocate about his position on nuclear power. *Nucleonics Week*, the industry's leading trade publication, wrote in November 1977, "In the opinion of many, the giant U.S. nuclear industry is slowly, very slowly, bleeding to death." Before long, the business and the daily press began printing stories with a similar angle. And although President Carter and his aides repeatedly assured industry representatives in private that the administration favored nuclear power, the industry did not believe them. "When the administration people talk to us, they say they are supporting nuclear power," said GE nuclear vice-president Bertram Wolfe. "But the fact is that the public doesn't perceive that, Carter himself has never said it, and the actions of the administration don't lead you to believe that."

As proof that the Carter administration was "fundamentally against a thriving nuclear industry," industry representatives pointed most often to Carter's opposition to reprocessing and to the Clinch River breeder reactor. They concluded that since both reprocessing and breeders were necessary if the industry was to survive past the turn of the century, Carter actually wished unobtrusively to phase out nuclear power in the United States.

The dispute came to a head during a high-level private meeting between the Atomic Brotherhood's government and corporate wings held in the White House on the morning of June 14, 1978.* President Carter's press schedule for that morning had listed only an ordinary-sounding meeting with two members of Congress: George Brown, a Democrat from California and long-time liberal, and Walter Flowers, a big-business Democrat from Alabama. Both of them chaired subcommittees of the Science and Technology Committee in the House of Representatives. But in fact, thirteen other men also were attending the meeting. Each was either the chief or number two executive of the nuclear industry's most important electric utilities, reactor manufacturers, or construction firms.

By 9:30 that June morning, all thirteen of these men had passed through the northeast gate of the White House. They convened in the Cabinet Room, where Congressmen Brown and Flowers, Energy Secretary Schlesinger, and President Carter welcomed them.

The meeting had been called because of a political deadlock. President Carter's request for funds in the fiscal year 1978 budget to cancel the Clinch River project had been denied by Congress. Despite the President's known objections, Congress has included $80 million in the budget to keep Clinch River alive. Carter vetoed that bill on November 5, 1977. Lacking the two-thirds majority needed to override his veto, Congress executed a neat end-run and secured funding for Clinch River by deleting the funds for the project from the energy budget and putting the $80 million into a catchall supplemental appropriations bill. Because that bill contained funding necessary for many other government projects, Carter had little choice but to sign it.

Realizing that he lacked the brute strength necessary to defeat the pro–Clinch River forces, Carter authorized Schlesinger to negotiate an acceptable compromise. Schlesinger first approached Congressman Olin E. Teague, a Democrat from Texas, who then chaired the all-important House Science and Technology Committee through which all Department of Energy authorizations must pass. While a warm friend to the industry and a hearty supporter of the Clinch River project, Teague was also a political realist.

Carter personally telephoned Teague in March 1978 to assure him of his support for a strong breeder research and development

---

* The full story of this meeting written by the author, appeared in *Mother Jones*, June 1979.

program. Over the next month, negotiations between the Department of Energy and the Science and Technology Committee were an almost daily occurrence. The negotiations focused on a letter from Schlesinger to Teague explaining in detail the administration's proposed compromise plan to "direct the nation's breeder program." This position later became known as the Flowers amendment:

- First, the Clinch River breeder reactor would still not be built, but design and testing of its components would be completed.
- Second, $55 million would be spent on a two-and-one-half-year study to plan and design a breeder reactor several times larger than the Clinch River reactor, which might use a less dangerous fuel than plutonium.

Both Teague and Flowers saw the amendment as a way to break the stalemate over Clinch River. However, it was narrowly defeated in the Science and Technology Committee because the administration would not promise in advance actually to *build* the larger reactor.

Refusing to give up, Teague proposed that the President meet the industry leaders to discuss the matter. His May 25 letter to Carter is a masterpiece of behind-the-scenes political entrepreneurship. Teague maintains a properly respectful tone throughout, and refers to his March telephone conversation with Carter as "my privilege." He uses the salutation "Mr. President" five times in a three-page letter, and his "suggestions" to Carter are "respectfully" tendered.

Behind the delicate etiquette, Teague is quietly turning the screws. He offers a clear analysis of the Clinch River situation and its consequences, along with a "respectfully suggested" solution. He describes his futile attempts to secure passage of the Flowers Amendment and laments that his own understanding of Carter's position—that is, support of a big fast breeder but not of the Clinch River reactor itself—is a view not widely shared by either nuclear energy adherents *or* opponents. "Frankly, with all respect," he writes, "I must tell you that industry and Congressional leaders seem reluctant to believe my report to them that you do personally favor a strong breeder program. . . . So, I am convinced they must learn that directly in at least a brief personal conversation with you."

Two weeks later, the White House gave Teague the go-ahead. On June 10, telegrams were sent to the thirteen executives inviting them to the White House meeting on June 14.

Present at the meeting were the presidents of three of the most nuclear-oriented utilities in the country: James O'Connor of Commonwealth Edison, William Lee of Duke Power, and Sherwood Smith, Jr., of Carolina Power and Light. William Kuhns, who chairs the board of the General Public Utilities Corporation (parent company of Metropolitan Edison, owner of the Three Mile Island nuclear plant), and William McCollam, Jr., then president of the Edison Electric institute, were also present representing the utility industry. From the reactor manufacturers were Robert Kirby, chairman of Westinghouse; Willard F. Rockwell, Jr., then president and chairman of the board of Rockwell International; Walter Dance, vice-chairman of the board of executive officers of General Electric; Arthur Santry, Jr., president of Combustion Engineering; and George Zipf, president of Babcock and Wilcox. From the nuclear construction firms came Harry Reinsch, president of Bechtel Power; William Allen, president of Stone and Webster; and Kenneth Roe, president of Burns and Roe. Burns and Roe was the architect-engineer for Clinch River, and Stone and Webster the constructor.

In brief, the terms of the deal Carter suggested to the executives assembled in the White House were these:

- If industry would permit him to cut the Clinch River breeder reactor from the budget before the 1980 election, the administration would, in return, study and design an even bigger, better breeder reactor that could be built after the election.
- As a further sweetener, the Carter team offered what many nuclear executives said they needed more than anything else to counter the nuclear opposition movement: a strong public statement to the American people by President Carter *endorsing* the safety and necessity of nuclear power for the United States. This would be a major shift from Carter's earlier position to use nuclear energy "only as a last resort."

Carter opened the meeting that morning by affirming his belief in the importance of maintaining a strong domestic nuclear power industry. He said he had not, however, changed his mind that the Clinch River project should be canceled. He understood the industry's disagreement with this approach, and emphasized that his policy was not aimed at killing the future of the breeder reactor in general. In fact, he revealed that the only thing standing in the way of his full endorsement of nuclear power was the Clinch River issue.

Knowing of Carter's proliferation concerns, the executives bombarded him with arguments that the Clinch River reactor could use fuels other than plutonium to reduce proliferation hazards. Carter replied, "Gentlemen, my concern is not with the fuel cycle"—an apparent shift from his previous arguments that caught the industry men by surprise. Carter said he had originally opposed Clinch River on proliferation grounds, but had since altered his view. Now he claimed to oppose the project because the reactor cost too much and was less technologically sophisticated than other designs. In addition, the United States, in his view, was not faced with a time deadline for developing the breeder reactor, a position sharply contradictory to industry's.

Carter stressed that it was in both sides' interest to get the Clinch River conflict behind them so they could turn their joint attention and efforts to the "more serious problems that face the industry," such as radioactive-waste disposal, reactor licensing, and government policies on uranium enrichment. Carter wanted to delay until 1981 the final decision on whether a breeder would actually be built, and admitted such a decision would be politically difficult. "That decision should be made by a new Congress and a new President, whoever he may be," said a grinning Carter.

The executives were not afraid to argue with the President. Robert Kirby, the Westinghouse boss, interjected that the industry would lose five years' worth of progress if the Clinch River breeder reactor was scrapped, and fall behind the French breeder program. William O'Connor of Commonwealth Edison declared that the Clinch River reactor was 50 to 70 percent complete, and that utilities with light water reactors were counting on its being finished on schedule. Moreover, O'Connor stated, the nation needed the tremendous amount of energy available from fast breeders if it was to solve its energy problems.

The President listened politely to these objections, but gave no indication of changing his position. After reiterating his own confidence in the safety of nuclear reactors, he reminded the executives that there remained considerable political sentiment against nuclear power. He asserted that he was nevertheless doing tangible things to sell atomic energy to the public, citing as an example the administration's bill to expedite licensing of nuclear plants. Congressman Brown then remarked that Congress was divided over the issue of the fast breeder and that the pronuclear forces did not have the two-thirds majority necessary to override the veto. Congressman Flowers urged the industry to accept some compromise or risk having the project slowly dissolve.

After thirty-seven minutes the President left, and Schlesinger took over as the participants shifted to the Roosevelt Room for the meeting's last hour. Schlesinger underscored the firmness of Carter's decision that the Clinch River reactor would not be built, saying, "Look, the President of the United States has just told you he won't build Clinch River, so don't bother telling me how good it is." He made clear the administration's commitment to conventional nuclear power by ticking off promotional measures it had taken: efforts to speed reactor licensing, increased funds for general breeder research and development, a commitment in Carter's energy plan to have nuclear reactors generate almost 25 percent of U.S. electricity by 1985.

"That's true," responded an industry executive, "but the most important thing for us is getting a strong public pronouncement from the administration on nuclear technology." Schlesinger replied that Carter was prepared to make just such a statement if the industry would stop being so "divisive" on the Clinch River issue.

(Robert Hanfling, executive assistant to Deputy Secretary of Energy John O'Leary, confirmed separately that he had helped draft the statement back in February 1978. He, O'Leary, and Schlesinger had wanted the statement delivered in March, but White House aides had successfully blocked the move, arguing that the speech should be used as a bargaining chip in the struggle with industry over Clinch River.)

Schlesinger's offer came as no surprise to at least some of the executives. At a private caucus the night before, they had decided that if forced to choose between the presidential endorsement and Clinch River, they would hold out for Clinch River. This was partly because they did not trust Jimmy Carter. As one executive put it, "Mr. Carter and his associates are fundamentally against a thriving nuclear industry. If we give in on Clinch River, we aren't going to get anything in return, regardless of what they promise us." There was also the executives' conviction that sooner or later the government would *have* to meet their demands. Nuclear power was inevitable after all. Why trade Clinch River, the symbol and promise of the industry's future, for an endorsement that world events would force upon Jimmy Carter (or his successor) before long anyway?

After a few more minutes of general discussion, the meeting broke up around 11:00 A.M. There was no compromise. The Carter-Schlesinger team had offered two gigantic concessions from its April 1977 position: the commitment to design a bigger, better breeder and the presidential endorsement of nuclear power. The executives were not moved.

AN ACCIDENT JUDGED INEVITABLE

Despite the many serious problems facing them in the late 1970s, industry executives retained an enormous confidence in the future of nuclear power. The market's return was as certain as tomorrow's sunrise. The obstacles to nuclear's advance—skyrocketing construction costs, growing public fear and opposition, stagnating electricity demand, burgeoning interest in alternative energy sources, and an unsympathetic President—were weak and temporary compared with the historical momentum of nuclear energy. The business slump of the late 1970s had been unexpected and painful, but it would pass, like a bout with the flu.

If anything could have forced industry officials to rethink these articles of faith, it was the catastrophic events of 1979. In January, the Nuclear Regulatory Commission disavowed the conclusions of the Rasmussen Report, the prestigious study advancing the viewpoint that the odds of a major nuclear power plant accident were roughly equivalent to the likelihood that a person would be struck dead by a falling meteor. Then in March, the NRC ordered five nuclear plants to shut down because of doubts about their ability to withstand earthquakes. But these setbacks paled in comparison with what came next.

At 4:00 A.M. on Wednesday, March 28, the Three Mile Island nuclear power plant near Harrisburg, Pennsylvania, began undergoing what would become the most famous nuclear accident in history. Initial press reports that "above-normal" amounts of radiation had been released into the atmosphere gave way by Friday morning to the frightening announcement that there existed within the reactor a dangerous hydrogen bubble whose expansion might lead to the ultimate horror for a nuclear power plant: a core meltdown. Hundreds of nuclear engineers from the Nuclear Regulatory Commission and throughout the industry struggled against time to figure out what exactly had gone wrong inside the reactor and how to shut it down safely. The entire world was watching. Three Mile Island was on its way to becoming one of the biggest news stories of 1979.

People's suspicion and fear grew as the Metropolitan Edison Company, the utility operating the stricken reactor, and the NRC continued to disagree with and contradict one another in their statements about the cause and seriousness of the accident. The public was left to suspect what government transcripts later documented beyond dispute: the experts were not in control of the situation. On Friday morning, NRC Chairman Joseph Hendrie privately told his top aides, "We are operating almost totally in the blind, his [Governor Thornburgh's] information is ambiguous, mine is nonexistent and—I don't know, it's like a couple of blind men staggering around making decisions." Nevertheless, Hendrie rejected sugggestions by some of his staff to begin a precautionary evacuation of residents. And when the threatening bubble mysteriously began to shrink on Monday, relieved government and industry officials still could not agree upon why that had happened.

The nuclear industry had a disaster on its hands. Nuclear company stocks plummeted on the New York Stock Exchange. Night after night, Three Mile Island was the lead story on national television news broadcasts. Crowds streamed into movie theaters across the country to view the The China Syndrome, a fictionalized account of a possible nuclear meltdown accident that bore an eerie resemblance to what appeared to be happening in Harrisburg. In supermarkets and offices, at school and at home, the topic everyone talked about was the nuclear accident in Pennsylvania. Polls later revealed that 98 percent of all Americans had heard about it—an extraordinarily high rate of news recognition. And they did not believe they were being told the whole story. A CBS poll taken a week after the accident began found that 66 percent of all Philadelphians thought the danger posed by Three Mile Island was greater than government and industry officials publicly admitted. A joint CBS–New York Times poll delivered even more ominous news to the nuclear establishment: "Only 46 percent of Americans now favor further development of nuclear power, compared with 69 percent who were asked the same question in a July 1977 Times/CBS poll.

Meanwhile, the Secretary of Energy displayed a remarkable

sense of timing by telling congressional investigating committees that nuclear power continued to be an essential element of the U.S. energy program and that they should pass the administration's bill to speed up nuclear plant licensing. Secretary Schlesinger also urged President Carter to include in his forthcoming major energy speech a strong statement supporting nuclear power. Carter was politically astute enough not to mention nuclear power in his national television address on April 9, but reporters pinned him down on the issue at a Washington press conference the next day. Carter told them that the United States "cannot abandon nuclear power in the foreseeable future" and that he would continue to press for quicker licensing of nuclear power plants. He also announced the formation of a special presidential commission to investigate the Three Mile Island accident and to recommend how the nation's nuclear safety standards could be strengthened.

The accident ignited explosions of protest around the world and quickly catalyzed the U.S. antinuclear movement into fresh bursts of activity. Organizers worked around the clock to bring more than 100,000 people from all across the country to the steps of the Capitol building in Washington on May 6, where they expressed their opposition to nuclear power and their support for safe energy alternatives. Local antinuclear groups picked up scores of energetic new members in the summer and fall of 1979 as newly concerned citizens sought to learn more about nuclear power and somehow do something aabout it.

An unmistakable change was taking place in the American mass consciousness. Nuclear power suddenly was a major political issue, and opposition to nuclear power a respectable political stance. Three Mile Island's effect on the American nuclear establishment was likened by *Washington Post* reporter Joanne Omang to what the Tet offensive had done to the American military establishment's support at home:

> Just as the nationwide Vietcong attack in South Vietnam was beaten back in February, 1968, so the uprising in the Metropolitan Edison Co. nuclear power plant in Pennsylvania was successfully contained in March 1979. Both the [U.S.] generals and the [nuclear] technicians claimed victory, but the public perception became just the opposite. . . . The Tet offensive washed away any illusions that Americans really controlled anything in Vietnam. As a result, new strength flowed to those who had been saying all along that we never should have tried to control the country in the first place.

The accident at Three Mile Island drastically shifted the grounds of the national debate over nuclear power, and proponents were put on the defensive like never before. Senate Majority Leader Robert Byrd outlined the problem facing the nuclear industry: "We've been assured time and time again by the industry and federal regulatory agencies that this was something that was impossible, that could not happen. But it did happen. There's going to be great difficulty on the part of the American people to feel absolutely reassured about nuclear power."

But through quick, decisive, unified action, the nuclear industry limited the political damage of Three Mile Island to far less than it might have been. With its tremendous power in Congress still intact, the industry handily defeated every significant legislative challenge made to the future of nuclear energy. For a time during May, it appeared that an amendment by Congressman Edward J. Markey, a Democrat from Massachusetts, prohibiting the NRC from issuing new construction permits for nuclear plants for six months beginning in October might pass the House. It sailed through the Interior Committee, and House Speaker Tip O'Neill predicted "overwhelming support" for it on the House floor. But nuclear industry lobbyists were waiting for the amendment at the Commerce Committee, where they launched a heavy effort against it. On June 6, the committee rejected the amendment 24 to 18, prompting George Gleason of the American Nuclear Energy Council to say relievedly, "We're encouraged by this vote [because] it means Congress will take a responsible attitude." By the time the Markey amendment reached the floor of the House on November 29, the industry had marshaled enough forces to crush the amendment 254 to 135. The industry also resoundingly defeated an amendment by Democratic Congressman James Weaver of Oregon that would have blocked the issuance of nuclear plant licenses in states that did not have emergency evacuation plans in place.

Soon after the accident, in an effort to show public officials and ordinary citizens that it took the accident seriously and was determined not to allow another one, the industry announced the establishment of two new nuclear safety centers. It also began preparing a multi-million-dollar national public relations campaign designed to ensure that, in the words of Edison Electric Institute vice-president Jack Young, "the appropriate lessons were learned about the Three Mile Island accident" by the American public. The campaign's messages stressed that nuclear power was safe and, more important, that doing without it invited unemployment, energy shortages, and general economic and national security disaster.*

But before the first of these ads could appear, the industry came under surprise attack on October 30 from the Kemeny Commission, the group President Carter had appointed to investigate the Three Mile Island accident. Given that only one of its twelve members— Dr. Theodore B. Taylor, a nuclear scientist at Princeton University—could remotely be considered an opponent of nuclear energy, the Kemeny Commission's report was an amazingly strong indictment of the nuclear industry and the Nuclear Regulatory Commission. The report specifically did not state whether the country should proceed with nuclear power. But it did affirm that "if the country wishes, for larger reasons, to confront the risks that are inherently associated with nuclear power, fundamental changes are necessary if those risks are to be kept within tolerable limits." Given the manifold deficiencies uncovered in reactor designs, regulatory oversight, reactor-operator preparedness, and numerous other areas of the nuclear establishment's day-to-day activities, "an accident like Three Mile Island was eventually inevitable," the Kemeny Commission concluded. Before there could be a reasonable expectation that similar accidents could be prevented in the future, "fundamental changes will be necessary in the organization, procedures, and practices and—above all—in the attitudes of the Nuclear Regulatory Commission and, to the extent that the institutions we investigated are typical, of the nuclear industry."

Although eight of the Kemeny Commission's twelve members at different times favored recommending a moratorium on the construction of new nuclear plants, the commission chair, Dartmouth College president John G. Kemeny, kept such a measure from passing by changing the voting procedures at the last minute and then repudiating his own previously expressed support for such a moratorium. The commission ended up issuing recommendations far milder than its conclusions might have supported: that all pending reactor licenses be re-examined in light of the lessons learned at Three Mile Island; that no utility be given an operating license for a new reactor until state and local emergency response and evacuation plans were reviewd and approved by the Federal Emergency Response Agency; and that the NRC be restructured, replacing the current five-member board of commissioners with a

* The full story of how the industry planned and implemented its post–Three Mile Island comeback strategy is told in chapter 8.

single chief executive officer and placing the entire organization under the control of the executive branch.

A few days after the report was released to the public, Congressman Morris Udall and Senator Gary Hart—who both chaired key nuclear subcommittees on Capitol Hill—announced that it had caused them to reconsider their previous positions; they would now support a three-year halt to all new nuclear plant construction. The beleaguered NRC also claimed to have been born again; it proclaimed a temporary "pause" in the granting of construction and operating licenses until it could develop and adopt new safety, siting, and emergency response standards. Atomic Industrial Forum president Carl Walske responded by blasting the NRC for introducing "yet another unsettling element" into the nation's energy situation, and warned that the licensing freeze posed "the threat of an open-ended delay in nuclear licensing [that] the nation can ill afford."

The public reaction of Walske and other leading industry officials to the Kemeny Commission report was a mixture of pious contrition and self-serving distortion of the commission's conclusions. Conveniently overlooking the fact that only Chairman Kemeny's questionable procedural maneuver had kept the commission from recommending a reactor construction moratorium, the industry claimed to agree strongly with the report. In press releases and full-page ads in leading newspapers such as the *Washington Post* and the *New York Times,* the industry misrepresented the commission's message regarding nuclear power, claiming it was "Proceed, but proceed with caution." This prompted an angry letter to the editor from commission member Russell Peterson, who protested that the commission had given the industry no such "yellow light."

However wrong it was for the industry to try to rewrite history, it was also completely understandable. After all, the industry was fighting for its life, and conventional wisdom believed it was losing. Politicians, Wall Street investment analysts, nuclear critics, the mass and the business media—most believed that, regrettably or not, nuclear power was on the way out. Three Mile Island was seen as the final and fatal blow to an industry already suffering from widespread public opposition, a five-year de facto moratorium on new orders, and sharply declining demand for its products.

The industry itself thought the death sentence a bit premature. This was made clear to me in an interview I held, barely forty-eight hours after the accident began, with Leo Yochum, one of the top six executives of Westinghouse. Yochum's official title was Senior Executive Vice-President for Finance, and his responsibilities included managing the billions of dollars that flowed in and out of Westinghouse's treasury every year and maintaining good relations with the large Wall Street banks and insurance firms that were the corporation's most important investors and financiers.

When we had arranged the week before for Yochum to telephone me at 11:00 A.M. on March 30, we naturally had no idea that by the time we talked, nuclear power would be making headlines around the world. In fact, as I sat waiting for Yochum's phone call, I half expected that the emergency at Three Mile Island would cause him either to forget about or to beg off from our scheduled appointment. His company was, after all, the world's number one nuclear firm, and he, as one of its very highest executives, was probably busy deciding Westinghouse's response to this latest and most serious threat to the future of nuclear power.

But then the telephone rang and a woman with the crisply polite voice common to executive secretaries informed me Mr. Yochum was calling from Pittsburgh. If Yochum was worried about what was happening a scant two hundred miles away in Harrisburg, his relaxed voice did not betray the fact. He spent the next forty-five minutes unhesitatingly and directly answering questions about Westinghouse's decades-long relationship with its investment banks First Boston and Lehman Brothers Kuhn Loeb, the $500 million credit line it secured in 1974 from fifteen of America's biggest commercial banks, the profitability of its nuclear business, and its overall investment strategy. I asked about future nuclear investments. Many observers, pro and con, believed that nuclear power was all but finished, and now there was the accident at the plant near Harrisburg. Was Westinghouse having second thoughts about staying in the nuclear business?

"I just don't understand this talk about nuclear being dead," responded Yochum with a hint of annoyance in his voice. "There is a nuclear imperative in this country. We know it, Wall Street knows it, and we're prepared to meet it. With today's energy situation, nuclear power just has to play an important part in meeting our future energy needs. The investment community is cautious about it in the short run, but they know nuclear is necessary for the long-term picture."

The interview lasted only a few more minutes. At the end of it,

Yochum confirmed that Westinghouse planned to invest approximately $300 million in the nuclear business over the next five
years.

Is that a pretty firm estimate?

"Right now, I don't see anything that would cause us to shift
away from that plan," he replied calmly.

Not long after Yochum hung up, Pennsylvania Governor Richard
Thornburgh went on the radio and advised that children and pregnant women be evacuated from the five-mile radius surrounding
the Three Mile Island nuclear plant. Before the immediate crisis
ended the following week, 60,000 Pennsylvanians had fled their
homes in fear of the technology Yochum termed "imperative" to
America's future.

5

A Sideline Business

I think we could be profitable without any new
orders, forever.

GORDON HURLBERT
President Westinghouse Power Systems Company

The single-minded, absolutely unshakable determination of the
men who run America's nuclear power industry was typified by
Leo Yochum's demeanor during our interview. In the days and
months that followed the Three Mile Island accident, their message became increasingly clear: America's leading nuclear corporations were not giving up. Utterly convinced of the future inevitability of nuclear power, the corporate side of the Atomic
Brotherhood hoped then and continues to hope to ride out the
current slump and cash in when the business revives a few years
hence.

But how do they survive in the meantime? After all, virtually no
nuclear power plants have been ordered in the United States for
seven years. Most companies would go bankrupt after seven weeks
without business, mush less seven years, yet America's nuclear
corporations say they are willing and able to wait years into the
future for their business to regain its old vitality.

How can they do it?

THE DIVERSIFIED GIANTS

The nuclear industry's fantastic tenacity is made possible by two
closely related features that have distinguished the corporate half
of the Atomic Brotherhood since its very beginnings. First, it is an
oligopoly, a business where just a handful of firms control nearly
all production and sales. And second, its members are some of the
most powerful and diversified multinational corporations on earth.
Most were giants of American capitalism long before the Nuclear
Age began. In fact, it was their decades of dominance over the
most strategic sectors of the U.S. economy and in particular over

nuclear's foundation industries—chemicals, heavy electrical machinery, and construction—that gave them the technical expertise, political connections, and above all, the tremendous size and wealth necessary to gain control over the emerging nuclear business. Today they sell hundreds of billions of dollars' worth of countless kinds of products every year, in markets throughout the world. To these titans, nuclear power is, financially, but a sideline business that provides only a small fraction of overall corporate sales. Consequently, if they so choose, they can subsidize their nuclear divisions for years while waiting for America's nuclear imperative to assert itself.

The nuclear industry is one of the most advanced expressions of a general trend that during the last century has fundamentally altered the economy of the United States: the transition from competitive to monopoly capitalism. What makes the industry so remarkable is that it represents the combination of at least five separate oligopoly industries into one cohesive superoligopoly. Just four companies—Westinghouse, General Electric, Combustion Engineering, and the Babcock and Wilcox subsidiary of McDermott—have supplied virtually every nuclear reactor ever purchased by U.S. electrical utilities. The same four, plus Exxon, completely control the market for ready-to-use nuclear fuel. Three giant construction firms—Bechtel, Stone and Webster, and the United Engineers and Constructors division of Raytheon—have built more than 75 percent of America's nuclear power plants. Five companies, including oil companies Gulf, Kerr-McGee, and the Conoco subsidiary of Du Pont, own almost half of the nation's uranium reserves. Nearly 70 percent of U.S. uranium-milling capacity belongs to Exxon, Atlantic Richfield, Kerr-McGee, the Utah International subsidiary of General Electric, and United Nuclear. And even these figures understate the extraordinary economic concentration within the nuclear industry, for most of these market leaders hold a commanding position within at least two of nuclear's subindustries, and some, like General Electric, are involved in nearly every step of the process, from uranium mines to power plants.

The twenty-four firms that dominate the nuclear industry* constitute what may be the single largest and most powerful business enterprise in history. They sold a staggering $400 billion worth of products in 1981; only six of the world's nations—the United States, the Soviet Union, West Germany, Japan, France, and China—boast

---

* The firms are listed in appendix 2, along with information on the extent of their nuclear involvement and on their overall size and profitability.

larger gross national products. They hold commanding market shares in such crucial industries as chemicals, mining, weapons, computers, construction, heavy machinery, communications, investment banking, and life sciences. They dominate the production of conventional fossil fuels—oil, natural gas, coal—and the development of solar and other forms of renewable energy. Full-fledged transnational corporations, they have long conducted a significant portion of total business overseas, and they aim to maximize profits on a global, not a national, basis. Their managers and executives are the best money can buy, and they possess the financial resources and trained vision to plan years and even decades ahead. All but five of the firms rank among the one hundred fifty largest corporations in America, and seven rank among the top seventeen. Their enormous influence over the American economy is amplified still further by numerous close associations with Wall Street's leading financial institutions. Eight of the nation's nine biggest banks, its seven largest insurance companies, and many of its top investment banks and law firms serve the nuclear corporations through such mechanisms as long-term multi-million-dollar credit lines; they share members of boards of directors, and regularly provide one another with confidential legal and investment counsel.

None of the nuclear industry's ruling corporations depend upon nuclear-related sales for more than 10 percent of total revenues, and for most the percentage is in the 0 to 5 percent range. That balance, combined with generally sparkling profit performances and bright future growth prospects in the rest of their business portfolios, makes it fairly painless for these giants to absorb current losses while waiting for the Great Nuclear Revival. And they can wait a long time. Take General Electric, for example. GE sells about $600 million worth of nuclear equipment and services every year, enough that, were its nuclear division an independent company, it would rank about 400 in the *Fortune* 500. But at GE, which enjoyed over $27 billion in sales in 1981, nuclear amounts to 2 percent of total sales. According to the best estimates of Wall Street investment analysts who track the corporation, GE in the late 1970s was losing around $30 million a year on its nuclear business. Although an inconceivably large sum to the average wage earner, that amounts to pocket change to GE. As of October 31, 1979, the corporation held, *in cash alone,* over $2.5 billion—enough, in theory, to subsidize its current nuclear losses for eighty years.

There was nothing consciously conspiratorial in these giant cor-

porations taking over the nuclear industry and organizing themselves into tight oligopolies; rather, these trends were made inevitable by the laws of capitalist economics and the nature of nuclear
technology. Nuclear power was a business whose scale of operations and capital investment requirements were both so huge that
only the very largest and most technically accomplished corporations could reasonably hope to succeed in it (and then only with
billions upon billions of subsidy dollars from the federal government). Moreover, although the eventual profits were assumed to
be enormous, they were also, as one executive put it, "way out in
the future," and available only to those rich enough to subsidize
the start-up costs out of general corporate funds for many years.

"We had business plans from the beginning characterized by
what we call the hockey stick," says General Electric nuclear vice-
president Bertram Wolfe, "which means there's a long negative
cash flow." The initial negative cash flow is represented by the
bottom blade of the hockey stick and depicts the fact that the
company's total investment is greater than total revenues. Where
the blade turns into the stick's handle is the break-even point; the
handle itself represents the breakthrough into overall profitability.
With a technology as costly and difficult to tame as nuclear fission,
only corporations possessing tremendous financial stamina could
follow the curve to the elusive break-even point and reap a profitable reward.

Furthermore, again because of the great cost involved, this feat
was possible only if the corporation sold a very large quantity of
reactors and related equipment at healthy profit rates. GE, for
example, has sold nearly one hundred reactors, plus fuel and services, over the past two decades, without achieving cumulative
profitability. A major reason for this was the fact that GE was forced
to share the market with three other suppliers, which was at least
one too many, as Wall Street has always correctly suspected. With
the market divided four ways, it has proved impossible for all
vendors except perhaps Westinghouse to sell the amount of products required to reach cumulative profitability. Perhaps, had the
obstacles of public protest and stagnating electricity demand not
arisen to thwart reactor sales in the 1970s, the market could have
sustained all four producers, but no more than four. Only as a
tightly controlled oligopoly did the reactor manufacturing business
ever have even a chance of turning a profit.

The advantages of oligopoly are obvious. The fewer firms there
are in a certain market, the more business there is for each of them

and the easier they find it (in theory) to avoid the price reductions that full and free competition tends to bring. Oligopoly is the natural result of the competitive rhythm of a capitalist economy. Competition necessitates the search for new ways to cut costs in order not to fall behind; inevitably, some capitalists are more successful at finding these solutions than others. The fortunate are rewarded with an increase in their sales and share of the total market, while the unfortunate suffer decreased sales and market power. The result is that the market gradually comes to be dominated by fewer and fewer firms, each of which controls a greater and greater share of the market. This tendency towards oligopoly is evident in the history of many of America's major industries; automobiles and steel are two classic examples of markets that originally were served by dozens of individual companies but today are dominated by just a handful of firms.

Once a company has attained some oligopoly power, it is only good business practice to use the extra-large profits it tends to deliver to consolidate and expand its business empire. Theodore Quinn, a top General Electric executive during the 1920s and 1930s, has revealed in some detail how GE employed this strategy during his years with the company. Quinn had witnessed and helped carry out such plans while at GE. A genuine *Wunderkind*, he was just thirty-four years old when top management chose him to head GE's new refrigerator department in 1927. By 1930, his division was doing an amazing $50 million worth of business every year; his successes propelled Quinn up the GE corporate ladder to the vice-presidential level and to positions as chairman of the sales committee and vice-chairman of the GE Supply Corporation. But Quinn resigned in 1936. An ardent believer in free enterprise, he was disgusted by the way GE and other giant corporations deliberately and ruthlessly acted to limit competition, buy up smaller companies or drive them out of business, and then impose inflated prices on the consuming public.

In one of the numerous books he authored after leaving GE, Quinn wrote:

> The secret of GE's predominance and growth [rested] upon two foundations:
> 1. As a J. P. Morgan combine originally (like General Motors and U.S. Steel) it had abundant capital, including access, through Morgan, to life insurance funds.
> 2. It had high-profit, monopoly lines which enabled it to finance other lines until they, too, could reach volumes that

would assure their continuance on a self-supporting and profitable basis.

In its early days as a company (J. P. Morgan created General Electric in 1892 by merging the Edison General Electric Company and the Thompson-Houston Electric Company), GE typically forced its way into new businesses by acquiring, with Morgan money, one or more of the independent companies then serving that particular market. GE would gradually secure a major share of the new market by having its subsidiary undersell and perhaps buy up weaker competitors. Once the competition had been thinned, the subsidiary boosted prices and began generating the extra-large profits associated with oligopoly; before long, these profits more than made up for initial losses.

By the time Theodore Quinn joined the company in the 1920s, GE had been enriching and enlarging itself in this way for nearly three decades. It had attained oligopoly positions within enough major markets that, as implied in Quinn's point 2 above, it could finance some of its future growth and diversification internally, without resorting to dependence upon Morgan money. Quinn points to GE's light-bulb business as a major profit center, where net profit on investment at times approximated 50 percent.

> It was from its lamp profits that General Electric financed its entry into the home appliance field. There was no purpose or advantage of efficiency involved. Because it had access to capital, it proceeded, as practically all of the other giant corporations have done, to purchase and absorb other corporations, driving companies with little capital out of business or forcing them into mergers.

The phenomenon Quinn refers to here is known in the jargon of economics as "cross-subsidization."* It is the mechanism by which oligopoly power and corporate growth and diversification feed upon and reproduce one another, and it has been a standard operating procedure for America's largest corporations for decades. There is nothing particularly mysterious about it: the bigger a corporation, the more easily it can buy its way into oligopoly positions. More oligopoly leads to greater sales and profits, which make possible still more oligopoly, and so on and on.

---

* Dr. John Blair, who served as chief economist of the U.S. Senate Antitrust Subcommittee for many years, has defined this term as "the use of profits obtained by a conglomerate corporation in industries in which it possesses substantial monopoly power to subsidize sales made at a loss in competitive industries."

It was only through gaining and exploiting oligopoly power within their original base industry that today's nuclear corporations grew large and wealthy enough to compete for a place within the nuclear oligopoly. GE and Westinghouse, for example, had long been giants of the electrical business, selling a wide range of products that produced, distributed, or consumed electricity, before they entered the nuclear business. Babcock and Wilcox and Combustion Engineering had overwhelmingly dominated the production of steam boilers and other sorts of heavy electrical equipment for years before they added nuclear reactors to their product lines. Du Pont and Union Carbide were among the country's biggest chemical companies and Goodyear one of its leading rubber firms before they expanded into uranium mining, enrichment, and reprocessing. And of course, Exxon, Gulf, Atlantic Richfield, Standard Oil of Ohio, Kerr-McGee, and numerous other leading uranium companies first made their fortunes in the petroleum business.

But the diversification into nuclear power was different from previous cross-subsidizations in the same way that the All-Star Game is different from regular season baseball games. For this time GE, Westinghouse, and the other would-be nuclear corporations were pitted, not against smaller, weaker firms such as they had effortlessly gobbled up in former expansions, but against other giants like themselves—rich, powerful, addicted to the treasures of oligopoly, and well-schooled in the methods of achieving it. Each of the dozen or so giants that wanted to get into the nuclear reactor business in the early 1960s knew the market could not possibly support all or even most of them. Yet, the try was worth it. For the few victorious survivors would, it was believed, acquire a substantial share of an enormous market, sell hundreds of millions of dollars worth of products that delivered especially large profit margins, and control an industry that figured to become as strategically important to the American and world economies over the next half-century as the petroleum industry had been during the previous fifty years. Thus, it is not surprising that the struggle for control of the nuclear industry was a particularly vicious one and that the industry never really passed through a competitive stage. Instead, like a man who emerges from his mother's womb in full physical and mental development, the industry, when it emerged from its government-nurtured gestation into the world of private commerce, was already a superoligopoly, ruled over by the kings of American capitalism.

A couple of months before the Three Mile Island accident ruined his company's reputation as a reactor manufacturer, Nelson Embrey, the head of marketing and business planning for Babcock and Wilcox's Nuclear Power Generation Division, outlined his strategy for boosting his company's share of the reactor market from the 15 percent it had held during the 1970s to around 25 percent. The centerpiece of Embry's plan was Babcock's model 205 standardized reactor, a machine capable of 1,200 to 1,300 megawatts of electricity and boasting, according to Embrey, a 5 percent higher fuel efficiency than comparable reactors sold by his competition. Embrey further disclosed that Babcock planned to emphasize "efficiency, reliability, and high-quality support of the reactors we already have in service" in its marketing offensive. But, strange as it may sound for a company aiming to fight its way up from the bottom of the heap, Embrey did not mention reducing prices as a way to woo customers away from the competition.

His omission was not really surprising, for price competition has been virtually unheard of in the nuclear reactor business since the turnkey era of the early 1960s. This is not to say that prices have never been reduced, nor that the Big Four reactor vendors have never competed with one another. They have competed—continuously and viciously. But they have drawn each other's blood with weapons other than price, for they knew from previous experience that under oligopoly conditions, what begins as price competition can easily degenerate into mutually destructive price warfare. As economists Paul Baran and Paul Sweezy explain:

> If firm A lowers its price, some new demand may be tapped, but the main effect will be to attract customers away from firms B, C, and D. The latter, not willing to give up their business to A, will retaliate by lowering their prices, perhaps even undercutting A. While A's original move was made in the expectation of increasing its profit, the net result may be to leave all the firms in a worse position.

Oligopoly corporations have responded to this predicament, Baran and Sweezy go on to suggest,

> by the simple expedient of banning price cutting as a legitimate weapon of economic warfare. Naturally this has not happened all at once or as a conscious decision. Like other power taboos, that against price cutting has grown up gradually out of long and often bitter experience, and it derives its strength

from the fact that it serves the interests of powerful forces in society.

The advantages of banning price cutting as a legitimate weapon of economic warfare are obvious. If price competition can be eliminated, firms in an oligopoly industry can collectively establish prices that maximize the profits of the group as a whole. Since the legal authorities frown on such activities, companies wishing to conspire on prices and market shares often do so in secret. Such practices are hardly foreign to the nuclear industry's ruling corporations; many of them have been centrally involved in some of the most audacious price-fixing schemes in U.S. corporate history.

The most notorious example, of course, is the international petroleum cartel. Ever since Standard Oil boss Walter Teagle invited the heads of British Petroleum and Royal Dutch/Shell to Scotland's Achnacarry Castle in 1928 to avert the price war that each dreaded would ruin them all, the world's major oil companies have conspired on a global basis to limit production, allocate supply, and thereby tacitly fix prices at levels far higher than would pertain in a free market. Of the perpetrators, Exxon, Gulf, Standard Oil of Ohio, Getty Oil, the Conoco subsidiary of Du Pont, and Atlantic Richfield are now active in the nuclear business. Less widely known are the numerous instances of secret collaboration between General Electric and Westinghouse. On December 9, 1930, at a meeting in GE's Paris office, the two firms joined with numerous foreign "competitors" in forming an international electric equipment cartel. All agreed to meet regularly to discuss and establish prices and terms of sale and, in certain cases, to allocate sales among themselves in an effort to control global competition. Both GE and Westinghouse left the cartel after World War II, but the two did not stop colluding between themselves. During the mid-1950s, they were the ringleaders of an overt conspiracy to fix the prices of a wide range of electrical equipment, "from two-dollar insulators to multi-million-dollar turbine generators." In all, the U.S. Justice Department brought twenty indictments against twenty-nine corporations and forty-five top managers and executives, charging violation of the 1890 Sherman Anti-trust Act. General Electric pleaded guilty to all major indictments against it, and with the government's consent, nolo contedere to thirteen "minor" ones. The other major companies did the same. Then there was the international uranium cartel, formed in 1972 by a group including Gulf Oil, Kerr-McGee, the huge, British-based Rio Tinto

Zinc, and the partially state-owned firms in Canada, Australia, and South Africa. The cartel's secret meetings to allocate supplies and boost prices were exposed a few years later in congressional hearings.

Yet secrecy and written agreements are not always necessary in restricting price competition. Oligopoly firms can easily administer unfairly high prices by employing a form of tacit collusion known as "price leadership." One firm, usually the strongest in the industry, takes the lead in announcing a price change; the others then simply fall into line and adopt the change themselves. While there are many variations on this practice (the individual firms may take turns initiating price changes or, if the group as a whole believes a proposed change is unwise, it may refuse to endorse the change and force the initiator to rescind it), all have the same result: price competition is eliminated.

The pricing patterns and forms of competition that have characterized the reactor-manufacturing industry strongly suggest the Big Four reactor vendors may have engaged in such tacit collusion over the years. Competition among the reactor manufacturers has always focused primarily on reactor efficiency and reliability rather than price. Decades of selling heavy equipment to the utility industry had taught each reactor manufacturer that it made profits only by helping its customer make profits, and that the many criteria by which a utility selected one piece of equipment over another ultimately boiled down to one question: Which machine will cut our costs and increase our revenues the most over its lifetime? Given this calculus, the actual factory price of a reactor mattered far less than its anticipated operating efficiency. (One need not be a Harvard Business School graduate to realize that it pays to invest a few million dollars more in a reactor if that reactor's superior efficiency promises over the long run to cut a utility's generating costs and boost its revenues by tens of millions of dollars.)

The ability to boost prices in the face of stagnant demand is an undeniable sign of collusive, administered pricing. Under competitive conditions, one would naturally expect a fall in demand to cause manufacturers to reduce prices and cut profit margins in order to rejuvenate demand. Yet despite the collapse of the reactor market in 1974, reactor prices continued to rise sharply through the end of the 1970s. In their official explanations, the reactor manufacturers blame the threefold price increase during these years on general inflation and on government regulations requiring additional safety features for reactors. Doubtless there is some truth to this defense. Yet James Deddens, a top nuclear executive at Babcock and Wilcox, implied privately that there was another reason as well. "The NSSS [nuclear steam supply system, the technical name for a nuclear reactor] vendors were trying to get the price levels up and the profit margins up," he said. "There was an element of 'Hey fellas, we can probably get the price levels to be fairly high,' even though the competition was still fairly fierce."

Industry officials recognize that even if there is a nuclear comeback, it will not be large enough to sustain all four reactor vendors at profitable levels of operation. "There will not be enough business for four nuclear systems suppliers between now and the year 2000," declares William Connolly, Combustion Engineering's senior executive vice-president for corporate and investor relations. "Somebody's going to have to stop taking new orders. We don't predict who is most likely to drop out first, other than to say that it most definitely won't be Combustion."

Leaving the nuclear reactor business is a touchy subject for the four vendors, and their statements concerning that possibility vary according to their audience. When talking to government officials, they paint a bleak picture of an industry at the end of its rope, unable to continue without tangible evidence that the government is committed to nuclear power playing a major role in meeting future U.S. energy needs. To Wall Street and inquiring journalists a slightly different story is told. Because they do not wish to appear to be giving up (in the business world, such rumors are often self-fulfilling), each vendor insists that, while it is constantly re-evaluating its position and future prospects within the nuclear business, it remains determined, in Babcock and Wilcox executive Nelson Embry's words, "to tough it through this thin period." At an April 1982 conference sponsored by the nuclear trade publication *Nucleonics Week*, high-level executives from each of the Big Four said their firms were committed to staying in the nuclear business indefinitely. John West, nuclear vice-president at Combustion Engineering, said Combustion had not yet shut down any of its nuclear facilities because it wanted to be ready "for when [the business] revives—not if, but when." Philip Bray of General Electric said that GE also was "preparing for the future re-emergence of nuclear projects in America," explaining, "We were the first. We aren't going to stop now."

The problems confronting the vendors are real enough. None of

them, except perhaps Westinghouse, has yet sold enough reactors
to recover the billions of dollars invested over the years in the
factories, equipment, and most important, personnel necessary to
produce nuclear reactors. Their capital investment has not yet been
completely recovered, much less begun to generate profits. The
mid-1970s orders slump seems to have come just as the vendors
were ready to turn the corner. As Combustion's William Connolly
says, "The most confounding thing in this business has been the
moving target of finally breaking even. You look out five years [into
the future] and it should be then, but every two or three years, that
point moves out another few years, due to the shrinkage of the
market." Bertram Wolfe of GE goes a step further: "It's questionable whether we [GE] will ever be cumulatively profitable,
whether the future returns on the business will ever make up for
our losses plus the interest they would be accruing." Only Westinghouse has said it is making any money in the nuclear power
business. Gordon Hurlbert, president of the Westinghouse Power
Systems Company, contends, "If you neglect our uranium difficulties, the business has been very profitable, more profitable than
the corporate average, both cumulatively and on a day-to-day
average."

Reactor manufacturers face two particular structural problems
during prolonged sales slumps, Mans Lonnroth and William
Walker explain in their report for the Rockefeller Foundation and
the Royal Institute of International Affairs entitled *The Viability
of the Civilian Nuclear Industry*: "the one of maintaining adequate
teams of designers and engineers in their own organizations, the
other of ensuring that supplies of bought-in component parts remain available." The problem of keeping one's team together is
already serious and promises to grow progressively difficult as the
vendors work off their backlogs of previous reactor orders. Westinghouse and GE, not surprisingly, have by far the largest backlogs.
Westinghouse is scheduled to deliver thirty-five reactors, GE
twenty-two, Combustion nine, and Babcock six. It is true that many
of these reactors will not actually go on line until the early 1990s,
but the vendors will actually run out of work long before then.
According to Bertram Wolfe, all the engineering and manufacturing
for the plants in GE's backlog will be finished, and virtually all
the equipment shipped, by 1985–86. Babcock and Wilcox finished
the manufacture of components for its civilian nuclear plants in
1982, leaving only the engineering work needed to get the plants
operating still to be completed.

The vendors have responded by reducing, but not eliminating, their nuclear production capacity. Babcock and Wilcox closed down its nuclear components plant in Mount Vernon, Indiana, in the spring of 1979 and began doing non-nuclear work in its Barberton, Ohio pressure vessel factory. GE and Chicago Bridge and Iron agreed in late 1980 to open the Memphis, Tennessee pressure vessel facility they jointly own to non-nuclear manufacturing work, and GE converted part of its Wilmington, Delaware nuclear fuel and components plant to produce aircraft engines. Westinghouse had to completely scrap its Tampa, Florida steam generator factory because the cost of converting it to non-nuclear work was prohibitive.

Many of these facilities could, however, in the event of a nuclear comeback, be reoriented to nuclear work fairly quickly and cheaply. "There's no level at which you go subcritical," asserts Philip Bray of General Electric. "There are ways to close a facility or divert it to other uses [so that] it can be brought back in[to nuclear work later]." A far greater and more immediate problem for the vendors is holding on to the thousands of engineers and highly skilled shop-floor personnel who work in producing reactors. These workers, Lonnroth and Walker write, "are in much demand in the market place, and are therefore as easy to lose as they are difficult to recruit. . . . Once they start leaving, it is feared by the vendors that there could be an avalanche, with design and engineering capabilities severely eroded."

The avalanche apparently has already begun. *Nuclear News*, the industry trade publication, reported in a November 1981 cover story that "some segments of the U.S. nuclear industry have more positions available than qualified people . . . to fill them." Enrollment in university nuclear engineering programs has been steadily falling since the mid-1970s, a trend that *Nuclear News* blamed on increasingly negative public perceptions of the nuclear industry. Nor is it only young people who are skeptical of nuclear power's long-term employment security.

One former GE employee tells how, back in 1977, "résumés were shooting out of the nuclear division like crazy, because the engineers saw the end was coming. Mangement tried to calm them down by issuing internal reports saying it planned more investment in nuclear, but most people didn't believe them." When asked about the incident, Bertram Wolfe smiles and answers, "When the market bottomed out, we decided we had to cut back in some areas, such as marketing. We understood that younger fellows with

career orientations and family responsibilities may be hard pressed
to stay in nuclear power. It's not exactly a growing business with
possibilities for promotions."

Why, then, do the reactor vendors keep at it? Why, after seven
years without new orders, multi-million-dollar annual losses, and
the attendant problems of trying to maintain a reactor-manufacturing capability, do the Big Four not simply take the path of least
resistance and give up?

The executives point out that their decision to stay in the nuclear
reactor business is made by judging its future profitability prospects, not by moaning about its past losses. Those losses, says GE's
Bertram Wolfe,

> are all past history. It's true there's no market for [nuclear]
> steam supply systems right now, but the costs of staying in
> over and above meeting our past obligations is very small.
> And the potential of that having a profitable effect in the future
> is reasonable. We certainly don't have to stay in the reactor
> business. We've got our backlog under control, and could stop
> taking any orders. We've not made that decision. We think the
> steam supply system business may be profitable in the future
> because the character of the business has changed. [The GE
> boiling water reactor] is a standardized product, the manufac-
> turing plants are in place, so there's really no new investment
> needed to cash in on a revived market.

And a revived market is exactly what the nuclear executives are
counting on. Fifteen orders per year would probably sustain the
entire industry, provided market shares remained roughly the
same. Nelson Embrey of Babcock and Wilcox says that his company
"can be very interested with three orders a year." The same is true
of Combustion Engineering. GE says it needs four orders a year
to run a profitable reactor business, but that it could manage with
three—although that would require changing the business structure substantially. Westinghouse refuses to disclose its minimum-
orders threshold, but executive nuclear vice-president Theodore
Stern says Westinghouse has reduced its capacity from ten reactor
orders a year to three and adds, "I don't think we'll reduce below
that." Stern's boss, Westinghouse Power Systems president Gordon
Hurlbert, declares:

> We could operate very profitably in a market of thirteen orders
> a year. It's like a single boy—there's more pretty girls out
> there than you could possibly love. We have more opportun-

ities to put both strategic funds and capital funds than we can possibly invest. . . . With our background, our base, and our cost structure, it looks like nuclear is a very good place to put a good portion of our money.

Many nuclear executives point out that even if they wanted to leave the business, they could not without severely damaging their corporate reputations and customer relationships. GE's Bertram Wolfe worries that Wall Street might perceive a GE evacuation of the reactor business "as an admission that GE isn't a high-technology, forefront company." The vendors are also keenly aware that many of the larger electric utilities want nuclear power to be at least an option later in the 1980s. Westinghouse, Combustion Engineering, and McDermott (Babcock and Wilcox's parent company) each depend on the utilities for over a third of total corporate sales (for GE, the ratio is about 15 percent). Under the circumstances, to abandon nuclear could cost a reactor manufacturer millions of dollars in non-nuclear sales. As one Babcock and Wilcox executive explained, "We can't cut our own throats by leaving nuclear. We depend on the utility business."

Bertram Wolfe likened GE's staying in the nuclear business to the dilemma of a man clutching the tail of a tiger—the only thing worse than holding on is letting go:

We've got thirty-five plants in our backlog we've got to build, extending until 1990, and these things take ten years to build. The company has a lot of pride, and the message we get from corporate headquarters is to do that job and make sure they're good products, and the company has backed us financially to the hilt. . . . A lot of the new testing and development facilities we've put in [at GE's San Jose, California nuclear division headquarters] aren't because we see a glorious new product out there, but to maintain the quality level of the present products. The hope is that the present product will give returns in the future.

The orders backlog is more than a contractual duty: it represents over $8 billion worth of revenues that will invigorate the vendors' nuclear cash flows throughout the next five years. And as these plants come on line, they will gradually double what is by far the vendors' most lucrative area of operations: the refueling and servicing of existing plants. Not only are refueling and servicing constantly growing markets, but the profit rates on such work are about one and one-half to two times greater than the 10 to 12 percent pretax margin that vendors earn selling the reactors themselves.

This is especially true of the spare parts business, where the customers are captive, and, as GE international salesman Adrian Fioretti dryly puts it, "you don't have the normal day-to-day competitive pressures."

James J. Taylor, vice-president of Westinghouse's Water Reactor Division, projects that the entire nuclear fuel market will be worth $1.5 billion a year by the late 1980s; the servicing business will be worth another $1 billion. If Westinghouse maintains its present share of the market, says Taylor, between the two markets it should annually garner approximately $1 billion in nuclear sales. Assuming, conservatively, a 15 percent return on these sales, that translates into $150 million worth of nuclear profits every year for Westinghouse, even if it never sells another reactor. GE expects equally bountiful revenues. Because they have sold fewer reactors in the past, Combustion and Babcock will have to be content with less refueling and servicing work. Yet John West, senior vice-president for Combustion Engineering's Nuclear Power Systems Division, expects $200 million worth of such business a year by the early 1990s, and emphasizes that refueling and servicing "are very important. They are the sustaining areas of the [nuclear] business, and as they become more important, a lower level of systems [reactor] sales will do."

Fuel and service sales are already helping the vendor's nuclear cash flows. GE, for example, sold $200 million worth of fuel alone in 1980, $80 million of it to overseas customers. As the competition for the refueling and servicing business has intensified, the vendors have striven to increase the efficiency and reliability of their fuel bundles. The resulting research and redesign work has had the fortunate side effect of partially solving the problem of keeping design teams together. Ironically, the Three Mile Island accident, because it led the Nuclear Regulatory Commission to revise and add safety regulations, also provided work for nuclear engineers and boosted vendor revenues. "One industry observer forecasts an $8 billion retrofit market across the rest of the 1980's and says its is growing at 20 percent a year compounded," according to the Atomic Industrial Forum's 1982 year-end report.

Government research-and-development contracts also help the vendors keep their key nuclear design and production staff and facilities busy. President Reagan's commitment of $1.6 billion over the next five years to complete work on the Clinch River breeder reactor, along with his $500 million in annual funding for general breeder research, is intended not only to keep the United States from falling behind the French in breeder technology but also to keep the industry's production teams together while waiting for new orders. The nuclear work most vendors do for the military is also a great help. "Our naval nuclear work is very important," affirms John McMillan, vice-president of Babock and Wilcox's Nuclear Power Generating Division. "It gives us a base-load of work with which we can maintain our manufacturing skills and technology and keep together a cadre of good, experienced manufacturing people. It's certainly a key ingredient for us in terms of our staying power within the nuclear business."

As companies who routinely think, plan, and operate on a global scale, each of the Big Four (except Babcock and Wilcox) also regards overseas sales as an important potential means of survival. Exports have always been essential to the nuclear industry, as we have seen, but they are especially crucial now. Since 1975, both Westinghouse and GE have sold more reactors abroad than at home. With no new orders coming from U.S. utilities, exports are "the name of the game in keeping the United States vending industry alive," says Dickson Hoyle, Westinghouse's director of international nuclear affairs.

The export market has its own problems, however. "With today's unemployment, no industrial country is going to import a product which it can manufacture itself," explains Westinghouse international nuclear sales executive John Kreuthmeier. "So the only markets open right now are in the Third World." But most Third World countries with electricity markets large enough to accommodate a nuclear power plant simply cannot afford the tremendous expense. Brazil, for example, apparently is scaling down its nuclear construction program partly because it does not want to increase its already staggering foreign-debt burden, which at $60 billion is the second largest of any developing country. The largest debt belongs to Mexico, which until its economic crisis of 1982 was considered the most promising overseas market for U.S. reactor manufacturers. In November 1981, Energy Department Deputy Secretary and former Bechtel Corporation nuclear executive W. Kenneth Davis led a high-level U.S. government delegation to Mexico in an attempt to win American firms the inside track on the first two of twenty-odd nuclear plants scheduled to be ordered there over the next decade.

It is the nuclear vendors' flexibility and adaptability, along with the promise of a large, growing, and lucrative future nuclear fuel and reactor-servicing market, that leads executives like Gordon Hurlbert of Westinghouse to declare:

I think we could be profitable without any new orders, forever. We've got a decade's backlog. By then the [heavy machine tool] equipment will be written off, and you lay off the
people, and put a new product in there. . . . Look, this isn't
like distribution transformers—you sell 'em like you do crack-
ers out of the A&P. You have 'em out in the warehouse, they
[the utilities] come and they get 'em and you fill it up again
and you push 'em like that. And if you don't sell, why, you
write off while you're in big trouble. But we've got a lot of
lead time on this [nuclear business]. We're planning our manpower needs right now for three years ahead, on the assumption that we might not ever get another order, and then on a
reasonable assumption, and then a very optimistic assumption. But there's going to be so much fuel business and so
much repair and service business. And [if there are no orders]
you just have to close up your facilities and get rid of the
people.

Of course, neither Hurlbert nor most other top nuclear executives
believe there will not be more reactor orders in the 1980s. True,
there probably will not be enough to support all four vendors, but
there should be plenty to keep at least one or two happy. The
question, then, is not who can wait, but who can wait the longest.
    There has been speculation that GE was preparing to abandon
reactor manufacturing ever since 1976, when the company significantly tightened the terms and conditions under which it would
sell nuclear reactors. It is true that GE has thought long and hard
about leaving the nuclear business. Indeed, in 1978, Thomas
Vanderslice, then GE's vice-president for power systems, told a
group of Wall Street investment analysts that GE was all ready to
go and its exit plan was so smooth that "the Street" would not even
hear it leave; there would be no noticeable impact on corporate
finances. In early 1982 GE chairman John Welch went a step further when he told a meeting of New York security analysts that the
company's planning "does not anticipate any new nuclear plant
orders" in the United States for the rest of the decade. Nevertheless, GE is still not leaving the nuclear business.* Company offi-

* The speculation about GE's imminent departure has always been at least partly
wishful thinking on the part of other vendors, which perceived GE's re-evaluation
of the nuclear business as an unusual move with propitious consequences for them.
This was a misreading, according to Bertram Wolfe. "GE is a very introspective
company. Ever since I've been here, we've been constantly re-examining whether
we should stay in or go out of the nuclear business. That happens with all of our
businesses."

cials say it plans "to be in the business indefinitely in regards to fuel, services, and support for our operating reactors," and GE is pushing strongly for export sales to keep its reactor-manufacturing facilities and staff occupied. The company is demonstrating its commitment to the future by continuing the campaign it began in the mid-1970s to improve the boiling water reactor's performance and reduce its "down-time" (the amount of time a reactor is out of service). In four years, GE succeeded in raising the operating-capacity factor of boiling water reactors an astonishing 21 percent, from 47 percent in 1975 to 68 percent in 1979; meanwhile the performance of its competitors' pressurized water reactors was dropping from 65 percent to 56 percent.

"We still remain optimistic that the nuclear option will come back," says Bertram Wolfe, "and with respect to sticking power, there's nobody that can stick like GE. We can stay in indefinitely. . . . The real question is, How long can B&W and Combustion stay in? Their backlogs are very small compared to ours, and their financial resources are very low. Clearly those two companies are the most vulnerable."

The one company everyone agrees will remain in the nuclear reactor business until the bitter end is Westinghouse. It is the undisputed industry leader, ahead on reactor sales, the learning curve, and fast breeder development, and far and away the vendor most committed to nuclear power, in both rhetorical and invest-ment terms. The uranium fiasco dealt the corporation a severe blow, but Westinghouse landed on its feet afterwards and even managed to squeeze nearly $100 million in compensation out of Gulf Oil and other members of the international uranium cartel, which preferred to avoid a protracted, costly, and probably embar-rassing courtroom battle.

Although Westinghouse is but one-third as large as GE, it is twice the size of Combustion Engineering and McDermott, and considerably more diversified. For 1981 the corporation reported earnings of $438 million on worldwide sales of $9.4 billion. The productivity of Westinghouse's 140,000 employees grew by 4.5 percent in 1981, outstripping not only U.S. industry as a whole but also the rates in the three industrial nations where productivity is growing fastest: Japan, West Germany, and France. Westinghouse is wealthy enough that Power Systems Company president Gordon Hurlbert dismisses a $50 million investment in a new nuclear fuel plant as "not a lot of capital." The corporation projects spending $1.5 billion on capital investment during the first five years of the

1980s, without having to borrow a nickel of it from outside financiers. For Westinghouse, as for GE, staying in the nuclear reactor business is a question of will and determination, not capability.

The rest of the nuclear industry is also dominated by diversified transnational corporations, but these are even less troubled by the continuing market slump than are the Big Four. In the business of engineering and constructing the gigantic power stations that house nuclear reactors, just six firms—Bechtel, Stone and Webster, United Engineers and Constructors, Ebasco Services, Daniel International, and Brown and Root—control virtually the entire U.S. market, and the top three command 75 percent of it. (See appendix 2 for precise market shares.) Towering above the rest is Bechtel, which controls an overwhelming 40 percent of the domestic market—nearly twice the share of its closest rival, Stone and Webster—and has built seventeen nuclear plants overseas, more than any other U.S. company. It has also been the engineering and construction company most active in building conversion, reprocessing, and other nuclear-fuel-cycle facilities.

In an interview conducted in 1979, before he became the number two official in Ronald Reagan's Department of Energy, W. Kenneth Davis, Bechtel's vice-president for nuclear development, admitted that Bechtel was "concerned over the present market hiatus," but said the slump had not yet caused any major problems for the company. "The principal difficulty is we stopped expanding as rapidly as we had been," he remarked. "But we have considerable confidence that nuclear power will continue to be used on an increasing scale, despite the present hiatus." A permanent nuclear moratorium in the United States would hurt Bechtel, but the damage would likely be neither severe nor lasting, because, in Davis's words, "we could shift many of our engineers from nuclear to coal [plant] designs without much problem." Ashton O'Donnell, vice-president of Bechtel's Nuclear Fuel and Operations Division, added, "As a company we have no particular axe to grind. . . . If somebody says there'll be no more atomic plants, well, there'll still be coal plants, oil plants, and solar plants and tidal plants. They all call for good, solid engineering-construction management and know-how."

The nuclear architect-engineers are, uniformly, exceedingly wealthy companies whose corporate reach extends far beyond the electricity business. "In good times, construction companies have always been prodigious cash producers because they require no expensive inventory and can finance their day-to-day business with their clients' cash," *Business Week* enthused in September 1980. "But now, their cash flow is almost an embarrassment, Fluor (whose Daniel International subsidiary ranks fifth among nuclear architect-engineers), for example, paid cash for its $100 million headquarters building and is still sitting on a $222 million wad." The *Business Week* article went on to predict that "the engineering-construction industry cannot fail to profit mightily" in the 1980s as the big oil companies rush to rebuild and expand their refineries and the massive, government-sponsored synthetic fuels program takes off.

Bechtel, which has 30,000 permanent employees, has operated in more than one hundred countries, building steel mills, deep-water ports, dams, oil pipelines, and, in Jubail, Saudi Arabia, an entire industrial city the size of Toledo, an undertaking that ranks as the largest single construction project in history. Fluor performs 90 percent of its work overseas; this includes a $4.2 billion coal conversion plant the company is building for the apartheid government of South Africa. Stone and Webster built a billion-dollar petrochemical plant for Libya, and Halliburton's Brown and Root subsidiary is one of the world's leading builders of offshore drilling and production platforms for oil and natural gas. Back in the United States, Raytheon, the $3.7 billion parent company of number three nuclear architect-engineer United Engineers and Constructors, stays healthy by annually consuming over a billion dollars' worth of U.S. government weapons contracts. Enserch, parent of number four Ebasco, is the fourth largest natural gas utility in the country and deeply involved in petroleum exploration, production, and services. And Ebasco, while waiting for an upsurge in electric power plant orders, has successfully shouldered its way into the synthetic fuels business.

If the key to the staying power of the nuclear construction firms is their flexibility, that of the uranium companies is their market's stability. After all, if there were a moratorium on new reactor orders, functioning plants would still require fueling and waste disposal services. As Lonnroth and Walker point out,

> the front-end of the fuel cycle . . . is insulated to a degree from economic cycles since, once nuclear power is reasonably established, its business arises out of the routine operation of the installed stock of nuclear power plants. It therefore has a

reasonably secure cash-flow even when new nuclear facilities are not being ordered. ... The fuel cycle industry's income is thus related to the size of the stock of nuclear power plants ... while the reactor industry's income is related to the incremental change in that stock.

Yet the fuel cycle industry is not completely invulnerable to market slumps. Nowadays the uranium mining and milling industries exist primarily to supply nuclear power reactors. According to Richard Holway, manager of uranium marketing for Homestake Mining, "electric utilities now account for 99.9 percent of all uranium ore sales." An end to nuclear power would eventually bring uranium mining to a halt, but the process would be gradual, says Robert Moyer, marketing manager for Pathfinder Mines, the uranium subsidiary of Utah International, the gigantic multinational minerals firm General Electric purchased in 1976. "If there is a moratorium on new nuclear power plants, it will first halt new exploration. There are enough plants now on line that it would gradually increase competition in the existing market. But over a gradual time period, it will phase out the entire industry. However, the uranium-mining business isn't all that different from other businesses, so the companies would just transfer their personnel into other mining businesses."

The uranium and nuclear-fuel-cycle industries today are dominated by Exxon, Gulf, Kerr-McGee, and other big oil companies, which used their enormous previously accumulated oil profits to buy up uranium reserve lands and acquire existing independent uranium companies in the late 1960s and early 1970s. Big oil's tight grip on the uranium business is clearly demonstrated in appendix 2, which provides exact data on market shares. Even these figures understate the oil companies' power, says their trade association, the American Petroleum Institute, because they do not take into account the fact that oil companies own most of America's lower-cost (easier to mine) uranium reserves. The institute reports that, in fact, oil companies own 71.8 percent of available reserves below $20 a pound. Oil companies also control approximately 60 percent of the country's uranium-milling capacity, and undertake over 60 percent of the industry's exploration.

The uranium-mining industry, unlike the other industries in the nuclear business, did not begin as an oligopoly of giant firms. In 1948, the Atomic Energy Commission set out to spur domestic uranium production so that the massive atomic weapons program it was about to launch would not be dependent on foreign uranium sources. (Most of the uranium for the Manhattan Project had been imported from the Belgian Congo and Canada.) Despite attractive subsidy programs, the large mining companies failed to respond because they believed U.S. uranium deposits were too small and geographically scattered to make finding and mining them profitable. It was not until 1952, when a solitary prospector named Charlie Steen hit a lucky strike in southern Utah, that big firms began to show interest. Although giants like Union Carbide, which was already running the government's Oak Ridge enrichment plant and laying plans to manufacture nuclear reactors, were quick to get in on the early 1950s uranium boom, there remained opportunities for small independent firms to profit as well.

By the end of 1957, it was clear that U.S. reserves were sufficient to meet military requirements, so the AEC announced a slowdown in its uranium purchasing. To cushion private uranium producers, the AEC instituted an allocation plan to divide its reduced demand among the various U.S. producers. The slowdown naturally hit hardest at those small producers that lacked the political muscle needed to gain a healthy settlement from the AEC and the financial stamina to wait until the creation of the commercial nuclear power industry revived uranium demand.* By the early 1960s, most of the small companies and independents had been forced out of the business.

In 1964 Congress amended the Atomic Energy Act to allow private ownership of nuclear fuel. That move, coupled with the mid-1960s surge of nuclear power plant orders, revitalized the potential profitability of the uranium business and rekindled the interest of oil companies like Gulf, Exxon, Continental, and Getty that had very briefly been in the business in the 1950s. Beginning with the phase-out of AEC uranium price supports in 1968 and continuing into the early 1970s, these oil giants quietly and successfully set about obtaining commanding positions in both ura-

* One company that did not lack the required political influence was Kerr-McGee, the oil and gas company that Robert Kerr of Oklahoma had founded in the 1930s. Kerr-McGee, which had entered the uranium business in the early 1950s, was originally awarded only a modest share in the AEC's allocation program, owing to the company's relative lack of what the AEC defined as "economically recoverable reserves." But by this time Robert Kerr had been elected a U.S. senator and had risen to become one of the most powerful men on Capitol Hill. There is no record of why it happened, but less than a year after the AEC announced its original allocation plan it suddenly withdrew it because of "inequities." Kerr-McGee fared substantially better under the new allocations.

nium mining and milling. Atlantic Richfield's cash purchase of leading uranium and copper company Anaconda in 1976, the same year GE acquired Utah International, was the final stroke in big oil's takeover of the uranium mining and milling businesses.

The same pattern of oligopolistic domination by gigantic and vertically integrated corporations repeats itself throughout the rest of the nuclear fuel cycle. Uranium conversion, which prepares milled uranium for enrichment, is undertaken in the United States at only two facilities. The largest, which accounts for 60 percent of production, is owned by Kerr-McGee, the same company that is number one in uranium mining and milling. The second plant is operated by the Allied Corporation (formerly Allied Chemical Company), which like Kerr-McGee, has substantial oil interests. More important, it was the lead company in the Allied General Nuclear Services consortium that began but eventually abandoned construction of the reprocessing and waste disposal plant at Barnwell, South Carolina. Allied Chemical owned 50 percent of the joint venture; the other half was split equally between two of the Seven Sisters, Royal Dutch/Shell and Gulf Oil. Gulf also happens to be the second largest holder of U.S. uranium reserves.

A few years ago, Exxon, the giant of all oil giants, laid plans to construct its own reprocessing plant (Bechtel was commissioned to do preliminary design work), but shelved the idea after President Carter prohibited reprocessing in 1977. If Exxon ever does build the plant, it will have achieved a degree of vertical integration within the nuclear business second only to General Electric. Exxon is a leader in uranium mining, milling, and fuel fabrication already. Along with Bechtel, GE, Westinghouse, and others, it made a strong bid in the early 1970s to take over the enrichment business from the federal government (see chapter 4 for details). Reprocessing is the only major step in the cycle that has yet to bear the unmistakable imprint of Exxon's footsteps.

Because Nixon's enrichment privatization scheme failed, the enrichment industry remains under the ownership of the U.S. Department of Energy. The government's three facilities are, however, operated for profit by two giant companies, Goodyear and Union Carbide. Union Carbide, besides operating the Oak Ridge, Tennessee and Paducah, Kentucky enrichment plants, also is a leading uranium miner and miller, possessing 20 million pounds of reserves and the country's seventh largest milling capacity.

Nuclear waste disposal likewise remains officially under U.S. government control but is performed by private corporations for

profit. The waste storage facility at Hanford, Washington, for example, which handles high-level nuclear waste generated by the
weapons program, is managed by Rockwell International, a leading
Defense Department contractor and developer of the fast breeder
reactor. Rockwell took over from Atlantic Richfield in 1977. Altogether, Rockwell is responsible for over 100 million gallons of high-
level waste at Hanford, slightly more than the 98 million gallons
that chemical giant Du Pont is watching over at Savannah River,
South Carolina.

THE WALL STREET CONNECTION

Giant corporations are social organisms. Like people, they maintain
networks of close friends and associates upon whom they depend
for certain vital needs. An important part of the reason why Exxon,
Union Carbide, Westinghouse, and the other giant corporations
who run the nuclear industry remain so wealthy and powerful—
and hence able to absorb nuclear-related losses fairly painlessly—
is their close and longstanding ties to an elite group of law firms,
banks, and insurance companies that themselves rank among the
mightiest members of the American financial establishment.

    The following table lists financial institutions that held signifi-
cant amounts of stock in the top twenty-four U.S. nuclear corporations as of year-end 1980. (The specific holdings of the larger
institutions, as well as other relevant financial information, are
detailed in appendix 4.)

Financial Institution	Fortune Ranking	Number of Nuclear Companies in Which a Leading Stockholder
J. P. Morgan (bank)	5	14
Bankers Trust (bank)	8	11
Teachers Insurance & Annuity (life insurance firm)	10	–
Manufacturers Hanover Trust (bank)	4	14
Prudential Life (life insurance firm)	1	11
Citicorp (bank)	1	14
Lord Abbett & Co. (investment company)	–	–
Chase Manhattan (bank)	3	6
Chemical Bank (bank)	7	5
First National of Boston (bank)	17	7
Bank of America (bank)	2	9*

* 1978 figure.

Many of the same names reappear in the following table, which lists the nuclear industry's most important moneylenders.

Financial Institution	Number of Nuclear Companies in Which a Leading Debtholder	Lending Exposure $ Millions
Prudential Life (life insurance firm)	13	$1,242.6
Metropolitan Life (life insurance firm)	12	1,211.2
J. P. Morgan (bank)	10	258.1*
New York Life (life insurance firm)	10	231.8
Chase Manhattan (bank)	8	461.8*
Manufacturers Hanover Trust (bank)	8	401.2*
Citicorp (bank)	8	154.0*
Aetna Life (life insurance firm)	4	258.1
John Hancock Mutual (life insurance firm)	3	156.0
Equitable Life (life insurance firm)	3	155.3
Connecticut General Life (life insurance firm)	6	150.1
Bank of America (bank)	6	92.5*

* The debt data are as of year-end 1977. The asterisks in the right-hand column indicate that some estimation was used in determining those amounts. Those involve conservative estimates of the extent of the institution's participation in one or more consortium loans. A complete listing of each institution's loans is available in appendix 4.

One important caveat: the extensive and overlapping web of relationships binding America's leading financial institutions to its leading nuclear companies was created neither recently nor specifically because of these corporations' nuclear involvement. In many cases, such as the J. P. Morgan bank's extremely close relationship with General Electric, the connections predate the emergence of the nuclear power industry by many decades. Furthermore, the greatest strength of the corporations that run the nuclear industry is their immensely profitable domination of numerous other businesses throughout the U.S. and global economies. To be sure, any financial institution contemplating a loan offer to or stock purchase in one of these companies would certainly factor that company's nuclear involvement into its decision, but only occasionally would that involvement tip the balance one way or the other.

Although the figures on corporate debt are, unfortunately, dated and incomplete (borrowers and lenders that operate at the multimillion-dollar level are notoriously closed-mouthed about their dealings), they nevertheless are sufficient to identify some of the main financial backers of the nuclear power industry. Let us start with the J. P. Morgan corporation, whose $53.5 billion worth of assets make it America's fifth largest bank. Morgan owns billions of dollars worth of stock in nineteen of the nuclear industry's top twenty-four companies. Aside from being the top stockholder at Halliburton (parent of nuclear construction company Brown and Root), Morgan is number 2 at Combustion Engineering, Kerr-McGee, and UNC Resources, number 4 at General Electric, Getty Oil, Rockwell International, and Union Carbide, number 6 at Du Pont and Allis-Chalmers, number 7 at Exxon, number 8 at Standard Oil of Ohio, number 10 at McDermott, and number 11 at Gulf Oil. In addition, Morgan held over $258 million worth of debt to nuclear companies at year-end 1977. It was, for example, the lead bank in organizing for Allied Corporation a six-year, 125 million Eurodollar loan that runs until 1983. In 1978, it joined with various other U.S. and European banks to sign a $200 million, seven-year loan agreement with Atlantic Richfield, the huge oil company to which it had lent $25 million in 1973. And when Westinghouse decided in 1974 to secure a $500 million line of credit to meet short-term corporate borrowing needs, Morgan was one of fifteen major banks that put their money at Westinghouse's disposal.

Bankers have a well-deserved reputation for prudence and caution. They do not lend out millions of dollars to someone without first being sure both of how the money will be spent and of the borrower's ability to repay it. It is unlikely that in the case of the Westinghouse loan, where the average share of each participating lender was $33 million, the loan officers of Morgan, Chase Manhattan, and the other participants would not have requested, received, and very carefully evaluated confidential Westinghouse financial records and business projections before recommending that their bank participate in the arrangement. Such loan transactions not only provide the banks with vast inside knowledge about the borrowing corporation, they also foster a community of interest among the parties involved; the bankers acquire a direct financial interest in the borrower's future success and profitability.

Arguing along these lines, one could make a respectable case that the Prudential Life Insurance Company, for example, has as much of a stake in a revival of nuclear power as do some nuclear corporations. Its $62.5 billion worth of assets make Prudential America's largest life insurance company. With over $1.2 billion worth of credit extended to thirteen of the industry's top thirty corporations, it is also the nuclear industry's top financier. Among its heaviest borrowers are uranium miner Standard Oil of Ohio ($356.6 million), uranium enrichers Goodyear ($166.6 million) and Union Carbide ($156.5 million), reactor vendors McDermott ($102.4 million) and Westinghouse ($76 million), and uranium king Kerr-McGee ($48 million). Prudential also holds what can only be described as a very impressive portfolio of nuclear industry stocks. It is the number 1 stockholder at Raytheon, number 3 at Gulf Oil and Union Carbide, number 4 at Atlantic Richfield, Du Pont, and Fluor, number 6 at General Electric, number 8 at Westinghouse and Halliburton, number 9 at Exxon, and number 18 at Combustion Engineering.

The job of investment banks is to help corporations when they decide to raise fresh capital not by borrowing but by floating a bond or issuing new shares of stock. It is not uncommon for up to two dozen investment banks to join in distributing a single securities offering, but there are always one or two that oversee and organize the whole transaction. These "lead" banks usually have been associated with the corporation for years previously and act as its ambassadors to the rest of the financial community.

It follows that the more dependent a company is on outside financing, the more critical are its involvements with investment banks and, by extension, its links to the rest of the financial community. During the half-century preceding World War II, such Wall Street financiers as George F. Baker and J. P. Morgan were able to exert enormous influence over the activities of even very large corporations, precisely because the corporations then urgently needed outside help in financing their expansion and diversification drives. The balance of power gradually shifted away from the banks, however, as the corporations' efforts to gain market dominance began to pay off in the form of a steady flow of monopoly profits. As a result, today most giant corporations, including those which run the nuclear industry, are able to meet their routine financial needs with internally generated funds. This is not to say they no longer borrow from banks. But nowadays giant corporations negotiate their loans from a position of strength, secure in the knowledge that the banks need them at least as much as vice versa.

There are few business relationships more intimate than that between a corporation and its investment bank, for the latter also advises and assists the former on mergers and acquisitions. To make intelligent recommendations about which companies should be taken over, the bank obviously must possess detailed inside knowledge of the corporation's strengths, weaknesses, and long-term objectives. Indeed, the very process of seeking out prospective conquests involves the investment bank at the highest levels of corporate planning and policymaking. Yet the same investment banks as a matter of course advise, place debt, and arrange mergers for corporations that are said to be competitors. Morgan Stanley, for instance, has been the primary investment bank for Exxon, General Electric, and Union Carbide for decades, and served as lead bank in debt offerings for Continental Oil, Shell, and Standard Oil of Ohio. Goldman Sachs, another top Wall Street investment bank, has collaborated with nine of the nuclear industry's leading corporations, including GE, Union Carbide, Allied Chemical, Goodyear, Enserch, and Rockwell International. And First National of Boston has close ties with uranium miners UNC Resources and Gulf Oil as well as reactor manufacturers Combustion Engineering and Westinghouse.

To be sure, the existence of such relationships does not ensure constantly and smoothly coordinated policy; occasional collisions are inevitable when two or more corporations want to control the same market; the day is long past when string-pulling bankers could dictate settlements of such disputes from above. To paraphrase Edward Herman, professor of finance at the Wharton School, financial institutions are the powerful servants, not the masters, of giant corporations. Their power is real, but usually indirect. Their role is not to control corporations but rather to shape their general objectives and strategies and synchronize them as much as possible with those of other corporations. Gentlemen's agreements, insider deals, mutual understandings, private collusion—all the devices by which competition is limited—are naturally easier to arrange and execute when the corporations involved share links with the same small group of powerful financial institutions.

What makes these banks and insurance companies particularly important here is their close relationships with the nuclear industry's sole customer: the electric utility industry. The utilities are a key exception to the abovementioned general rule about corporate independence from outside financiers. Indeed, because centralized electricity generation is, next to preparing for war, the economy's most capital-intensive activity, utilities must appeal to Wall Street every time they wish to construct a new power plant, nuclear or other. And when they do, thirteen of them, including four of the most heavily nuclear utilities in the United States—Duke Power, Carolina Power and Light, Commonwealth Edison, and Virginia Electric Power—use as their investment banker Morgan Stanley, the firm that also serves GE, Union Carbide, Exxon, and nine other leading nuclear suppliers in the same capacity. The same pattern is evident in First Boston's representing nuclear suppliers Combustion Engineering, Gulf, Du Pont, and Westinghouse simultaneously with assisting (nuclear-dependent) electric utilities Baltimore Gas and Electric, Long Island Lighting, and the New England Electric System. Moreover, the nuclear industry's leading commercial bankers and insurance companies are among the utility industry's leading stockholders. Teachers Insurance and Annuity ranked in the top ten stockholders at fourteen electric utilities, Prudential Life at thirteen, Chase Manhattan at ten, Lord Abbett at seven, and Citicorp, Bankers Trust, and Connecticut General Life each at six separate utilities. Add to these mechanisms of direct influence the enormous ability Chase Manhattan, Bankers Trust, Chemical, Prudential, et al. have to influence Wall Street opinion in general, and the full potential powers of the industry's financial backers over the ever capital-hungry electric utilities becomes obvious.

One last layer of affiliations undergirds the nuclear industry, and it more than any other molds the industry into a coherent political and economic force: interlocking directorates. An interlock occurs when a corporation or bank elects an executive or director of another corporation to serve on its board of directors. The sociologist C. Wright Mills thought interlocks were important because they "permit an interchange of views in a convenient and more or less formal way among those who share the interests of the corporate rich." More specifically, interlocks between competing firms make possible the joint planning of their industry.

Interlocks often occur through third-party institutions. For example, on the board of directors of Citicorp we find Roger Milliken, the president of Milliken and Company, one of America's oldest textile firms. At board meetings, Milliken, who is also a director of Westinghouse, joins with Citicorp chairman Walter Wriston, who himself happens to be a director of General Electric, to set Citicorp policies. They are assisted in that endeavor by two representatives from Exxon, including its chairman and chief executive officer, Clifton Garvin; by the chief executive officers of nuclear-related firms Du Pont, Halliburton, and Standard Oil of California, and by a representative of the nuclear construction firm Stone and Webster.*

At the other major New York banks the situation is similar. Chemical Bank shares directors with GE, Westinghouse, Exxon, and seven other major oil firms. Manufacturers Hanover is linked twice to Westinghouse (Manufacturers Hanover president John McGillicuddy sits on Westinghouse's board) and once each to GE, McDermott, and Goodyear. J. P. Morgan shares no less than three directors with its cousin company GE, two with Union Carbide, and one with Goodyear, and was tied to Bechtel through George Schultz, who before becoming Ronald Reagan's Secretary of State served on Morgan's board by virtue of his position as president of Bechtel. Finally, there is Chase Manhattan, the bank of the Rockefellers, which has interlocks with Exxon, GE, Union Carbide, Metropolitan Life, Allied Chemical, and Stone and Webster.†

Examining interlocks from a corporation perspective shows General Electric interlocked an astonishing seven times with Union Carbide, a firm it supposedly competes against in the uranium market, as well as in numerous other non-nuclear product lines. GE is interlocked four times with Exxon and Westinghouse, twice with Combustion Engineering, Rockwell International, and Goodyear, and once with McDermott. Westinghouse, in addition to its four interlocks with GE, is linked six times to Union Carbide, five to Exxon, three to Goodyear, twice to McDermott and Rockwell, and once to Combustion Engineering.

* The chairman and chief executive officer of uranium producer Conoco also used to sit on Citicorp's board before Conoco was gobbled up in 1981 by Du Pont, after a bloody takeover battle with Joseph E. Seagram and Sons and Mobil Corporation.
† Rockefeller family interests have supported nuclear power from the very beginning. The Rockefellers got their start in nuclear in 1950, when they hired Lewis Strauss, recently resigned Atomic Energy Commission member, as their investment adviser. Strauss served them until 1953, when President Eisenhower called him back to chair the AEC. In 1954, Laurance and David Rockefeller founded the United Nuclear uranium company, and Chase Manhattan became the first bank to establish a nuclear power division. In 1955, Nelson Rockefeller, who was then serving in the White House as President Eisenhower's special assistant, persuaded Eisenhower to reinvigorate and expand the Atoms for Peace program to include more training for foreigners and increased funding for exporting U.S.-manufactured research reactors. As governor of New York between 1959 and 1973, Nelson worked hard and successfully to stimulate, through state subsidies, the private development of nuclear power in New York. And in 1975, as vice-president, he pushed for creation of a federal Energy Independence Authority, a $100 billion program of government subsidies and loan guarantees intended to stimulate U.S. domestic energy production. Most of the money was targeted on such nuclear-related projects as breeder reactors, uranium enrichment, and fuel reprocessing.

How these various financial and personal affiliations translate
into real decisions and actions is difficult to determine precisely;
outside observers do not know enough about what goes on in the
boardrooms and executive offices of big business to prove specific
linkages, and the gentlemen directly involved are not interested
in supplying the missing information. However, one can sometimes
piece together enough publicly available information to hazard
educated guesses about how corporate and financial institutions
work in concert to promote and protect one another's interests. A
group of New England antinuclear activists calling themselves the
New Manhattan Project claim to have done that in regard to the
First National Bank of Boston, the biggest bank in New England
and the sixteenth biggest bank in the United States. First National
has been a central player in New England's nuclear power industry
since the mid-1950s, when it led the consortium of banks and
insurance companies that provided half the financing for the Yankee Rowe plant built in western Massachusetts. Today, First National is the lead bank in a consortium that has extended a $115
million line of credit to the Public Service Company of New Hampshire for the construction of the embattled Seabrook nuclear power
plant and that has loaned $500 million to finance Boston Edison's
Pilgrim 2 nuclear project.

The New Manhattan Project charges that First National has financed these nuclear plants—even though they are, according to
the Project, "a poor investment from a business point of view"—
largely because of the bank's "huge investment in the continued
prosperity of the nuclear industry" and because almost half of the
members of its board of directors are heads of major nuclear companies. The activists point out that First National's trust department
holds large blocks of stock in Boston Edison, Northeast Utilities,
Exxon, Citicorp, Halliburton, and the Virginia Electric Power
Company. (They could have added Atlantic Richfield, Combustion
Engineering, Du Pont, General Electric, Kerr-McGee, and Mc-
Dermott to the list as well.) On First National's board sits the
president of the New England Electric System, a utility company
that owns 10 to 25 percent of four of New England's seven operating nuclear plants. In fact, New England Electric's presidents
have been on First National's board continuously since 1954, when
New England Electric was the lead utility in the formation of the
Yankee Atomic Company that built the reactor at Rowe. The president of Boston Edison also sits on First National's board, while
the bank's president, William L. Brown, is on Boston Edison's

board. Furthermore, First National chairman Richard Hill serves on the board of Raytheon, whose United Engineers and Constructors subsidiary was awarded the job of chief architect-engineer for the Seabrook project. The president of Raytheon in turn sits on the First's board, and the First's trust department is Raytheon's leading stockholder. Also on the First's board is the president of Stone and Webster, the nation's second leading nuclear designing firm. Stone and Webster and United Engineers and Constructors have designed between them 35 percent of the nuclear plants in the United States; but in New England, their combined market share is almost twice as large. How much of the difference is due to the two companies' close ties to First National? Would First National have financed nuclear power stations if it did not hold hundreds of millions of dollars' worth of stock in nuclear corporations? We do not know.

The informal partnership between Amerca's nuclear corporations and its largest banks and insurance companies is an awesome one, and not only because of the enormous economic power it involves. The same financial institutions that are linked to the nuclear corporations enjoy similarly intimate relationships with the nuclear industry's ostensible competitors in the oil, coal, and natural gas businesses, with its customers in the electric utility industry, and indeed with the most powerful corporations throughout all sectors of the American economy. They are thus able to encourage among all their corporate colleagues a unity of outlook and policy that transcends individual interests and serves the needs of American business as a whole. More important, because they play the decisive role in determining the size and direction of capital flows in the U. S. economy—who receives how much money to pursue what sorts of investment projects—they are well-positioned to turn their vision of what U.S. energy policy should be into reality.

6

Building
America's Pyramids

If you're a fifty-five-year-old chairman of the board
of a utility company, do you want to have your last
ten years before retirement tied up with fighting a
nuclear plant through the courts?

HUNTER CHILES,
formerly Manager, Market Research and Analysis,
Westinghouse Power Systems Marketing Division;
currently Director, Office of Policy,
Planning, and Analysis,
U.S. Department of Energy

Sometime during the middle of the twenty-sixth century B.C., King
Cheops, Pharaoh of Egypt, decided to construct a grand stone
structure in which he and selected members of his royal court
would be entombed at the end of their earthly days. It was important that the burial place be as magnificent and comfortable as
possible because Cheops would reside there forever. The King,
like the pharaohs who ruled Egypt after him, was considered a god
incarnate, and received eternal life by divine right.

Cheops found the most brilliant mathematicians and engineers
in the realm and ordered them to design a suitably monumental
edifice. Every year for approximately the next two decades the
King conscripted 100,000 Egyptian peasants to construct the awesome funerary complex that the modern world would come to know
as the Great Pyramid. The peasants worked on the burial palace
three months a year during the late summer, when the flooding of
the Nile prevented them from farming. They could not refuse the
King's orders, nor did they receive wages for their backbreaking
toil. The ruling authorities did console them with the promise that
their labor on the project increased their chances of attaining eter-

nal life. When the peasants died, King Cheops or his descendants could intercede for them with the god Anubis, who led the dead into the other world.

Thus inspired, the peasants set about their task. The work was grueling and the standards exacting. Each of the pyramid's four sides was to be 756 feet long at the base, and the maximum allowable error was a scant few inches. Working completely without scaffolding or machinery, the peasants piled over two million blocks of limestone, each weighing two and one-half tons, on top of one another until the pyramid, when finally completed, covered more than thirteen acres and rose 480 feet into the air.

King Cheops's burial mansion and the other pyramids constructed for later pharaohs have humbled visitors for more than forty-five centuries now. Begotten through an extraordinary combination of regal narcissism, envisioned immortality, scientific and engineering brilliance, and human sacrifice, they remain lasting monuments to the best and worst of the Egypt of the pharaohs.

Much the same can be said of nuclear power plants and modern America. Westinghouse executive Jean-Claude Poncelet has called nuclear power stations "the ultimate symbol of technocracy," and he is right. Ranking among the most amazing technological achievements of their time, they are epitomes of twentieth-century man's ability to dominate the natural world around him and rearrange it according to his wishes. As with the pyramids, one cannot help but marvel at the incredible human achievement they represent. But they also have a darker side. Nuclear fission offers humanity relief from the age-old scourges of scarcity and endless toil. But if humans misuse it, it can deliver the void of death just as easily as the abundance of life.

Like the pyramids, nuclear power stations are historical artifacts of enormous richness, for they vividly embody the basic economic and social relationships of the society that produced them. The Atomic Brotherhood, which brings these power stations into being, is itself a creature of those relationships. As such, it cannot be comprehended separately from them. There is no better way to understand the men and institutions who build America's nuclear power plants, and the crisis now confronting them, than to observe them in action. Just as studying how the pyramids were built educates archaeologists and historians about the pharaohs' Egypt, so can tracing how nuclear power plants are built yield crucial insights into the Atomic Brotherhood and modern America.

THE ELECTRIC REVOLUTION

Since the primary function of nuclear power stations is to produce electricity, it is not surprising that the central actors in the creation of nuclear power plants in the United States are the companies that produce the nation's electricity. The electric utilities are the ones that initially decide whether and where a community will build a nuclear plant; choose nuclear over alternative sources such as coal or conservation; hire the companies who finance, design, manufacture, and construct the plant; pay other companies to dig up and process the uranium that fuels it; and operate the plant and sell the electricity it generates.

Through their control over electricity, these companies have influenced the shaping of modern American society as profoundly as King Cheops did ancient Egyptian society. Although few would go as far as Combustion Engineering vice-president John West's statement that "electricity is the most marvelous thing to come along throughout history," there is no disputing the enormous role electricity has played in the making of twentieth-century industrial society. Electricity literally revolutionized how people lived, worked, and moved about. To the home it brought the convenience of such labor-saving appliances as refrigerators and washing machines; to the factory it brought motors whose precision and flexibility multiplied industrial productivity many times over. Electrified streetcars allowed workers for the first time to live and work in separate places and thereby radically transformed urban geography; electric lighting liberated the night for human activity. Electricity's influence on the economy was just as profound as on daily life. In the history of American economic development, only the steam engine, the railroad, and the automobile can be credited with stimulating waves of economic expansion more massive and enduring than that which followed the introduction of electricity during the late nineteenth century. Like those three innovations, electricity both required and made possible the production of many new goods and services, and thereby created vast new markets and investment opportunities. Elevators, for example, were rarities before the development of electric motors. And without elevators, the skyscrapers that today dominate city landscapes would still be but an architect's dream. Aluminum, the light, tough metal used in automobiles, airplanes, and hundreds of other industrial products, could not be economically produced before Edison invented the electric power station. Television, the telephone, and other machines of mass communication would all fall silent without electric current.

Mass production of electricity was destined for technical and economic reasons to be a monopolistic enterprise. The production process itself was mysteriously simple. Running water or steam drove a turbine that in turn spun a coil of wire within a magnetic field; the current thus generated could then be transmitted by wire to distant locations and perform an enormous variety of useful mechanical tasks. One characteristic of electricity, however, complicated matters: once produced, it could not be stored. Thus, a power station had to be large enough to accommodate "peak" demand exactly when it was required, even though that meant that most of the time the station would operate at but a fraction of full capacity. Yet power stations were so expensive to build that they were economical only in large sizes and only when run at nearly full capacity. The solution that finally emerged was to centralize electricity production facilities and guarantee each power station a sufficiently ample and stable demand to ensure its efficiency. This required the prohibition of competition, a move that was practical in more ways than one. After all, what sense did it make to string two or three sets of competing transmission lines across a city when one could do the job? Electricity was a natural monopoly, like telephone networks, sewer systems, and natural gas.

But who would control this monopoly? Bitter struggles over this strategic commodity began in the late nineteenth century and centered upon whether electricity production and distribution would be run by public or by private enterprise. The initial success of private entrepreneurs around and after the turn of the century led economist and social activist H. S. Raushenbush to complain, "Except in those cases where cities insisted on having these services before the companies were willing to give them, or where the companies got too stubborn about their rights to charge more than the traffic would bear, we have let the privately owned companies furnish the service." The cities attempted to prevent the companies from taking unfair advantage of their monopoly status by establishing regulatory agencies empowered to determine what rates the companies could charge. But as the companies grew beyond their original urban franchises, they were increasingly able to avoid such regulation and charge what they pleased. States then began establishing their own regulatory commissions; these were often staffed with officials more loyal to the companies than to the public.

Meanwhile, the idea of "public power" was also spreading; by the end of World War I, there were nearly 3,000 municipally owned electric utilities in the United States. During the 1920s, the privately owned utilities mounted a nationally organized attack aimed at eliminating the competitive threat these public systems posed. The National Electric Light Association (NELA) sponsored a massive public relations campaign, which, bragged one of its administrators, employed every known method of publicity but skywriting, and focused on the supposed "socialist" nature of public control. A memorandum drafted by an Illinois affiliate group described the campaign's stategy: "My idea would be not to try reason, or logic, but to try to pin the Bolshevik idea on my opponent." A subsequent Federal Trade Commission investigation exposed power companies' efforts to influence schools and universities, manipulate the press, and buy favor from various state legislatures. In addition to decrying "socialist" public utilities, NELA also coordinated merger and takeover moves and used its political and economic leverage to block public agencies from access to capital.

These tactics reduced the number of public power systems in the country to less than 1,900 by the late 1920s. And although public power made a comeback during the New Deal years of the 1930s, most notably with the establishment of the Tennessee Valley Authority, it never regained the ground it had lost. Today, approximately two hundred investor-owned utilities—or, as former Senator Lee Metcalf used to call them with tongue in cheek, IOUs—generate more than 75 percent of America's electricity and control nearly $300 billion worth of its productive assets.

THE NUCLEAR CHOICE

How and why did electric utility companies first begin buying nuclear power plants? A fear of "creeping socialism" was the main impetus, according to a view widely held among both industry executives and nuclear critics. "There was a substantial threat," claims Fitzgerald D. Acker of Combustion Engineering. "The government said [to the utilities in the 1950s] if you don't go in and start developing nuclear reactors, we'll do it ourselves, and we will build our own plants and sell the power." A desire to neutralize Washington's threat led utilities to press such traditional heavy-equipment suppliers as Combustion Engineering to develop nuclear reactors, says Acker. "I don't think [Combustion] could have avoided going nuclear and still satisfied our commitments to the utility industry. They were trying to get us into the nuclear business long before we went in. . . . They were pushing when I came to the company in 1956."

Substantial evidence suggests, however, that the threat of government ownership, while significant, was *not* the major stimulus of utility industry interest in nuclear power. Electric utilities had in fact been intrigued by the possibility of atomic electricity ever since the end of World War II. As we have seen, the industry's trade group, the Association of Edison Illuminating Companies, lobbied Congress in 1945—unsuccessfully—for permission to begin exploring nuclear energy's commercial applications immediately. And when the Atomic Energy Commission did grant private firms access to classified technology in 1951 through the Industrial Participation Program, a number of utilities jumped at the opportunity. True, the utilities did not respond to the AEC's subsequent Power Reactor Demonstration Program as enthusiastically as some government officials would have liked, but that was largely because the utilities thought the AEC's contract terms were too stingy. Traditionally risk-averse companies, they were unwilling to gamble scarce research and development funds on a still unproven technology. They remained keenly interested in nuclear power, but demanded that the government bear the cost of developing it into a competitive power source. As Albert F. Tegen, president of the General Public Utilities Corporation, stated in an Atomic Industrial Forum report evaluating the 1953 Joint Atomic Energy Committee hearings on atomic power plant development and private enterprise: "We want atomic power if it is economical. We can absorb large quantities of it. The sooner we get it, the better we like it."

The more farsighted executives in the electric utility industry were quick to recognize what nuclear power could do for them. Like other great technological innovations before it, nuclear fission promised to revolutionize the production process of a commodity— in this case, of electricity—to produce a vastly greater output at a significantly lower cost while expending far less human labor. Nuclear reactors *were* substantially more expensive machines than traditional fossil-fueled steam boilers, but they were capable of mind-boggling fuel efficiency; scientists in the early 1950s were estimating that 1 pound of raw atomic fuel could generate as much power as 1,500 *tons* of coal. AEC Chairman Lewis Strauss's jubilant prediction in 1954 that nuclear energy would mean electricity "too cheap to meter," however naïve it may sound in retrospect, was

nevertheless a genuine articulation of the great admiration vision-
ary scientists and businessmen had for fission's awesome potential.

Besides its efficiency advantage, nuclear power was also seen as
environmentally superior to coal, the primary fuel used by most
electric utilities in the 1950s. Thomas Ayers, former chairman and
chief executive officer of the Chicago-area Commonwealth Edison
Company, recalls that his company's interest in nuclear power was
initially sparked in the early 1950s because "we were concerned
with how, over the next projected twenty-five years of growth, we
would transport and what we would do with all the by-products of
the coal we would have to burn." In 1951 Commonwealth received
one of the three contracts awarded under the AEC's Industrial
Participation Program and, working with scientists and engineers
at the Argonne National Laboratory in Chicago, did much of the
original work that eventually led to the development of the boiling
water reactor.

"Around 1953, we organized the 'Nuclear Power Group,' which
consisted of three other utilities—American Electric Power, Union
Electric, and Illinois Power—and a big construction company,
Bechtel. In 1956 we decided to build [our first nuclear plant]
Dresden One, with some capital from each of these utilities, and
with General Electric agreeing to deliver the plant at a certain
overall price." Ayers is proud of the fact that Dresden One was the
first completely privately financed nuclear power plant in the
United States, and one of the most economical. "We wanted to
make it very reliable, and not push the frontier of technology with
this particular unit. . . . Other people in the business were trying
to take steps ahead, like the Fermi [fast breeder] plant. . . . We
used to say we wanted to build the Model T."

Most electric utility executives were even more cautious about
nuclear power in those days, Ayers recalls. "Most people in the
industry thought we were nuts. I used to say kiddingly, 'Either
we're going to be smarter than hell in the seventies, or you fellas
should save me a sweeper's job, because I'll be looking for one.'
And everybody thinks now we were lucky, but we weren't lucky.
We did our homework, made very advantageous contracts to build
these plants, built them on very favorable terms, and they're very
efficient, low-cost power producers just like we expected."

"It was out of our experience with Dresden One that we decided
we had an absolute gold mine for making low-cost power," Ayers
explains. Dresden One came on line in 1960; it took most U.S.
utilities another few years to conclude that Commonwealth had

been right about nuclear power after all. The less timid ones began ordering nuclear plants in 1964, under the fixed-price, "turnkey" contracts General Electric and Westinghouse were offering. By the end of the 1960s, most of the rest of the utility industry had climbed aboard the Great Bandwagon of nuclear power despite, as we have seen, a paucity of data on actual operating costs for reactors.

Why, despite the inconclusive evidence on costs, did American utilities buy so many nuclear power plants during the second half of the 1960s? Part of the answer is simply that more power plants were needed to satisfy the country's constantly growing appetite for electricity. Demand was increasing by about 7 percent per year; to keep up, utilities had to double generating capacity every ten years. The demand growth stemmed from the tremendous vitality of the U.S. economy and the steadily declining real cost of producing electricity. To increase demand still further, General Electric, Westinghouse, and many electric utilities launched advertising campaigns extolling the virtues of the all-electric home. Toothbrushes, blankets, knives, can openers, typewriters, lawn mowers, razors, and countless other gadgets were electrified as evidence of electricity's wonderful versatility and convenience.

A key factor in the utilities' decision to use nuclear power to help meet this demand was the belief that nuclear plants, being more capital-intensive, would produce greater profits than coal-fired plants. (According to the formulas used by government regulators, the more capital a utility invested in power stations, transmission lines, and the like, the higher its revenues would be.) The executives also trusted that as time passed nuclear would produce cheaper and cheaper electricity, thereby boosting demand and encouraging the utility industry's long-term growth.

But ironically, nuclear power's greater capital expense was initially a hindrance. Because its fixed cost was so high, nuclear was competitive with coal only when it enjoyed substantial economies of scale, that is, at very large power-plant sizes. It was not until the American economic boom of the mid-1960s that many utilities were large enough to purchase such plants. As *Forbes*, the business magazine, explained in June 1966:

What has made nuclear energy competitive is not any sensational development in technology, but the vast expansion of the electrical utility business and the development of power pools. It has long been possible to build nuclear plants with the capacity they need to operate efficiently. Until recently, however, very few utilities were big enough to want plants of that size . . . they were afraid to make so much of their generating capacity dependent on a single unit. More and more power companies have enough demand to afford that risk now. In addition, power pools enable three or four relatively small companies to join in building a nuclear plant with a capacity of 800,000 kilowatts or more.

This quotation hints at another reason for the utility industry's powerful attraction to nuclear energy: the opportunity it gave large, privately owned power companies to expand their service area and profit-making base. Smaller utility companies, unable to afford the giant new plants, could more easily be squeezed out of business. The resulting vacuum would be filled by the large, investor-owned utilities whose Wall Street connections could arrange the massive financing needed to build nuclear plants. Nuclear power thus promised to hasten the trend towards concentration of the nation's electricity supply in fewer and fewer hands. (By the late 1960s, more than two-thirds of the approximately one thousand companies that supplied electricity in 1945 had been gobbled up by larger competitors.) The AEC encouraged this trend by exempting nuclear power plants from antitrust laws.*

An additional attraction of nuclear power for the utilities was the greater bargaining leverage it gave them over their traditional, primary suppliers in the coal and electrical manufacturing industries. In the early 1960s, over half of U.S. electricity came from burning coal. Nuclear power's supposed competitiveness with coal, *Forbes* understated in the article quoted above, was "alarming news for the U.S. coal industry. . . . It is also ominous for the railroads that depend heavily on coal hauling fares." Every nuclear reactor displaced 45 million tons of coal a year. The coal companies at first tried to forestall nuclear's invasion of the utility market by cutting prices and cooperating with the railroads to introduce cheaper, more efficient methods of mine-to-power-station transportation. But by the end of the Great Bandwagon sales surge in 1968, they had given up the fight. Belief in the historical inevitability of

* The AEC got around the law by employing a legalistic artifice: it licensed nuclear power plants, not as commercial facilities (this would have subjected them to antitrust restrictions), but as experimental research projects under the medical therapy section of the Atomic Energy Act. The experimental licenses were good for forty years. See H. Peter Metzger, *The Atomic Establishment* (New York: Simon & Schuster, 1972), pp. 247–49.

nuclear power was by then so widespread within the business community that even the coal and railroad interests accepted the expansion of nuclear power production as an unwelcome but unavoidable fact of life.

America's electric utility companies have traditionally had a direct financial interest in building as many power plants as they could. Government regulatory formulas reinforced the "more is better" mentality by tying a utility's revenues to the amount of capital it invested. The more plants built, the more money made. These formulas also gave utilities an incentive to build nuclear rather than coal-fired plants, since nuclear plants were more capital-intensive and therefore promised, at least in theory, larger revenues.

But regardless of whether a utility decided to build a nuclear or a coal plant, outside financing was always necessary. Although electric utilities are among the very wealthiest members of American society, even they do not have nearly enough money to pay for power stations out of their own pockets. "The electric utility business is the most capital-intensive of all American businesses," explains Thomas Ayers of Commonwealth Edison. "To get one dollar of annual sales in the oil business requires an investment of 69 cents. For automobiles it's 53 cents, in steel it's 83 cents. But in the electric utility industry it takes an investment of three dollars and 26 cents. If you went back over time, you'd find that year in and year out 32 percent of the new money raised for plant expansion in the United States was for the electric power business. And 50 percent of the new stock issued annually is from utilities."

Wall Street, the nation's main marketplace for the buying and selling of money, is where a utility goes to borrow the necessary funds to build a nuclear power plant. In practice, says Sherwood Smith of Carolina Power and Light, "we don't raise money for a specific plant. Each fall we meet with our financial advisers and lay out our construction plans for the next ten years, and then they help us decide when to issue the necessary securities and what the mix should be among common stock, preferred stock, and bonds. We look at things such as when interest rates are likely to be low, and then we'll decide, for example, to issue a bond in July, stock in the fall, and another bond in December." Wall Street's most prestigious investment banks bid against one another for the privilege of serving as lead underwriter on such securities offerings. "If I had a small company, I'd probably use just one [investment bank]," boasts Ayers of Commonwealth Edison. "But we're so big, they all want the business."

The lead underwriter ("underwriter" is actually a glorified term for middleman), joined by a group of other investment banks that may number as high as thirty or forty, buys the securities at a wholesale price from the utility and then sells them to other investors at a markup. "Fifty percent of our stockholders live in Commonwealth Edison's territory," Ayers explains. "But [common] utility stocks are also bought by banks and trust companies. Preference stocks are bought primarily by insurance companies, because they have a tax advantage in buying them. And bonds are bought by institutions—pension funds, trusts, insurance companies—with big blocks of money to put out."

For many years electric utility stocks were greatly valued on Wall Street because they promised high, albeit not spectacular, returns and very low risks. They paid out steadily rising earnings so consistently that they became known as "widows' stock"—the perfect thing to leave behind to keep the wife and kids financially secure. But all that changed when a series of unexpected developments in the mid-1970s caused the cost of electricity to rise sharply, the demand for it to fall just as sharply, and the utility industry to sink, as if in quicksand, into the most serious crisis in its history. Higher fuel costs, courtesy of the OPEC cartel and the major oil companies, were the first culprit. But at least as damaging was the threefold increase in power plant *construction* costs. The federal government, under public pressure, had ordered that power stations be made less dangerous to the workers who ran them, the people who lived near them, and the environment that surrounded them. The additionally required safety equipment not only cost extra money itself, it also delayed construction schedules;* plants once built in six years began taking twice as long to complete. As a result, inflation penalties and interest charges—the "paper costs" a utility paid for the hundreds of millions of dollars' worth of borrowed capital it had tied up in construction projects—escalated wildly. The problem was made much worse by the persistently

---

* Consider what would happen when the Nuclear Regulatory Commission ruled, for example, that a piece of piping that the utility had already installed and embedded in concrete must have a diameter of ten inches rather than six inches. The architect had to redesign the equipment; the engineer had to reorder it from the manufacturer, wait for it to be produced and delivered, rip the old piping out of the concrete, replace it with the new, and cover it up again. All that would cost time and money, throw the project off schedule, and add to inflation and interest cost penalties.

high inflation and interest rates that plagued the American economy during the 1970s.

Public utility commissions in most states responded to the crisis by allowing companies to pass along higher fuel costs to their customers. This had the unintended effect of removing industrial consumers' incentive to use more electricity. Most commissions also provided massive rate increases for residential and commercial customers, and some began allowing utilities, under a procedure called "construction work in progress," to charge ratepayers for unfinished power plants as if those plants were actually generating electricity. Angry citizens responded by decreasing electricity consumption and organizing themselves to resist future rate increases.

From 1974 to 1980, the nation's demand for electricity grew at only about half the traditional 7 percent rate. As a result, utilities now have 35 percent more generating capacity than is required to meet peak demand; that is nearly double the normal "reserve margin" of 20 percent. *Business Week* described the gravity of the situation in a May 1979 cover story entitled "A Dark Future for Utilities." The continuing slump in electricity demand meant less investment, slower growth, and reduced profits for the utility industry. With profits down, companies would also find it harder to attract the outside risk capital needed to finance what construction they did have planned. "Lenders and investors are growing increasingly troubled by the industry's inability to boost profits," the magazine explained, "and stock prices have sagged."

Precisely because of the capital-intensiveness that had previously made it so appealing to utilities, nuclear power plant construction became almost impossibly expensive during this period. Economist and nuclear critic Charles Komanoff has calculated that from 1971 to 1978 capital costs of building nuclear plants increased 13.5 percent a year, over two times as fast as the general inflation rate and roughly twice as fast as capital costs for coal-fired plants.

The likelihood of continued upgrading of nuclear safety regulations leads Komanoff to predict that nuclear capital costs will continue to rise faster than coal costs in the 1980s and that by the end of the decade nuclear electricity will cost at least 20 percent more than coal-produced electricity. The Nuclear Regulatory Commission had identified more than 100 generic safety defects in nuclear plants that would require new design standards to correct; some 140 additional requirements were issued following the Three Mile Island accident alone. These new regulations have helped cause more frequent shutdowns of operating reactors, shutdowns that hurt utility profits and in some cases raised customer bills. In 1981, for example, U.S. nuclear plants were on an average forced to shut down nearly one day out of every eight they theoretically should have been in service; in 1977, the rate was one day out of thirteen. Another difficulty surfaced in 1981 when government inspectors discovered that radioactivity bombardment had rendered steel piping in some older pressurized water reactors dangerously brittle. As a result, some utilities may be forced to shut down their older reactors purchased from Westinghouse, Combustion Engineering, and Babcock and Wilcox well before they have fully amortized their investments.

Wall Street appears already to be preparing for a shift away from nuclear power. Following the 1979 Three Mile Island nuclear accident, a significant number of nuclear utilities had their bond ratings downgraded and saw their stock prices fall more sharply than those of the industry as a whole. A report prepared in late 1979 by a research department of Bache Halsey Stuart Shields, a major Wall Street investment house, stated, "We anticipate that the uncertainty of costs will escalate to the point where nuclear plants are an unattractive financial proposition. . . . Nuclear plants may either be too expensive to build, or their payoff too uncertain, to compensate investors adequately for the risks taken."

It is not that the investment community opposes nuclear power. As Leonard S. Hyman, vice-president of Merrill Lynch, patiently explained to a House Interior and Insular Affairs Committee in October 1981:

> Merrill Lynch and the investment community in general are neither for nor against nuclear power. We are charged with meeting the objectives of the American investing public. Those objectives never change. In short, each investor seeks the maximum return commensurate with the risk involved on the dollars that he or she has to invest. . . . Investors do not decide whether to build or not to build a nuclear power plant. They simply indicate at what price the money is available and let the managements and regulators decide whether the investment is worth making at that cost of money.

Some utilities have been forced to conclude that borrowing the capital necessary to finish even nuclear plants already under construction was not worth it. For example, in August 1981 the Northern Indiana Public Service Company abandoned plans to complete the Bailly nuclear plant near Gary; the following month, the Boston Edison Company stopped working on the Pilgrim 2 plant in Plymouth, Massachusetts. The *Wall Street Journal* reported in January 1981 that the Washington Public Power Supply System, builder of the country's most ambitious nuclear project, was "floating on an ocean of debt so vast that officials say they face a crisis in raising enough money to finish construction." The price tag for the five nuclear plants being built by WPPSS (pronounced "whoops" by cynical New York bond traders) has more than quadrupled in the last decade to $17 billion, and is still growing. WPPSS was forced to mothball two of the proposed plants and abort plans for a new bond offering in August 1981 after Wall Street underwriters indicated that investors would not buy. Sixteen planned nuclear plants were canceled in 1982 alone.

The precarious financial conditions are forcing many companies to do something previously unheard of for electric utilities: urge their customers to use less electricity. Conservation and better peak-load management are intended to delay the need for additional plant construction until the companies can once again afford it. Yet in their own minds utility executives are clear that these measures are disliked, short-term necessities, to be abandoned as soon as possible. As the chairman of the Florida Power and Light Company told an energy industry meeting in 1980, "We cannot conserve ourselves into prosperity."

Utility profitability remains dependent upon building more power plants. Executives claimed in 1981 that $365 billion worth of construction would be necessary by 1990 if the country was not to run short of electricity. Companies have begun devising new and innovative techniques to attract outside financing, including adjustable-interest-rate bond placements and borrowings in the Eurodollar market. State regulators are coming to the utility industry's aid, granting rate increases of $6 billion in 1980 and $8 billion in 1981. According to utility analyst Alden Meyer of the Environmental Action Foundation, utility companies received 87 percent of the total rate increases they requested between 1979 and 1981, compared with only 40 percent during the mid-1970s. President Reagan's 1981 tax bill also helped utilities' cash flow tremendously, as should the Federal Energy Regulatory Commission's 1981 recommendation that all U.S. utilities be allowed to charge ratepayers for "construction work in progress." (FERC even began considering whether the monopolistic utility industry should be deregulated to allow greater marketplace earnings.)

Whether these maneuvers succeed in restoring the financial

health of the nation's electric utilities is of decisive importance to
the future of nuclear power in the United States. A sick electric
utility industry inevitably means a sick nuclear industry. Before
utilities can resume ordering nuclear plants, three things must
change. First, there must be a demonstrable and publicly recognized need to build more power plants. Short of such dramatic
events as power blackouts or another oil embargo, this would require that electricity demand begin growing again by at least 3
percent, year in and year out. The growth need not occur nationwide, however. Strong growth in the Sunbelt region would suffice.
Second, if utilities are to afford these new plants, they must regain
their financial soundness and balance. Here, much will depend
upon the overall performance of the American economy. The Reagan administration's tax breaks and other favors notwithstanding,
the utility industry cannot prosper in an economy beset by continuing high interest rates and inflation. Finally, if utilities are to order
nuclear rather than coal plants, nuclear's tremendous and rising
capital costs must be markedly reduced, a step that will require
drastic changes in government safety regulations.

THE INDUSTRY PECKING ORDER

Once it has arranged the initial loans, a utility building a nuclear
power plant hires an architectural firm to design the facility and
an engineering firm to construct it. Often, the same company performs both functions and is known as the architect-engineer. Finding an architect-engineer the utility trusts is exceedingly important,
for that company occupies the most strategic post in the entire
mammoth operation. In consultation with the utility, it decides
which companies will be awarded the contracts to supply the materials, labor, and equipment necessary to erect the plant, and how
generous those contracts will be. It is also responsible for keeping
the project on schedule and within its budget, and for assuring that
the final result is a plant that is safe.

After drawing up the plant's design specifications, the architect
sends them to each of the Big Four reactor vendors. With hundreds
of millions of dollars' worth of business at stake, it is understandable that the bidding procedures and contract negotiations for a
nuclear power plant are fiercely competitive. The first objective,
obviously, is to win the contract. After that, says Jim Jones, the top
lawyer in Babcock and Wilcox's nuclear division and a man who

has negotiated numerous multi-million-dollar contracts, "Everybody has the same goal—you want to transfer whatever risk you might have to the other party."

Almost a year passes from the day the utility first decides to build a nuclear plant until it has bids in hand from all four reactor vendors. It then calls in representatives from each vendor for technical discussions, which last another six months. "After about three months of technical discussions, the utility has usually narrowed it down to a choice between two vendors," Jones relates. "That's when the serious negotiations begin, and the utility plays off one vendor against the other, trying to get as many concessions as possible out of us."

Jones winks and chuckles when asked how he knows who the other finalist is. "You ask the receptionist. Has she seen the guys from GE lately? No? How about Combustion? It's not too often the utility will tell you, 'Your competition will do this or that.' But towards the end of the negotiations, after going over a certain spec for the sixth time, we might say, 'I don't think you can get what you're asking from anyone in the industry,' and they'll reply, 'I can tell you you're wrong.' Then you know the other guy offered that."

It is the job of lawyers like Jones "to keep the utility from ratcheting us into promising something we can't deliver" while still winning the contract. "Sometimes the utility will find it doesn't need the reactor to begin operation until six months later, so it'll tell its negotiators to keep on us and see what else they can get out of us." Although the reactor happens to be the single most important piece of equipment in a nuclear plant, the same contentious ritual precedes the awarding of all major contracts.

But the supplier companies and the utility are not the only ones involved in the preconstruction negotiations. Because a nuclear plant has such a massive potential impact on a community's environment, economy, health, and safety, construction cannot advance until governmental authorities at the local, state, and federal levels grant their approval. "Do you know we have to get permission from sixty-seven different government agencies in order to build a nuclear plant?" asks Duke Power president William Lee incredulously. Not only that, but private citizens have a legal right to intervene during the Nuclear Regulatory Commission's licensing hearings to oppose, delay, or demand additional safety features for the plant or plant site in question.

The citizens' first intervention opportunity comes when the utility applies for a permit to construct the plant. (This occurs approx-

imately eighteen months after the initial decision to build.) At this
stage, the utility is required to submit to the NRC an environmental-impact report outlining the effects that plant construction and
operation will have. It also submits a Preliminary Safety Analysis
Report (PSAR)—basically a rough sketch of the plant design that
is supposed to inform the NRC about the plant's safety. The utility
must also demonstrate that it has the financial capability to complete the project, and that the construction and operation of the
plant will not violate antitrust laws. The NRC and other federal
agencies, such as the Environmental Protection Agency, then review these documents and, upon finding them satisfactory, hold
public hearings before a three-member Atomic Safety and Licensing Board. "The construction permit hearings can take anywhere
from three months up to two years," explains Robert King, the top
lawyer for Combustion Engineering's Nuclear Power Systems Division. "We hoped that standardization [of plant design] might cut
the time for this in half, since you can submit a PSAR that the
government has already seen once. But it probably won't work out
as well as we hoped just because of the nature of the beast. Things
never seem to shrink when you're dealing with a bunch of bureaucrats."

The utility must go through the same process again once the
plant is constructed and ready for operation, in order to obtain a
license to operate the plant. During this second set of hearings,
interveners "can raise the very same issues which were resolved
during the first hearing," King complains.

The resulting delays cost time and money, and frustrate industry
officials to no end. "One of the industry's criticisms of the licensing
process has been that the NRC has bent over backwards to ensure
public participation," declares Combustion Engineering's Edward
Scherer. Alvin Kalmanson, former legal counsel for Babcock and
Wilcox's Nuclear Power Generating Division, goes a step further
and calls for the elimination of public participation in the licensing
process. "The public should rely on the NRC to carry out the task
it is charged with: protecting the public. The public must have
confidence that those people are doing their jobs, and if they're
not, to get new people to do it. But to have housewives coming
into these highly sophisticated technical decisions [approving
nuclear plants] is just ridiculous."

While industry officials view the licensing process as a costly
annoyance, the record shows that it nevertheless eventually tends
to operate in their favor. In the scores of cases where citizens have

intervened in a nuclear plant's licensing process, the utility has always persevered; neither the AEC nor the NRC has ever turned down an application for an operating license. The most that citizens have accomplished is to delay reactors and force the addition of more safety features.

To the extent that the public has succeeded in forcing the industry to bear more of the health and environmental risks of nuclear power plants, there has been a constant struggle among the various sectors of the industry to shift the cost of those risks onto other companies. The vendors, for example, demand that the utility purchasing a nuclear plant take financial responsibility for nearly all changes in government safety regulations that occur after the day the contract is signed. The utilities have tried to fight back by insisting on phased contracts, which allow them to delay buying a reactor until they are sure they need it. But the balance of power remains weighted in the vendors' and the constructors' favor. "Sure, you've got cancellation privileges," huffs Ayers of Commonwealth Edison. "But they're such that you'd rather not talk about them, because the guy building the plant is sure as hell going to get all his money out, plus what he planned to make on it."

Contract maneuverings such as these offer fascinating insights into the pecking order that prevails within the nuclear industry. Electric utilities, long regarded by antinuclear activists as the main villains in the nuclear drama, are in fact decidedly less powerful than their larger collaborators, the architect-engineers and reactor vendors. Occasionally reactor company executives will admit, albeit not for attribution, that they have something less than a high regard for their counterparts in the utility industry. What is implied in snickering private comments is that utility company executives are second-rate, minor-leaguers, and to put it bluntly, not too bright. After trying twice to say this politely and failing, one reactor executive confided, "Look. Just ask yourself this. What kind of guy gets out of school and goes to work in a regulated industry?" A regulated industry means lower profits, lower salaries, less freedom and excitement—in short, less power and prestige.

Until the early 1970s, a utility usually bought the uranium fuel it needed from the same vendor from which it had bought its reactor. The Big Four vendors acted as middlemen between utilities and mining companies like Utah International, Kerr-McGee, and Homestake Mining. The Four bought the uranium, paid to have it refined and enriched, fabricated the fuel into the rods that are placed inside the reactor, and sold bundles of these rods to the utilities.

Although the Big Four (along with Exxon) still control the fuel fabrication stage of the nuclear fuel cycle, they rarely act as uranium retail outfits any longer. Now most utilities purchase their own uranium, and they contract with the Four for fabrication services the same way they contract with other companies at the mining, milling, and conversion stages of the nuclear fuel cycle. "Ever since the mid-1970s, about 80 percent of our sales have been to utilities and only about 20 percent to the fabricators," says Robert Moyer, marketing manager for Pathfinder Mines Company, the uranium division of Utah International.* "Some utilities have gone back even farther in the product cycle, and have actually begun exploring for and developing their own properties. There's not too many that have actually bought mines, although Commonwealth Edison did buy the Cotter Corporation [a fairly small uranium producer that owned one mine and one mill]."

The search for uranium takes geologists from Pathfinder and other companies all over the world. "For most U.S. companies, Pathfinder included, the United States is the site of most of their production facilities," Moyer explains. "But we explore worldwide. Exxon not long ago purchased a significant share of Australia's future production and also found some material in Canada, as did Gulf. It looks like Canada's is low-cost uranium [to produce], but we aren't moving into that market." When asked why not, Moyer replies, "Pathfinder doesn't need uranium for kicks—we explore for it so we can produce it and make money. And there is such heavy government involvement in Canada that we just thought our money would be better used elsewhere."

One place where Pathfinder and other uranium companies are exploring is southern Africa, despite U.S. government restrictions against further investment in support of South Africa's apartheid regime. "Of course we're concerned about the political stability of the government there," Moyer concedes. "In fact, we're concerned about the whole continent, and this would probably keep us from investing much money past the exploration stage. On the other

---

* In what qualified at the time as the largest merger in American financial history, General Electric purchased Utah International in 1976 for $1.2 billion. The Justice Department ruled that the merger did not violate antitrust laws so long as, among other stipulations, Pathfinder Mines did not sell uranium to GE.

hand, minerals are funny things. You have to look for them where they are."

In the case of uranium, that means four countries. Eighty-seven percent of world uranium reserves that can be cheaply mined are located in the United States, Canada, Australia, and South Africa (including Namibia). There are serious political, bureaucratic, or geographic obstacles to conducting profitable mining operations in each of these regions. In Canada there is the government owner-ship that cramps a company's style and drains its profits. Any in-vestment in South Africa or Namibia is likely to be nationalized if the black majorities seize power there. And in Australia and the United States, much of the uranium is located beneath land that is owned by indigenous peoples—Aborigines in Australia and Native Americans in the United States—who in many cases are adamantly opposed to mining.

No matter where it occurs, uranium mining is a dirty and dan-gerous business. Townspeople and miners alike risk contracting cancer from "radon daughters," highly radioactive solid particles that form out of the radon gas inevitably released during uranium mining. These "daughters" endanger miners because they seep into the mine atmosphere during excavation, and they endanger townspeople because they remain behind in "tailings," a fine grey sand that is left over after the uranium has been extracted from the mined ore. Huge piles of these tailings lie around uranium mills throughout the western United States; the wind blows the radio-active dust onto surrounding communities and the rain leaches it into the surface and ground water. Because neither the federal nor the state governments monitor radon dosage around uranium mills, the carcinogenic effects of these tailings dumps have yet to be precisely measured. As for miners, Charles C. Johnson, Jr., admin-istrator of the Consumer Protection and Environmental Health Service of the U.S. Public Health Service, said back in 1969 that "of the six thousand men who have been uranium miners, an estimated six hundred to eleven hundred will die of lung cancer within the next twenty years because of radiation exposure on the job."

To protect the miners, the federal government in the late 1960s finally mandated tougher occupational health and safety and en-vironmental regulations. Those regulations drastically increased production costs for uranium companies. The companies have been hurt the most in the mines, according to Richard Holway of Home-stake Mining, but building mills is also tougher now. In 1979

Holway projected that his company's costs would continue to rise 30 percent faster than government price indices, and so he was pushing for as much production as possible before the government raised safety levels even further. He noted that waiting for the new regulations was self-defeating. "You can't afford to do that type of thing. I guess that's one of the disadvantages of our competitive system—the good guy who tries to obey the rules gets run out of business."

Another problem for uranium companies is that much of the high-grade uranium ore in the United States appears to have already been mined. "The quality of the uranium now being mined has fallen tremendously," Holway states. "In 1960, we were getting six pounds of uranium out of every ton of dirt we mined. Now we only get three pounds." This has forced greater reliance on uncertain foreign sources of uranium, and it caused some observers in the late 1970s to question whether sufficient amounts of uranium could be found to fuel the world's light water reactors for the rest of their lifetimes.

Thanks mainly to the continuing global slump in nuclear reactor sales, such fears have now been quieted. Recent studies indicate that there is little likelihood of running out of uranium anytime soon. The International Energy Studies Group at the Massachusetts Institute of Technology has concluded "there is little basis for worry about [uranium] supply during the next 10 to 20 years." A 1980 report by the Department of Energy concurs, stating that if prices are allowed to rise to $50 a pound, sufficient uranium will be available to supply U.S. reactors through the year 2020.

Robert Moyer of Pathfinder dismisses all talk about running out of uranium as nonsense. "Taking a snapshot that accounts for how many reserves there are now isn't going to be accurate," says the Pathfinder manager. "Reserves are only a matter of relative price. Deposits remain deposits until the price goes up high enough for them to become reserves. And we don't go out and find all the deposits we can, because it's not economically sensible to do that. If we prove reserves out for fifty years ahead, what we've done basically is spend money that we won't get back for fifty years. But as the price of uranium goes up, we'll find more."

And yet, because of the slump in reactor orders, the price of uranium in recent years has actually been plummeting. From a record high of $52.00 a pound in 1978, the spot price of uranium fell to $23.50 a pound by late 1981, a six-year low. The *Wall Street Journal* reported in November 1981: "Since early 1980, U.S. uranium output has been cut by about a third, and the work force has shrunk to fewer than 14,000 from 22,000. . . . Exploration activity has sunk to a 10-year low, and some major producers are considering getting out of the business altogether."

What comes out of a uranium mine is basically piles of dirt containing sprinklings of uranium. Since it costs so much to transport the dirt, a company usually locates its mill right next to the mine. Inside the mill, the ore is crushed and ground and concentrated into a mixture of uranium oxides known as "yellowcake." The mining company's final contractual responsibility is to transport the yellowcake to one of the two uranium conversion plants in the United States. "At that point," Moyer explains, "the material becomes the property of the utility purchasing it, although he doesn't actually take possession of it until it has been fabricated into fuel rods."

The utility pays the owners of the conversion plant (either Allied Chemical or Kerr-McGee) to transform the yellowcake into uranium fluoride gas, which they then ship to one of the three government-owned enrichment plants for further purification. The government charges the utility a below-market-cost fee for the enrichment service.* The enriched fuel then goes to a fuel fabrication plant where operators, working by remote control to avoid radiation contamination, solidify it into small ceramic pellets, which are loaded into thin metal rods. The utility company finally takes physical possession of its uranium once the completed fuel rods are released from the fabrication plant; it transports the rods back to its construction site and stores them under armed guard until the time comes to load them into the reactor.

The dangers at these stages in the nuclear fuel cycle include not only contamination of workers but also the organized theft of bomb-grade uranium. For example, this has apparently occurred at the fuel fabrication plant in Apollo, Pennsylvania, where two hundred pounds of material have been unaccounted for since 1969. Internal CIA documents reveal that intelligence officials believe the material was diverted to Israel, where it was used in making nuclear weapons. There are worries that similar heists could take place during transport. From the moment it leaves the enrichment plant

---

* The price utilities pay for enrichment is also skewed in that it does not reflect the costs of the tremendous amounts of electricity needed to operate the enrichment plants. Nuclear critic David Comey once estimated that the three enrichment plants consume about 3 percent of all electricity produced in the United States—the equivalent of all the electricity used by New York City.

and throughout its travels by truck to the fuel fabrication facility, the power plant, and ultimately to a waste disposal site, nuclear fuel is of weapons-level potency. Partly because of the obvious hazard this poses but also because of fear about the health effects of a leaky transport tank or a traffic accident, numerous municipalities around the country moved during the late 1970s to prohibit the shipment of radioactive materials through their environs. Bans against nuclear transport passed by the East Coast seaport cities of Miami, Charleston, Morehead City, and New York jeopardized international trade as well as domestic commerce. *Nuclear News* worried in its November 1979 issue that the bans would paralyze the industry by making it impossible to transport nuclear materials at all. But the Department of Transportation seems to have quieted that fear. In January 1981 it announced that the federal government would, if necessary, override all local restrictions against transporting radioactive materials.

A society that relies upon nuclear energy for some of its electricity is taking a risk—how large a risk is open to debate—that the plants will never undergo a major accident that would take thousands of lives and irreparably devastate the surrounding countryside. When the Nuclear Regulatory Commission awards an operating license, it is implicitly saying that it trusts that utility to prevent such accidents. Living up to that trust is the greatest responsibility a utility can have, greater even than producing electricity for its customers or dividends for its stockholders.

Much obviously depends upon the men (and an occasional woman) who operate and maintain the plant. The Kemeny Commission concluded that the Three Mile Island accident demonstrated that operators were not adequately prepared to handle emergency situations and that human error posed a far greater threat to safety than mechanical error. The nuclear industry had reached the same conclusion months earlier and had embarked on a major campaign to "combat human error in nuclear plants." To prevent such goofs as inadvertently discharging radioactive steam into the air over the plant parking lot, losing track of 350,000 gallons of radioactive water, and having two of four on-duty reactor operators sleeping on the job (all incidents that occurred at the Dresden One nuclear power station near Chicago in early 1981), the industry moved soon after the Three Mile Island accident to upgrade the training and discipline of reactor operators.

But Joseph R. Egan, a station-certified nuclear engineer who worked at the Dresden One plant when the new measures were imposed, says workers were skeptical of them. "There was something comical," he later wrote, "about professors and bureaucrats and consultants entering the control room for the first time to tell nuclear plant workers why they've been making mistakes all these years. Nobody bothered to ask workers what was behind human error." Egan agrees that a nuclear plant's mechanical structure is not responsible for safety problems, but claims its social structure is. "Can a nuclear plant ever be operated safely in an environment where conflict is the norm, and where the very technology must be designed to sidestep labor-management antagonisms?" Antagonism between management, workers, and engineers—normal at any industrial facility—prevents the "integration of hand and mind [and] cooperation between workers and engineers" that is essential for safe operation, Egan claims. "If, for example, an engineer discovers that an instrument has drifted out of calibration, automatically stopping routine maneuvers, he knows that the reactor is in an undesirable state that can lead to overheating of the core if prolonged. But the only thing he can do is phone the on-call instrument mechanic, who may arrive an hour later to rotate a single screw on the instrument a half-turn, a function that the engineer or operator could have performed in seconds."

Another special problem for companies operating nuclear power plants is security. An Associated Press story in 1979 reported: "The men who guard the Indian Point nuclear power plants [located thirty-six miles from New York City] warn that it is there for the taking." Guards interviewed by the AP revealed, among other things, that alarms around the plants were often turned off, and because of heavy traffic the ones turned on sounded so often that "no one pays much attention." In 1980, free-lance reporter Jeff Stein decided to test the story by attempting to infiltrate Indian Point; he succeeded, with the help of an NRC document available at the local public library. The *Barrier Penetration Database and Barrier Technology Handbook* not only contained the basic design of Indian Point, it also, Stein wrote, offered "instructions on how to surmount 32 security fences, walls, floors, doors and windows, [and its] detailed appendices showed me how to slip through corridors and scurry up ladders carrying a valise full of burglar tools." The success of a mock raid in 1980 on the nuclear weapons plant at Savannah River, South Carolina, indicates that the government is no better at nuclear security than private industry. Using forged credentials, seven government counterterrorist experts infiltrated the plant, seized hostages, and took over the control room of a large atomic reactor before calling off the security drill.

The nuclear production process does not end with the generation of electricity. During normal operations, a reactor disgorges twenty-five to thirty tons of fuel rods, one-third of a core, every eighteen months. These rods, which have become too radioactive to be efficient heat producers, are stored temporarily in a deep enclosed pool of water known as the spent-fuel pool, located next-door to the reactor. The rods must cool down for four to six months before they can be handled, and even then all operations must be done by remote control to prevent worker contamination.

The nuclear industry has always planned to reprocess the rods and extract the reusable uranium and plutonium before turning them over to the government for final storage. But all commercial ventures into reprocessing have failed dismally, and in 1977 the Carter administration banned reprocessing altogether on the grounds that, since it produced plutonium that other nations or terrorist groups could fashion into nuclear bombs, it constituted an unacceptable risk to American national security.

The industry was thus faced with a dilemma. It either had to find some means of disposing of the spent fuel that was piling up at nuclear plants around the country, or begin shutting some of these plants down, perhaps as soon as 1983. The Energy Department estimated in 1982 that by the end of the decade as many as twenty-eight reactors in the United States could run out of storage space. Some utilities had been able to delay the day of reckoning by rearranging their spent fuel so that more rods could fit in their storage pool, but this was only a stopgap measure. Industry officials suggested transporting the spent fuel to centrally located, "away from reactor" storage pools. These AFRs could buy time until commercial reprocessing was revived.

Thanks to the Reagan administration and the industry's strong support in Congress, both the spent-fuel and the reprocessing problems now appear on the way to solution. The Nuclear Waste Act of 1982, passed in December over the objections of environmentalists, allows for temporary AFR storage of up to 1,900 tons of spent fuel, enough to tide the utilities over until the permanent waste-disposal facilities mandated by the bill are ready later in the decade.

Another potential crisis point for the industry concerns the disposing of the biggest single nuclear waste product there is: the power plant itself. Thousands of years after King Cheops's temporal death, the pyramids he built are at least still nice tourist attractions. Not so for a nuclear power plant. After its thirty years of useful life are up, the plant is so radioactive that it must be quarantined from human beings for many centuries. André Crégut, the French nuclear engineer who directed construction of the Phoenix breeder reactor, has asked, "Do we have the moral right to leave these plants in place knowing that it will take hundreds, perhaps thousands, of years before they cease to be dangerously radioactive?" In 1978, the then fifty-year-old expert decided to clear his conscience by devoting his remaining working years to finding ways to take the plants apart safely. Crégut disputes the conventional options for "decommissioning" a worn-out plant. Covering it with concrete (entombment) is not acceptable because "there is no way to be certain that after 500 or 600 years the protective casing will be physically maintained or guarded." Welding a plant shut and placing it under permanent guard (mothballing) has the same drawback and does not prevent the radioactivity inside from leaking into the environment. Thus the only real solution is complete dismantling and permanent storage of the facility, a tremendously costly, difficult, and dangerous job. A used reactor has been bombarded by so much radioactivity that it cannot be dismantled for decades; even then, its walls are so radioactive that they can be cut up only under water and with remote-controlled welding arms.

The ultimate cost of decommissioning is unknown. But the Department of Energy has estimated that it will cost $25 to $30 million annually for the next one hundred years to decommission the four hundred of its nuclear facilities that were obsolete by 1981. Industry estimates vary from $46 million to $210 million per plant. The law requires utilities to set aside sufficient money to cover these costs, but industry executives themselves admit they have failed to do so. Then there is the additional expense of decommissioning the numerous other facilities that make up the nuclear fuel cycle—uranium mills, enrichment plants, fabrication facilities, reprocessing plants, and so forth. Since no commercial nuclear facility has ever been decommissioned, it is impossible to know what the total, final cost of this last stage of the nuclear industry's operations will be.

The industry's final and perhaps most vexing crisis point is nuclear waste disposal. As of October 1981, the federal government had spent over 3.6 billion taxpayer dollars trying—without success—to find a safe, permanent way to dispose of nuclear waste. The Energy Department is now considering several geologic formations as potential waste-burial sites, including the salt domes and beds of Utah, New Mexico, Texas, Louisiana, and Mississippi and the granite formations in the Great Lakes region.

The passage of The Nuclear Waste Act of 1982 gave the industry an important boost. According to the Atomic Industrial Forum, "this legislative largesse exceeded the fondest hopes of many nuclear energy partisans" and left them "celebrating the prospects of a brighter future." The bill calls for the Department of Energy to conduct environmental assessments of five potential disposal sites and recommend three of them for more detailed study by January 1, 1985. The President will be expected to pick the first site by 1987 and the second by 1990. Individual states have the right to veto their selection for a site, and that veto would stand unless both houses of Congress voted to override it.

President Reagan hailed the bill as "an important step in the pursuit of the peaceful uses of atomic energy." Yet the controversy over nuclear waste is likely to continue. Political maneuvering will grow more contentious and citizen protest more vocal as the federal government moves closer to picking the mandated two disposal sites over the next seven years.

Opinion polls consistently identify nuclear waste disposal as Americans' number one concern about nuclear power, and efforts to allay this concern have met with suspicion. Many states take the understandable position that any nuclear waste dump should be put in someone *else's* backyard. The industry's political problems have been compounded, according to energy writer Elaine Douglass, by resistance from the federal nuclear weapons bureaucracy. Although the public by and large blames the commercial nuclear industry for the waste problem, the government's weapons program is in fact equally responsible; in the course of producing plutonium for weapons over the last thirty-five years, the Atomic Energy Commission and now the Department of Energy have generated about as much nuclear waste as private industry. Responsibility for watching over these military wastes has rested with the Energy Department, and it was able to do pretty much what it liked with them. It determined its own health and safety criteria for military-waste storage facilities, without any oversight from the Nuclear Regulatory Commission (which must license and regulate all commercial waste sites) or the public.

The new law stipulates, however, that the *final* disposal repositories for military waste be licensed by the NRC, and furthermore, that these repositories handle both military and commercial waste, unless the inclusion of military waste is deemed inimical to "national security." The weapons bureaucracy has been in no great hurry to see such repositories established. Indeed, the Energy Department and its congressional comrades, the House and Senate Armed Services Committees, have strenuously opposed all efforts to expand even modestly the NRC's authority over military waste, arguing that NRC oversight would indeed jeopardize national security. Critics retort that the national security claim is a sham; the real reason for the weapons bureaucracy's resistance is that NRC oversight would, in NRC Commissioner Victor Gillinsky's words, "be the camel's nose in the tent." The weapons makers fear that public and congressional scrutiny of their waste dumps might lead eventually to criticism and curtailment of the source of those wastes—the Energy Department's expanding nuclear weapons production program.

The nuclear waste dilemma illustrates two of the three main causes for the commercial nuclear industry's continuing stagnation: citizen resistance to nuclear power, and incompatibility between the industry's immediate needs and the federal government's broader desires and responsibilities. A review of the major obstacles to producing nuclear power plants demonstrates that, where the industry is in trouble, it is often because citizens have organized against activities they perceive as threats to their daily lives. The one crisis point where this is not directly obvious is the nation's declining growth in electricity demand, which is due primarily to the near-collapse of the American economy in the late 1970s, the third major reason for the industry's stagnation. Yet even here, the slowdown in demand growth is partly due to conservation by consumers and businesses rebelling against rising electricity costs. The industry's second crisis point, the ever-rising real costs of nuclear power plants, can be traced to the public's distrust of industry safety claims and to the government's decision to make nuclear power production safer. Mining and processing uranium, and transporting it around the country, have also been made far more difficult and expensive by pressure from what Richard Holway of Homestake Mining calls the "antinuke types." Usually this pressure has been exerted against the government, which has responded by occasionally mandating changes inimical to industry interests. (In two important cases—development of the fast breeder reactor and, as we shall see, reactor exports—the government has restrained the industry not so much because of public opposition as because of its own overriding concerns about American national security and long-term global dominance.)

The production and sale of nuclear technology is an inherently risky and expensive enterprise. The secret of the nuclear industry's early success was to shift many of that enterprise's risks and costs onto the society at large. Now some of them are being shifted back onto the industry. That is the ultimate threat posed by citizen resistance, and it is that resistance the industry must overcome if it is to continue building nuclear power plants.

7

The Nuclear Imperative

I'm counting on nuclear power to pay my pension
when I retire.

GORDON HURLBERT,
*President, Westinghouse
Power Systems Company*

Like countless visionaries before them, the men of America's
Atomic Brotherhood are sustained during the darkest hours of their
struggle by a deep faith in the justness of their cause and the
certainty of their eventual triumph. When they affirm their belief
in the inevitability of nuclear power, they speak with the calm
conviction of fundamentalist Christians prophesying the second
coming of Jesus Christ. As they recite the many reasons why the
United States and the rest of the world cannot avoid heavy reliance
on nuclear energy in the decades to come, they exhibit the patient
self-assurance of men who believe themselves in perfect harmony
with the motion of history. Their faith is unshaken by those who
doubt their message; their anger is kindled by those who resist it.
Their ultimate victory is certain, they reason, because destiny cannot be denied.

Their belief in a nuclear imperative is fundamental to the Brotherhood's guiding ideology—the unique combination of values,
opinions, and ways of thinking that shapes how they look and act
upon the surrounding world—and to their determination to press
on, even in the face of considerable and growing countervailing
evidence. For in the minds of nuclear executives, what is at stake
in the struggle over nuclear power is not just the profitability of
their own corporations but the future of American capitalism, technological society, and indeed Western civilization.

THE WAGES OF "NO NUKES"

"A large percentage of the people involved go through the frustrations of this business because they fundamentally believe that what is at risk is American society," declares General Electric's nuclear vice-president Bertram Wolfe. The nuclear faithful are sustained by an absolute certainty that, deep down, a majority of the American people agree with them; but unfortunately Americans have been led astray in recent years by hysterical antinuclear activists and sensationalistic media coverage, and now industry officials must find a way to win them back. "We know that philosophically we're right," says Wolfe, "that what we're trying to bring to the table is what the public really wants. At industry meetings we ask ourselves how to get our position across to the public better and tell it, 'Look, what you want is a better life—more freedom, not less—and we can provide something that will help you get there.' "

The urgency of the cause imbues the executives with a sense of mission and a genuine devotion to their work rare in the corporate world. "People in this business wouldn't trade jobs for anything," exclaims Charles Sheehan, chief financial officer for GE's Power Systems Sector. "It's exciting, it deals with national issues, and it's a place where you can make a real contribution to the good of the country."

Fundamental to the nuclear imperative is the notion that doing without nuclear power will deeply and perhaps irreparably damage the U.S. economy and gravely endanger the national security. Industry officials claim that without nuclear energy, the United States is sure to suffer energy shortages in the years and decades ahead, which will cause, at the very least, economic slowdowns, and more likely, outright economic collapse. The immediate danger is the threat of widespread electrical blackouts. In November 1979, just a few months after American motorists had once more been forced, ostensibly by the cutoff of oil supplies from revolutionary Iran, to wait in long lines to buy gasoline at jacked-up prices, Atomic Industrial Forum vice-president Paul Turner said, "Just take a look at what happens when you cut gasoline 5 percent. . . . And nuclear is a hell of a lot more important to the economy than gasoline—it supplies 5 percent of the *total* energy. You can't so easily dismiss that, especially in places like Chicago and New England which depend on nuclear for over half of their electricity. There would be a revolutionary situation in New England tomorrow if we cut off nuclear power."

"All of our forecasts indicate that we will have a power shortage in this country in the mid-1980s," William Connolly, senior vice-president for investor relations at Combustion Engineering, said in 1979. "The utilities and the utility suppliers will be sitting in 1985 in the same place where the oil companies were in 1974. People will be asking, 'Why didn't you tell us?' And we sit here in abject frustration, because we are trained to think five, ten, twenty years into the future, and the American consumer and politician is not." Nuclear power is a crucial component in the industry's long-range vision of America's economic future; take it away and the equations no longer balance out, the columns no longer match up. "We've got a population we've got to employ, house, feed, and do everything else to," says Bechtel nuclear fuel vice-president Ashton O'Donnell. "I think we have to go nuclear."

Nuclear power is not seen as the only must. Chauncey Starr, vice-president of the utility industry's Electric Power Research Institute, told the U.S. House Energy Research and Production Subcommittee soon after the Three Mile Island accident that the country would have to more than double its electricity-generating capacity by the year 2000—to a level of 5,000 billion kilowatt hours—or face massive power shortages. Starr emphasized that these figures were based on a "pessimistic" 3.8 percent rate of annual growth in electricity demand and that the actual rate would likely be higher. Meeting the 5,000 billion target would require a doubling of coal-fired power plants—a perhaps logistically impossible feat given the serious regulatory, transportation, labor union, environmental, and public health obstacles that must be overcome. National security and price considerations preclude enlarging the contribution of oil and natural gas beyond their present 13 percent. Hydroelectric power, Starr projected, could provide about 7 percent of the year 2000 demand, and geothermal energy (heat from the earth's interior) another 2 percent. That leaves, besides nuclear, only solar power, a source Starr claimed could meet only 2 to 6 percent of the expected demand. Much of the public, however, seems to think solar electricity is capable of making a far greater contribution. The prevalence of that belief, Starr told the subcommittee, is "a major obstacle to the necessary development of the nuclear option." Attacking "the anti-nuclear partisans [who] have promulgated the simplistic fantasy that clean and limitless solar energy is now available, with only the stupidity, greed, or inertia of the establishment holding up the transition," Starr warned that "deep and long-lasting national injury" would result if this "deceit" was allowed to obscure the fact that "the current choice is between nuclear, expanded import of oil, or not enough electricity to meet minimal needs."

Such a shortfall would have ugly social consequences indeed, according to industry leaders. Energy shortages bring not only relatively minor inconveniences like waiting in line for gasoline but also massive unemployment, high inflation, and human suffering. Factories and schools will close down for lack of electricity; millions, especially poor people, may freeze in the dark. In private, industry officials worry most about the impact of power shortages on the business sector, which consumes two-thirds of America's electricity. In a speech before the Business Council, a group of top executives from leading U.S. companies, Starr predicted that electricity shortages would reduce industrial productivity, encourage capital flight to foreign countries, and quickly throw the nation into a "dangerous downward economic spiral." Business then could not supply a sufficient number of jobs, and "our social fabric could be torn apart."

A "no nukes" policy would also increase the nation's already perilous vulnerability to a cutoff of foreign oil, claims the industry. John Simpson, one of the half-dozen most important executives in the nuclear industry's history owing to his twenty-one-year leadership of Westinghouse's nuclear division until his 1974 retirement, articulated this argument to me one day during the 1979 Atomic Industrial Forum's annual conference. Speaking about the national security imperative of nuclear power, he said, "You know, even if we killed hundreds of people a year, we'd still have to go nuclear. There's just no other way. The Russians could take a hundred people and paralyze this country overnight—just send 'em in to wreck the Middle East oil fields. We fix 'em and they wreck 'em again. The United States just can't stand for that."

Nor, according to the nuclear imperative, is it only the United States that is in danger. Unless something is done very soon to reduce drastically the excessive dependence on foreign oil of all capitalist nations, the international financial system could well collapse, the world economy totter into an intractable depression, and the Western Alliance fragment and dissolve. In an article entitled "The Petro-Crash of the 1980s," which appeared in November 1979, *Business Week* analyzed in its usual comprehensive and candid way what the oil crisis means to the future of the world economic system. "This year, more than ever before, OPEC has captured the power to drain money—petrodollars—from the consuming countries at will," the magazine observed. As a result, "there is something very close to open economic warfare among nations. . . . Just as the U.S. and the West lost control of energy in the 1970s, so too are they in danger of losing control over the world's flow of capital and wealth in the 1980s." The sudden appearance of a global oil glut two years later quieted such fears, but only temporarily. Despite impressive conservation efforts, Western nations, especially Europe, and Japan are destined to remain heavily dependent on oil for many years to come. And to obtain oil, they will have to deal with OPEC, which along with the major international oil companies continues to control supply. Even during the glut of the early 1980s, oil prices remained around $30 a barrel; if demand revives slightly, they may well begin rising again. Thus the dangers foreseen by *Business Week* in 1979 seem likely to persist. Rising oil prices will spur inflation, which politicians will fight through imposing austerity measures that may well cause them to be voted out of office. "Protectionism and trade wars on a scale not seen since the interwar years" may result, according to the magazine, as oil-importing nations "are faced with enormous balance-of-payments deficits that only heavy borrowing and fierce attempts to export can alleviate."

What, then, is to be done? On January 1, 1975, Secretary of State Henry Kissinger warned that the United States might intervene militarily if the flow of Middle East oil was interrupted. The idea of U.S. military action to protect the Middle East oil fields was again seriously discussed after the Soviet Union's invasion of Afghanistan. In his 1980 State of the Union address, Jimmy Carter proclaimed that the United States would repel "by any means necessary, including military force," an attempt by "any outside force" to gain control of the Persian Gulf. The Reagan administration has made similar threats. Doing without nuclear power, then, may be seen as leading to the greatest national security threat conceivable: war in the Nuclear Age with the only other country capable of destroying civilization.

Given these grim circumstances, nuclear executives cannot comprehend how anyone can fail to perceive the national interest in an immediate and substantial expansion of nuclear power. Indeed, they themselves see their patient and costly policy of waiting for nuclear's return as an act of genuine patriotism. Says Bertram Wolfe of General Electric: "The feeling in the company is that unless we have to [leave the nuclear business], we should maintain that option for reasons of national welfare. . . . That doesn't mean that if

there were large financial debits we would use stockholder money
to subsidize the government, but where there's a coincidence of
objectives, there is a feeling of social consciousness that it wouldn't
be right for us to just abandon nuclear power." Indeed, according
to one highly placed source at GE, nuclear energy was, at least
during the late 1970s, set aside from other divisions during the
annual budget process and made all but immune to funding reductions. This remarkable policy was announced in a decision
handed down from "the very highest level of the company"—
meaning, presumably, then chief executive officer and chairman
Reginald Jones and the GE board of directors.

Many other experts, however, are far less gloomy about the dangers of doing without nuclear power: they point out that, thanks to
conservation efforts induced by the massive price increases of the
1970s, the U.S. economy is now consuming significantly less energy than experts had previously predicted. Furthermore, consumption is expected to decline even further in the future, perhaps
to a level of virtually no growth by 1990. The Department of
Energy announced in March 1981 an anticipated energy consumption growth rate of 1 percent a year through 1990; two years earlier,
it had forecast a rate of 3 percent. Part of the savings stemmed from
a 15.4 percent improvement in energy efficiency achieved by the
nation's ten most energy-intensive industries (the group includes
steel, aluminum, and chemicals) since 1972. Roger W. Sant, director
of the Energy Productivity Center at the Carnegie-Mellon Institute
of Research, commented on the 1979 figure of 2.8 percent growth
in national electricity demand: "I think what we've seen in the
last year is probably the precursor to the 1980s—much, much lower
growth rates. I suppose 3 percent growth is now the conventional
wisdom, but my guess is that it will be quite a bit lower than that."
Yet this decline is not expected to halt economic growth. Sant's
Mellon Institute expects a 2.6 percent annual growth of gross national product in the 1980s, despite a zero energy-growth rate.

Nuclear executives are hardly unaware of the trend towards
greater energy efficiency. In fact, they are handsomely profiting
from it. Westinghouse, for example, is a leading seller of industrial
heat pumps that recover waste heat, of factory computer systems
that automatically adjust heating, cooling, and lighting at different
times of the day, and of a vast array of other products designed to
increase energy efficiency. Du Pont and Ebasco are offering similar
services to industry, and Union Carbide and General Electric are
actively working on cogeneration, the industrial process whereby

steam is used twice—for heating and for running a turbine to generate electricity. GE, the leading manufacturer of the turbines used in cogeneration, expects the process to account for as much as 50,000 megawatts of electricity in the United States by the year 2000; that is roughly equivalent to the output of forty conventional nuclear power plants. In addition, many electric utilities are encouraging cogeneration and other forms of increased energy efficiency among their customers in order to forestall costly capacity additions to their own systems.

All this being the case, what justifies the cry for the necessity of nuclear power? Although one obvious answer—because the corporations will profit handsomely if the cries are heeded—certainly must be kept in mind, that explanation fails to account for the executives' perseverance in the face of continuing multi-million-dollar nuclear-related losses. Something deeper is at work. Part of the answer, I believe, lies in the fact that these men's opinions and attitudes were formed in the pre-OPEC era of cheap energy, when national economic growth and their own corporations' sales and profits increased in direct proportion to overall energy consumption. And although those economical relationships are clearly beginning to change, it is only natural that the consequent change in consciousness occurs somewhat more slowly.

"Growth" remains for nuclear executives (and proponents) a good and necessary thing. Their instincts tell them that within an economic system predicated on growth, conservation cannot possibly be more than a minor source of energy in the long run. As Joseph Dietrich, the former top nuclear engineer at Combustion Engineering, said, "If we [are to] keep making more and more stuff needed to expand our standard of living, I think you come to the end of where conservation can help." While the nuclear executives support and are profiting from the drive to increase energy efficiency, they nevertheless strongly believe that conservation must be viewed as an addition to, not a substitute for, other forms of energy production. As Bertram Wolfe of General Electric says about future energy supplies, "There *is* no one solution. You're going to need all of everything you can get."

THE PRICE OF PROGRESS

The nuclear imperative is founded not simply on fear of the consequences of doing without nuclear power but also on the conviction that nuclear power is the very embodiment of progress and enlightenment. Nuclear executives see themselves as pioneers in humankind's never-ending struggle for a better life and see the nuclear enterprise as an inevitable development in the natural evolution of human civilization. Nuclear energy is an idea whose time has come, an integral part of the larger scheme of things. Demanding vision, intelligence, and courage, it stands for all that is noble and unique about human beings. It offers solutions to the age-old problems of scarcity and want. Because it is new and somewhat risky, it may take some decades for ordinary people to get used to it. But get used to it they must, for the way forward is blocked without it.

The idea that nuclear power is somehow meant to be has been part of the Atomic Brotherhood's ideology from the very beginning. Robert Oppenheimer, the father of the atomic bomb, in his 1945 farewell address to subordinates at the Manhattan Project's Los Alamos weapons facility, advanced the view that scientists were not free to desist from the historic task of developing nuclear power:

> But when you come right down to it the reason we did the job is because it was an organic necessity. If you are a scientist you cannot stop such a thing. If you are a scientist you believe that it is good to find out how the world works; that it is good to find out what the realities are; that it is good to turn over to mankind at large the greatest possible power to control the world and to deal with it according to its lights and values.

Like Oppenheimer's, the perspective of today's nuclear officials is rooted in a technologically determinist view of the world and of history. It is a view that sees humankind's choice of actions as being, in essence, already largely determined by past technological developments, the sequence of events they unleashed, the consequent material conditions of today's world, and the objective requirements of future civilization. According to this outlook, to resist the historical momentum of nuclear energy is to flail futilely at forces independent of human control. Far wiser is to understand and accept those forces, and harness them for the good of humanity.

"It's sort of philosophical, I guess," Herbert Sprague, a young nuclear fuel executive at General Electric, says with a grin, "but I really have faith that nuclear power has just got to be the energy of the future. It's the logical next step." Thomas Ayers, former chairman and chief executive officer of the Commonwealth Edison

Company, explains, "We're in a time when the basic energy [source] is about to shift. We went from wood to water to coal to oil. And now I think we're going to go into nuclear, breeder-nuclear, fusion, and somewhere along the line, hydrogen." *Not* making the shift would mean severe social problems and human suffering on a global scale as early as the turn of the century, according to GE's Bertram Wolfe. "By the end of the century, you see world oil production down, increasing population around the world, and an aspiration worldwide for the better things in life," says Wolfe. "And you look at that and wonder how you're going to satisfy it. Nobody really believes that solar is going to solve the problem. . . . We should be moving quickly on things like the breeder [reactor] right now, if we want it ready in time, because it traditionally takes forty to fifty years to switch energy technologies."

The men of the nuclear industry argue that their technology offers the only hope of maintaining the abundance and leisure of industrial civilization. The planet's stock of hydrocarbons, they point out, is rapidly being depleted. It is not so much that we will run out of coal, oil, and gas as that they will become prohibitively expensive to use to fuel our entire societies. Moreover, these hydrocarbons are actually far more valuable as feedstocks for producing plastics, ammonia, and other petrochemicals that are central to the workings of advanced industrial economies. Indeed, to continue to use them as fuel is wasteful and selfish and, in the words of one nuclear advocate, "will very probably force our descendants to return to the industrial economy of the early nineteenth century."

The theme of nuclear power as the natural and welcome successor to today's fossil fuels was subtly, persuasively argued in a 1979 film commissioned by the Atomic Industrial Forum entitled *A Play Half Written: The Energy Adventure.* Obviously intended for a mass audience (its twenty-six-minute length makes it perfect for television), the film champions energy and technology. Its central message is that human progress through the ages has depended directly upon making such technological advances as nuclear power. A narrator stands on a deserted theater stage musing about "the great cosmic plan" that humanity has been acting out for thousands of years; the film quickly cuts to shots of all kinds of human faces—old, young, in-between, American, Asiatic, African, laughing, weeping, placid—and then to images of great human achievements—*Mona Lisa,* Stonehenge, jet airplanes, the Apollo Spacewalk. The narrator informs us, however, that something is missing here, "something without which the human drama would have closed in rehearsal." The missing element is energy: "Since the very first scenes of the human drama, our progress has been dependent upon our success at finding new sources of energy to power our invention. It has been a natural progression from age to age, from the Stone Age to the Nuclear Age. [First] muscles, then animals, then burning wood, wind, water, then on to the burning of coal, oil, and natural gas, and more recently transforming these fuels into electricity. And now we're moving into another of these natural transitions—to nuclear fuels."

"Our energy decisions in the future will shape not just technology but our art, entertainment, and our whole way of life," exclaims the narrator as the film cuts to hilarious excerpts from old Buster Keaton movies and then to a symphony orchestra performing Beethoven's Ninth. "We must create a social, environmental climate where people can reach their full potential. And as always, that will take more energy—not less—if our characters are to have the opportunity to develop as they wish." Enter nuclear energy, and in the nick of time: "This domestic source of energy was developed just when we needed it, when supplies of oil and gas were running out."

How we take advantage of nuclear power and other energy technologies, declares the narrator, will determine the degree of our liberation from poverty, ignorance, disease, and injustice. The camera follows him strolling through a restored turn-of-the-century American town, telling the audience that, before the era of the steam engine, life expectancy was thirty-eight years; men worked an average of seventy-two hours a week, women an exhausting ninety-eight. And even that relative hardship was a far more hopeful situation than that of many in today's world, where two-thirds of humanity is severely malnourished or actually starving. The lesson of all this: "Where people exist upon the invisible line stretching from the most primitive to the most advanced society depends upon the energy and tools available to them." Ergo, nuclear power equals human progress.

The debate over nuclear energy, Westinghouse executive Jean-Claude Poncelet told a 1980 Atomic Industrial Forum meeting, is really a debate over the future of technological society. "The nuclear controversy," the young French scientist argued, "[is rooted in the] ill-defined and almost subconscious sense of malaise and dissatisfaction that permeates modern industrialized societies. This malaise is characterized by a growing feeling of alienation, a fear of increasing dehumanization in our society, and a deep apprehension that the individual is losing control over his individual destiny, that perhaps no one is really anymore in control."

The men of the Atomic Brotherhood believe in nuclear energy and they believe in technological society. So did most Americans for many years. But over the last decade or so, many have professed growing skepticism. Doubt about the virtues of technological society has crept into the minds of millions among the public, and they are beginning to wonder whether the comfort and convenience technology brings are worth the social, psychic, and environmental costs it exacts.

While conceding there are risks to their technology, nuclear executives argue that these are actually quite small—far smaller, for example, than driving one's automobile. And these risks fade into insignificance when considered against the enormous positive potential of nuclear power. What is more, this energy source has arrived at just the right moment. "Here's a throwaway product," says an exasperated Thomas Ayers. "It has no other use. It's almost a miracle that it came along when it did. And here we are, sitting around talking about whether it's hurting us. To me it's damn ludicrous."

The reason many executives think fear of nuclear power ridiculous is their firm conviction that it is they who control nuclear technology, and not the other way around. The conviction is most obviously manifested in the feelings of incomprehension, pity, and contempt nuclear officials have about those who *are* frightened. At the Atomic Industrial Forum's 1980 annual conference, for instance, psychiatrist Robert DuPont told hundreds of head-nodding executives that fear of nuclear power—"the primary problem facing this proud industry," according to DuPont—should be understood as a phobia, as "a fear of fear itself," which could be overcome by making nuclear power less remote and unfamiliar. (Apparently unaware of his own pun, DuPont suggested to the executives, "You should expose more people to the plants themselves, and especially to the normal Joes who work there, so they can see there's nothing to be scared about.") Nuclear waste disposal is another bugaboo, say industry officials. Antinuclear hysterics and government indecision have convinced most Americans there is no solution for the waste problem. Yet the real trouble, according to John West, the vice-president in charge of Combustion Engineering's nuclear division, is not that there is *no* solution but that there are too many good solutions and the federal bureaucracy, as usual, cannot bring itself to select one. "I have a vulgar analogy," the executive confided. "It's kind of like you have a blonde, a brunette, and a redhead, real glamorous gals all lined up for action, and you can't decide which one you'd like to go to bed with. They're all good."

John Siegal of the Atomic Industrial Forum argues that toxic chemical waste is actually much nastier than nuclear waste. "It sounds weird, but the nice thing about nuclear waste is that it's radioactive," Siegal states. "That means you always know where it is, and you know it will eventually decay away. Chemical wastes last forever, and they're easy to lose track of."

One top nuclear executive cannot understand what all the fuss is about nuclear waste in the first place. After six hundred years, he reasons, the dangerous materials decay down to where they are "pretty innocuous," so why are governors, legislators, and citizens around the country declaring their states off-limits to nuclear dumping? "To me it's the craziest thing," he exclaimed. "Neither they nor their descendants are going to be there at the time when anything could conceivably go wrong. If you do a halfway decent job of disposing of it, it's at least a few hundred years before anything could go wrong, and they won't even be there then."

He summed up the industry's safety approach in the phrase "defense in depth." "You use multiple barriers to [prevent] the dangerous occurrence," he explained. "Now, some of the antinukes and academics look at this and criticize it because not each of the barriers is foolproof. But that's just not the approach. The idea is that the multiple barriers will catch any problem somewhere along the line."

"Defense in depth," bespeaks nuclear engineers' confidence that scientific method, carefully applied, can permanently triumph over human fallibility. The key assumption behind this approach is that nuclear experts can anticipate each and every sequence of events that might lead to serious accidents. Armed with that foreknowledge, they can construct systems that no combination of human error or natural catastrophe can compromise. Perhaps the most impressive evidence of the sincerity (if not the validity) of this belief, is that nuclear executives are involved along with the rest of the public. "Finally, you have to say that I live here too, and my family, so why would I be motivated to do something that would make the environment unsafe for my family?" asks John Kreuthmeier of Westinghouse.

Although industry executives are confident nuclear energy is safe, none claim it is absolutely without risk. Indeed, that is the crux of their safety argument. In a world where nothing is without risk, the rational man—and nuclear executives are above all else rational men—seeks not to eliminate but to minimize risks. The public's refusal to recognize that nuclear poses far smaller health and environmental risks than do coal and other energy sources is a real frustration to industry officials. "Just once I'd like to answer the phone, 'Atomic Industrial Forum, Coal Kills,'" exclaimed one staffer at the industry's trade association. The nuclear men point out that coal plants actually release more radiation during operation than do nuclear plants, as well as pollute the air with smoke and soot; that hundreds of miners are poisoned, maimed, and killed every year digging up coal; and that burning coal may through a process known as "the greenhouse effect" eventually alter the earth's atmosphere sufficiently to induce catastrophic climatic changes. Thus, if society's true goal is to build a safer and more ecological energy system, it should limit use of coal and other fossil fuels, not nuclear energy.

Most industry officials are confident Americans will eventually get used to nuclear power and accept the minor risks associated with it as merely the price of progress. "The nuclear industry is not going to go away under any circumstances," declares Kemp Fuller, an investment banker at Moseley, Hallgarten and Estabrook, who has closely followed the industry's development. "People are going to have to learn to live with nuclear power, just like they learned to live with the gas combustion engine, which impinged on people's previous notions of tranquillity." Nuclear executives argue that smoking cigarettes, flying in airplanes, and driving automobiles are far more dangerous than living near nuclear power plants, and yet people willingly take those risks every day because the activities are familiar to them. The executives hope that over time nuclear power will achieve a similar degree of familiarity and hence acceptance among the populace, yet they realize such a scenario is likely only in the absence of major accidents.

That raises a problem, one which Alvin Weinberg, former head of the Oak Ridge National Laboratory and one of the grand old men of the Atomic Brotherhood, addressed in a speech to colleagues from around the world at the twentieth anniversary gathering of the International Atomic Energy Agency in 1977. Weinberg predicted that by the year 2050 the world would have 5,000 reactors in place. Given the Rasmussen Report's probability of a major accident every 20,000 reactor-years, humanity could then expect a catastrophe every four years. Clearly, such a barrage would destroy public acceptance of nuclear power. To prevent it, Weinberg suggested the formation of a "nuclear priesthood," a carefully chosen cadre of specially trained experts who would be given extraordinary authority, including police powers, to ensure nuclear safety through the ages.

Nuclear critics have attacked Weinberg's proposal as a threat to civil liberties and a step towards an authoritarian society run by a technocratic elite. Here again, industry officials suggest that people adopt a cost-benefit approach. Alvin Kalmanson, the former lawyer for Babcock and Wilcox's nuclear division, agrees that nuclear energy is a technology geared towards experts and the concentration of social power, but argues, "That's a price you pay to live in an advanced industrial society. You give up some freedom and some control."

THE CLASH OF PHILOSOPHIES

When French journalist Daniel Singer wrote, "An old ruling class always looks strangely bewildered when faced with a new massive social movement," he was remarking on the Polish Communist Party's reaction to Solidarity, the independent trade union formed in 1980. But the insight applies equally well to the American nuclear industry's response to the antinuclear movement. For although that movement has been a significant political force since the early 1970s, it remains something of an enigma to most industry officials. Methods powerful men have traditionally used to vanquish opponents—ignoring, ridiculing, spying and infiltrating, disrupting, defaming, outspending—seem only to have strengthened the antinuclear movement, and nuclear executives are not sure why. What they are sure of is that the movement has hurt them, badly, and that it must be subdued if the nuclear imperative is to be realized.

The executives grant the antinuclear movement the grudging respect due a tested and worthy adversary. Although he does not think the activists can permanently stop nuclear power, William Connolly, Combustion Engineering's senior vice-president for investor relations, does admit, "They've been even more damaging than they realize." John McMillan, vice-president of Babcock and

Wilcox's Nuclear Power Generating Division, concurs: "I think they've been effective. There's no question about that."

But top executives are divided on the more subjective questions of what motivates antinuclear activists and what their intentions are. Combustion's John West, for example, derisively terms them "an anti-growth, sleeping-bag society." Nelson Embrey, a top manager in Babcock and Wilcox's nuclear power division, nearly jumps out of his chair when asked his view of antinuclear activists. "What are they about?" Embrey repeats rhetorically. "They are [an] anti-government, anti–big business, anti-technology movement. [Their goal] is a pure socialist form of government that has nothing big about it. Anything that's big is bad, a simpler way of life."

William Connolly disagrees: "There are those who will tell you that this is part of a worldwide commmunist conspiracy. I don't adhere to that. People who are in the movement are well-intentioned. I think they are a lot of misguided intellectuals ... who don't deal realistically, or live in the real world. A lot of them have private income sources, and have the luxury of thinking rather than doing. It's about the only remaining outlet for those people who want the greening of America. . . . But the environmental movement is a movement for which I have a lot of sympathy, because I do feel that we have been abusing this planet. I'm a follower of Cousteau and all the others. I have a son who is an environmental studies major at the University of Vermont who keeps me on the straight and narrow. But I really think [the antinuclear movement] is the vestiges of a misguided minority of the population."

The industry finds it difficult to understand the antinuclear movement primarily because the two are so thoroughly different from one another. But the industry and the movement do have one thing in common, and it is this shared trait that makes the nuclear struggle so fascinating to watch and endows it with something of the appearance of a modern-day holy war. Both the activists and the executives are absolutely certain they are right, that theirs is the moral and just cause, and that therefore they are destined to triumph while their opponents are destined to fail. The executives regard nuclear power as humankind's salvation and feel honored to help bring it into being. They shield themselves against castigation and ridicule by reassuring one another that societies have always reacted hostilely to those who, like themselves, were ahead of their times.

Yet they do take offense at the sometimes vicious verbal assaults

nuclear opponents heave against them. "There's no compromising
with the antinuclears in this country," says R. F. Von Hollen, a top
manager in Combustion Engineering's nuclear division. "They're
rabid. They just want everything shut down. . . . It's very hard to
deal with a class of people whose only intent is to put you on the
defensive and make you look bad, and tell you everything you've
done is no good, and no matter what you do, it isn't going to satisfy
them. And if you ask them what to do instead, you never get an
answer. 'Just don't do anything. Stop doing what you're doing and
we'll let nature take its course.'" Such an uncompromising and
passive approach to the physical environment is simply incompre-
hensible to the rationalistic, ordered mind of nuclear engineers.
"You have to understand an engineer," Von Hollen pleads. "An
engineer is a practical man. He is resigned to using science for the
betterment of mankind. And he's used to making trade-offs. Cost-
benefits are put into him from day one of engineering school—if
you do this, you'll get that, is it worth it?"

Because the engineers could not believe that any rational person
in possession of all the relevant facts could sincerely be against
nuclear power, the industry at first blamed the public's uneasiness
about nuclear power on itself. It had simply failed to communicate
adequately the full truth about nuclear power. And while this is
still the prevailing viewpoint in regard to the public at large, industry officials have since come to believe that most antinuclear
activists are simply beyond the reach of sensible argument and
debate and, furthermore, are not genuinely worried about the dangers of nuclear power at all, but actually are opposed to *all* forms
of energy production. Industry officials became convinced of this,
recalls Babcock and Wilcox's former nuclear lawyer Alvin Kalmanson, when the Sierra Club forced the Southern California Edison
Company in 1977 to cancel the largest order for coal-fired power
plants in U.S. history. The utility, after previous hassles with the
Sierra Club over a proposed nuclear plant, had instead decided to
build four gigantic coal units and to locate them, not in densely
populated southern California, but on Native American lands in
southern Utah. According to Kalmanson, the people in Utah welcomed Edison with open arms because they needed the employment the plants would provide. "But then the Sierra Club found
out about it," says Kalmanson, "and bused people in and demonstrated and paraded and made speeches, and put heavy pressure
on Secretary of the Interior Andrus, and finally Southern California
Edison canceled the plants. That's when we started to realize the

objection wasn't particularly to nuclear, because it was the same groups who were marching against the nuclear plants."

A more sophisticated and thoughtful elaboration of this viewpoint comes from Bertram Wolfe of General Electric: "They're against nuclear power, but if you look a little deeper you find they're also against coal power, offshore oil, Alaska oil, western coal. They're basically against any new large endeavor. . . . Nuclear power is just the high-visibility cutting edge that they go after, but really their thrust is very broad social changes. The idea is if they can stop this society, they can then move it in the direction they want." Referring to a manifesto published by Friends of the Earth, a major antinuclear-environmental group, Wolfe declares, "I must say I admire them at least for putting it down. If people read that and took it seriously, they'd be absolutely horrified. This is a document that says 'Let's go back one hundred years.' It talks about an educational system that so far as I can see is what they have in China and Cuba now, about an agricultural system that is labor-intensive, and on through the whole social gamut. If someone said to you, 'This is the system we want' and you looked at it in any real detail, you'd be horrified, because it's another Jonestown they're talking about."

Wolfe's explicit reference to the most ghastly horror story in American culture's recent history reveals just how deeply appalled nuclear executives are by the alternative society envisioned by their opponents. To Wolfe and other far-sighted industry executives, it is clear that the antinuclear-environmental movement threatens far more than nuclear energy and individual nuclear corporations. "They're against the whole structure of our present society," Wolfe explains. "They're certainly against big business, against capitalism as we see it. And they certainly want to distribute the wealth in a more egalitarian way."

Wolfe is right that the antinuclear movement's basic values and priorities are at odds with American capitalism itself. Opposing nuclear power plants or petroleum pipelines on safety or environmental grounds, for example, directly challenges the essential capitalist canon that nothing is more important than producing. What is ironic, however, is that the antinuclear activists themselves by and large seem not to grasp the anticapitalist implications of their own philosophy. They are protesting the *consequences* of growth for growth's sake without realizing such behavior is endemic to a capitalist economic system. One might say they are anticapitalist in effect, not intent. The executives, on the other hand, perceive those same anticapitalist implications so immediately and clearly, so instinctively, that they assume their adversaries must as well. This leads some executives to conclude that the activists are consciously, secretly planning the overthrow of American capitalism and that stopping nuclear and other forms of energy is but one part of their strategy for achieving that goal.

"They're not really against nuclear power," snorts Nelson Embrey of Babcock and Wilcox. "It just happens to be the first soft white underbelly they saw." The environmentalists' plan, according to a speech written by H. Peter Metzger after he stopped writing books and became manager of public affairs planning for the Public Service Company of Colorado, and distributed by the Atomic Industrial Forum, is to stop every form of energy production and, in the ensuing economic chaos, install themselves as society's new and absolute rulers:

> Their plan is to strangle our society, under the guise of study and regulation, by stopping everything which we need to grow, and that is: water, coal and nuclear power, land use, and new industry, particularly pipelines and refineries. In the acknowledged economic chaos which *must* follow such a course, they hope we will all wake up to the inherent good sense of their Utopia (however vaguely defined) and simply climb aboard their bandwagon; we will have, they figure, no alternative.

The nuclear industry has attempted to defend itself against the environmentalists by portraying them as enemies of economic growth. In another speech distributed by the AIF, entitled "Environmentalism: What Is It Really About?" William Tucker, a contributing editor for *Harper's*, charges that environmentalism is the self-serving ideology of what neoconservatives are calling "the new class." This class, according to the theory, sprouted up between the rich and the working class sometime during the 1960s and is composed of, in Tucker's words, "professional people, well-educated, with high incomes, mobile, not particularly tied to one place or job, yet still not 'rich' in the classical sense of making a living from owning *things*. They still depend on employment or professional fields for their income, rather than owning property or simply clipping coupons." This new class, Tucker argues, cynically employs environmentalism to protect its own position of relative privilege within the social hierarchy; by limiting overall economic growth through environmental restraints, it effectively blocks the only means of social advancement open to the lower middle class and the poor. Through the rhetoric of liberalism, the new class has cunningly managed to establish a strategic and beneficial alliance with the poor, even though the two groups' interests are diametrically opposed. No less deceitful, the affluent have passed off environmentalism as a trendy, progressive concern when, in fact, "It's major direction . . . has been to work against the interest of the lower middle class and the poor, and for the people at the top end of the scale." The task facing the nuclear and indeed the entire energy industry, according to Tucker, is to assemble "a careful documentation of the effects of economic stagnation on broad numbers of people, in order to show the vast majority of the public that environmentalism is not necessarily in their interests." As we shall see, this message is central to the industry's post–Three Mile Island comeback campaign.

Perhaps the nuclear executives are simply deluded victims of their own rhetoric and, like countless other powerful men throughout history, are simply unable to understand and accept that their time of glory and power is passing. Perhaps. But they sincerely believe they will win the nuclear struggle. They are savvy enough to realize that if nuclear energy makes a comeback in the United States, it will not be because Americans actively like nuclear power—those days are gone forever, thanks to Three Mile Island—but because they believe the country cannot do without it. The industry is confident that Americans can be made to perceive and respect the supposed connection between nuclear energy production and economic prosperity. "Americans are a pragmatic people," states John McMillan, of Babcock and Wilcox. "When the blackouts start and the economy gets worse over the next few years, the antinuclear movement will be lost in the shuffle. The majority of middle-class Americans who depend on the growth of the economy for their jobs are going to make their voices known so strongly that the politicians will have no choice but to go nuclear."

8

The Great Comeback

You know, President Coolidge once said that "The slogan 'Press On' has been the solution to all problems in human history," and I think that will be the cause with nuclear power, too.

FREDERICK L. WEBBER,
*Executive Vice-President for Government Affairs,
Edison Electric Institute*

Serious as it was, the Three Mile Island accident did not cause nuclear industry leaders to re-examine the fundamental assumption that underlay all their decisions and actions: that the United States and the rest of the world should, must, and would rely heavily on nuclear power in the future. But Three Mile Island did shock nuclear executives into realizing that their nuclear imperative was not necessarily a self-fulfilling one. If that imperative was to materialize, the industry would have to work for it. And despite the many serious difficulties facing them, the executives remained confident of ultimate success.

The Atomic Industrial Forum's 1979 annual conference, held the second week of November in San Francisco's posh St. Francis Hotel, convened under the stubbornly optimistic theme "Moving Ahead with Nuclear Power." As the following excerpt from the conference brochure's incredible welcoming message shows, the industry was no less determined than ever that nuclear power would be a major future energy source for the United States:

> History will record 1979 as a watershed year for nuclear power when its mettle was severely tested. To the credit of the underlying technology and the people in industry and government who are responsible for applying and controlling that technology, history will also record that nuclear power stood the test.

As a result, nuclear power will gain through adversity. . . . Nuclear power is already committed to play an important role in meeting our future electric energy needs. It remains for the industry to determine how the job can be done most effectively and in an environment not only of public need but of public acceptance and desire as well.

Cynics may dismiss it as a pathetic example of rationalization and self-delusion, but this view of Three Mile Island as a blessing in disguise was voiced repeatedly at the AIF conference. The tough times had engendered a fresh spirit of unity and determination. As one General Electric official marveled, "The mood at this year's conference is so much more alive and upbeat than the last couple of years. I guess we had to have a scare thrown into us before we really got off our duffs."

As he spoke, the GE man stood by the picture window of his company's hospitality suite on the top floor of the St. Francis Hotel, surrounded by a roomful of fellow executives. He looked out over the lights of San Francisco for a few moments, quietly searching for the right words, before turning to say, "I think these guys are tired of being kicked around. After Three Mile Island, they're ready to stand up and fight."

All things considered, the accident probably *was* a blessing for the men of the Atomic Brotherhood. For not only did it shock them into action while there was still time to win the nuclear fight, it also made the fight a test: Were they strong enough to pick themselves up and keep fighting? Did they have the endurance, the will, the intangible something extra that truly great competitors have always called upon in order to come from behind and win? Did they want victory badly enough? The men of the Brotherhood believed they did. And noses bloodied, adrenaline pumping, they bounced to their feet, eager to prove it.

LIKE IT OR NOT

Two weeks to the day after the Three Mile Island accident, they had already begun planning their counterattack. On April 11, 1979, the Board of Directors of the Edison Electric Institute (EEI), the trade association of the nation's privately owned utility companies, met at the Hyatt Regency Hotel in Atlanta and established what later came to be called the TMI Oversight Committee. The board asked Floyd Lewis, chief executive officer of the Middle South Utilities Company and a man widely respected throughout the industry, to chair the committee as it coordinated the industry's response to the accident. According to William Lee, president of the Duke Power Company and a leading force in the Three Mile Island recovery effort, the Atomic Industrial Forum also was closely involved in Oversight Committee operations from the start, and committee members "received input from all segments of the nuclear industry."

The committee's first and overriding concern was, in the words of EEI senior vice-president Jack Young, "to ensure that appropriate lessons were learned from the accident." Recognizing that anything close to a repeat performance of the Three Mile Island accident would bring nuclear power to a permanent halt, the Oversight Committee moved quickly and decisively to upgrade the safety of nuclear power plants. It established the Nuclear Safety Analysis Center (NSAC) and gave it a $3.5 million budget to investigate the accident and determine what it implied about safety issues generic to all nuclear plants. Soon thereafter, it asked companies from throughout the nuclear industry to contribute $11 million more to set up the Institute for Nuclear Power Operations (INPO), which would improve the training of nuclear plant operators.

Paul Turner, AIF vice-president for public affairs, hinted at the dual purpose of these safety initiatives when he explained in an interview: "In the kind of society we have, the perception of Three Mile Island is at least as important as the facts of Three Mile Island." To be sure, the new safety centers would improve nuclear safety. But perhaps more important, they would also give nervous Wall Street investment analysts, probing government regulators, and an angry American public the impression that the nuclear industry took the accident seriously and was determined that such a mishap would never happen again.

But how could the industry get that message across? "We found it difficult to get media coverage of steps like NSAC and INPO," said EEI's Jack Young, "but we needed to let people know that these changes were being made." And this had to be done quickly, before irreparable public relations damage was sustained. "We were just astonished by what the press was saying," recollected one staff member of the Oversight Committee. "There was a complete avalanche of misinformation that had to be corrected."

Twelve of the nuclear industry's top public relations specialists began meeting soon after the accident to attack the problem. Jack Young of EEI and Paul Turner of the AIF cochaired the group, which included representatives from each of the Big Four nuclear reactor manufacturers, the Bechtel Corporation, the American Nuclear Energy Council lobby group, and electric utility companies and trade associations. The group went by the awkward name of the Public Relations Steering Committee of the TMI Oversight Committee. One of its first decisions was to set up yet another committee, this one to be called the Committee on Energy Awareness (CEA), which would carry out on a day-to-day basis the directives of the Steering Committee.

The CEA's marching orders were agreed upon during the Steering Committee's May 30 meeting at the Bechtel Corporation's San Francisco headquarters. A memo from Paul Crane, Bechtel's top public relations officer, to his boss, Bechtel president Harry Reinsch, reporting on the meeting provides a description of the CEA's internal structure, budget, and future plans. (A dissident Bechtel employee leaked the memo to a reporter for the *San Francisco Chronicle*.) Various nuclear companies had pooled resources to provide the CEA with a $1.6 million budget for the last half of 1979. Companies also "loaned" some of their top executives for periods of one to six months, thereby absolving the spin-off organization of considerable labor costs. There were over twenty programs the Steering Committee wanted the CEA to initiate, including private briefings for business and political leaders; round-table discussions with the editorial staffs of leading newspapers; outreach to college campuses, local labor leaders, and senior citizen groups; and development of local, pronuclear grass-roots groups.

The CEA's public outreach materials would include four messages. The first two were designed to reassure Americans and reestablish their trust in nuclear power:

- The nuclear industry is making an all-out effort to increase nuclear safety as a result of lessons learned at TMI;
- The industry continues to seek ways to minimize potential exposure to radiation and to develop acceptable ways to transport and store nuclear waste.

The second two were designed to persuade Americans of the dangers of doing without nuclear power:

- The electrical power industry is working to develop alternative energy sources; however, the Nation cannot meet the growing demand for electricity without utilizing nuclear energy;

- Individuals, as well as the Nation, will suffer economically, socially, and environmentally if it abandons nuclear energy.

The number one priority for the CEA, according to the Bechtel memo, was to shore up support for nuclear power within the American business community. The CEA sent its first team of industry executives to Wall Street on Monday, July 23, 1979, to give a speech to a record-setting gathering of the New York Society of Security Analysts. The speakers, Harry Blundell, president of the Utah Power and Light Company, and H. L. Culbreath, president of the Tampa Electric Company, were chosen specifically because their firms had no nuclear commitment. "We are here, not to protect a particular nuclear investment, but instead to argue the *national* case for nuclear power, and to ask the support of the financial and investment community in that endeavor," declared Messrs. Blundell and Culbreath. The two utility presidents got the security analysts' full attention within the first thirty seconds of their presentation when they warned that a nuclear moratorium "could greatly influence the profitability of the companies you follow, and your ability to predict their performance accurately." Such a moratorium, they argued, would increase electricity costs and shortages, reduce the gross national product, throw one and one-half million people out of work, increase oil imports, and raise energy prices. Furthermore, it would increase American dependence upon foreign oil supplies and thus imperil American national security and the strength of the Western Alliance system. Blundell and Culbreath later made similar presentations to investment analysts in Atlanta, Hartford, and other cities.

The CEA took its message further up the corporate hierarchy on October 13, when Dr. Chauncey Starr, vice-chairman of the Electric Power Research Institute and a leading member of the TMI Response Committee,* went to Hot Springs, Virginia, to address a Saturday meeting of the Business Council, an organization composed of top executives of some of America's biggest banks and corporations. The council's chairman at the time was Reginald H. Jones, the head of General Electric. The chief executive officers of Bechtel and Exxon, two other leading nuclear companies, served as vice-chairmen. Other council members included David Rockefeller, chairman of Chase Manhattan Bank; Thomas A. Murphy, chairman of General Motors; Walter B. Wriston, chairman of Citibank; and J. Paul Austin, chairman of Coca-Cola.

* The TMI Response Committee was an outgrowth of the TMI Oversight Committee.

Dr. Starr declared to this august collection of American business leaders that "the issue of nuclear power policy is a concern not only to the electric utilities, but has vital impact on the American business community generally. . . . What is at issue is the future availability of sufficient energy supply to permit the production of industrial goods and services under realistic projections of the growth of the national economy." Without nuclear power, the nation would suffer electricity shortages and "undoubtedly slide into a dangerous downward economic spiral." The economy would not grow enough to absorb new workers into the labor force, and the nation's "social fabric could be torn apart" as the disadvantaged took to the streets to press their demands. Starr recounted the new safety initiatives undertaken to assure the public that nuclear power is a safe and controllable technology, but lamented that even these steps might not be sufficient to turn the tide "unless the public is convinced of the need for nuclear power." For that, the "active, high-priority support of the business community" is needed. "The ultimate blow will land on you," Starr warned before closing with the entreaty "Will you help us?" Council chairman Reginald Jones thought so much of Starr's speech that he made hundreds of copies of it for his many associates throughout the upper levels of American business and government. In his gracious thank-you letter Jones congratulated Starr: "The case for nuclear (in the *national* best interest) has never been made more soundly or more clearly in the unavoidably harsh light of reality."

An equally enthusiastic response greeted William Lee, president of Duke Power and, like Starr, a key member of the TMI Response Committee, when he traveled to Wall Street on November 6, 1979, to make the second CEA-arranged presentation to the New York Society of Security Analysts. In fact, the analysts were so engrossed in Lee's message that they remained asking questions for an extra hour past the scheduled 1:30 P.M adjournment. Lee informed the group about NSAC and INPO, as well as the TMI Response Committee's proposal to develop a new form of insurance to protect electric utilities against prolonged nuclear plant shutdowns. He also reviewed the most important of the scores of nuclear information activities that the Committee on Energy Awareness had mounted over the summer. Lee said the CEA-sponsored activity that received the greatest media attention was the "Energy Truth Squad" that trailed radical activists Jane Fonda and Tom Hayden during their fall 1979 national political tour. At each Fonda-Hayden stop, two nuclear spokespersons called a press conference to refute the activists' denunciations of nuclear power and to articulate the CEA message. The CEA also supplied the local utilities with camera-ready ad copy for placement in the local newspapers following a Fonda-Hayden appearance.

Just two days after Lee's November 6 speech, the CEA took another important step when it launched a $700,000 pronuclear national advertising campaign. The CEA placed full-page ads in the *New York Times,* the *Los Angeles Times,* the *Washington Post,* the *Washington Star,* and the *Boston Globe* that asked, "Where Is the Energy to Come From?" A week later, readers of the same papers learned about "What Really Happened At Three Mile Island." Three other ads, on radioactive waste disposal, nuclear-plant radiation emissions, and the need for nuclear power, appeared later that winter, and were reprinted in *Time, Business Week, U.S. News and World Report,* and *US* magazines. The first appeared the day after the fifty-four American hostages were taken in Iran, and the men of the nuclear industry seized the opportunity to emphasize to an outraged and indignant American public how nuclear power could prevent similar humiliations in the future. The industry seemed almost to welcome this new illustration of the dangers of dependence on foreign energy sources. In fact, when the Atomic Industrial Forum was considering to whom it should grant its annual Statesman of the Year award, the Ayatollah Khomeini was suggested only half in jest as the most deserving recipient. During the spring of 1980, television viewers in certain target areas around the country began to see CEA commercials that featured ominously unflattering camera shots of Khomeini and other Middle East leaders and asked whether Americans really could risk their energy security with such men. "Nuclear power?" asked a gruff masculine voice at the end of the spot. "Yeah—because America needs energy."

The CEA's spring electronic advertising campaign, an internal report boasted, was a "resounding success" and "a precedent-setting achievement." "The populations of 19 markets in six states and Washington, D.C. were exposed to over three weeks of saturated exposure to hard-hitting pro-nuclear ads." In addition, a three-part series on the industry's response to TMI was aired on 151 stations, reaching nearly 10 million viewers. Previously, explained the report, the electronic media were virtually inaccessible to the nuclear industry and other private interests like Mobil and Exxon who wished to affect public policy by sponsoring "even relatively non-controversial messages." Nuclear critics could usually " 'scare' broadcasters into either rejecting pro-nuclear ads or providing free response time by using threats of complaints to the Federal Communications Commission on Fairness Doctrine grounds."

The CEA combined brains with money to get around that obstacle. It notified all target radio and television stations that its two agents—the Smith and Harroff advertising agency and the highly respected Kirkland and Ellis law firm—would provide the stations free counsel on how to handle critics' requests for free air time. The CEA's argument that the pronuclear ads were necessary to correct imbalanced network news coverage of Three Mile Island prevailed in nearly every case. The lesson learned, exulted the CEA's internal report, "is that *the Fairness Doctrine works on behalf of the nuclear industry*" [emphasis in original].

Other parts of the nuclear industry had also taken it upon themselves to inform the public. The most remarkable example was a two-page ad that appeared in the July 31, 1979 issue of the *Wall Street Journal.* "I was the only person injured at Three Mile Island," read the headline above the picture of Dr. Edward Teller, the noted nuclear scientist and father of the H-bomb. Teller had suffered a heart attack following the accident, a result, he claimed, of the twenty-four-hour days he put in refuting the "propaganda that Ralph Nader, Jane Fonda, and their kind" were spreading to frighten an unsuspecting public away from nuclear power. Teller pooh-poohed the idea that the accident had endangered any lives and proclaimed that nuclear power was necessary for the survival of a free society. The credibility of Teller's statement was shaken, however, when NRC Commissioner Peter Bradford wrote the *Journal* a letter refuting many of Teller's claims and pointing out a piercing irony: Dresser Industries, which paid for the Teller ad, was the company that manufactured the valve whose failure led to the accident at Three Mile Island.

The basic message of the Committee on Energy Awareness was that nuclear power is safe and necessary. Even at Three Mile Island, the safety systems had worked and nobody was killed. And the industry was already studying and working to make nuclear power even safer for the future. Meanwhile, in a world filled with uncertainties and threats ranging from the Ayatollah Khomeini to Soviet adventurism, America simply could not eliminate nuclear power from the future energy equation if it was to avoid economic collapse.

Nowhere was this point of view more powerfully articulated than in the keynote speech Robert Kirby, the chief executive at Westinghouse, gave before the November 1979 annual meeting of the Atomic Industrial Forum. That Kirby chose to speak at the AIF meeting himself rather than dispatch a lieutenant as he had done the year before demonstrated the high significance he attached to reviving nuclear power. Kirby appeared on the same opening-day panel as did Senator James McClure, the strongly pronuclear Republican from Idaho. The glib senator warmed up the crowd with some well-placed attacks on the antinuclear forces. Nuclear opponents were an affluent, selfish new class, he charged, that wanted "to limit economic growth so that no one else's advancement will infringe upon their own enjoyment." Conceding that nuclear opponents did have the initiative, McClure nevertheless asserted that "things can be swung to our side" through a combination of factual communication and bold leadership. But "this struggle for nuclear energy cannot be won if nuclear proponents continue to surrender the moral position to our opponents," declared McClure to a long ovation.

The room grew quiet when Kirby stood up to deliver his speech, entitled "The Future of Nuclear Power." Kirby looked older, tougher, and heavier than in his official photographs. Unlike the other panelists, who chatted among themselves or with old friends as the conferees trooped into the St. Francis's huge ballroom, he passed the time staring intently into the crowd, smoking an endless chain of cigarettes, and muttering to himself. His eyes never rested on any one object for very long, and he seemed to be observing the crowd as a group rather than searching out individual faces within it. His mouth was a thin line pulled taut across his face; his hair, the silver-grey color of a ten-cent piece. He wore a three-piece dark blue pin-striped suit and moved deliberately as he approached the microphone.

The hall lights dimmed, and on the screen behind Kirby there appeared the image of a stick man, hanging from a noose and swaying to and fro. Kirby began to speak in a creaky voice that clashed with the rest of his image: "During the Watergate crisis an image was created for the American public of a man hanging—and twisting slowly, slowly in the wind." A global map appeared on the screen as Kirby said, "Today, it is the United States which hangs, hangs in the winds of fortune, held high by a thin line of ships bringing foreign oil to our ports and refineries." A thin white line stretching from the United States to the Middle East, illustrating the fragility of America's energy supplies, was added to the map. "In the 1950s, we left an age of innocence and entered an age of imminent nuclear disaster. In the 1970s, we entered the age of imminent catastrophe. Russian bases and ships are located strategically so that they can cut the bulk of our overseas oil supplies in hours." When he uttered the word "Russian," a blood-red hammer and sickle the size of the Atlantic Ocean exploded onto the screen, blotting out American's oil lifeline. Under today's conditions, continued Kirby, "imposing any moratorium on nuclear power, a source of oil independence, is absolutely ludicrous."

The dramatic introduction was a fitting prelude to the remainder of Kirby's remarks, which outlined clearly and comprehensively a strategy for nudging America back down the nuclear path. The starting assumption was that the United States and the rest of the world need to produce ever greater amounts of energy to assure economic growth; Kirby cited estimates that the world will need nearly two and one-half times as much fuel by the year 2000 as it is consuming today. Growth itself was an unquestioned virtue. For poor nations, Kirby reminded the crowd of affluent American business executives, growth is an escape from poverty; for the United States, it is "the only demonstrated way to continue pursuing the most idealistic and elusive political goals in man's history."

Referring specifically to electricity, Kirby asserted that it will be necessary to more than double present supplies during the next two decades. Oil is too unstable to rely upon for that, and new sources such as solar, geothermal, and wind, according to the Westinghouse boss, remain uneconomical. Coal cannot do the job alone. Even if it could, "We would be foolish as a nation to place all of our electrical eggs in one basket." Although most of the country's electric utilities now possess more electricity-generating capacity than is necesary, Kirby predicted that by the early 1990s these bloated reserve margins will have become much smaller. Because it takes at least a decade to bring a new generating plant on line, Kirby set 1983 as the date by which decisions about new power plants will have to be made. "In the short period between now and then," he told his colleagues, "we have a job to do."

The battle over nuclear power and, ultimately, economic growth is, in Kirby's words, "worthy of the best of us. And we don't have much time to resolve it." Kirby identified the realization "that a second TMI could change the public's reasonable fear into hostility" as the basic lesson that industry must learn from Three Mile

Island. The most pressing immediate need is to act upon that lesson, and Kirby applauded INPO, NSAC, and the other safety initiatives launched by the TMI Response Committee as important steps in that direction. But of equal importance "is the need to inform the public about the positive benefits—in effect the truth—of nuclear power." Kirby acknowledged that critics would portray nuclear power as an imminent source of disaster being impelled by corporate greed. His suggested response to that attack was a repetition, in starker terms, of the major themes embodied in the Committee on Energy Awareness's materials: "The public must be told that it will have to choose . . . between nuclear energy and some tough alternatives. Alternatives like inflation, higher unemployment, no economic growth, and national insecurity." Kirby pointed out that such an "economic slowdown" would blast minorities, women, and youth first and hardest.

With the stakes and options thus neatly arranged, Kirby assigned responsibilities for the fight ahead. Washington should hurry up and solve the problem of radioactive waste disposal. Public officials must make "reasoned judgments" about safety regulations that will "assure safety on one hand and energy availability on the other." The government's constant stream of new safety regulations must stop. The twelve-year licensing process for a nuclear plant could be cut in half, Kirby charged, and public safety would actually be enhanced. The Westinghouse leader closed by urging the entire nuclear industry, and particularly the electric utilities, to renew their faith in nuclear power. "Those who are calling for a national energy program," declared Kirby, "should get one—our way, not theirs."

Kirby's speech was a favorite topic of conversation that night in the plush hospitality suites that Westinghouse, Bechtel, and other industry giants rented as temporary headquarters during the three-day conference. The St. Francis Hotel's thirty-first floor swarmed with activity as executives scurried among the various suites, drinking, seeing old friends, renewing business contacts, and talking shop. At the Bechtel suite, Ashton O'Donnell, the vice-president in charge of Bechtel's nuclear fuels business, could not say enough about Kirby's presentation. "I've never heard the nuclear argument made any better," O'Donnell enthused. "I told Bob afterwards that I thought he should use that speech whenever he gives talks around the country. It included a lot of things that many of us in the industry have been thinking but haven't been able to articulate as well as he did. It's very, very important."

Unlike the Atomic Industrial Forum's annual conference in San Francisco three months before, its conference on "Nuclear Power and the Public" in Boston in February 1980 was not announced to the press. This was a working conference, where participants talked freely about what communication tactics had worked for them and what future directions should be followed. Its purpose was to teach the nuclear industry's small army of public relations officials how to convince a freshly skeptical American public of the safety and necessity of nuclear power.

The need for such instruction was demonstrated by an incident I happened to witness en route to the conference. Coincidentally, I had chosen the same flight from Washington to Boston as the entire Atomic Industrial Forum staff and found myself assigned to sit right next to two of the AIF's male staffers. I did not hear how the exchange began, but at one point the younger staffer got involved in a discussion with a young woman seated cross the aisle in the row ahead of him. She didn't like nuclear power and was especially concerned about the cancer-causing effects of nuclear radiation. The young man's response was straight out of the public relations textbooks: he was gently assertive without being threatening and projected the impression of being open to differences of opinion. "Well, either I'm confused or someone's confused," he replied, "because the overwhelming weight of all the respected scientific opinion that I've read concludes that nuclear power is not a great cancer risk. In fact, did you know that coal-fired electricity stations actually let off more radiation than nuclear plants?" "Oh, really," the young woman murmured, through a polite smile. Apparently sensing the futility of further discussion, she turned away, unconvinced, and busied herself with a magazine. Her quick, graceful exit left the young nuclear apostle bewildered and disappointed.

Before industry public relations officers could make the nuclear argument to the American public, they first had to understand and believe it themselves. Thus, the two and one-half days of workshops and panels at Boston's Copley Plaza Hotel served as a sort of short course in why nuclear power is safe and necessary and how that message should be communicated. For example, the two safety issues industry officials believe are of greatest concern to Americans—radiation and nuclear waste disposal—were each the subject of individual workshop sessions. At the panel on "Our Role in America's Future," the audience heard Dr. Harvey Brooks, a Harvard professor who cochaired the National Academy of Sci-

ence's prestigious study of America's future energy options, explain
that all collaborators on the study agreed that while conservation
should be the top priority, it could not do the job alone. "Even in
the most drastic conservation strategy, you can't meet the goals of
economic growth without some nuclear energy," he assured the
crowd. Later, right-wing journalist Arnaud de Borchgrave sounded
the alarm about the national security ramifications of Western Europe's growing energy dependence on the Soviet Union. The
United States could protect Europe from Soviet political blackmail,
suggested de Borchgrave, only by defining the Persian Gulf as "a
vital interest of the entire Western Alliance" and embarking on "a
real energy policy" at home that would include dramatically increased reliance on nuclear power.

The conference next focused on the terrain where the battle to
save nuclear power would be fought: American public opinion.
Jonathan Carlson, a young associate at Cambridge Reports, Incorporated, offered a detailed analysis of "What Americans Are Saying" about nuclear power and how the industry should respond.

"I have bad news and I have good news," Carlson began. "The
bad news is that Three Mile Island was an unmitigated public
relations disaster. But the good news is that 1980 offers the chance
to regain the support you lost during TMI." After stating the obvious—that the future of nuclear power is inextricably intertwined
with public opinion—Carlson explained that the reason the industry could hope to regain support was the sharp increase during
1979 in the public's perception of the seriousness of the energy
crisis. "The more seriously people view the crisis, the more willing
they are to bite the bullet," said Carlson. "Even many opponents
of nuclear favor construction 'if it is needed.' That phrase, of course,
is a key factor in the whole debate. . . . Many Americans clearly do
not expect to need nuclear because [they think] solar is just around
the corner."

A chorus of groans went up and many in the audience dejectedly
shook their heads when Carlson reported that "more than one in
six Americans expect solar to be the dominant [energy] source in
ten years." According to Carlson, these people tend to be the same
ones who oppose nuclear power. To prove the point, he offered a
detailed breakdown by income level, age group, sex, race, education, religion, political ideology, geographical area, and urban/rural
residence of the supporters and opponents of nuclear energy. Men
are much more likely than women to approve of nuclear power

plants; women opposed them by 46 to 33 percent margin. The eighteen-to-thirty-five age group opposed nuclear, while older respondents favored it. Those making $25,000 or more annual salary clearly supported nuclear, while views were mixed among those in lower-income brackets. Blacks tended to oppose nuclear, although more than one in three replied that he or she "didn't know" whether more nuclear plants should be built. Opposition was strongest in the Northeast region of the United States; support was most evident in the Pacific region and the South.

Three Mile Island's impact on public attitudes about nuclear power, Carlson reported, was major and negative: "About four in ten Americans are less favorable to nuclear development as a result of TMI." The initial reaction to the accident, measured in April 1979, grew even more negative when the Kemeny Commission's initial findings were released later that summer. But in the fall sentiment began to swing back, and by the end of the year it appeared that nuclear power had lost only about 8 percent of the support it enjoyed previous to the accident. However, the "hard-core" opposition to nuclear power plants rose from 10 percent to 20 percent of those surveyed, and remained constant throughout the year.

Americans who opposed nuclear power did so because they feared its dangers, especially those of cancer-causing radiation leaks and radioactive waste disposal, said Carlson. Those who supported nuclear emphasized the country's need for energy. "The issue hinges on the trade-off between safety versus the need for energy. . . . Almost 30 percent of those who in theory oppose nuclear power will accept more plant construction if they believe that the country needs the power." Carlson termed that "the bottom line" on Americans' views about nuclear power.

In closing, Carlson emphasized that nuclear power was an issue that would be decided in the public arena and that "the antis will be out there against you." Westinghouse executive Jean-Claude Poncelet later briefed the audience on exactly "What to Expect from the Antis" in the coming years. In listing the strengths of nuclear opponents, Poncelet acknowledged they enjoyed high public credibility, were "sincere and highly motivated," followed a strategy that was "well-thought-through and effective," and were "well-organized" and "well-funded." He went on to predict that the antinuclear movement would form coalitions with peace, welfare, and other liberal groups in an "attempt to create the reality,

or perception, of a 'people's movement' against nuclear power";
would "increasingly draw a link between nuclear power and nuclear war"; would "become more explicitly anticorporate" and attempt to halt "the flow of capital to nuclear power projects through
actions directed at banks, insurance companies, pension funds,
etc."; would "continue extensive lobbying and litigation activities
at both state and federal levels"; and would, through increased
international cooperation and actions, "attempt to create the
impression of a 'worldwide movement' against nuclear power."

Nevertheless, Poncelet assured his audience, "the antinuclear
movement, as such, must fail." Many nuclear opponents regarded
the Three Mile Island accident as "the beginning of the end for
nuclear power," and this had led them to adopt an attitude of
"arrogance, cockiness, and . . . a self-righteous sense of self-confi-
dence" that the industry could use against them. "Perhaps the
major weakness of the opposition," said Poncelet, "is their refusal
to compromise, attesting to an intolerant and elitist attitude." He
argued that this inflexibility would not only turn the general public,
politicians, and the press against the movement eventually but
would also allow the industry to anticipate and deflate the movement's planned actions and arguments in advance.

Poncelet concluded by appealing to the industry's pride and
warning it against becoming its own worst enemy: "What would
do us in, so to speak, in this battle over nuclear power is not the
actions of the antinuclear movement, but more so our very own
actions. . . . For nuclear power has a very bleak future if indeed
we do not get our own house in order and utilize and manage this
technology with the standards of quality and excellence that we
cherish and are fully capable of upholding, and if we do not properly inform and respond to the valid concerns and questions of the
general public."

Exactly how the industry planned to communicate with the public was outlined by a panel chaired by Paul Turner, the AIF vice-
president and key architect of the industry's post–Three Mile Island public relations effort. When Turner introduced Boston Edison president Frank Staszesky to inform the audience about the
Institute for Nuclear Power Operations, Staszesky was pleased to
note, "I don't recognize many of the people in this audience. That
means there is a new generation ready to pick up the cudgels and
communicate our message. And I want to say that you people have
the most important job in our industry during the next two years."

The new director of the Committee on Energy Awareness, William Perkins, spoke next and brought the conferees up to date on what the CEA had been doing over the eleven months since Three Mile Island. Perkins, who worked for Paul Turner as an AIF communications specialist before taking on the CEA job, began by offering his opinion that Three Mile Island "was mostly a public acceptance disaster," not a technological, life-threatening disaster. When Perkins quoted the lead Walter Cronkite used on his broadcast the evening of March 28, 1979—"We are faced with the remote but very real possibility of a nuclear reactor meltdown"—the crowd groaned its frustration and displeasure at what it saw as Cronkite's sensationalistic distortion of the facts. After reviewing the CEA's past achievements, Perkins disclosed that in the future "our top priority is to reach some specific groups who have a definite stake in adequate energy." The first group was women. The plan for changing the opinions of women, a plurality of whom are opposed to further nuclear development, called for meeting with female editors of women's magazines and the "life-style" sections in daily newspapers and impressing upon them the connection between the availability of cheap and plentiful energy, a dynamic, growing economy, and women's progress towards equality. Similar reminders were to be offered at local women's group meetings across the country, perhaps by members of Nuclear Energy Women, a group created by the Atomic Industrial Forum and headquartered in its Bethesda, Maryland office. Perkins said that the CEA was developing other ideas for reaching blacks, senior citizens, and Hispanics, but cautioned that the industry must not expect immediate benefits. "These programs are invisible," he said. "We won't see their results anytime soon, but they are important and worthwhile."

Another top priority was "trying to place pro-nuclear speakers in situations where they can relate to the public without the filter of editors and reporters." To circumvent normal coverage from a medium that the industry believed was by and large unfair and negatively biased, the CEA planned to place eight to ten radiation experts on daily talk shows geared to housewives and to develop television commercials presenting the arguments for nuclear power. A second level of CEA communications work would be aimed at shoring up support for nuclear power within the labor unions, encouraging the creation and blossoming of local nuclear advocacy groups across the country, and pressing the nuclear case within the mass media. The latter involved plans to conduct more editorial roundtables with the media chiefs who determine what is and is not news in America, and attempts to place more pronuclear articles in major publications.

Following Perkins, Thomas Saunders of California's Pacific Gas and Electric Company spoke about his company's fantastic successes on Nuclear Energy Education Day, an event the AIF's Nuclear Energy Women sponsored on October 18, 1979, to promote public acceptance of nuclear energy. Nuclear Energy Education Day—with its conveniently appropriate acronym, NEED—received front-page coverage in the AIF's *Press INFO* newsletter, which claimed that over 100,000 people across the country had attended NEED coffees, brunches, rallies, and other social events. There had even been a thirty-five-mile energy jog in California, in which the runners wore T-shirts that proclaimed "Nukes Keep America Running." The press release painted a picture of a massive, spontaneous outpouring of popular support for nuclear energy; but if the northern California example on which Mr. Saunders confidentially reported to the AIF conference is indicative of a broader trend, it appears that much of the public response actually was orchestrated by private companies with very direct interests in nuclear energy.

Saunders appears to be in his late fifties, old enough to have a couple of grandchildren who would delight in his chipper optimism and twinkling smile. He has a long history of involvement in Democratic Party politics in California, having managed successful campaigns in 1962 for Governor Pat Brown and in 1964 for President Lyndon Johnson. It was easy to see how he did so well in politics. Very much at home in front of an audience, Saunders immediately put everyone in the Copley Plaza's large ballroom at ease by joking that he came from California, where the biggest obstacle to nuclear power was the Abalone Alliance, an antinuclear group "which someone described as forty people, a press list, and a rock band." In his role as senior representative in Pacific Gas and Electric's Governmental and Public Affairs Department, Saunders was the senior official most directly responsible for organizing his company's NEED activities. He proved his communications expertise that afternoon.

Saunder's film slides were drawn in a gay, multicolored, inviting style and made their points subtly, usually through the charming human characters they featured. But the story embodied in his cartoons and accompanying narrative was rather less endearing. It told how a group of private corporations led by PG&E spent a good deal of time and money creating and developing what was intended to be perceived as an independent, popular movement supporting nuclear energy. According to Saunders, a woman in the General Electric Company's Public Affairs Department named Sara Morabito was the one who first realized and convinced PG&E's top management of the tremendous public relations potential of NEED. Saunders spoke of Morabito with fatherly affection, saying "she was an inspiration to us all." Deciding that it needed help with financing, PG&E management searched out others likely to support the concept of NEED. Before long, the biggest corporations and banks in California had signed on. These included, according to Saunders, not only nuclear industry leaders General Electric and Bechtel but also Kaiser Aluminum.

The corporations quickly decided to establish Citizens for Adequate Energy, a group that could organize local citizens more credibly the corporations and could continue operating past the October 18 Nuclear Energy Education Day. They were joined in this endeavor by three more giant corporations: Bank of America, Levi Strauss, and the Wells Fargo Bank. Saunders emphasized that Citizens for Adequate Energy was not technically a grass-roots group, since it was paid for with corporate funds, started with leadership from the top, and didn't expect to pick up bona fide grass-roots support until later, after NEED. "We're working very hard to establish local chapters," Saunders told the audience, "because, believe me, they have about eight thousand times more credibility with their peers than some voice out of San Francisco or Washington."

The corporate backers all agreed that Citizens for Adequate Energy should espouse, not an exclusively pronuclear "line," but rather a more balanced energy approach emphasizing conservation and the need for adequate energy to maintain current living standards. Supplying "adequate" energy required utilizing all possible energy sources, including nuclear. It was also agreed that Pacific Gas and Electric was best equipped to handle the preparation of all literature and activities for NEED, since it was in closer contact with and had a better feel for the public to be reached. "Once those decisions were reached," said Saunders, "it was all downhill."

"For about six weeks, NEED was the number one priority for PG&E management," Saunders related. Employees were asked to serve as hosts or discussion leaders for the many informal gatherings that would take place on NEED. Over 840 PG&E workers volunteered; the company provided fourteen three-hour training sessions, complete with sample questions and answers and speeches, in order to prepare them for the endeavor. "The training sessions had their own reward in terms of corporate morale," exclaimed Saunders. The 20,000 guest kits that PG&E prepared for employees to hand out at the various NEED gatherings were snapped up very quickly. Saunders made special mention of how the materials inside the kits, such as the Citizens for Adequate Energy membership cards and the *Energy News* tabloid, were professionally produced—slick and good-looking.

All this preparation made for a fantastic success on Nuclear Energy Education Day. Over 1,400 gatherings—more than one-third of the total number nationwide—took place within the PG&E service area alone. More than 20,000 members of the public attended, and Citizens for Adequate Energy picked up hundreds of new members. As for future plans, Saunders confided, "we'll go public with our backing of the group when we have twenty-five to thirty companies involved. We can say that the anti side is financed by government grants and we're financed by the people who use energy."

A "PEOPLE'S INITIATIVE"

The election of Ronald Reagan and a significantly more conservative Congress in November 1980 did not cause the nuclear industry to relax its public relations efforts. American Energy Week (AEW), an ambitious national education program masterminded months in advance by CEA executives, was held as planned on March 15–21, 1981. AEW's red, white, and blue promotional literature described the U.S. oil import bill as "a $100 million 'tea tax' which we must free ourselves from just as our founding fathers did in 1776." It portrayed conservation as a necessary, well-intentioned, but inadequate step towards that goal; a complete solution required drastically increased production of nuclear power, coal, domestic oil and natural gas, and other U.S. energy sources.

The primary organizing goal of the AEW was to get millions of Americans to sign a "Declaration of Energy Independence" that charged, "The excessive American dependence on imported oil . . . jeopardizes the independence and welfare of our nation and the well-being of each citizen," and called for "eliminating energy waste and encouraging development of all our energy resources," including nuclear power. AEW planners convinced the U.S. Jaycees, the General Federation of Women's Clubs, and other national organizations to urge their local affiliates to conduct signature drives. Westinghouse sponsored a signature-gathering contest among 125 energy advocacy groups.

A second AEW focus was the congressionally mandated National Energy Education Day, March 20. Between 8,000 and 10,000 elementary and secondary schools across the country participated in the event; energy fairs, exhibits, and workshops were held to "promote greater community awareness about energy." The 1,400-member Shopping Center Network supported AEW by distributing its own energy quiz to an estimated 4 million shoppers visiting three hundred malls nationwide. Scores of other organizations, ranging from the U.S. Chamber of Commerce and the Shell Oil Company to the Alliance to Save Energy and the United Methodist Church, organized their own AEW programs. The Conference Board, the New York-based business-advocacy research institute, educated opinion leaders with a series of six all-day energy briefings in Atlanta, San Francisco, Detroit, Denver, Boston, and Dallas. And in New York City, General Electric, Consolidated Edison, and the Power Authority of the State of New York hosted a luncheon at the Plaza Hotel on March 19 for some 250 of New York's most influential business executives, politicians, labor unionists, and other opinion leaders. That high-powered group heard James Edwards, Reagan's new Energy Secretary, deliver the administration's first major policy speech about energy.

In all of its promotional literature, AEW described itself as a "people's initiative." It was, in fact, by executive director Jack Betts's own admission, a spin-off organization of the Committee for Energy Awareness. The idea of organizing an American Energy Week was first raised at a CEA planning meeting in the fall of 1979. "There was a group of us sitting around talking," Betts recalled, "and we began to see that the problem we were fighting was much broader than just the electrical industry. Our concern was to dispel the idea that just because there aren't gasoline lines anymore, there is no longer an energy crisis. Energy needed to have a much higher priority in our nation's thinking, and to bring that about we needed to form a broader coalition, outside the electrical industry."

The first need of any fledgling organization is money. According to Betts, who immediately came on to help direct AEW, it got its start-up funds—$100,000, to be precise—from the nuclear industry's three main public affairs outfits: the CEA, the Atomic Industrial Forum, and the Edison Electric Institute. To make future

corporate contributions tax-deductible, AEW incorporated as a nonprofit organization. Its new president was Paul Turner, the AIF's
vice-president for public affairs. Treasurer was Jack Young, Turner's counterpart at EEI. Executive vice-president was Don Mc-
Cammond, formerly vice-president for public affairs at the heavily
nuclear-dependent Virginia Electric Power Company. Senior vice-
president was Jack Betts. The four men had worked together before; each was a member of the steering committee that set policy
for the CEA.

The AEW's fund-raising strategy was a model of efficiency and
common sense. "We figured out which cities had the biggest clus-
ters of *Fortune* 500 company headquarters, and then we planned
fund-raising lunches for those cities," explained CEA staffer Ellen
Lepper. Jack Betts added, "We'd get a chief executive officer of a
major company who was interested in our subject to host the luncheon, and he'd invite the various other leading companies in the
city to attend. We'd get anywhere from 40 to 150 people at these
lunches, and either Don McCammond or I would give a talk explaining American Energy Week."

The luncheon in Pittsburgh, for example, was hosted by W. H.
Krome George, chairman and chief executive officer of Alcoa, and
Robert Kirby, chief executive officer of Westinghouse, a pairing
that perfectly symbolized the overarching appeal of AEW's pro-
energy (rather than simply pronuclear) message. Westinghouse, the
nation's leading nuclear reactor manufacturer, was primarily an
energy producer, while Alcoa, by virtue of its electricity-intensive
aluminum operations, ranked as a leading energy consumer. Their
guests at the fund-raiser included representatives from all sorts of
Fortune 500 companies, including U.S. Steel, the Mellon Bank,
Gulf Oil, PPG Industries, and the H. J. Heinz Company.

Luncheons were held in over a dozen cities. In Cleveland, the
Chessie Railroad System and the conglomerate TRW were the
hosts. The Crocker Bank coordinated things in Los Angeles, Chicago Bridge and Iron in Chicago, and LTV in Dallas. In Atlanta, it
was Continental Telephone. Duke Power and Carolina Power and
Light, two heavily nuclear electric utilities, sent out invitations in
Charlotte, North Carolina. No luncheon was held in New York
City—"New York's impossible unless you plan six months in advance," explained Don McCammond—but Ebasco, a nuclear construction firm, and Merrill Lynch did send letters encouraging their
many corporate neighbors to support American Energy Week.

American Energy Week marked a second stage in the nuclear

industry's comeback effort. For the industry was now augmenting its previous outreach to the business community and its mass advertising with political organizing and coalition building at the grass-roots and national levels. This was a new departure, aimed directly at the source of the antinuclear movement's strength and vitality. Industry officials believed, rightly or wrongly, that the opposition derived most of its political strength from millions of Americans who shared with it nothing more than a vague, phobic fear of nuclear power. The average citizen simply did not buy the movement's overall political philosophy. If projects like AEW could persuade these average Americans that nuclear power was crucial to their standard of living, the industry would be a big step closer to politically isolating and emasculating its opponents.

The ultimate justification the men of the Atomic Brotherhood advance for risking the hazards of nuclear power is what they call the nuclear imperative. The immediate imperative is to protect the United States from the string of calamities that would follow another cutoff of oil imports. In the medium term—say, over the next two decades—nuclear power is said to be necessary to avoid an energy shortage that in this country would encourage stagnation and cause special suffering for the poor and working classes, and overseas would condemn countless millions to continued misery and hopelessness. In the long run, nuclear power is held to be essential to human progress. Nuclear power is the most worthy candidate to replace petroleum because it is potentially the most efficient and abundant energy source available.

The men of the Atomic Brotherhood believe profoundly that preparing for the nuclear imperative is the right thing to do, that they are acting in the common good. There is of course nothing new about an elite proclaiming that its own interests are identical with those of the society as a whole; the tactic has been central to the domination of the many by the few for centuries. But it may well prove difficult for the industry to convince the American public of this new logic, for there is growing evidence, often gathered by traditional supporters of nuclear energy, that the United States could in fact move away from dependence on nuclear power without causing energy shortages and human suffering. Indeed, such a move might well improve the U.S. economy, environment, and national security. (The case against nuclear power is even more compelling in poor countries, which lack the industrial infrastructure and finances nuclear power requires.)

Nuclear power in 1980 provided just 3 percent of this country's total energy, ranking it below even firewood as an energy contributor. The 3 percent figure derives from the fact that nuclear fission, unlike more flexible energy sources such as coal or oil, can produce only electricity. Since electricity amounts to about one-third of the country's total energy consumption, and nuclear plants generate 12 percent of all U.S. electricity, nuclear's share of total energy equals 3 percent. The 3 percent figure hardly qualifies nuclear as the "major" energy source that its backers term it and, in fact, casts doubt on their assertion that widespread energy shortages would result from its elimination.

The argument that nuclear power will protect America from OPEC strangulation, while it probably appeals to many Americans on a gut level, is simply at odds with the facts. *Energy Future,* the best-selling analysis of America's future energy options produced by the Energy Project of the Harvard Business School, states emphatically that "nuclear power offers no solution to the problem of America's growing dependence on imported oil for the rest of this century." Nuclear is prevented from ever being able to save much oil by two simple facts: very little of the oil the United States consumes (under 10 percent) is used to make electricity; and, despite the 1970s oil-price explosion, oil and gas still run vehicles, furnaces, and factories far more cheaply than nuclear-generated electricity could. According to the American Petroleum Institute, oil and gas supplied 73 percent of total U.S. energy in 1980. Even if every oil-fired power plant in the country were torn down and nuclear plants erected in their place, this figure would only fall to 67 percent. (The savings would actually be considerably less, because the type of oil that would be displaced by the nuclear plants, a gooey substance known as residual oil, is too "heavy" to be diverted to other uses such as home heating or gasoline for automobiles and would, therefore, go to waste.)

The only remaining hope for nuclear power displacing significant amounts of oil is substituting nuclear-generated electricity for oil in industrial processes where electric power has not been heavily used previously. But the price of oil would have to rise to $100 a barrel before such a nuclear trade-off would make economic sense, and that calculation does not take into account the near-certainty that the cost of nuclear electricity will continue to climb faster than the inflation rate in the years to come. Finally, even if nuclear power *could* save us lots of oil, it would be quite a few years before those savings could be realized. It now takes twelve years to license and build a nuclear plant. If, after declaring a national energy emergency, the President and the Congress gambled on safety and cut the process in half, it would still be at least six years before any additional nuclear plants could replace the oil stations.

Quicker, easier, and cheaper escapes from continued dependence on foreign oil exist, and are already being pursued. Conservation has traditionally been associated with an austere, back-to-the-caves life-style. Recently, the idea has been repackaged as "increasing energy productivity." Either way, it amounts to the same common-sense notion: being more efficient in how we use energy and thus getting more end-use, or work, out of the same amount of fuel.

The most forceful and compelling advocates of increasing energy efficiency reside in the business world itself. None other than the Harvard Business School has concluded that conservation is the "key energy source" to meet future U.S. and world energy needs. *Energy Future*, the school's recent publication, stated that conservation "could perhaps 'supply' up to 40 percent of America's current energy usage." That is ten times larger than nuclear's present contribution. Not coincidentally, *Energy Future* assigns nuclear power a marginal role at best in the country's future energy picture. "There is simply no reasonable possibility for 'massive contributions' from nuclear power for at least the rest of the twentieth century," writes Harvard economist Irvin C. Bupp.

The government's Council on Environmental Quality (CEQ) concluded in a 1979 study cheerfully entitled *The Good News About Energy* that the U.S. economy could operate on 30 to 40 percent less energy without any reduction in economic growth or human comfort. CEQ Chairman Charles Warren, in announcing the study, said that "with a determined national effort to conserve energy, we can do well, indeed prosper, on much less energy than most people imagine." While many previous analyses had estimated that the United States would more than double its energy consumption by the end of the century, the CEQ study found that, by increasing energy productivity, the country could still have a healthy, expanding economy in the year 2000 while using only about 10 to 15 percent more energy than is used today. Not only would increased energy efficiency relieve the pressure on the environment and allow the United States to cut petroleum imports from what they otherwise would have been, but it would also spur economic growth: "Instead of investing an ever increasing share of funds in new energy production facilities, we can adopt less costly conservation options, and in the process make capital available for more socially useful and job-producing investments." The CEQ study added that conservation would "buy the time needed for the introduction of preferable renewable energy alternatives."

Throughout its history, the nuclear industry has claimed that the atom provides cheap, clean, and safe energy. The Three Mile Island accident forced the official industry line to shift to "We need nuclear energy—like it or not." Within two years of the accident, the Committee for Energy Awareness had already communicated that new message to millions of Americans. And that was just a beginning. In May 1982 Georgia Power executive Robert Scherer, chairman of the board of the Committee for Energy Awareness, asked utility industry leaders to support a nuclear public relations campaign "far beyond" current efforts. "There is no reason to be defensive about nuclear power," Scherer told his colleagues. "It is not the technology that has faded but the country's vision of it. . . . Coca-Cola spends $100 million a year to prove 'Coke Is It.' We can spend $30 million to $40 million to prove nuclear power is essential to our well-being." But, in fact, it is not the industry but electricity consumers who will pay for the massive national campaign of pronuclear television commercials Scherer envisions. The CEA admitted at a January 1983 press conference that $21 million of the first $25 million funds it received came from utility companies' rate bases. The industry's far greater reliance on the powerful mass medium of television will, however, be balanced by continuing local efforts across the country to build grass-roots support for nuclear power. Industry planners are realistic enough to know that even this greatly expanded public relations offensive will take years to bear fruit, but that does not discourage them. Winning back public support for nuclear power is, as one industry official concedes, "a long-haul job."

9

Washington:
Creator, Betrayer ... Savior?

> You know, we Jeffersonian democrats have great
> faith in the common man. More fun with the com-
> mon woman, but great faith in the common man.
> We'll get the right kind of laws.
>
> GORDON HURLBERT,
> *President,*
> *Westinghouse Power Systems Company*

"We are now bullish on nuclear power," Theodore Stern, executive vice-president of Westinghouse's nuclear operations, exulted soon after the 1980 election. It was not hard to see why. The men of the industry needed nothing less than the government's full support if their comeback effort was to succeed, and now that Ronald Reagan was President they seemed certain to get it. The events of the 1970s had given the executives a new appreciation of how crucial federal support had always been to their industry. After four years of Jimmy Carter, the fact that a true friend of nuclear power was now the most powerful man in Washington did much to boost the executives' spirits and to inspire them for the difficult struggle ahead. As General Electric vice-president Bertram Wolfe explained, "It's a helluva lot more pleasant now that we have a guy in the White House who philosophically agrees with us." The executives felt they could trust Reagan, for he was of their world and viewed things more or less as they did. He would not abandon them when the going got tough; his support for nuclear power was genuine, enthusiastic, ideological.

The new President had pledged during the campaign to help revive nuclear power, and he lost no time in fulfilling his promise. Nuclear energy was the only major program, besides the military, that Reagan completely spared during the first year of his campaign

to reduce federal spending. While cutting $40 billion primarily
from such social programs as public housing and food stamps,
Reagan raised the fiscal year 1982 budget for nuclear energy 36
percent, to $1.6 billion. Meanwhile, funding was sharply reduced
in every other Department of Energy program. Money for solar
energy was slashed 67 percent, support for conservation 75 percent.
The administration lobbied hard for $240 million to continue work
on the Clinch River breeder reactor, and allocated a whopping
$500 million for long-term breeder research.

President Reagan went on to announce a nonproliferation policy
that tacitly endorsed the nuclear industry's fundamental criticism
of the previous Carter policy: that restricting U.S. manufacturers'
exports of nuclear reactors and fuel actually encouraged the spread
of nuclear weapons. Reagan planned to regain influence over proliferation by "re-establishing the position of United States as the
world's prime nuclear supplier." Towards that end, restrictions on
exports to such supposedly trustworthy nations as Switzerland and
Japan would be relaxed. Policymakers would instead concentrate
on limiting transfers of nuclear materials to those countries Washington suspected were aiming to build a bomb. This would be
accomplished partly through establishing "better cooperation
among nuclear-supplier countries."

More good news for the industry came in October 1981 when
Secretary of Energy James Edwards delivered for President Reagan what executives had long said they needed more than anything else: a strong presidential endorsement of the safety and
necessity of nuclear power, along with policies designed to ensure
that its potential was realized. Reagan's statement avoided any
mention of the Three Mile Island accident and the rising public
opposition to nuclear power. Rather, it focused on nuclear's economic potential, calling it "essential" to the nation's energy future
and blaming its current difficulties on government meddling in the
marketplace. "The federal government has created a regulatory
environment that is forcing many utilities to rule out nuclear power
as a source of new generating capacity. . . . Nuclear power has become entangled in a morass of regulations that do not enhance
safety but that do cause extensive licensing delays and economic
uncertainty."

Reagan's proposed solution was to "streamline" the licensing
process so that nuclear plants could be built in six to eight years
rather than ten to fourteen. Electric utilities would then find it far
easier to afford new plants; and Reagan's tax bill, already signed

into law, would help them attract the risk capital needed to finance them. He promised to remove two more "regulatory impediments" to nuclear development by "lifting the indefinite ban which previous Administrations placed on commercial reprocessing activities" and ordering the Energy Department to "proceed swiftly" to build a nuclear waste repository. The only major obstacle to nuclear power's commercial recovery not directly addressed in Reagan's statement was the decline in U.S. electricity-demand growth; but administration policymakers assumed this problem would take care of itself once their economic policies had propelled the American economy into a fresh period of sustained growth.

Reagan's bold actions seemed to re-establish a unity of approach between the government and corporate wings of the Atomic Brotherhood that had not existed since the days of the Nixon presidency and the old Atomic Energy Commission. Industry executives were understandably pleased about the rapprochement, yet they remained cautious about the future. After all, it would take even a Ronald Reagan some time to reverse the momentum created by previous federal nuclear policies. And some executives wondered whether even Reagan's program was sufficiently generous to make nuclear power commercially viable again.

These concerns faded into the background, however, when word leaked out in the fall of 1981 that the Reagan administration was seriously considering a step that industry men feared would completely undo any progress they might otherwise make. The government needed vast new quantities of plutonium for the thousands of nuclear warheads Reagan wanted built over the coming years, but its traditional supply sources were drying up. Military planners at the Department of Energy suggested that the government obtain the additional plutonium by reprocessing the waste products of commercial nuclear power plants. In theory, the proposal would help the industry as well as the government, since it would get rid of the spent fuel accumulating at power plants around the country, but executives opposed it because they feared it would ignite massive new public opposition to nuclear power. Government officials countered that the waste-into-weapons scheme might be required on grounds of national security.

Thus after less than a year of the Reagan presidency, the newly forged, still fragile sense of unity between the government and the nuclear industry was already in danger of dissolving. And the cause of the difficulty was the sudden reappearance of the two basic contradictions that had troubled the Atomic Brotherhood since the end of World War II: the organic link between nuclear power and nuclear weapons, and the closely related conflict between Washington's view of nuclear energy as primarily a tool of foreign policy and the industry's view of it as a commodity to be bought and sold for a profit.

THE MEN IN CHARGE

The key nuclear-power policy positions within the Reagan administration were without exception filled with men either drawn directly from the nuclear industry or very sympathetic to its plight. This was in keeping with the philosophy Alfred S. Bloomingdale, multimillionaire Diner's Club founder and old personal friend of Ronald Reagan, articulated while serving on Reagan's transition team in November 1980: "Running the government is like running General Motors. It's twice General Motors or three times General Motors, but it's General Motors. . . . What we are doing is just trying to find the best guy for the job—the ones we'd hire for our own business."

But politics being what it is, exceptions were inevitably made. James Edwards, the man Ronald Reagan appointed Secretary of the Energy Department, appears to be such an exception. What background Edwards had in energy he had gained between 1974 and 1978 while serving as governor of South Carolina. The Savannah River facility, a key part of the Energy Department's nuclear weapons production chain, was located in South Carolina; so were eight conventional nuclear power plants and the abandoned commercial reprocessing plant at Barnwell. James Edwards used to brag that South Carolina was "the world's nuclear energy capital." Such outspoken support of nuclear power made him attractive to Ronald Reagan, as did Edwards's philosophical preference for a "free market" solution to the nation's energy problems. Appointing Edwards would also allow Reagan to placate powerful Southerners in Congress, notably Senator Strom Thurmond.

But before Edwards had been Secretary of Energy for a month, other Reagan administration officials were questioning his qualifications and competence, complaining that his expertise in energy matters was limited strictly to nuclear power, and leaking to the press unflattering information apparently intended to force his resignation. Edwards angered State Department officials, for example, when he sent a message of congratulations to the Saudi Arabian oil minister, Ahmed Zaki Yamani, after the Saudis persuaded OPEC to adopt a unified—and higher—$34 a barrel crude-oil price. As one high-level State Department official fumed, "It isn't the traditional role of the U.S. Energy Secretary to congratulate OPEC for raising our prices."

Controversy again swirled around Edwards after he remarked to a reporter that he would like to "get rid of these strident voices" that are blocking nuclear energy development, because "subversive elements are using these people." Expressing a view remarkably similar to that of many nuclear executives, Edwards went on to assert, "There are a lot of people who would like to do to us economically what no military force in the world could do: bring us to our knees [by halting nuclear power and other forms of energy]." The Soviets, Edwards warned, are "building these [nuclear] installations as fast as they can."

Edwards claimed he did not want to be labeled a "nuclear person," but then selected for his deputy secretary (Energy's number two post) W. Kenneth Davis, a vice-president at the Bechtel Corporation, the world's leading nuclear construction firm.* Davis had begun his nuclear career in the 1950s working for the Atomic Energy Commission, where he quickly rose to become the AEC's director of reactor development. He held that influential post from 1954 to 1958, an especially critical time when the AEC was determining the future course of reactor development. The knowledge and experience Davis gained at the AEC made him extremely valuable to firms hoping to enter the nuclear business, and in 1958 Bechtel hired him away to head its fledgling nuclear division. He remained with Bechtel for the next twenty-two years, while also serving terms as president of the Atomic Industrial Forum and vice-president of the National Academy of Engineers. He actually came to the Reagan group before his future boss Edwards did— Davis was a key adviser on energy and nonproliferation policy to the Reagan transition team—and Edwards's poor performance once in office reinforced the impression that Davis was the real power behind the throne.

Davis's domination of the Department of Energy put former top officials of Bechtel in control of all three Cabinet positions most central to nuclear power and national security policy. Caspar Weinberger, formerly Bechtel's top lawyer (as well as Richard Nixon's Secretary of Health, Education, and Welfare), was Ronald Reagan's

---

* The man Edwards selected to do the Energy Department's long-term energy planning was J. Hunter Chiles. Before becoming director of the department's Office of Policy, Planning, and Analysis (a position one step below Kenneth Davis's), Chiles was the top market analyst for the Power Systems Division of Westinghouse.

Secretary of Defense. George Schultz, who had been president of
Bechtel for eight years before Reagan asked him in July 1982 to
replace the resigning Alexander Haig, was Secretary of State.

Domination of government policymaking by big business is an
old story in the United States, but rarely if ever has a single company achieved the extraordinary control that Bechtel gained within
the Reagan administration.* Political cartoonists lampooned the
Bechtel takeover (one cartoon printed during Schultz's confirmation hearings portrayed the White House with a sign on the front
lawn reading "A Subsidiary of the Bechtel Corporation"), and such
publications as *Rolling Stone* criticized it as "an obscene expression of how narrow economic interests dominate our government,"
but the mainstream press and the Congress remained respectfully
silent. When Philip Habib, President Reagan's special Middle East
envoy, also was revealed to be on the Bechtel payroll, Republican
Senator Larry Pressler of South Dakota was the only member of
Congress to demand that Habib resign. The Senate as a whole
voted 97 to 0 to confirm George Schultz as Secretary of State. One
of the few pointed questions asked of Schultz during his confirmation hearings was whether he felt qualified to make U.S. policy
on nuclear nonproliferation, given the fact that nuclear exports
were a major source of business for Bechtel. Schultz's artfully
intimidating response: "If I'm not qualified to deal with that subject, then I'm not qualified to be Secretary of State. You need
somebody else." In other words, yes, Schultz did intend to make
policy. And not surprisingly, the policies set by Schultz and his
fellow Bechtel alumnus Kenneth Davis have been very favorable
to the nuclear power industry and their old company in particular,
as we shall see.

Davis had in fact been widely viewed within Washington energy
circles as the likely successor to James Edwards after Edwards
announced in the summer of 1982 that he would leave the administration to become president of the Medical University of South
Carolina. That likelihood declined sharply, however, after George
Schultz was named Secretary of State in June, reportedly because
President Reagan was reluctant to name a third former top Bechtel
official to the Cabinet. Instead, Reagan chose as his new Secretary
of Energy Donald P. Hodel, a man who was less well known than

---

* Schultz, Weinberger, and Davis were but three in a long line of top U.S. officials
closely linked to Bechtel. Richard Helms, for example, the former CIA director and
ambassador to Iran, was retained as a senior Bechtel consultant in 1979.

Davis but no less predisposed to energy industry interests. Environmentalists and consumers criticized Hodel as "a James Watt clone" because he had served as Watt's right-hand man and undersecretary at the Department of the Interior since Reagan's election. Hodel was from 1972 to 1977 top administrator of the quasi-public Bonneville Power Administration, which coordinates electricity supply in the Pacific Northwest, before founding his own firm, Hodel Associates, Inc., which did consulting work for a number of major western utility companies. He then went on to direct the National Electricity Reliability Council, the utility industry's main research organization, from 1978 to 1980 before joining the Reagan administration. Initial evidence indicates that as Energy Secretary, Hodel will pursue policies similar to those of Edwards and Davis. He will not, however, be aided by Davis, who resigned from the administration in January 1983.

For the other top nuclear job in his administration, the chair of the Nuclear Regulatory Commission, President Reagan chose Nunzio Palladino, head of the Department of Nuclear Engineering at Pennsylvania State University. Palladino had joined Westinghouse immediately after receiving his master's degree in mechanical engineering in 1939. He spent the next twenty years with the company, and was a member of the original group of engineers executive Charles Weaver dispatched to the government's Oak Ridge National Laboratory in 1946 for training to become Westinghouse's "nuclear cadre." Palladino later designed the reactor core for each of the two projects that accounted for Westinghouse's early dominance within the nuclear industry: the *Nautilus* nuclear submarine and the first U.S. power reactor at Shippingport, Pennsylvania. He left Westinghouse in 1959 for Penn State, where he created and built a new Department of Nuclear Engineering. Later in his career, he served as president of the American Nuclear Society and as a member of the Advisory Committee on Reactor Safeguards, which counsels the NRC on technical matters.

The retirement of Commissioner and Acting Chair Joseph M. Hendrie enabled Reagan to fill a second slot on the NRC with Thomas Roberts, the treasurer of Vice-President George Bush's unsuccessful 1980 presidential campaign. From 1969 to 1978 Roberts ran the Southern Boiler and Tank Works, a company for which making steel liners for nuclear-reactor containment buildings constituted 85 percent of total business. Peter Bradford's retirement in 1982 allowed Reagan to appoint a third new commissioner as well: James Asselstine, formerly a Republican aide for the Senate

Committee on Environment and Public Works. The White House hurried Asselstine through his Senate confirmation hearings so that he could participate in a March 1982 NRC vote on an Energy Department proposal to allow work on the Clinch River breeder reactor to begin before permit hearings were held. But Asselstine surprised and disappointed the White House by voting against the proposal. Nevertheless, these appointments should assure an NRC generally sympathetic to industry concerns.

The President himself has been a vocal nuclear advocate since his days as goodwill ambassador for General Electric between 1954 and 1962. Reagan hosted the company's weekly television program, *GE Theatre*, and made hundreds of appearances every year before chambers of commerce, civic clubs, and groups of GE factory workers, where he spoke out against labor unions, government regulation, Social Security, and godless communism. Following his unsuccessful attempt to gain the 1976 Republican Party nomination for President, Reagan kept his name in front of the voters by doing nationally syndicated radio commentaries. His broadcasts about nuclear energy read like industry press releases. Fission, Reagan told listeners, was an "economical, inexhaustible source of electric power" that saved the nation 450 million barrels of imported oil each year and thereby reduced our trade deficit by $6 billion. Consumers paid between $2 and $3 billion less on their electric bills every year thanks to nuclear power. The savings would have been even greater except for the "paperwork and the multitudinous permits required by the government," which unnecessarily added seven or eight years to the process of constructing nuclear plants. Safety was no problem: "Since the first nuclear power plant went on line twenty years ago, there has not been a single nuclear injury. . . . The waste from one nuclear plant in a year would take less storage space than a dining room table. . . . Paper, not nuclear waste, is our real storage problem. The legal work for the Seabrook plant in New Hampshire alone has generated a five-foot shelf of state hearing transcripts." Most of nuclear power's problems were "the result of placard-carrying demonstrators." Although many of these "modern-day Luddites" were sincerely motivated, "their movement is run by strategists who are cynical and not sincere and who have a motive not announced to the ground troops who go out and get arrested." Exactly what that motive was, Reagan did not specify, but he did say that the protesters were "the unwitting victims of Soviet designs" and wondered why they didn't "start some demonstrations in East Germany or Czechoslovakia, or Russia, for that matter."

Reagan's appointments marked a continuation of the traditional practice of staffing the government's nuclear agencies with men who were drawn from or sympathetic to the industry, who appreciated the connection between atomic energy's military and industrial applications, and who grasped the importance of atomic energy to the broader objectives of American economic and foreign policy. Most of those who have held the top jobs over the years—Chairman of the AEC and NRC and Secretary of the Department of Energy and its predecessor organizations—were previously investment bankers, businessmen, lawyers for businessmen, scientists who directed the government's nuclear national laboratories, or trusted high government officials. True members of America's power elite, they have glided from the top of the business and financial world into the most strategic and sensitive agencies of the government and back again, all the while reinforcing a basic unity of outlook that endures long after they themselves have moved on.

Charles W. Duncan, Jr., for example, was president of Coca-Cola, head of his own investment bank, and then deputy secretary of defense before Jimmy Carter appointed him Secretary of Energy in July 1979. The man Duncan replaced, James R. Schlesinger, was in charge of national security programs at the Office of Management and Budget before President Nixon asked him in 1971 to chair the AEC. Schlesinger then went on to fill two more of the government's most powerful and sensitive jobs—CIA director and Secretary of Defense—under President Ford before Carter appointed him Energy Secretary in 1977. Upon leaving the government, Schlesinger became an energy consultant for Lehman Brothers, one of Wall Street's top investment banks. His second in command at the Energy Department, John F. O'Leary, joined the Board of Directors of the General Public Utilities Corporation, owner of the Three Mile Island nuclear facility. Schlesinger's predecessors as U.S. energy czar—Frank G. Zarb, Robert W. Fri, Thomas Sawhill, and William Simon—all had backgrounds in Wall Street investment banking. Three of the five officials who preceded Schlesinger as AEC commissioner also came from the ranks of big business or high finance.

John McCone, AEC chairman from 1958 to 1961, for example, was closely tied to the Bechtel Corporation before taking the AEC job, and upon leaving it he became director of the CIA for John F.

Kennedy. McCone, by his own admission, was the man who in 1970, while a board member of the International Telephone and Telegraph Corporation, communicated to National Security Advisor Henry Kissinger and CIA Director Richard Helms the offer of ITT's chief executive officer, Harold Geneen, to contribute $1 million in company money to help U.S. operatives overthrow the government of President Salvador Allende in Chile.

The nuclear industry and Congress have had their differences over the years, but they have remained close partners through it all because they always agreed on the important things. Theirs has been a long and amiable relationship, based upon mutual generosity and loyalty. Despite the Three Mile Island accident, nuclear power's deteriorating economic performance, and the fact that more than half of all Americans oppose the construction of more nuclear power plants, Congress today remains solidly pronuclear. The average member of Congress votes the industry position seven times out of ten, according to an analysis of ten key 1981 votes by Critical Mass, the antinuclear research group sponsored by Ralph Nader.

Jimmy Carter discovered how loyal Congress was to the industry when he tried to cancel the Clinch River breeder reactor in 1977. As we have seen, Congress funded the project over Carter's known objections, then neutralized his veto with a clever parliamentary procedure that forced Carter to fund the project. Left with no alternative, Carter called nuclear industry leaders to a closed White House meeting and, along with his Energy Secretary, James Schlesinger, offered as a compromise the pledge to build a bigger, better breeder after the 1980 elections. But the executives did not trust Carter to keep his word. They rejected his offer, confident that their traditional relationship with Congress would deliver the funds necessary to complete the project.

David Stockman, President Reagan's federal budget director, also was taught to respect the industry's clout on Capitol Hill. Citing fivefold cost overruns and projections that it would cost taxpayers at least $3.3 billion if it was ever completed, Stockman suggested that Clinch River be deleted from the first Reagan budget in 1981. Stockman believed the administration had to appear even-handed, demanding sacrifices from rich and poor alike, if its effort to reduce federal spending was to succeed. Clinch River seemed the perfect target; even many supporters of nuclear power thought it made no economic sense. "A white elephant," the *Wall*

Street Journal called it. "A colossally mismanaged boondoggle," jeered *Time*. But the White House did not heed Stockman's advice, in his view largely because it feared the wrath of Howard Baker, the Senate majority leader. "It just wasn't worth fighting," Stockman later explained in his candid interview in *The Atlantic*. "[The Reagan economic program] will go nowhere without Baker, and Clinch River is just life or death to Baker."

Baker has long been a powerful ally of the nuclear industry. His home state of Tennessee holds the government's massive nuclear complex at Oak Ridge, and Clinch River is scheduled to be built there if construction ever begins. Baker had threatened in 1977 to oppose Jimmy Carter's emergency energy plan because it failed to include Clinch River, and he was no less adamant that the project continue under Reagan. He led the tricky floor fight that preceded passage of the Clinch River appropriations bill on November 4, 1981. Working with another long-time friend of the nuclear industry, Senate Energy Committee Chairman James McClure, a Republican from Idaho, and with the White House, Baker steered the bill to a 48 to 46 victory, the narrowest margin in Clinch River's history. "It was good old-fashioned arm-twisting," said a Senate aide who worked against Clinch River. "We just got out-muscled. There's no other way to explain it."

Clinch River opponents were not just out-muscled, however; they were also outspent. The five main companies building Clinch River had funneled $279,505 in campaign contributions to the members of the House of Representatives who participated in a July 1981 vote approving funds for the project 206 to 186. General Electric gave the most money—$106,130—but fellow subcontractors Westinghouse and Rockwell International gave $86,425 and $53,550 respectively, and the project's design and engineering firms, Burns and Roe and Stone and Webster, each contributed about $15,000.

There is of course nothing new, or illegal, about business interests using their wealth to try to influence government policy. Moreover, just as the appointment of an industry veteran like Nunzio Palladino to Nuclear Regulatory Commission chairman does not mean the industry will get its way on every issue before the NRC, neither do massive campaign contributions to a generally very supportive Congress guarantee the industry absolutely smooth sailing on Capitol Hill. Government decision making after all is a complex process in which officials are influenced from many sides and ultimately must choose among mutually exclusive options. On the other hand, campaign contributions and friendly political appointments do assure that the industry's requests are considered carefully by men who are predisposed towards granting them. And that advantage is amplified by another important source of political leverage: big business's control over large and crucially important areas of American economic life. No government will lightly antagonize interests as powerful as those running the nuclear industry, and for obvious reasons. A remark by the chairman of the editorial board of *Fortune* magazine back in 1952 is, if anything, even more applicable today: "Any president who wants to seek a prosperous country depends on the corporation at least as much as—probably more than—the corporation depends on him. His dependence is not unlike that of King John on the landed barons at Runnymede, where Magna Carta was born." Jimmy Carter's June 1978 White House meeting with industry leaders, for example, was a tacit admission on his part that they and their corporations were simply too powerful for him to ignore. Carter did not invite antinuclear leaders to the White House until May 7, 1979, one day after they publicly demonstrated *their* political power by bringing 100,000 demonstrators from around the country to the steps of the Capitol in Washington to protest government support of nuclear power.

ECONOMY AND SAFETY

It is now fashionable among those who predict the impending demise of nuclear power to blame the downfall on nuclear's disastrous economics. "Nuclear power is sinking in this country," wrote Anthony J. Parisi in the *New York Times Magazine* in early 1981, "not because of chaotic financial markets, public protests, or bureaucratic tangles, but under its own economic weight." Nuclear power is "the victim of an incurable attack of market forces," proclaimed antinuclear analysts Amory Lovins, Hunter Lovins, and Leonard Ross in the summer 1980 edition of *Foreign Affairs*. "The global nuclear power enterprise is rapidly disappearing [because] nuclear power is not commercially viable." Indeed, capital costs of constructing nuclear power plants in the United States have doubled in the last decade, stretching to the limit the financial capabilities of even the largest private utilities. Cautious Wall Street investment banks are shying away from utilities that seem overly dependent on nuclear power. Even the chairman of the Edison Electric Institute, Frank W. Griffith, concedes that "any electric utility president who orders a new nuclear unit has certainly got to do an awful lot of soul-searching as to whether or not it's a prudent decision."

Obviously, there will be no revival of nuclear power until it is made economically attractive and profitable again. But the foregoing statements notwithstanding, this is not an impossible task. The argument that nuclear power's economic problems are irreparable overlooks the central fact of nuclear political economy: it is Washington, not Wall Street, that determines the marketplace cost of nuclear power. There are two main mechanisms by which Washington exercises its economic influence: subsidies and safety regulations. Through extensive use of both, the Reagan administration is moving to reduce nuclear power's marketplace price by shifting more of the health and financial risks and costs onto the society at large.

Reagan's decision in 1981 to single out nuclear power as the only major nonentitlements program besides the military to receive a budget increase demonstrates the importance he attaches to reviving it. The following year (fiscal year 1983) Reagan allocated another $1.02 billion—an amount the Atomic Industrial Forum nevertheless criticized as "no boon for commercial nuclear energy, contrary to some perceptions," because it was less than the previous year's. The administration also continued its campaign to discourage solar energy and conservation, nuclear's would-be competitors; solar funding, which had peaked at $578 million under Carter in fiscal year 1981, was slashed to $70 million, while conservation, $558 million under Carter, fell to only $19 million.

The nuclear industry has grown accustomed over the years to such presidential generosity on the taxpayers' behalf. Every president since Franklin Roosevelt has decided that nuclear energy promised enough benefits to America's national security and the economy that the federal government should subsidize the costs of producing it. According to a Department of Energy study written in 1980 by economist Joseph Bowring, the government has spent almost $40 billion since 1948 subsidizing industrial nuclear power production. Reactor research and development has claimed $23.9 billion, almost two-thirds of the total amount. The second largest subsidy has been for uranium enrichment. Bowring estimates that the government has spent $7.1 billion over the years making "enrichment services available to the industry at substantially less than the price that would be charged by a private supplier." Another $2.5 billion went to subsidize the production of uranium ore through such devices as price supports and import restrictions. A fourth subsidy category, assistance to foreign reactor sales by U.S. manufacturers, is listed at $237 million, a figure that includes monies spent under the Atoms for Peace and Euratom programs as well as U.S. contributions to the International Atomic Energy Agency, but excludes another $6.6 billion worth of low-interest loans with which the Export-Import Bank has helped finance foreign nations' purchases of U.S.-produced nuclear power plants. Finally, the government has spent $6.5 billion on various problems related to nuclear waste disposal, including research and development of a method of permanent disposal, storage of spent fuel, cleaning up uranium-mill tailings spills, and not requiring nuclear utilities to recover plant decommissioning costs from their customers. Bowring concluded that without the subsidies, nuclear electricity would be one and one-half to two times as costly today and unable to compete even with oil-fired electricity.

But even more important than such direct subsidies is Washington's authority to decide how safe the industry must make nuclear power production. Nuclear energy's total social cost includes not only such direct financial costs as reactor research and development but also "external costs" such as nuclear waste disposal and "external risks" such as those to the health and safety of people working within and living near nuclear power plants. These external costs and risks stem from the extraordinary health, financial, and environmental hazards of nuclear power production. Yet the notion of "total social cost" is hardly unique to nuclear power. The cost to society of automobile production and use, for example, includes not only the labor, knowledge, and raw materials embodied in the finished vehicles but also the unhealthy and unsightly pollutants they spew into our air supply when driven, as well as the loss of vast expanses of countryside to parking lots and freeways.

It is appropriate for the government to decide how much of the total social cost of producing some goods or services must be borne by the producers and thence the marketplace and how much by society at large. Where the government draws that line greatly affects the product's marketplace cost. Car prices rose, for example, after the government demanded antipollution devices; nuclear reactor prices also rose owing to stricter government safety requirements. But the equation works in reverse as well: before issuing those tougher regulations, the government was silently subsidizing automobile and nuclear power production in an amount precisely equivalent to the cost to society of the consequent dirtier air and more dangerous reactors.

By assigning many of nuclear energy's external costs to society as a whole, the government over the years has provided a subsidy to its marketplace cost far beyond the $40 billion detailed in the Bowring study. The precise monetary value of this extra subsidy is impossible to calculate, for a number of reasons. First, nobody is sure yet how much permanent disposal of nuclear waste, to take but one example, will ultimately cost (although the Department of Energy projects spending $23 billion on it over the next twenty years). And how safe does the disposal method have to be? Honorable people on all sides of the nuclear debate could under the best of circumstances disagree on the slippery question how safe is safe; that billions of dollars and public acceptance of nuclear power rest upon the answer inevitably makes the issue even more contentious and subject to misjudgment. Furthermore, what price tag do we as a society put on preventing such tragedies as the cancer cases or birth deformities that might result from low-level radiation or a major accident? Conversely, what price on maintaining an adequate, affordable supply of energy to run the society? Another dilemma: cancers often do not appear until twenty years after the event; how to be certain whether a cancer was due to radiation releases or, say, to cigarette smoking? It was precisely because of such uncertainties involving the health and environmental effects of nuclear power that corporations were unwilling to invest substantially in the technology until the government made it clear these risks would be socialized. And that is the final reason no dollar figure can be affixed to nuclear subsidies; without them there would have been no nuclear power industry in the first place.*

Nowhere has the government's determination of how safe nuclear power production must be had a greater impact on nuclear economics than in regulation of power station design. Industry executives fondly remember how it took just five or six years to construct the first wave of nuclear plants during the 1960s. Yet as these and subsequent plants came on line, revealing previously unsuspected safety problems and underscoring the seriousness of recognized but unresolved issues, government regulators became

---

* A prime example is the Price-Anderson Act, which relieves the nuclear industry of nearly all liability in the event of a major reactor accident.

increasingly worried that unless reactor design was improved, the likelihood of an eventual nuclear accident would rise to dangerous levels. The more and larger reactors there were, the greater the danger. Under the circumstances, the only way to limit the overall accident probability was to reduce and keep reducing the accident risk for each individual plant. That demanded a continual upgrading of nuclear safety requirements, an endeavor that occupied government regulators throughout the 1970s. As industry executives and such nuclear critics as economist Charles Komanoff alike agree, this upgrading was the primary cause of the drastic increase during those years in the cost of building nuclear plants in the United States.

The crucial question for the future of nuclear economics is whether the government will continue to tighten safety regulations. Nuclear critics believe present regulations still are not stringent enough. The economic argument implicit in the critics' position is that the upgrading of the 1970s forced the marketplace to absorb more but still not enough of nuclear's total social cost. The risk of an environmental or public health disaster remains unacceptably large. Nor is it only nuclear critics who hold this view. In a celebrated article following the Three Mile Island accident, nuclear pioneer Alvin Weinberg declared, "For nuclear energy to grow in usefulness, the accident probability *per reactor* will simply have to diminish."

For their part, industry executives will occasionally concede privately that reactor standards were too lax in the 1960s and that at least some of the subsequent upgrading was necessary, if only for public relations reasons. As one Babcock and Wilcox executive put it, "There's a price to be paid for keeping public confidence, and that's overly redundant safety regulations. Everyone in the industry realizes that." But now the good idea of tighter regulation, it is thought, has been carried too far. What bothers industry men is not so much the regulations themselves, but rather the speed and unpredictability with which they change. Nuclear power plants could be constructed both safely *and* economically if Washington would only, in Westinghouse chief executive officer Robert Kirby's words, "finally and absolutely stop the era of uncertainty with regard to regulations . . . and approve *the* [regulatory] blueprint for the future." By "standardizing" adequate safety specifications once and for all, the government could cut construction time and, more important, costs in half and return nuclear power to favor among electric utilities and on Wall Street.

This Ronald Reagan is committed to doing. Administration officials have pledged on numerous occasions to reduce the time needed for building nuclear plants to six to eight years, and the goal is shared by the industry's closest friends in Congress. The Nuclear Regulatory Commission's first step towards quicker licensing of nuclear plants was to restrict citizens' rights to intervene during public licensing hearings. Specifically, during the second set of hearings for a plant's operating license, interveners may no longer question the utility's financial capability to operate the plant safely, nor the need for the plant's electricity. The NRC went even further when it submitted to Congress a "Nuclear Standardization Act of 1982." The legislation reportedly borrowed heavily from a General Electric proposal to certify standardized plant designs for operation anywhere in the United States and thus limit regulatory oversight to siting issues. This would eliminate operating-license hearings entirely, thereby allowing "one-step licensing," a change the industry has long requested.

The administration took a similar approach to nuclear waste disposal, a problem that industry opinion polls identify as the public's major concern about nuclear power. To quiet the public's fears, Reagan ordered that the Department of Energy stop studying nuclear waste and get on with proving that it can in fact be safely stored. In explaining the President's plan to the annual meeting of the American Nuclear Society in November 1981, White House science aide John M. Marcum declared, "We can no longer afford further iterations of technical programs looking for every different and slightly improved solution. This unfortunately has been the thrust of [the Department of Energy's] approach to date, and has served to reinforce the public's misperception that we can't find a technical solution."

The Reagan administration is likely to find, however, that slashing nuclear safety regulations is easier said than done. Many others involved in the national nuclear controversy doubt that all the technical problems have been solved, and are unlikely to be swayed merely by presidential assurances to the contrary. As a *Washington Post* editorial pointed out, "what is holding up the construction of a waste site is state and local opposition to having one and a serious debate over what technical criteria such a facility should meet to be licensed by the NRC. The [president's] plan to brush all this aside by quickly building an unlicensed facility is destined to fail." Those who reject Reagan's quick-fix solution to nuclear waste disposal are implicitly arguing that without further studies and a better disposal plan the risk of a catastrophic mishap remains unacceptably high, and that the cost to the nuclear industry of waiting for these is simply an unavoidable part of the total social cost of nuclear power production. The same basic argument applies to those opposed to cutting nuclear plant licensing time in half.

Even Reagan's own Nuclear Regulatory Commission chairman seems leery of the consequences of drastic regulation reduction. In his first official address to the nuclear industry since assuming his NRC post, Nunzio Palladino told the Atomic Industrial Forum's 1981 annual conference that in his first five months on the job he had found deficiencies at some nuclear power plants that were "inexcusable" and showed "a surprising lack of professionalism in the construction and preparation for operation of nuclear facilities." Palladino scolded the assembled executives about "lapses of many kinds—in design analyses resulting in built-in design errors; in poor construction practices; in falsified documents; in harassment of quality control personnel; and in inadequate training of reactor operators." The NRC chief assured the industry men that he still supported streamlining of the licensing process, but warned that such action would accomplish nothing unless the industry improved its own performance: "If the nuclear industry does not do its part, no amount of regulatory reform will save it from the consequences of its own failures to achieve the quality of construction and plant operations it must have *for its own well-being* and for the safety of the public it serves" (emphasis added).

Palladino's stern lecture revealed both why he had not been the industry's choice for NRC chairman and why he was nevertheless the perfect man for the job if nuclear power was ever to be revived. Palladino had devoted his entire professional life to the advancement of nuclear energy; he referred in the last line of his AIF speech to "the crucial role of nuclear energy in [our nation's] future." It was precisely because he strongly believed in nuclear energy that he felt the need to be tough with the industry. Thirty-five years of experience in the nuclear field had taught him much about both nuclear safety and the nuclear industry. Palladino was honest enough to admit there existed grave "deficiencies" in the industry's safety practices, smart enough to recognize they had to be corrected if the public's confidence in nuclear power was to be regained, and shrewd enough to know the industry would make the necessary corrections only if government forced it to do so. In both tone and intention, Palladino's tongue-lashing was similar to his predecessor James Schlesinger's 1971 declaration before the American Nuclear Society that the AEC would not bow to industry wishes and ignore the requirements of the recently passed National Environmental Policy Act. The executives' indignation notwithstanding, both Schlesinger and Palladino were in fact performing a crucial but rarely acknowledged role of government regulatory agencies: protecting the regulated industry's long-term interest by forcibly restraining its short-term greed.

ATOMS FOR PEACE, PHASE II

Less than five months after assuming the presidency, Ronald Reagan was given an unforgettable lesson in the frightening implications of the connection between nuclear power and nuclear weapons. On June 7, 1981, Israeli warplanes roared across the desert into Iraq and in a surprise attack over Baghdad destroyed a research reactor that Israel claimed was preparing to manufacture material for nuclear bombs. The raid powerfully illustrated something American strategists had known for over three decades: that the worldwide proliferation of nuclear technology gravely endangered global peace and stability in general and U.S. strategic interests in particular. Who could be certain that the Iraqis and other representatives of the Arab League might not retaliate by imposing another oil embargo or launching a military counterattack (say, against Israel's nuclear facility at Dimona) that would once again embroil the Middle East in war? The Arabs responded far less militantly this time, although Saudi Arabia did pledge to help Iraq rebuild the shattered reactor. But the Israeli strike caused many Western observers to worry aloud about the possiblity of similar raids elsewhere, perhaps by the Soviets against the Chinese nuclear installation at Lop Nor or by the Indians against the Pakistani reactors in Kahuta. Once again attention focused on the perilous and stubborn problem of how to halt the global spread of nuclear weapons capability, but compelling answers were not forthcoming.

Five weeks later, while workmen were still clearing away the rubble of Iraq's shattered Osirak reactor, President Reagan announced a new U.S. strategy for solving the problem. The President sought to have the best of both worlds—to increase U.S. exports of nuclear equipment and fuel while preventing any diversion of them to weapons uses. The key phrase in his official policy statement was his commitment to "re-establish the United States as a reliable and credible nuclear supplier." How this would translate into actual policy was first explained in a speech Assistant Secretary of State James Malone delivered September 4 in London to the Uranium Institute. The fundamental assumption underlying the Reagan policy was, in Malone's words, "If we [the United States] are to maintain our influence in the international community on nuclear issues, we must be an active participant in nuclear trade and commerce." Towards that end, the administration had already dramatically increased funding for breeder reactor research and development, scrapped restrictions against commercial reprocessing of spent nuclear fuel, and outlined measures to expedite the granting of federal licenses for nuclear exports.

These steps were in sharp contrast to the nonproliferation policy pursued by Jimmy Carter, and Malone indicated that Reagan strategists had in fact attempted to learn from what they saw as the previous administration's mistakes. Among the "essential lessons from the history of the past several years" the Reagan people had drawn, said Malone, was that the United States could not "unilaterally dictate the shape and content of world nuclear commerce." Instead it had to "work more effectively with other nations to inhibit transfers of sensitive materials and technology, particularly to countries and areas of proliferation concern."

Carter, of course, had made a similar pledge to cooperate more closely with the other nuclear supplier nations. But his effectiveness with them had been damaged, in the Reagan view, because he had refused to trust them any more than he trusted such unstable, weapons-hungry nations as Pakistan. Carter had been just as adamant, for example, about dissuading Japan from building fast breeder reactors and reprocessing plants as he had been about prohibiting the export of such technologies to South Korea. The Reagan policy, by contrast, would "distinguish among regions" that were a proliferation risk and those that were not. Moreover, it would "recognize in deed as well as in word the desire of nations to fulfill their energy security needs." Thus, the Reagan administration would not "seek to inhibit or set back civil reprocessing and breeder reactor development abroad in nations with advanced nuclear power programs where it does not constitute a proliferation risk," that is, in the nations of Western Europe and Japan. The result, Reagan officials hoped, would be more effective cooperation within the club of nuclear supplier nations to keep the bomb out of the hands of the world's poor countries.

Yet Malone and other top Reagan strategists had also concluded from recent history that to "attempt to control and limit acquisition of nuclear technology is not by itself a practical option." It was also necessary to "reduce [other countries'] motivations for acquiring nuclear explosives." Most countries wanted nuclear weapons because they feared for their national security; the Reagan administration would seek to quiet these fears "by working to improve regional and global stability." It would provide trouble-spot countries with additional conventional weaponry or with stronger guarantees of U.S. assistance in the event of attack, and would also seek to resolve those regional disputes that gave countries an incentive to try to obtain nuclear weapons in the first place. For example, the administration had proposed a $2.5 billion military and economic aid package for Pakistan, a country that was repeatedly denied U.S. assistance by President Carter because of its efforts to build atomic bombs.

The Reagan administration's nonproliferation policy represented a major triumph for the nuclear industry. It had been advocating such a policy, unsuccessfully, ever since the mid-1970s, when India's nuclear explosion and West Germany's offer to provide Brazil with uranium enrichment and reprocessing facilities had alerted Washington that its traditional nonproliferation strategy was flawed and obsolete. The industry view, as we saw in chapter 4, failed in the ensuing fight over how U.S. policy was to be changed. Here it is worthwhile to review the industry's argument as well as the position that ultimately persevered, because the two viewpoints have dominated official U.S. thinking about nuclear proliferation ever since.

Both sides agreed, of course, on the need to contain the spread of nuclear weapons; where they diverged was on how to achieve that goal. The first group, which included key members of the Ford administration and Congress, argued that Washington could stop the proliferation of nuclear arms by force, influence, and example. Stricter safeguards on the export of conventional light water reactors were necessary, and the export of enrichment, reprocessing, and breeder technology must be explicitly and absolutely prohibited. The United States should use its overall political muscle and especially the tremendous influence it derived from being the world's leader in nuclear technology to persuade other nuclear supplier nations to adhere to the same set of tougher guidelines. Elements of this approach later became official U.S. policy, as when Congress passed, at the Carter administration's urging, the Nuclear Non-Proliferation Act of 1978. President Carter also decided the United States would defer development of breeder reactors and commercial reprocessing. That move was first proposed by a Ford Foundation study authored by a number of Trilateral Commission members who later joined the Carter Cabinet. It was intended in part to convince other supplier nations that U.S. calls for tighter nuclear safeguards stemmed from genuine, serious proliferation concerns, not greedy commercial ones.

Opponents of this position, foremost among them the nuclear companies, charged that it was grounded on an arrogant, naïve, and outdated view of the world and would in fact unwittingly accelerate nuclear proliferation. It was easy for the United States to forswear the breeder and reprocessing; it was sitting atop a seemingly inexhaustible treasure chest of oil, coal, natural gas, and shale reserves. What about the energy needs of countries like Japan, which had to import nearly all the energy they consumed? Especially after OPEC's development, both industrialized and underdeveloped countries saw nuclear power as a necessary element in their future energy policies, and they were determined to acquire it. For the United States to attempt to block this worldwide rush for energy independence would be not only selfish but self-defeating. Like it or not, the overwhelming U.S. military and economic dominance of the 1950s and 1960s was greatly diminished and the ability to influence other nations' nuclear policies through general political pressure no longer certain. Moreover, the days of America's atomic monopoly were over; there were now others that would gladly supply enriched uranium and advanced nuclear technology if the United States did not. An American renunciation of developing and trading these technologies would only force other countries to intensify development of their own nuclear industries, drain away American industry's technological leadership, and thus leave the United States with little if any influence over global nuclear power development and commerce.

It was a compelling argument for why the Carter policy was doomed to failure, but the industry lacked any alternative prescription. Indeed, when during interviews for this book I asked industry executives what should be done to solve the proliferation problem that was hampering their commercial expansion, I invariably received the accurate but insufficient reply that "proliferation is a political problem, not a technical one." The one exception was General Electric nuclear vice-president Bertram Wolfe. His suggestion for how the United States should go about containing nuclear weapons proliferation is contained in an article in the January 1980 issue of the *Bulletin of the Atomic Scientists*. The United

States, he argues, should take the offensive on nuclear power, revive its export program and the development of advanced nuclear technology, and strive to regain the unquestioned technological superiority that was the key to its nuclear power hegemony up through the 1960s. Wolfe advocates, in short, that the United States "reinvigorate its Atoms for Peace program." Under his plan, the United States "would promise to take a leadership role in developing commercial reprocessing, recycle and breeder technology and would promise to make the benefits of such technology available to others, subject to appropriate institutional arrangements to assure availability of supply when needed, while minimizing proliferation risks." The GE executive straightforwardly answers the cynic's question—"Are these suggestions not a means of aiding an ailing nuclear industry of which my company is a part?"—by arguing that limited proliferation is impossible without a strong U.S. nuclear industry. New and more stringent nuclear development and trade guidelines will be necessary to control future weapons proliferation. Only by regaining technology superiority (of which a strong nuclear industry is but the physical embodiment) can the United States negotiate these agreements from a position of strength rather than weakness.

The parallels between Wolfe's proposal and the original Atoms for Peace program of 1954 are indeed striking. The genius of both was to transform proliferation from an argument *against* further development of the U.S. industry into an argument strongly *in favor of* it. Both were advanced a few years after global events had clearly demonstrated that the United States no longer held a monopoly on nuclear power technology and thus could no longer expect to hoard its knowledge from the rest of the world. In both eras, the assumption was that the rest of the world hungered insatiably for the magic secret of nuclear power and would find a way to get it, if not from the United States then from the Russians or, in the 1980s, from the French, the Germans, or any number of other potential suppliers. And once they got it, they would use it to make bombs. Since monopoly and renunciation of nuclear technology were therefore no longer feasible strategies, the only way the United States could hope to prevent weapons proliferation was through control, control based on overwhelming and obvious technological superiority. Achieving this superiority would require many billions of dollars in federal subsidies for reactor research and development, export promotion, and the like. In both cases the expense was justified on the grounds that there existed an identity of interest between the national security of the United States and the global expansion and technological advancement of its nuclear power industry.

Although the Reagan administration has not formally launched an Atoms for Peace, Phase II program, the similarities between its policies and Wolfe's proposals are too striking to ignore.* The administration has rejuvenated development of the breeder reactor and commercial reprocessing, for example. And it has opened up nuclear export trade opportunities that never would have been explored under Carter. In the fall of 1981 the White House ordered the U.S. Export-Import Bank to offer Taiwan especially generous financing for two nuclear plants it planned to order. The administration also relaxed previous U.S. restrictions against such countries as Brazil and South Africa, neither of which has signed the Nuclear Non-Proliferation Treaty. Vice-President George Bush told Brazil the United States would not object if Brazil broke its exclusive U.S. supply contract and instead purchased enriched nuclear fuel, absent full safeguards, from non-U.S. sources. A high-level State Department group met with South African officials to discuss the possibility of U.S. shipments of enriched fuel for that country's Koeberg nuclear station. The President himself approved the sale of classified enrichment technology to a private consortium in Australia seeking to start an enrichment business. Energy Secretary Edwards secretly authorized the export of a computer system Argentina needs before it can operate its heavy water nuclear plant, a facility expected to come on line in 1984 that is capable of producing weapons-grade materials.

Credit for the more permissive Reagan policy must go largely to W. Kenneth Davis, who while still employed by the Bechtel Corporation helped draft the Reagan transition report that later became

---

* Moreover, its approach to the threat posed by the U.S.-U.S.S.R. nuclear weapons buildup is also remarkably similar to that which Wolfe suggests for containing nuclear proliferation. Reagan strategists believe that the Soviets are ahead in the arms race, that their nuclear superiority gravely endangers the security of the United States, and that they will never willingly agree to relinquish that superiority. The Soviets are thought to understand and respect force and might, not noble-sounding diplomatic entreaties. The Reagan administration is determined to force the Soviet Union to back down by escalating the arms race to such a tempo that the Soviet economy will be unable to stand the strain. Once the Soviets recognize the folly of trying to keep up with the vastly more productive American economy, according to the administration, they will become docile enough for the United States to negotiate a real arms control agreement that reduces armaments on both sides without compromising American national security.

the basis for the administration's nuclear nonproliferation and trade policy. One of that report's major recommendations was that the United States share enrichment and reprocessing technology with friendly nations that had "a legitimate need" and did not "constitute a proliferation risk"—a recommendation which, as we have seen, President Reagan adopted. Less than a year after Davis passed through the revolving door between Bechtel and the Reagan administration and became deputy secretary of the Energy Department, one of his old colleagues, Bechtel vice-president Harry Browne, wrote to the department asking for permission to negotiate with Japan about building a large reprocessing plant there. Browne's letter was sent while George Schultz was still president of Bechtel, and Schultz was aware of the proposal, according to a Bechtel spokeswoman. In April 1982 Bechtel received a tentative but positive reply: the Energy Department was reviewing its plutonium policy but expected, once that review was completed, to be able to grant "a favorable decision on the Bechtel request." That request would also have to be approved by the State Department, but not before the revolving door whisked Schultz from Bechtel to the State Department.

The Reagan administration's nonproliferation proposals were widely attacked as a relaxation of the United States' commitment to halting the spread of nuclear weapons and as a giveaway to the nuclear industry. A *Washington Post* editorial complained, "In the insiders' jargon of [the nuclear] business . . . 'reliable supplier' suggests not letting non-proliferation concerns interrupt nuclear trade." Former President Carter charged that it was those who would "benefit financially" from the "lucrative" trade in nuclear reactors who had convinced Reagan to relax nonproliferation controls, and that as a result global stability and U.S. security would be threatened.

Yet, ironically, the administration's nonproliferation strategy was actually considerably tougher than previous statements President Reagan himself had made on the issue. In a press conference in Florida during his election campaign, Reagan said the United States should not stand in the way of countries wanting to develop nuclear weapons. "I just don't think it's any of our business," said the candidate. And after the Israeli attack against Iraq's nuclear reactor, Reagan publicly expressed his skepticism that international mechanisms intended to prevent the spread of nuclear weapons— in particular, the Nuclear Non-Proliferation Treaty and the International Atomic Energy Agency—could actually do so. "How many countries do we know that have signed the non-proliferation treaty that very possibly are going ahead with weapons?" Reagan asked. He added that he himself supported nuclear exports, but realized it meant that "you have at least opened the door where someone can proceed to the development of weapons."

THE WEAPONS CONNECTION

A commercial nuclear industry could not exist in America, much less flourish, without public support—that much had been clear from the beginning. To gain that support, the Atomic Brotherhood and particularly the old Atomic Energy Commission had promised Americans many things in the 1950s; while electricity "too cheap to meter" was the grandest and most memorable, even more important were the Brotherhood's calm reassurances that atomic power was and always would be completely different and separate from atomic weapons. This was the crucial claim that had to be believed before citizens would allow atomic power plants to be built in their communities. Americans had generally supported the use of atomic weapons on Hiroshima and Nagasaki (after the fact, of course), but they also remembered the horrible consequences of that usage. They were thus unlikely to sanction the creation of an industry that would deploy among them machines they believed capable of accidentally wreaking the same kind of wanton destruction. Hence the need for reassurances.

But in fact government leaders knew very well that there was no firm line dividing atomic energy's military and nonmilitary uses. Comforting rhetoric about "the peaceful atom" was for mass public consumption. The government elite itself recognized that nuclear power and nuclear weapons could never be *totally* separated— they were after all merely different uses of the same extraordinary energy force, atomic fission—and from the beginning they based U.S. nuclear power policy on that fact. As Under Secretary of State Dean Acheson and Atomic Energy Commission Chairman David Lilienthal concluded in a classified 1946 report, "The development of atomic energy for peaceful purposes and the development of atomic energy for bombs are in much of their course interchangeable and interdependent."

This interdependence has meant that many of the same private corporations and government agencies that produce nuclear power also inevitably produce nuclear weapons as well.* The Atomic Energy Commission, for example, managed both nuclear weapons production and commercial power development until its abolishment in 1975. And even then, when the AEC's commercial power *regulatory* authority was transferred to the new Nuclear Regulatory Commission, its power *development* function remained tied in with weapons production and eventually became the job of the new Department of Energy.

An internal memorandum by a top energy official in the Carter administration charged that making the Energy Department responsible for nuclear weapons work inevitably biased its approach to solving America's energy problems. The nuclear weapons program, according to the memo, typically consumed more than a third of the department's total budget and exerted "a profound and disturbing influence upon the Department and its attempts to develop effective national energy policies." In particular, the memo argued, the weapons work biased the department toward advocating nuclear power as a major solution to U.S. energy problems while downplaying or ignoring the potential contributions from conservation, solar, and other renewable energy sources. Two specific examples of weapons bias cited by the memo were that weapons research frequently took priority over energy system development in the Energy Department's national laboratories and that a majority of the department's outside research and development contracts were awarded to large aerospace and military contractors.

Military dominance within the Department of Energy is most obvious, however, in the department's budget. Fully 60 percent of the $11.8 billion the Reagan administration proposed for the Energy Department's fiscal year 1984 budget was devoted to such military activities as the development and production of nuclear weapons, including the Trident, the Pershing, and the MX. Meanwhile, as in previous Reagan budgets, substantial cuts were proposed for solar, conservation, and fossil-fuel programs, while nuclear power continued to dominate the department's energy work with $1.5 billion in funding.

From the time uranium leaves the mine to the time it leaves the enrichment plant, the companies that handle it are the same, re-

---

* It has also meant that nuclear power and nuclear weapons production pose many of the same health and environmental dangers. Uranium miners and factory workers risk cancer regardless of whether the radioactive materials they handle are used to illuminate living rooms or to buttress America's military might.

gardless of whether the uranium's ultimate destination is the core of a power reactor or the inside of a warhead. (Such major U.S. uranium producers as Gulf Oil and Atlantic Richfield may protest that none of their uranium has ever been used to make weapons; that is true because they and other oil giants did not enter the uranium business until the late 1960s—*after* the Atomic Energy Commission had already acquired enough uranium for all its future weapons needs.)

From the enrichment stage onward, the uranium bound for power reactors follows a different course than the uranium bound for warheads. Therefore, companies involved in these later stages of nuclear power production are not automatically also weapons producers, though it turns out that most of them do weapons work just the same. General Electric and Westinghouse, the two main suppliers of commercial reactors and fuel, are forty-year veterans of the nuclear weapons program. Now Westinghouse is competing with Gulf subsidiary General Atomic (which also is trying to sell commercial reactors) for the privilege of building a massive new plutonium-production reactor for the Department of Energy. General Electric manufactures one of the key components in hydrogen bombs. Both GE and Westinghouse, as well as the other two commercial reactor manufacturers, Combustion Engineering and Babcock and Wilcox, are also heavily involved in producing aircraft, submarines, and other "delivery systems" for U.S. nuclear warheads. Babcock and Wilcox is also a prime supplier of fuel for the Navy's nuclear submarines. Rockwell International, one of the main subcontractors on the Clinch River breeder reactor project, oversees a nuclear waste dump for the military. So does Du Pont, whose recently acquired Conoco subsidiary is also a major uranium producer.

The essential oneness of nuclear power and nuclear weapons notwithstanding, industry leaders recognized that the existence of their industry depended on maintaining a distinct separation between the two in the public mind. Thus when Assistant Secretary of State James Malone warned industry executives in his September 1981 speech, "The economic and political costs of nuclear programs that become linked, however ambiguously, to military uses will ultimately be borne by us all, to the detriment of peaceful nuclear development," it was like telling a platoon of infantrymen to make sure their rifles were always clean and in good working order. Malone's warning to keep nuclear power separate from nuclear weapons was something executives had first learned so long ago that it had become second nature to them. They had repeated the claim so often they had come to believe it themselves.

The industry men thus were surprised and alarmed to learn that, at the time Malone was giving his speech, other high officials in the Reagan administration were already seriously considering a proposal that the industry faithful regarded as not only a cardinal sin but political suicide. The proposal in question called for recycling the waste products of commercial nuclear power plants in order to obtain plutonium needed for the next generation of nuclear weapons. The idea went to the heart of both U.S. military and U.S. energy policy, and would require the specific approval of the President before it could be enacted. If Reagan did approve it, he would be ordering the most profound change in U.S. nuclear energy policy in over a quarter-century. Ever since President Eisenhower announced the Atoms for Peace program in 1953, the Atomic Brotherhood's central claim to Americans and to the world at large had been that nuclear power and nuclear weapons were two separate creatures. Reprocessing commercial nuclear waste into weapons— in effect, turning every U.S. power reactor into a bomb factory— would expose that claim as utterly false. Not only would it link nuclear power and nuclear weapons in the public mind; it would positively highlight the intrinsic connection between them.

The idea of turning waste into weapons was a direct product of the accelerating arms race with the Soviet Union. If the American Atomic Brotherhood was to keep building more weapons, it needed more plutonium; but its old supply sources were drying up. For thirty years, the government had obtained its plutonium from a handful of production reactors located at the Hanford nuclear complex in Washington State and the Savannah River plant in South Carolina. But now these "dedicated production facilities" were beginning to wear out, just as any piece of machinery eventually does; they could be kept in operation for another decade or so if they were "patched up," but this would only buy time until new facilities could be built.

Military planners in the Department of Energy, the government agency responsible for manufacturing nuclear weapons, had been considering various options for future procurement since the mid-1970s. Their search grew urgent, however, in 1980 when a desperate President Carter ordered development of the MX and cruise missiles and the neutron bomb. This massive arms buildup, which

Ronald Reagan later endorsed and greatly expanded,* would require vast quantities of plutonium. The Energy Department could
choose to fill the increased demand through the tried and true
method of building additional dedicated production facilities. Each
of these would take about a decade to bring on line, and would
cost anywhere between $5 and $12 billion. But a breakthrough at
its Lawrence Livermore Laboratory in Berkeley, California, gave
the department a second, and potentially cheaper and quicker way
to close the projected "plutonium gap." (A third option—importing
five tons of plutonium from Great Britain—could provide short-
term relief while military planners decided upon a long-term solution.)

Through a process called "laser isotope separation" (LIS), the
Department of Energy could instead exploit the enormous stores
of plutonium that remain "locked up" in used nuclear power-plant
fuel rods. When uranium atoms split to create nuclear energy,
neutrons released in the reaction are absorbed by the remaining
uranium atoms, thus producing plutonium. The average commercial power reactor produces in this way about five-hundred pounds
of recoverable plutonium a year. It was always assumed by industry
executives that this plutonium, once reprocessed, would be used
to fuel the next generation of nuclear technology, the fast breeder
reactors. But it could, if further purified, also be used for nuclear
warheads. Previously such purification, although technically feasible, was prohibitively expensive. But the laser isotope separation
process, which would use lasers to upgrade the reactor plutonium
to weapons-grade purity, promised in theory to perform the task at
a fraction of the cost of previous methods. A further potential advantage of LIS, according to Lawrence Livermore reseachers, was
that it might be available for use as soon as the late 1980s, years
earlier than new dedicated production facilities.

Because the LIS research had been highly classified, few if any
people outside the secretive nuclear weapons bureaucracy knew
that the Energy Department was considering such an approach
until 1981. In an October 1 hearing before the Subcommittee on
Oversight and Investigation of the House Committee on Interior
and Insular Affairs, Charles Gilbert, the assistant secretary for defense programs at the Energy Department, confirmed that the department wanted to spend $560 million over the next three years

---

* The Reagan military buildup will demand that 4,000 more nuclear warheads be
built by the early 1990s than President Carter had planned.

to accelerate the LIS program and to build an LIS production facility by 1987. Additional evidence came a week later, when Energy Secretary James Edwards delivered President Reagan's official nuclear-power policy statement. Under persistent questioning from reporters, Edwards conceded that the idea of using commercial spent fuel as s source of plutonium for the weapons program was in the "conversational" stage within the administration. That was a gentle way of putting it. Over a month earlier, Edwards himself had specifically endorsed the idea in a private meeting with the department's Energy Research Advisory Board. "We are going to be needing some more plutonium for our weapons program, and the best way I can see to get that plutonium is to solve the waste problem," said Edwards. "Reprocess [the waste], pull out the plutonium, and you may have to upgrade that. . . . We could also use the plutonium in the breeder reactor and get that technology proven and we would solve two problems at one time. It just makes a lot of sense to me to go that route."

Edwards was exaggerating greatly when he said that turning waste into weapons would "solve" the nuclear waste problem, but his basic point—that the scheme promised to benefit the industry as well as the government—was correct. Reprocessing commercial spent fuel into weapons-grade plutonium would enable the Energy Department to dislodge two of the biggest obstacles hindering the nuclear industry's recovery. The more pressing of these was what electric utilities should do with accumulating spent fuel that they were quickly running out of room to store. They could not reprocess the fuel because the United States had no commercial reprocessing plant; they could not get rid of it because the government had yet to make a final decision on permanent nuclear waste disposal. By 1983, they would either have to spend many scores of millions of dollars constructing their own additional temporary storage facilities or start shutting down their reactors. If it implemented laser isotope separation, the Department of Energy could take this unwanted fuel off the utilities' hands. And although the long-term problem of disposing of high-level nuclear waste would remain, the department would have bought itself a few extra years to build a permanent storage repository for it. Secretary Edwards, then, was half right: going the LIS route *would* solve the nuclear waste problem, at least in the short term.

Turning waste into weapons could also give a much-needed boost to the commercial viability of nuclear reprocessing. A major goal of President Reagan's new nuclear policy was to encourage private companies to enter the reprocessing business and, in particular, to buy the unfinished reprocessing plant sitting idle in Barnwell, South Carolina.* But there was a problem. Barnwell's current owners, the Allied General Nuclear Services Corporation, a consortium composed of Allied Chemical, Gulf Oil, and Royal Dutch/Shell, had lost an estimated $360 million they had invested in the plant after President Carter indefinitely prohibited commercial reprocessing in April 1977. As a result, "Nobody is going to buy Barnwell until they get assurances the next administration won't screw them like Carter did," according to GE nuclear vice-president Bertram Wolfe. The industry had pressured Reagan soon after he took office to approve government purchase of the Barnwell plant, but the President had declined, citing his preference for a "free-market" solution. He did, however, instruct Energy Secretary Edwards to meet with industry leaders to "determine which regulatory barriers [were] of greatest concern" to them and to "develop recommendations for my further review on how to create a more favorable climate for private reprocessing efforts."

There were, it turned out, three major obstacles to private investment in the reprocessing business. First, executives were uncertain about what health and safety standards the government would force them to meet before granting an operating license for the Barnwell plant. Before investing, they wanted a clear, fixed set of what they considered reasonable guidelines from the Nuclear Regulatory Commission, specifying how the plant would be built and operated. Second, they feared that a future administration or Congress might "pull a Carter" on them and reinstate the ban against commercial reprocessing; they wanted protections against such a move. Finally, because of the fall in uranium prices and delays in breeder reactor development, executives questioned whether there would be sufficient demand for the plutonium that Barnwell would eventually produce. No executive could risk corporate funds on Barnwell without far greater assurances that its products would find a market and the investment yield a profit.

* If all efforts to encourage private ownership and operation of Barnwell failed, the Reagan administration had one other option for meeting the Energy Department's plutonium needs. *Inside Energy* revealed in September 1981 that high-level officials in the department's Defense Program Division were considering a proposal to modify the government-owned Savannah River plant so that reprocessing of commercial spent fuel into breeder-grade or weapons-grade plutonium could be done there. Previously Savannah River had reprocessed only military and Energy Department research-and-development fuels and had provided plutonium only for the weapons program.

Enter once again the Bechtel connection, in the person of Deputy Energy Secretary W. Kenneth Davis. By summer 1982 Davis had persuaded his boss, Secretary Edwards, to send to the White House an extraordinary proposal that met each of the executives' demands and promised to create a virtually risk-free environment for private investment in Barnwell. The Energy Department proposal offered (1) a certain market, through guaranteed government purchase of the plutonium produced at Barnwell, (2) significantly weakened and permanently binding safety regulations, and (3) complete financial compensation—in other words, a money-back guarantee—of all money invested in Barnwell in the event that a future Congress or administration decided once again to prohibit commercial reprocessing.

The company most eager to revive and buy into Barnwell was none other than Davis's old firm, Bechtel. Bechtel had originally designed the Barnwell plant; in the fall of 1981 it began studying its financial and operating data and the regulatory barriers to commercial reprocessing. According to Frank Deluzio, a private consultant and key figure in the effort to encourage private purchase of Barnwell, Bechtel was "talked to by DOE" about doing the study and was told by a subcontractor who analyzed the question that the Barnwell plant could by its third year of operation be making $60 million to $80 million a year in profits. Ashton O'Donnell, Bechtel's vice-president for nuclear fuel operations, denied that the department had approached Bechtel. O'Donnell said the study "was paid for and instigated by Bechtel, for our own purposes," and refused to divulge any of its findings. He did emphasize, however, that Bechtel "was not prepared to endorse the idea that it is economically sensible to run Barnwell only if it reprocesses spent fuel for nuclear weapons."

That apparently was *not* the view of James Buckham, president of the Allied General Nuclear Services consortium that was abandoning Barnwell. According to Buckham, the government's breeder program could consume only half of Barnwell's total plutonium output. Would the government use the other half to make nuclear weapons?

When the news that the Reagan administration was indeed considering that option leaked out in the fall of 1981, it swiftly provoked a widespread negative reaction. Expressing a viewpoint shared by virtually all opponents of the proposal, the Natural Resources Defense Council (NRDC), a respected environmental group, charged that it "would render the distinction between atoms

for peace and atoms for war totally meaningless." The primary
concern of most critics was that the plan would encourage the
global spread of nuclear weapons. Senator Gary Hart, for example,
in a letter to Energy Secretary Edwards, protested that "implementation of this plan would set an example that could render
virtually ineffective any efforts of the United States to discourage
nonweapons countries from using their commercial nuclear power
programs to develop a nuclear weapons capability." Similar concerns were voiced by the Nuclear Club, a newly formed group
opposed to nuclear proliferation, and by the NRDC, which charged
the plan "would destroy whatever credibility" the United States
had on nonproliferation issues. NRDC also worried that the plan
"could lead to a militarization of the entire back end of the civilian
fuel cycle." Such a development, the group warned, would (1)
endanger public health and safety because militarized facilities
would be able to avoid NRC licensing requirements and public
accountability, (2) encourage increased police surveillance of nuclear workers and antinuclear groups, as well as other infringe-
ments on civil liberties, and (3) constitute an undeserved, unfair
government bailout of the faltering commercial nuclear industry.

Friends of nuclear power also disliked the idea because they
feared it would impede commercial use of the atom. Sigvard Eklund, director general of the International Atomic Energy Agency,
sternly warned top U.S. officials that such a move by the United
States could unleash a new wave of hostility to nuclear energy in
Western Europe. The *New York Times* called the idea "not just
misguided but dangerous" because it threatened "setting off a joint
campaign, by people opposed to nuclear power as well as those
opposed to nuclear weapons, in the United States and Europe."

Nuclear industry executives were uncomfortable about the
Reagan administration's idea for the same reason. "This could be
a public relations disaster," said a spokesperson for the American
Nuclear Energy Council. Industry officials, like administration policymakers, did not accept the notion that turning commercial waste
into weapons would increase the likelihood of nuclear weapons
proliferation. But they did concede that it would, in the words
of GE nuclear vice-president Bertram Wolfe, "give the marchers one more reason to say nuclear power is leading to the end of
humanity."

Top industry strategists discussed the waste-into-weapons idea
at length at the fall 1981 meetings of the boards of directors of the
Atomic Industrial Forum and the American Nuclear Energy Coun-

cil. According to Wolfe, who attended both meetings, "You can certainly say the industry is not enthusiastic about the mingling of nuclear fission's commercial and military applications. The industry position and my own personal feeling is that we've really kept the commercial separate from the military for all these years, and that the advantages of merging them now would have to be damn large to make it worthwhile."

Yet despite their profound misgivings about the Reagan administration proposal, the industry refused, apparently on patriotic grounds, to criticize it publicly. "None of us felt we were in a position to say whether this was required for the national defense," explained Bertram Wolfe. "Some of the comments at the meetings were that if the national defense required this move, we could not as citizens oppose it just because it would be bad for the nuclear power industry." The Edison Electric Institute's press release took a similarly wary but cautious approach to the issue. It conceded that the nuclear industry believed "our nation's nuclear weapons needs and our nuclear power programs should be kept separate," but then went on to say that any decision to link the two was an issue of national defense policy. National defense policy was "understandably not the province of the electric utility industry" but was "established by the President and the Congress." The utilities did plead, however, that in making their decision the Washington lawmakers "take into consideration the course of action we have pursued in utilizing nuclear power for the production of electricity."

As it had been so many times in the past, the Atomic Brotherhood was once again plagued by a disagreement over the proper uses and purposes of nuclear energy. Members of both the government and the industry wings of the Brotherhood saw nuclear energy as a means of assuring energy independence and unending economic growth. But to the government men in general and the Reagan administration in particular, nuclear energy was also and more fundamentally the key to reviving U.S. military power and rejuvenating America's global power. And if achieving those lofty goals required reprocessing nuclear waste into weapons, the government men planned to do it, whether the industry liked it or not.

Seymour Shwiller was one of the men on the government side of the Atomic Brotherhood who believed U.S. national security might require reprocessing nuclear waste into weapons. A veteran staffer on the House Armed Services Committee that controls funding for LIS work, Shwiller dismissed the fuss about the proposal as uninformed and communist-instigated posturing. "I don't see how the plutonium knows whether it was born in a power reactor or a military reactor," he said. "And besides, if you're gonna get killed by a nuclear weapon, you don't really care. You just want it to be over with quick. The people who abhor nuclear weapons would abhor them even if we used sand to make them. The Soviet disinformation apparatus and the KGB have done a real job on this country. They're the ones who caused people to be against nuclear. My philosophy is nuke 'em all. I'm not going to be a Russian slave like my grandparents were."

For all the passion of his opinions, Shwiller was enough of a realist to be aware there would be significant opposition to the idea on Capitol Hill. "Sure, there's gonna be flak," he said, "but I think we just need to go one step at a time. First we let the scientists find out if it [LIS technology] is gonna work, and then we say that this is how we solve our weapons needs and the problems for the nuclear industry at the same time. You start by asking each member of Congress, 'Do you believe in the national security?' and go from there. 'Do you believe we need nuclear weapons? Yes? Well, do you want to spend $1 billion or $12 billion to build them?' You know," he concluded, "a lot of people forget that government workers pay taxes too. We're trying to save the country some money with this idea."

But were the potential financial savings worth the political costs? Even strong LIS supporters like Seymour Shwiller admitted that the government did not *have* to raid commercial spent-fuel pools in order to keep making weapons; it could just as well meet its plutonium needs by building new "dedicated production facilities" and renovating old ones. (A story leaked to the *Washington Post* in October 1981, apparently by a government official opposed to the waste-into-weapons idea, claimed the Energy Department was in fact planning to increase plutonium and tritium production 70 percent by 1985 through employing such measures.) True, $11 billion, or whatever the eventual savings yielded through LIS plutonium production might be, was no small sum. But then neither was the virtual certainty of massive new waves of opposition to nuclear energy a trifling matter. The two-million-plus people who filled the streets of Western Europe's major cities in the fall of 1981 had clearly demonstrated the enormous potential power of a political movement that linked nuclear power and nuclear weapons. And the lesson was not lost on the men of America's Atomic Brotherhood. As industry consultant Frank Deluzio confided nervously,

"The stuff in Europe could catch fire over here real easily. And then it'd be chaos."

There are great political risks and costs to the Reagan administration's attempting to implement such an unabashedly pronuclear policy in the 1980s. The first hazard is inherent in all controversial political issues: alienating voters who hold the opposite opinion. But Ronald Reagan has never enjoyed the support of environmentalists and nuclear opponents, and what little he did have began to erode after he named James Watt Secretary of the Interior. (Even the National Wildlife Foundation, whose membership chose Reagan over Carter by a 2 to 1 ratio, has demanded that Reagan fire Watt.) Unlike Carter, Reagan is not in the slightest degree beholden to the environmental movement. Political pressure aimed at softening his support for nuclear power thus is likely to succeed only if it comes from much broader and larger segments of the population than it has previously.

More serious is Reagan's gamble that safety regulations can be significantly cut without causing a major nuclear accident. If he wins that gamble, he begins to reverse nuclear power's economic tailspin and positions it to become a major future U.S. energy source. But if he loses, or even if there is another close call like Three Mile Island, nuclear power is finished in the United States. Similar reasoning applies to his encouragement of nuclear exports and advanced technology development. If all goes as anticipated, U.S. industry will once again be competitive in the world market, and Washington will be able to control the global flow of atomic technology and materials. But many observers, some holding positions of power in Washington, believe Reagan's policies are far more likely to encourage than to limit nuclear proliferation. If there is another attack like Israel's against the Iraqi reactor, if another country announces that it has acquired nuclear weapons capability, or worst of all, if a bomb is actually dropped by a "new" weapons state, Reagan will almost surely have to moderate his position in a manner damaging to industry interests.

Finally, and most serious of all, there is the gamble the Reagan administration will be taking if it decides to try to reprocess commercial nuclear waste into weapons. At a time when the public does not so much support as tolerate nuclear energy, such a policy all but invites public opposition to rise up and demand the elimination of nuclear energy once and for all. Yet indications are that the Reagan administration is still pursuing the idea. In its fiscal year 1984 budget request, the Department of Energy asked for $250 million to cover future purchases of plutonium from the Barnwell plant. Moreover, Congress increased fiscal year 1983 funding for the AIF program to $66.2 million, more than double the amount the administration had requested.

The future of the nuclear industry as it entered the 1980s thus remained darkly clouded. There were limits to what even as loyal a friend as Ronald Reagan could do for the industry; there were overriding pressures that could force him, as they could force any president, to take action contrary to the industry's best interests. Perhaps it was because he understood this that Atomic Industrial Forum president Carl Walske was publicly jubilant but privately cautious about the industry's future under Reagan. A week after Reagan's election victory, Walske and several hundred other guests attended what in the past few years has become the industry's major social function—the luxurious party hosted by Westinghouse at the close of every AIF annual conference. While waiting in line for a cherry crêpe suzette, Walske was greeted by a man who happily exclaimed in what sounded like an Indian accent, "Isn't it great news about Reagan?" Walske's face remained impassive as he cocked his head away from the man and murmured, "Well, we'll just have to wait and see."

10

A Nuclear America?

Our new objective must be to find a safer, "health-
ier" method of producing peaceful [nuclear] energy
by a method that also minimizes or eliminates the
present risk of furthering the spread of nuclear
weapons. If it is also cheap, or relatively cheap,
fine; but first it must be safe.

DAVID LILIENTHAL,
Chairman, Atomic Energy Commission, 1947–1952

The interview was over, his secretary had already called him twice
to leave for his next appointment, but Westinghouse Power Systems Company president Gordon Hurlbert was determined to im-
part one last message to his visitor. Suddenly shedding the bluff
manner and loud voice of the previous hour, this man who ranked
as one of the top five executives of America's thirty-third largest
corporation began speaking in a soothing yet urgent tone about
what he called "the great tragedy of our time."

What was he trying to get at? It took a few seconds before I
realized that the international spread of nuclear explosives, and
more particularly then-President Jimmy Carter's efforts to stop it,
were the objects of his apparent anguish. Hurlbert was distressed,
but not because Carter's actions had cost his company billions of
dollars' worth of lost nuclear export sales. No, what made the
spread of nuclear weapons capability not merely unfortunate but
truly tragic was that it did not have to happen: the U.S. government
could have prevented it. But instead, because of a moral failing on
its part—in Hurlbert's words, "an unwillingness to be sensitive to
other people's needs"—the United States had unwittingly ended
up encouraging it.

The fiftyish executive lowered his voice almost to a whisper as
he said, "We weren't sensitive that [the Japanese and other U.S.
allies] had the same hopes and fears we do for abundant, economical energy. And our unwillingness to be sensitive to their needs

caused them to say, 'Well, we're gonna go ahead with our own breeder reactor, with or without you.' And morally, I think Carter really believed [in] this. But the very action he took to reduce the probability of proliferation is the tragic thing that produced it. Because if we can't be trusted to be sensitive to their needs, then they're gonna have to go it alone."

Was it too late to repair the lack of trust?

"I think it's like your wife catches you in bed with another woman," Hurlbert replied. "It's never quite the same again. You can repair it, but not all."

That exchange took place on January 29, 1979, almost exactly two months before the Three Mile Island accident that changed the course of nuclear energy development forever. Four years of investigating and writing later, it seems to me that Mr. Hurlbert was wiser than even he knew that day. For in the midst of his transparently calculated monologue about global nuclear politics, he unwittingly identified what is the single most important obstacle to a revival of nuclear power in the United States: the difficulty of regaining lost trust.

The men of America's corporate-government Atomic Brotherhood now must face the political consequences of their past indiscretions. For years they assured Americans that nuclear power was safe. Atomic Energy Commission Chairwoman Dixy Lee Ray used to boast that nuclear power is much safer than eating; after all, three hundred people choke to death every year trying to swallow food. Most Americans believed such claims. As the years went by, they granted the men of the Brotherhood the benefit of the doubt despite serious and increasingly frequent lapses—such as their suppression and whitewashing of official reports documenting the true potential hazards of nuclear energy, the silencing of those few top scientists who were unwilling to endorse the official line about nuclear's supposedly "negligible" health effects, the decades of simply ignoring the minor problem of what to do with nuclear's lethal waste products. Americans responded to the mounting circumstantial evidence of betrayal with relative calm. The more gullible ones were taken in by the Brotherhood's pious protestations of innocence; most of the rest looked the other way and wished the whole messy business would just go away.

But there was no ignoring the Brotherhood's final and most damning act of infidelity: the accident at Three Mile Island. No longer could the risks of nuclear power be called exaggerated, nor its dangers abstract. As then–Senate Majority Leader Robert Byrd complained, the industry and the government had promised time and again that such an accident could not happen. Now that it had, how could Americans ever trust the nuclear men again? How could they believe any of their past, much less their future, claims? Gordon Hurlbert is right. Once the bond of trust is shattered, it's never quite the same again.

Lying is risky in a democracy; the men of the Atomic Brotherhood are paying today for their deceptions of yesterday. They bear the responsibility for their misdeeds, yet all judgments must be tempered with understanding. Once the men of the Atomic Brotherhood made the original fateful decision to tame atomic energy, they became subject to forces far beyond their control. Their great mistake was being too proud to admit this fact, too taken with their cleverness and accomplishments to remember they were still only human beings, with human frailties and limitations. Indeed, in retrospect, it is hard to see how they could have made fundamentally different choices than they did. Their freedom of action was limited by (1) the nature of fission technology itself, (2) the imperatives of the global capitalist economic system in which they operated, (3) the constraints imposed by America's system of democratic government, and (4) the ramifications of the United States' constant struggle to remain the world's dominant nation. What is curious is that the men of the Brotherhood, with a few notable exceptions, still do not recognize the enormous influence these forces have had on nuclear power; they themselves do not fully grasp how and why nuclear power has landed in its current predicament. (The same, incidentally, can be said of many nuclear opponents.)

Whatever one's position on the issue, thinking intelligently about the future of nuclear power is impossible without first coming to terms with its past. If the men of the Atomic Brotherhood fail to learn from the past, they will repeat their old mistakes and doom to failure their effort to salvage the technology they hold so dear. The Brotherhood's history holds equally valuable lessons for those who wish to banish nuclear technology. Knowledge is power, and nuclear opponents will need plenty more of both if they are to succeed in creating the better world they envision.

WHY THINGS WENT WRONG

The unprecedented crisis now facing nuclear power is rooted in the nature of fission technology itself, and particularly in three of its central characteristics:

- The inseparability of nuclear power from nuclear weapons;
- The tremendous dangers inherent in nuclear power production;
- The enormous expense of developing such a complex and capital-intensive technology safely.

Nothing has caused as many problems for nuclear power as its inseparability from nuclear weapons. This is ironic, since nuclear power probably would not have been developed at all, or at least not as rapidly, had there been no weapons program. Its inseparability from nuclear weapons made nuclear power, by definition, a national security issue. It both required and was used to justify the extraordinary secrecy that has always characterized the entire U.S. nuclear program; it was the predictable and repeated abuse of this secrecy that ultimately destroyed Americans' faith in nuclear power. The weapons connection also led to the postponement and even outright prohibition of certain actions that were vital to creating a prosperous nuclear power industry. In particular, the development of fast breeder reactors, of commercial reprocessing, and of a vigorous export program were impeded because government officials feared such steps would undermine U.S. national security and global power by encouraging the spread of nuclear weapons.

The need for nuclear secrecy was further reinforced by the tremendous potential dangers involved in using fission as a source of electricity. Whatever its merits, the argument now being advanced by nuclear advocates—that fissioning uranium is no more dangerous than burning coal or than other forms of energy production—is irrelevant to this point. The question at hand is not whether nuclear power is a tolerably safe energy source today; but rather whether Americans, if given all the available information about the potential dangers of nuclear power production in the 1950s, would have given their approval to the sort of all-out commercial nuclear program envisioned by the Atomic Brotherhood. The men of the Brotherhood apparently believed they would not, and so they conspired to keep the full truth of nuclear energy from the public—to "keep them confused," in President Eisenhower's words. This may have been a short-term tactical necessity. A reactor meltdown is such a frightening thought that many citizens probably would have opposed nuclear power development no matter how unlikely such meltdowns were said to be. Openly acknowledging *all* of the potential dangers of nuclear power production would have all but guaranteed public fear and opposition to nuclear power, especially had the Brotherhood admitted, as Charles Weaver concedes he and fellow Westinghouse executives did privately at the time, "that all questions [about nuclear safety] weren't answered." As it turned out, the Brotherhood's deceptions succeeded only in delaying the outbreak of widespread public resistance, and in making it worse than it otherwise might have been.

A different set of problems emerged from the complex and capital-intensive nature of nuclear power production. The first was that the industry was destined from the start to be an oligopoly dominated by some of the very largest multinational firms in the United States. A vast amount of capital had to be invested before nuclear power stations could be produced and used. Because the necessary front-end investment was so large, a manufacturer would recover it and begin to reap profits only after selling many, many units of fuel and reactors. The industry thus could support only a few firms, and these would have to be large and wealthy enough to be able to afford not only the enormous initial investment but also the years of waiting for that investment to pay out. Of course, once it did pay out, the profits promised to be enormous. But that was the catch. Making enough sales to turn a profit depended, for both individual firms and the nuclear industry as a whole, on three factors. First, access to not just a national but a global market was essential; export sales were vital. Second, that market had to keep expanding, especially in the industry's single most important sales area, the United States. Electricity demand therefore had to keep growing steadily and vigorously, as did the overall economy that gave rise to such demand. And finally, nuclear power had to seize and hold a good portion of this growing market; nuclear-generated electricity therefore had to be kept cheaper than electricity generated by the traditional base-load source, coal. As we have seen, each of these preconditions to nuclear profit making has been absent at one time or another in the nuclear industry's history.

Permanent and deep government involvement in the nuclear power business was made inevitable by the aforementioned central characteristics of fission technology. The weapons connection alone required Washington to retain at least veto power over the power industry's actions, while the costs and dangers of nuclear power production were simply too great to be accommodated within a purely private-enterprise framework. A technology that posed such huge potential health and safety hazards could not escape close government regulation. The consequences of a nuclear accident were so grim and far-reaching that the decision to risk such consequences was necessarily a social one, and thus could be made only by the federal government (which did precisely that by passing and twice extending the Price-Anderson Act). Nor could private corporations alone bear the cost of making fission a safe and economically competitive source of electricity. The amount of capital required and the risk that it would be lost if the atomic venture ultimately proved unsuccessful were both simply too large for even giant corporations. Massive subsidies, as well as a firm federal commitment to making nuclear power work, were essential to the creation and survival of a commercial industy.

The necessity of government involvement meant that corporations that wished to sell nuclear power could do so only with Washington's cooperation and blessing. Such corporations had no choice but to enter into the informal, special relationship with Washington that formed the basis for the Atomic Brotherhood. But as much as industry executives like to blame their problems on small-minded federal bureaucrats and spineless politicians, the temptation to term the Washington alliance a necessary evil for the corporations should be resisted. True, the industry has suffered often and sometimes severely at the hands of its federal partners; and perhaps most important, nuclear executives were forced to relinquish a corporation's usual freedom to plan and run its business more or less as it sees fit. Nevertheless, the overriding fact is that there never would have been a nuclear power industry without the enormous assistance, financial and other, provided by Washington.

Because they had separate and occasionally antagonistic interests in how nuclear power should be developed, clashes between the industry and the government were unavoidable. Corporate chieftains saw nuclear energy as a means to unprecedented riches; government officials saw it as a means to unprecedented power. To be sure, these two goals were not always contradictory. Government members of the Brotherhood were glad to help their industry brothers make profits. Washington also agreed that nuclear power was good for American capitalism as a whole; with its ability to produce virtually limitless amounts of energy through the breeder reactor, nuclear power in the 1950s and 1960s seemed likely eventually to lower production costs throughout the economony and thus encourage a massive and enduring wave of economic growth in the United States. Lower overall production costs would also give American corporations in all fields an advantage over their Japanese and European competitors in the struggle for control of the world market.

But long before these lofty goals were close to being realized, the drive to commercialize nuclear power collided with two more immediate and important responsibilities of the government. The first was Washington's commitment to uphold and expand the American global empire. Maintaining a congenial climate in foreign countries for American economic expansion had been a major aim of U.S. policy since the turn of the century; the overwhelming economic and military superiority the United States enjoyed after World War II gave its leaders virtually unlimited freedom to establish a world order that served American corporate interests above all others. Military interventions; CIA destabilization efforts; economic and military aid to client states; manipulation of the world's key currency, the dollar—these were but a few of the tactics the U.S. government used to influence if not absolutely control global events in the postwar era. At bottom, U.S. global military power rested on its atomic weaponry, the intimidation value of which was obvious to U.S. foreign-policy makers (and to the rest of the world) from the time the bombs were dropped on Hiroshima and Nagasaki in August 1945. U.S. policymakers believed that having a well-stocked nuclear arsenal at their disposal would help them fashion a world order where friendly foreign governments would guarantee access to petroleum, copper, and the scores of other raw materials vital to an advanced industrial economy, and where U.S.-based multinational banks and corporations could supply growing consumer markets and exploit cheap labor resources without fear of nationalization, guerrilla movements, and other disruptions. Nuclear weapons would, according to U.S. strategy, above all deter the Soviet Union from invading Western Europe or otherwise threatening U.S. global interests.

What brought all this into conflict with the needs of the nuclear industry was the inseparability of nuclear power from nuclear weapons. The industry's long-term survival depended upon being able to sell its products in the global market and upon being able to develop and use fast-breeder and reprocessing technology. Yet top government officials believed that these steps would make it easier for other nations eventually to obtain atomic weapons, which in turn would reduce the United States' relative power over the rest of the world and hence its ability to shape global events to its liking. Thus, the nuclear power industry was in a very difficult position. Its commercial success required actions that, by spreading nuclear weapons around the world, would disrupt and threaten the system of U.S. global dominance that enriched American big business as a whole. Washington could hardly allow that system to be compromised in order that one sector of the business elite could prosper, no matter how powerful that sector was.

The industry's development also clashed with the government's obligation to protect the public and the natural environment. If Washington forced the industry to install and pay for adequate safeguards against all the potential dangers of atomic fission, it threatened to destroy nuclear power's economic competitiveness. Yet if Washington excused industry from these costs, it had to cover them itself—an extremely expensive proposition for even the U.S. government—or face a greater likelihood of reactor meltdowns, radiation-induced cancer epidemics, and the like. Such disasters threatened not only to destroy public tolerance for nuclear power but also to foster among citizens a dangerous distrust of their government, a disrespect for its authority, and perhaps even challenges to its legitimacy.

The potential for conflict between the nuclear power corporations and the federal government was evident as early as 1946, the year Washington decided to delay indefinitely the private development of nuclear power. Government members of the Atomic Brotherhood made the ruling because they recognized the essential unity of nuclear power and nuclear weapons. They understood that nuclear power and nuclear weapons were not so much two different things as two different uses of the same principle. Both depended on the same secret: the fissioning of atoms to release vast amounts of energy. To be sure, nuclear power stations channeled that energy into electricity and useful work, while weapons used it to obliterate, but the difference was one of application, not essence. Because the knowledge and technology needed to produce nuclear power and nuclear weapons were, as Under Secretary of State Dean Acheson and soon-to-be Atomic Energy Commission Chairman David Lilienthal pointed out in their 1946 report, "in much of their course interchangeable and interdependent," a country could pursue whichever application it wished once it learned the atom's secrets.

Protecting the secret of atomic weapons thus required an equally vigilant safeguarding of the secret of atomic power; nuclear power and nuclear weapons inevitably ended up behind the same wall of secrecy after the war. The 1946 Atomic Energy Act institutionalized the extraordinary secrecy, centralization of authority, and strict security measures that previously had been justified as war-time necessities. (The act authorized the death penalty for those who disclosed atomic secrets of foreign governments.) Through frequent invocation of the sacred cause of "national security," both the Atomic Energy Commission and its toothless congressional watchdog, the Joint Committee on Atomic Energy, managed to insulate themselves from normal democratic processes and from any meaningful outside control. The repeated abuses of their priv-ileged position, which ultimately caused many Americans to turn against nuclear power, perhaps could have been prevented had the Congress not charged the agencies with both promotion *and* reg-ulation of nuclear power. Yet the alternative—to establish an independent oversight body—would have meant risking what gov-ernment officials saw as the transcendent danger: the compromis-ing of América's atomic secrets.*

When Washington dropped its ban against nuclear power devel-opment in 1954, it was not because government officials suddenly forgot the inseparability of nuclear power from nuclear weapons. In fact, that inseparability was the very basis of their decision to change course. They believed that to stay the world's number one nation, the United States had to remain number one in the world's mightiest technology. When the Soviet Union's bomb ended the U.S. atomic monopoly in 1949, President Truman responded by ordering a massive increase in nuclear weapons production, in-cluding the beginning of hydrogen bombs. Because nuclear power was inseparable from nuclear weapons, the United States had to stay ahead in power development as well. Thus, upon learning in the early 1950s that the Soviets, Europeans, and Canadians were exploring ways to produce nuclear-generated electricity, Washing-

---

*Because they flowed from the nature of fission technology itself, these same con-tradictions confronted every nation that launched a nuclear program. Peter Pringle and James Spigelman describe in fascinating detail in *The Nuclear Barons*, their international history of nuclear development, how the AEC's counterparts in Brit-ain, the Soviet Union, France, and Canada exhibited the same antidemocratic behavior. "In all except Canada," the authors explain, "their task was to develop both the peaceful and the warlike atom, and, because of the military connection, they became closed societies. Pledging national security, the powerful commission members were able to deflect legitimate and concerned public inquiry about their work; in the years that followed they would escape the normal checks and balances of democratic control." Even Canada, the one nation whose nuclear program was dedicated solely to commercial development, could not avoid secrecy. After all, though Canada was applying its atomic secrets peacefully, what would prevent a thief from applying them militarily?

ton decided it had to accelerate its own development of nuclear power. The Eisenhower administration's moves to encourage a domestic power industry and to launch the Atoms for Peace export program were the logical complement to the Truman administration's previous initiation of a nuclear armaments race. Both Presidents' actions were explicitly intended to reassert overwhelming U.S. superiority over the rest of the world in atomic energy. To be sure, officials like Secretary of State John Foster Dulles did not welcome the security risks of sharing atomic knowledge and technology with the rest of the world. But they found those risks preferable to what they saw as the greater threat to American global dominance that would follow from relinquishing U.S. nuclear superiority.

The 1954 policy reversal is of enormous historical importance, for it marked the beginning of twenty years of uninterrupted harmony and cooperation within the American Atomic Brotherhood. Washington still believed that nuclear energy was central to preserving and expanding U.S. global dominance. But new policies were needed now that its monopoly had been shattered. Washington's imperial interest no longer lay in outlawing nuclear power but rather in creating a strong domestic industry as rapidly as possible. Suddenly, what was good for the nuclear corporations was good for the American empire.

But down this seemingly sunny path lurked trouble for the Brotherhood. The basic contradictions of fission technology did not disappear merely because global events had caused Washington to change direction. Atoms for Peace had the most serious long-term ramifications, for it gave the rest of the world the ability to build atomic bombs eventually. Of course, U.S. officials tried very hard to prevent weapons diversions. Countries were forced to allow complete inspection of their nuclear facilities and were provided with uranium fuel enriched to 3 percent uranium-235 content, a level of purity sufficient for research and power reactors but not for weapons use. But these precautions, while effective in the short run, were doomed to eventual failure. No device could permanently divide nuclear power and nuclear weapons. Fissioning even the supposedly safe 3 percent U-235 fuel inevitably produced significant amounts of plutonium, the basic ingredient of atomic bombs. Training thousands of nuclear scientists and engineers inevitably provided foreign countries with knowledge that could be applied in secret to make weapons.

Washington's determination to race ahead of the rest of the world in developing nuclear power led to enormous strategic mistakes that did incalculable damage to the long-term prosperity of nuclear power within the United States. The first of these mistakes was the selection of the light water reactor design as the model on which the United States would base its global claim to technological superiority. As we have seen, the light water model was chosen for the first U.S. reactor at Shippingport for reasons of operating reliability, not economics: the government wanted to prove its atomic prowess to the world, not produce cheap electricity. It is true that other reactor designs were investigated and tested in the 1950s, but Washington's early support for the light water reactor prejudiced companies against adopting them. Westinghouse and to a lesser extent General Electric were already building a significant lead in light water technology by the end of the decade, and other firms feared they would never catch up if they wasted too much time exploring other models that might not work anyway. As a result, the industry based its future on a reactor design that even some proponents of nuclear power have since complained is badly flawed in many respects, especially in its vulnerability to accidents and weapons diversions.

The government's haste to commercialize nuclear power also led it to neglect its responsibility to protect public health and safety and to respond to public opinion. Promotion of nuclear power consistently took precedence over its regulation. The nuclear corporations naturally tended to underestimate the dangers of nuclear power production. They were in a rush to get nuclear plants produced and in service and to gain a commanding position within this booming new industry. They wanted to keep costs as low as possible. In a capitalist society, these are natural urges that it is the government's responsibility to counter. But in this case, Washington failed miserably, because it had its own reasons for sharing the corporations' desire for rapid commercialization. The AEC's idea of tough regulation was to prohibit the industry from building a power reactor in the middle of Queens, the densely populated borough of New York City (and even that decision had to be forced upon reluctant AEC officials). Anything that endangered nuclear power's competitiveness with coal-generated electricity or otherwise interfered with its rapid commercialization was resisted. The AEC ridiculed citizens who dared to question the safety of nuclear power even as it suppressed internal reports documenting nuclear's enormous potential health risks. It ignored such serious problems as waste disposal while it spent hundreds of millions of dollars developing the next generation of reactor technology, the fast breeder. Perhaps most important of all, it approved construction and operation of nuclear power stations without first researching, establishing, and enforcing a system of rigorous safety standards. The long-term costs of such actions greatly exceeded their short-term benefits. They left the impression that technical problems like waste disposal were insoluble, and forced safety improvements to be made gradually and retroactively, which was, in the long run, far more expensive than it would have been to build safe plants from the start.

But not all of nuclear power's problems can be traced back to government failings. The nuclear corporations, and the laws of capitalist production and oligopoly competition that they naturally obeyed, also deserve much of the blame. Their greed eventually crippled them. Although not often mentioned, part of the reason why construction costs of nuclear power stations rose so sharply throughout the 1960s and 1970s was the all-out war the Big Four reactor manufacturers fought to try to knock each other out of the business and gain larger market shares. One casualty of this war was the chance for the industry to develop and then mass-produce economical, reliable products. Bigger and bigger reactors were produced because they promised—on paper at least—to minimize electricity-generation costs and thus maximize profits for the industry's customers, the electric utilities. Instead, they caused the capital cost of the entire nuclear power plant to increase, primarily because construction was delayed while the AEC did what Combustion Engineering's Richard Von Hollen called a "custom review" of each new design. Safety also was compromised, as manufacturers in the megawatt race, in the words of Babcock and Wilcox executive James Deddens, "may have sold something that hadn't been tested as thoroughly as it would be today."

Competition for the global market brought another set of problems. In order to ensure future access to the markets of the advanced capitalist nations, General Electric and Westinghouse in the early 1960s signed licensing agreements with European and Japanese electrical equipment manufacturers, thereby supplying the very technology with which their overseas competitors would challenge the Americans' control of the global market a decade later. The corporations' transfer of technology also indirectly encouraged nuclear weapons proliferation, for it hastened the decline of U.S. control over global nuclear trade. Partly because of technical assistance from GE and Westinghouse, French and West German companies were eventually able to offer on the world market not just power reactors but enrichment and reprocessing plants, the technologies needed for large-scale weapons production.

It was during the 1970s that the Atomic Brotherhood's past finally caught up with it. The men of the Brotherhood had been able since 1954 to manage the contradictions of nuclear power in a way that served the interests of both industry and Washington. But now the chain of events set in motion by their previous actions was coming full circle, and those contradictions were re-emerging in sharper and more dangerous form. The latent conflict between what was good for Washington and what was good for the nuclear industry grew increasingly apparent as global events forced Washington to choose between its loyalty to nuclear power and its broader responsibilities.

The Brotherhood's dilemma was made worse by certain fundamental economic and political changes, three of which became particularly apparent in the 1970s. The first was the dramatic decline of the United States as the pre-eminent global power. To be sure, it remained the world's most powerful nation, but there were undeniable signs that its ability to control other nations was no longer what it had been during the twenty-five glorious years following World War II. Among those signs were the U.S. defeat in Vietnam; the decline of the dollar and collapse of the Bretton Woods monetary system that had enshrined it as the world's key currency; the growing strains within the Western Alliance as economic competition from Europe and Japan sharply increased; the rise of OPEC; severe economic stagnation in the United States itself; and the loss of the United States' previous overwhelming superiority over the Soviet Union in nuclear weaponry.

The decline in overall U.S. hegemony was paralleled by a decline in U.S. dominance of nuclear power development. Whereas in the 1940s the United States enjoyed a monopoly on nuclear technology and in the 1950s and 1960s was able to make or break the nuclear power programs of most other nations, by the 1970s its control over global nuclear commerce had lapsed to where it could not prevent even such Third World countries as India and Brazil from attaining the capability to produce nuclear weapons. The critical U.S. monopoly over enriched uranium had been broken. The Western Europeans and the Japanese now had their own reactor manufacturing industries that increasingly were challenging American firms on the global market. Third World countries were going nuclear just as the United States had been urging them to do since 1954; but by playing the advanced capitalist nations off against one another, they were obtaining not just power reactors but also the fuel cycle technology with which they could fashion atomic weapons. India already had the bomb, Israel and South Africa probably had it, and unless the international flow of nuclear technology and materials was quickly contained, many more countries were likely to obtain it during the next decade. It was to retard, if not prevent, this destabilizing global proliferation of nuclear weapons that Washington in the mid-1970s tightened export restrictions, deferred reprocessing, and, under the Carter administration, blocked the development of a plutonium-fueled breeder and attempted to redirect the breeder program toward a more proliferation-resistant design.

The second change that obliged the government to take a harder line against the industry was the emergence of an effective mass opposition movement. General uneasiness about nuclear power was beginning to creep into the mass consciousness by the mid-1970s. News reports about the Brotherhood's past deceptions reached Americans just when many of them were learning for the first time from Vietnam and Watergate that their government was perfectly willing to lie to them about anything whenever it felt circumstances required it. Because much of the opposition movement's support came from the politically potent middle and upper-middle classes, it was able to exert significant pressure on the government to upgrade safety requirements. Washington also had its own pragmatic reasons for tightening regulations. As reactors ordered during the 1960s finally began operation, government bureaucrats came to realize that thoroughgoing safety improvements were essential if the Brotherhood was to avoid the sort of major nuclear accident that would doubtless destroy public support of nuclear power forever. Continuous upgrading of government safety regulations was the single most important reason for the stretching of construction time for nuclear plants from seven years at the start of the 1970s to fourteen or more years by the end of the decade. The predictable result was a massive increase in the cost of nuclear power. The industry fought the safety improvements every step of the way.

The government's tougher stance came at the worst possible time for the industry: just when the industry needed help the most, the government was moving in the opposite direction. When the industry desperately needed export sales to offset the domestic market's decline, Washington was erecting obstacles to those sales.

When the development of breeders and reprocessing should have been moving full speed ahead, the government was hedging on its support for them. When the industry's customers, the electric utilities, were suffering the worst financial crisis in their history, the government was making it more difficult and expensive for them to purchase nuclear power plants.

Most industry executives reacted by angrily blaming their troubles on Jimmy Carter and his supposed personal vendetta against nuclear power. Carter was simply out to get them, they told one another. He was motivated by an irrational, quasi-religious belief that plutonium was somehow evil; were he not in a position of power, he would deserve their pity.

This was self-delusion. It was Gerald Ford's administration, not Jimmy Carter's, that first decreed restrictions against nuclear exports and commercial reprocessing, and Ford did so precisely because the prevailing political climate at the time left him no choice. Moreover, reactor design requirements were already being tightened while Richard Nixon, hardly a foe of nuclear power, was President. It is true Carter took these policies a step further, but the difference was one of degree, not kind.

The problem underlying the breakdown of the Atomic Brotherhood during the 1970s was far more serious than the relatively minor differences between individual U.S. presidents. The hard fact the nuclear industry refused to admit was that its needs were increasingly coming into conflict with the federal government's broader responsibilities to protect the public health and safety, buttress its own shaky political legitimacy, and uphold the faltering American empire. In fulfilling those broader responsibilities, both the Ford and the Carter administrations were forced to impose hardships of varying severity on the industry. Their actions were not intended to kill nuclear power, but rather to manage it more intelligently. Carter in particular seemed to understand the long-term need to bring nuclear power development into line with the imperatives of American global power, and to save it from itself by forcing it to be safer. But these distinctions were lost on industry executives.

Nor did the executives seem to appreciate that their biggest problem was something no American president could do much about: the decline of U.S. economic prosperity. Since the end of the Second World War, the United States had been enjoying perhaps the most tremendous period of economic expansion in human history, but by the 1970s the underlying forces that produced that expansion had finally exhausted themselves. After a quarter-century of explosive growth, the American economy plunged into a period of sluggish capital accumulation and lethargic investment, and encountered a new phenomenon referred to by baffled economists as stagflation: simultaneous high unemployment and high inflation. Recessions were the worst since the 1930s, yet inflation still raged out of control. The 1974 oil-price explosion made a bad situation worse, because it pulled prices of all forms of energy up with it, thereby pumping another surge of inflation through an economy already low on purchasing power.

The combination of general economic stagnation and sharply increased prices all but destroyed the market for new nuclear power plants. The timing was ironic: the fall occurred just before the time when superprofits were finally supposed to start gushing into reactor makers' treasuries. The unspoken assumption of the long-range business plans made by nuclear executives in the 1960s—that electricity demand would continue growing at 7 percent a year into the indefinite future—turned out to be quite wrong. Demand during the second half of the 1970s actually grew only half that fast, thus bloating the utilities' excess capacity margins to over 30 percent. Predictably, new reactor orders fell off and many previous orders were canceled or deferred.

Their unexpected fall from grace did not, however, cause the men of the Brotherhood to lose faith in what they called the nuclear imperative. Pioneering humanity's conquest of atomic energy *was* proving more difficult than they expected; the Three Mile Island accident in particular had hurt their cause. Still, nuclear power could not be stopped forever. It was essential not just to America's future but the world's. Without nuclear power, global scarcity was inevitable. And scarcity in the nuclear era would bring not just the usual poverty and civil strife but perhaps the war to end all wars. This was the message the Brotherhood had to get across to people. The corporations were willing to wait a few more years for people to come to their senses. Nuclear power after all was merely a sideline business for them; they were wealthy enough to absorb their nuclear divisions' minor losses for years if they wanted, and soon there would be no losses at all, thanks to the growing and lucrative business of refueling and servicing reactors already in service. When Ronald Reagan, a true believer in nuclear power if there ever was one, was elected President in 1980, the stage for the Brotherhood's comeback was finally set. The final, decisive act in America's struggle over nuclear power was about to begin.

THE REAGAN BACKFIRE

It would seem that Ronald Reagan and his crew of industry-bred advisers are the perfect candidates for the difficult job of reviving nuclear power from its deep and serious coma and nursing it back to full health. They do not see any contradiction between vigorously promoting nuclear power and fulfilling the federal government's broader responsibilities, as the Ford and Carter administrations did. Believing that a strong nuclear industry is good, even essential, for America and thus that the industry's interests coincide with the government's, they are providing virtually everything the industry has been demanding from Washington since the onset of the nuclear crisis in the mid-1970s: a commitment to cut the construction time and hence the cost of nuclear plants in half; the speedy announcement of a solution to the politically troublesome problem of nuclear waste disposal; the legalization and encouragement of commercial reprocessing of used nuclear fuel; the acceleration of fast breeder reactor research and development; and the active promotion of nuclear exports. These measures were intended to free the industry from the "excessive government regulation" that President Reagan in his first major nuclear policy statement charged was the prime cause of nuclear power's problems and to "enable nuclear power to make its essential contribution to our future energy needs."

But the Reagan prescription for how to cure the many ills of nuclear power is in fact destined to fail. One cannot accurately prescribe solutions without first having an accurate diagnosis, and Reagan's diagnosis of the causes and dimensions of the crisis of nuclear power is badly distorted by his romanticized, unrealistic assumptions about nuclear power and the American economy. Despite—in fact, largely because of—their good intentions, the program charted by the men of the Reagan administration may well make things worse for nuclear power rather than better.

Even industry leaders, who are understandably appreciative of what Reagan is trying to do for them, do not think his program will work. It is a revealing measure of just how severe and deep-rooted the nuclear crisis is that executives sincerely doubt that even policies as wildly generous as their old friend Ronald Reagan's will be enough to save them. Their doubts point to the most glaring—and ironic—flaw of Reagan's survival program: it does not provide sufficient assurances to restore private capital's confidence in the future profitability of nuclear power. And until that failure is corrected, the number one aim of the Reagan program—inducing a new wave of business investment in nuclear power stations—will certainly not be achieved. In fact, the Reagan program will actually perpetuate the political uncertainty that breeds investor wariness, because it promises to provoke still greater public opposition to nuclear power in the years ahead. Most important, it all but guarantees the eventual occurrence of a major nuclear reactor accident that will destroy public tolerance for nuclear power once and for all.

Reagan and his associates are blinded to the perils of their unrestrained pronuclear policy by their extraordinary faith in the inherent goodness of nuclear power. Unmoved by Three Mile Island and the other developments that made millions of Americans freshly skeptical during the 1970s, they stubbornly continue to believe the same atomic gospel that they and the rest of the Atomic Brotherhood have been preaching since the 1950s: nuclear power is a cheap, safe, and clean energy source that is vital to the American way of life; whosoever believeth in it shall be granted eternal (economic) life. Unless one makes the assumption that President Reagan actually welcomes the prospect of a reactor meltdown, or for that matter, a nuclear-armed Third World, one can only conclude that he and his advisers sincerely believe that safety standards can be slashed without producing a catastrophe and that nuclear exports and plutonium-based nuclear technology can be advanced without spreading nuclear weapons around the world. Perhaps fuure events will prove Reagan right on these points, but the historical record gives almost no reason to think so.

Reagan's international policy, for example, is intended both to increase U.S. exports of nuclear power equipment and fuel and to prevent any more nations from joining the nuclear weapons club. Administration officials do realize that improving cooperation with other nuclear supplier nations is crucial to limiting the spread of nuclear weapons, and the administration's blessing of Japanese and European plans for reprocessing and breeder reactors is intended as a positive step in that direction. By January 1983 the administration was, according to the *Washington Post*, close to reaching an agreement with the other major nuclear supplier nations on a "trigger-list" of weapons-related equipment that no supplier would export. Nevertheless, given the depressed global market for nuclear power, it remains highly questionable whether the supplier nations can achieve and maintain the high level of cooperation and self-discipline necessary to prevent future weapons proliferation.

To be sure, each of the advanced industrial nations has an interest in keeping the bomb away from non-weapons states, and thus could reasonably be expected to adhere to the mutual agreement mandating tougher safeguards and trade restrictions announced by the administration. Yet just as self-interest can lead capitalists to undersell each other and destroy mutually beneficial price-fixing agreements, so too could it lead the nuclear supplier nations to relax safeguards in pursuit of export sales. This is precisely what the French and West Germans did to break American firms' domination of the Third World nuclear market in the early 1970s. And such relaxing of safeguards is even more likely today, when reactor manufacturers in all supplier nations simply must have export sales if they are to survive the continuing depression in their home markets.

If self-restraint on the part of supplier nations offers scant hope of containing weapons spread, what about the second pillar of Reagan's nonproliferation policy: reducing other nations' motivation to acquire nuclear weapons in the first place? Reagan's State Department argues that other nations will not be tempted to violate the peaceful nuclear safeguards system if the United States guarantees their national security against external aggression; this was one of the major rationales for the administration's $3.5 billion program of conventional weaponry and economic assistance for Pakistan, a nation that had been denied such aide by the Carter administration because of its attempts to obtain nuclear weapons. Multi-billion-dollar arms shipments, however, are more likely to increase than reduce the likelihood that a leader like General Zia will succeed in acquiring the bomb for Pakistan, for such shipments strengthen the power of the country's military and often whet the military's appetite for even more and bigger weapons. The simple fact is that so long as some nations have nuclear weapons, and particularly so long as the two superpowers wield huge nuclear arsenals, other nations will want them—whether for protection, prestige, or power. To pretend, as the Reagan administration does, that nuclear have-not nations can be bought off with massive quantities of conventional weaponry is both wrongheaded and dangerous.

A third inconsistency of Reagan's nonproliferation policy is that its success depends heavily upon an enforcement mechanism that is simply not up to the task. The International Atomic Energy Agency, whose job it is to detect diversions of peaceful nuclear materials to military uses, has long been criticized by members of

Congress, journalists, and nuclear critics as hopelessly inadequate
to the task. The IAEA spends most of its time and resources promoting, rather than policing, nuclear power around the world; its
safeguards division is dismally understaffed, underfunded, and un-
derequipped; the nations it investigates can arbitrarily reject the
inspectors it sends or greatly limit the scope of their investigations;
and it is empowered only to detect and warn against weapons
diversions—it can do nothing to stop them. Even parts of Reagan's
own government are privately worried about the IAEA's shortcom-
ings. A study by the Nuclear Regulatory Commission "raised the
gravest questions about the IAEA's effectiveness," according to a
letter NRC Chairman Nunzio Palladino wrote to several members
of Congress.

Reagan's domestic nuclear power policy is as dangerous and
misguided as his international policy. It is rooted in a cynical and
false analysis of nuclear power's troubles, and seeks simple and
immediate solutions to what are complex and deep-seated problems. Its guiding assumption—that cutting federal red tape is the
answer to all of nuclear's problems, from waste disposal to economic competitiveness—is nothing less than reckless and may well
result in permanent political damage to nuclear power.

That the main reason why nuclear power plants cost four times
more today than they did ten years ago is that they take so much
longer to build—about fourteen years, compared with seven in the
early 1970s—is indisputable. But as we have seen, the prime cause
of the delays has not been legal citizen interventions in the licensing process, as Reagan and industry men claim, but rather the
constant stream of new safety regulations issued by the Nuclear
Regulatory Commission. The NRC, like the Atomic Energy Commission before it, issued these regulations to keep the probability
of a reactor meltdown tolerably low. Because of the Brotherhood's
premature and hurried commercialization of nuclear power in the
1960s, the NRC has still not caught up with where the industry in
its competitive frenzy has taken the technology: the NRC has identified over one hundred generic flaws in the light water reactor
design that need correcting, and more are being discovered as
reactor experience accumulates. Freezing regulations at their current level and heeding Westinghouse chief executive officer Robert
Kirby's suggestion to "approve *the* regulatory blueprint for the
future" thus will guarantee a growing likelihood of accidents as
bad as or worse than Three Mile Island. Slashing the NRC's inspection and enforcement functions will heighten the danger.

Reagan's attempt simply to impose a solution to the nuclear waste problem is another example of graceless, short-sighted policy that could hardly be better calculated to create a troublesome political backlash. It promises to further alienate and enrage many citizens and state and local officials around the country who are already understandably suspicious of the government's intentions. The *Washington Post*, a newspaper with an editorial position of consistent and strong support for nuclear power in the United States, tried to explain to Mr. Reagan that "what is holding up the construction of a waste site is [not bureaucratic inertia but] state and local opposition to having one and a serious debate over what technical criteria such a facility should meet to be licensed by the NRC. The plan to brush all this aside by quickly building an unlicensed facility is destined to fail."

Citizen resistance is the predictable legacy of the Brotherhood's decades of haughty inattention to safety issues. As a 1982 University of Washington study concluded, Reagan's enormous support for nuclear power, along with his destruction of federal programs for conservation and solar energy, "may well prolong the high level of opposition to nuclear power."

The nuclear industry's strategy for overcoming this opposition is, as we have seen, to divide and conquer: strip the antinuclear movement of its political support within the general population by waging a propaganda campaign designed to convince ordinary Americans that nuclear power is actually both a relatively safe source of energy and absolutely essential to economic growth and prosperity. The executives are probably right that mass opposition to nuclear power will be softened to the extent that Americans believe their "no nukes, no jobs" pitch. But there are two weaknesses to this energy blackmail strategy. The first is that with the electric utility industry facing a national average of 35 percent excess production capacity, there clearly is no desperate, immediate need for additional nuclear power plants. A much stronger case can be made that the United States will need more nuclear power in the middle-to-long-term future—say the 1990s and beyond. But Americans may well dismiss these long-term arguments precisely because the industry's claims about needing more nuclear power plants right away to avoid blackouts and freezing in the dark are so transparently false and self-serving. The second weakness is that the "we need nuclear" argument can work only if nuclear power is made much safer. Even if most Americans come to believe that the country will need nuclear power in the foreseeable future, it

is unlikely that they will jeopardize their health and safety today
in return for economic benefits they may or may not enjoy tomorrow. If there is another accident as bad as Three Mile Island or
worse, nuclear power is finished in the United States, no matter
what the industry says about the nuclear imperative.

The Atomic Brotherhood's top priority, then, if there is to be
nuclear power in America at the turn of the century, must be to
make the production of nuclear power much safer than it is today
and thereby slowly regain the faith of the general public in the
atom as a source of energy. However much the men of the Reagan
administration and the industry wish it were otherwise, it is simply
too late to smash or even discredit the antinuclear movement. Too
many Americans have learned too many disquieting things about
the atom; the movement itself is too large and well organized, and
it enjoys the political sympathies of too much of the general population. Ignoring public opposition to nuclear power, as President
Reagan is doing, will only cause it to grow in size, strength, determination, and militancy. If there is to be any hope of reviving
nuclear power, the Brotherhood must instead meet some of the
opposition's demands. Most important of all, Washington must order and enforce substantially tougher safety standards for nuclear
reactors and must spend whatever time is necessary to find a permanent solution to the waste disposal problem that will be widely
believed in and supported. In the short run these steps could quiet
the opposition by isolating activists who want nothing less than to
shut down all nuclear reactors from their more easily placated
sympathizers among the general populace. And in the long run,
these steps offer the best hope of preventing the catastrophic accident that would irreparably destroy Americans' tolerance for nuclear power.

Safety, however, is not enough. If nuclear power is to survive as
a commercial enterprise, it must also be made profitable again. But
here too the Reagan policy promises failure. Admittedly, charging
that the most exuberantly probusiness U.S. president of the twentieth century does not inspire business confidence is an extraordinary accusation. And yet, it is precisely Reagan's belief in the
"free marketplace," along with his related assumption that the
crisis of nuclear power can be overcome within the confines of the
traditional private-enterprise framework, that accounts for the in-
adequacy.

The villain in the nuclear drama according to administration
wisdom, is big government. What has destroyed investor confi-

dence in nuclear power, the President charged in his October 1981 nuclear policy statement, is "a morass of regulations that do not enhance safety but that do cause extensive licensing delays and economic uncertainty. . . . Government has created a regulatory environment that is forcing many utilities to rule out nuclear power as a source of new generating capacity." If these regulations are stripped away, according to Reagan, the nuclear industry will rise like a Gulliver freed from the bonds of the Lilliputians and tramp off, gaining strength with each step, to fight for and regain its rightful position in the marketplace.

The problem, as industry leaders recognize quite clearly, is that Reagan's world bears only a faint resemblance to the real world they inhabit. Invoking the glories of private enterprise is fine, in big business's view, if the purpose is to *justify* a certain government policy. But when it comes time actually to make and carry out that policy, rhetoric must be separated from reality. Reagan poses a dilemma because he does not just pay lip service to the values and principles of private enterprise: he genuinely believes in them. Before the men of the nuclear industry can obtain from Ronald Reagan the policies necessary to restore investor confidence, they must somehow make him see that the marketplace cannot and will not support nuclear power.

"The basic philosophy of the Reagan administration is, they try to remove the [regulatory] impediments and then let private industry take it from there. What we at GE question is whether that will happen," said Bertram Wolfe, top nuclear vice-president for General Electric. Wolfe was careful to emphasize that his pessimism did not stem from ingratitude for what Reagan had done for nuclear power during his first nine months in office: "It's a helluva lot more pleasant now that we've got a guy in the White House who philosophically agrees with us." But he went on in the course of a relaxed, one-and-one-half-hour chat in October 1981 to explain that he, his boss (GE's chief executive officer, Jack Welch), and other top industry officials nevertheless question whether Reagan's policies, however well-intentioned, will be enough to rescue their failing industry.

"This industry lives and dies according to shifts in government policy. Welch's conclusion is that you just can't divorce nuclear power from government policy. You know, in the 1960s we thought you could, we thought we'd grown up and we didn't see any reason why we couldn't be totally independent. Sure, Reagan brings a much better atmosphere, but it may be too late. Ten years ago [his program] would have been enough, but now I'm not sure. Much more direct government involvement may be necessary."

When asked whether he was talking about nationalization of the industry, Wolfe replied, "Well, I certainly hope it wouldn't come to that. But we *are* going to need at least a much stronger government carrot-and-stick policy to induce utilities to make nuclear purchases. It's questionable whether utilities can order any kind of large-scale projects any more, with 20 percent interest rates, one- or two-billion-dollar price tags, and a regulatory environment that's completely out of whack. And the nuclear venture in particular has a size and a time frame that make closer government involvement a necessity. We've got investments [in nuclear power plants] that stretch out over ten to fifteen years. In the case of something like Barnwell [the unfinished commercial reprocessing facility in South Carolina], it's more like thirty years. *It's not the government regulations themselves that bother us, it's that they keep changing.* If nuclear is going to make it, there will just have to be more direct government involvement. What I think we're eventually going to need is for the government to establish a set of energy objectives—how much energy we're going to need by the year 2000, how much of that will be electricity from coal, how much from nuclear, that sort of thing—and then set a plan on how to do it and provide the proper inducements to the private sector" [emphasis added].

Wolfe made one last comment that indicated he had not yet given up hope: "I really think this nation vitally needs nuclear power. We can't keep sending $80 billion [in annual foreign oil payments] abroad, and the world can't keep depending on the Middle East's oil. And nuclear makes good economic sense. But I just don't think you're going to see a revival of nuclear power until there's much stronger government involvement in the business."

One possible solution to these problems would be government planning of the industry. From the perspective of private capital, investing in nuclear power has become too risky. The experience of the 1970s—when nuclear plants ended up taking twice as long to build and costing twice as much as expected because of changing regulations, and when a $350 million investment in the Barnwell reprocessing center was suddenly rendered worthless by President Carter's ban against commercial reprocessing—taught investors just how vulnerable nuclear investments were to changes in government policy. Yet it is worth emphasizing that, as Wolfe explained, it is not the government regulations themselves that are the problem. Enlightened businessmen and investors understand the need for them, especially in an industry like nuclear power. What riles them is when the regulations change. When they are risking hundreds of millions of dollars on the basis of a certain government policy, they expect that policy to remain until the investment has paid out. With such huge stakes, government simply cannot change the rules in the middle of the game and expect private capital to keep playing. As Wolfe also explained, "Before anybody buys Barnwell [as President Reagan had been urging the industry], they're going to want assurances that the next administration won't screw them like Carter did."

Until it is assured of a stable investment climate, which means above all a stable government policy, private capital simply will not invest in nuclear power. Ronald Reagan, of course, is trying to assure just that through his slashing of safety regulations, and executives do appreciate his efforts, but they are not enough. Nor can they be, given the nature of nuclear power production. Reagan, after all, can only make promises for the four years he is President. But investments in nuclear power must be safeguarded from risk for ten, twenty, even thirty years. What happens if in 1984 or 1988 or later, Americans elect an antinuclear president or Congress that undoes all the good things Reagan is doing now? The unpredictability of democracy is too great; private capital will not risk billions of investment dollars unless it is protected from such dangers.

The only escape from the dilemma is via the sort of long-term government planning of the industry suggested by Bertram Wolfe. Massive federal subsidies would certainly be a key element in any such arrangement, though the nuclear industry will not be saved through a simple government bailout as, for example, the Chrysler Corporation was. To guarantee the long-term profitability of nuclear power, Washington will have to become even more actively and directly involved in its actual production than it already is. Along with industry, it must explicitly plan long-term production schedules—how many power reactors will be produced by the year 2000, how many reprocessing centers will be required, and so forth—and then it must do what is necessary to allow industry to meet these schedules.

The Reagan Department of Energy, under the astute leadership of former top Bechtel executive W. Kenneth Davis, adopted precisely this approach in its proposal to revive the abandoned reprocessing plant in Barnwell, South Carolina. The key element of the proposal was the offer of complete financial compensation in the event that a future administration or Congress should decide once again to ban commercial reprocessing.

The Davis proposal illustrates the fact that nuclear power cannot survive within anything even remotely resembling the "free market" so often praised by President Reagan. Rather, nuclear power requires the type of arrangement between government and private capital known as state capitalism, whereby the state enters into a tacit agreement with private capital to intervene in the marketplace, with money, legal authority, or both, to create and maintain conditions favorable to profit making. That is precisely the arrangement that has existed between the government and private capital since the creation of the commercial nuclear industry in the 1950s. But private capital feels that Washington stopped living up to its end of the bargain during the 1970s, and so it now is demanding an unmistakable reaffirmation of state support and a shifting of risk *out* of the marketplace and back into the society at large—in essence, a return to the conditions of the 1950s and 1960s—before going forward with any new investment in nuclear power. Because the industry needs a guarantee of generous and unwavering support for literally decades into the future, it must make its deal, not with politicians and governments that a capricious citizenry can vote in and out of power, but rather with the permanent institutions of the state itself. If it is to survive and prosper, the industry must greatly reduce its vulnerability to the citizen action and public pressure that can force changes in government policy. It must, in short, shield itself from democracy.

The immediate priority, however, is to stabilize the government regulations governing the design and construction of the industry's basic product: the nuclear power plants themselves. "The nuclear industry does not have a product that any utility in the United States can afford to buy," David Freeman, director of the Tennessee Valley Authority, told a closed meeting of top industry and Reagan administration officials in May 1982. Freeman pleaded with his audience to stop "blaming the messenger" of government regulation for nuclear power's ills: "The view that all the economic problems would disappear if only the regulators got off the industry's back is a smoke screen that's considerably more threatening to the industry's future than are the regulators." The real problem, Freeman asserted, is that the light water reactor is fundamentally flawed. Utilities cannot buy today's light water reactors "for the simple reason that the utility doesn't know what the total cost of electricity from such a plant will be or even when the power will be available. . . . The doubling and tripling of construction lead time [and hence of costs] only reflect the chaotic state of nuclear plant design, as the industry struggles to retrofit safeguards that experience has shown to be necessary." Nuclear power cannot be revived, Freeman warned, until corporate executives and government officials realize that "the real issue is the product itself. . . . The number one problem for the nuclear industry [is] a lack of standardization. . . . [It cannot continue] to patch the patches on our light water design." What the Brotherhood must do instead, according to Freeman, is incorporate the lessons learned since the Three Mile Island accident into a new design. Freeman did not rule out an improved light water design, but emphasized that such alternative concepts as the high-temperature gas-cooled reactor (HTGR) and the Canada deuterium uranium reactor (CANDU) deserve much closer consideration than they have received in the past. "We can't let the business interest of companies with massive investments in the light water reactors blind us to the possibility of developing a nuclear system that could serve mankind in a safer and more cost-effective manner." The future of nuclear power in the United States, Freeman concluded, depends upon "our choosing a more 'forgiving' nuclear design and then standardizing it."

THEIR OWN WORST ENEMIES

If the Atomic Brotherhood eventually triumphs, it will be because it finds a way to resolve the long-standing contradiction between making nuclear power profitable and making it safe. What is required is an approach that defuses political opposition while simultaneously restoring investor confidence.

Nuclear critics who scoff that this is an impossible task are both kidding themselves and greatly underestimating their opponents. W. Kenneth Davis's actions as Ronald Reagan's deputy secretary of energy, and Bertram Wolfe's and especially David Freeman's statements, demonstrate that the most farsighted and intelligent members of the Atomic Brotherhood already recognize essentially what must be done. The first step is to develop a standardized reactor that is significantly safer—in terms of both radioactivity releases and weapons diversions—than today's light water models. *Standardized* reactors are essential to regaining American *capital's* active support for nuclear power. They would allow a return to predictable and far shorter construction schedules, and thereby greatly reduce the cost of nuclear plants and increase their profit potential. They would protect investors from changes in government policy. They would, in short, deliver the stable investment climate without which private capital simply will not invest in nuclear power. *Safer* reactors, on the other hand, are essential to regaining the American *people's* trust in nuclear power. Safety must be upgraded not only in reactors but throughout the nuclear production process; and particular emphasis must be placed on finding a truly safe and final method of disposing of nuclear waste, including the decommissioning of the power plants themselves.

Nuclear power production cannot be made tolerably safe to the American people overnight, however. As David Lilienthal argued in his 1980 book, *Atomic Energy: A New Start,* what will be required is a serious, comprehensive, long-term research effort. "A new, different and safer alternative [reactor design] can hardly be widely available in less than ten or, more likely, fifteen years," he estimated.

Such a patient, long-term approach offers the men of the Atomic Brotherhood the best chance of reviving nuclear power as a viable commercial enterprise. As we have seen, the nuclear corporations possess the financial stamina required for this course of action. And the continuing slump in electricity-demand growth makes now the perfect time for them to begin. Given the overcapacity in the nation's electricity-generation system, utility companies will probably not be in a position to buy many new plants of any sort until the late 1980s anyway, no matter how much "excessive regulation" the Reagan administration hacks away. The self-interested thing for the Brotherhood to do in the meantime is to prepare for the eventual resurgence by developing nuclear power plants that are regarded as safe by the American public and that also are profitable to produce and operate.

But whether the men of the Atomic Brotherhood will act in their own long-term interest is by no means clear. Powerful men often prove to be their own worst enemies. The dilemma facing the men of the Brotherhood today is similar to the dilemma that confronted American business and political leaders during the Great Depression of the 1930s. Their own past excesses have landed them in the most serious crisis in their history, yet they are unable to consider making the short-term sacrifices required to save themselves. What makes this analogy particularly apt is the nuclear executives' claim that their technology is crucial to the future of American capitalism. They may be right. Certainly nuclear power is controlled and strongly supported by the most powerful forces in our society: the giant corporations and financial institutions that dominate our economy, and the military apparatus that wields such overwhelming influence over our political system and our future survival as a species. But capitalism has survived crises before. At present there appears little reason to expect that depriving American capitalism of nuclear power would cause it to crumble. As nuclear critics argue, an energy policy aimed towards a transition to solar energy in the long run is technically feasible, environmentally sound, and economically attractive. Getting from here to there *would* require a fundamental transformation in the governance of our society. In particular, it would require challenging what is a central canon of any capitalist society: the right of those who control the capital to decide when and for what purposes it will be invested. The giant corporations that plan and control the American energy system have not invested in decentralized solar technology for a simple reason: they do not perceive a decentralized solar economy to be in their self-interest. Profit maximization and constant growth are the guiding stars of their planning system. They favor centralized expensive energy technologies that only they have the wealth to develop—technologies like nuclear power. The present struggle between the corporations' private interest and the nation's public interest will determine America's energy path in the twenty-first century.

If the men of the Brotherhood truly believe nuclear power is essential to the capitalist economic system that has so richly rewarded them, they would do well to go back and study how capitalism escaped self-destruction in the 1930s. For just as fifty years ago capitalism had to be made less harsh to avoid being overthrown, so nuclear power today must be made much safer if it is to avoid being shut down permanently. Washington will have to take the lead on safety, because the corporations cannot do it themselves. Greed and the competitive urge prevent them from disciplining themselves on safety issues, just as they prevented capitalists fifty years ago from raising wages, encouraging trade unions, and supporting the redistribution of income required to stimulate economic demand and growth. Herbert Hoover did not understand this; Franklin Delano Roosevelt did. And while Roosevelt's New Deal reforms did not succeed in ending the Great Depression, they did save American capitalism from massive social unrest and rebellion long enough for the subsequent wartime mobilization to rejuvenate economic growth. Nevertheless, the financial oligarchy resisted Roosevelt's New Deal, just as most nuclear industry executives would resist a president who called for a New Start on atomic energy. So long as Ronald Reagan, our latter-day Herbert Hoover, is President, such a new start is inconceivable. From the standpoint of saving nuclear power, probably the best that could be hoped for from the Reagan administration is that it does not cause irreversible damage to the nuclear cause by precipitating, possibly through its slashing of safety standards, a major reactor accident or some other unforgivable catastrophe. But just as Hoover was replaced by Roosevelt, so might Reagan be replaced in 1984 by a more pragmatic politician better attuned to what big business in general and nuclear power in particular need to prosper in the modern era. In that event, the Brotherhood's nuclear imperative may well be realized after all.

Appendix 1

INDUSTRY OFFICIALS INTERVIEWED

I. Reactor and Component Manufacturers

WESTINGHOUSE ELECTRIC CORP.

ROBERT E. KIRBY	Chairman and Chief Executive Officer
LEO W. YOCHUM	Senior Executive Vice-President for Finance
GORDON HURLBERT	President, Power Systems Company
JOHN SIMPSON	Former Executive Vice-President, Nuclear Systems Division
THEODORE STERN	Executive Vice-President, Nuclear Systems Division
JAMES J. TAYLOR	Vice-President, Water Reactor Divisions
CHARLES WEAVER	Executive Vice-President for Corporate World Relations
HUNTER CHILES	Power Systems Marketing Division Manager
SAMUEL PITTS	Assistant General Counsel, Power Systems Company
JOHN KREUTHMEIER	Salesman, International Marketing Division
GEORGE HARTIGG	General Manager, Advanced Power Systems Division
DR. PETER MURRAY	Chief Scientist, Advanced Power Systems Division
DR. ROBERT OLSON	Program Manager, Water Reactor Division
ROBERT WEISSMAN	Assistant Manager, Regulatory and Legislative Affairs

GENERAL ELECTRIC CO.

DR. BERTRAM WOLFE	Senior Vice-President, Power Systems Sector
OSKAR THURNER	Manager, Domestic Marketing Division
ADRIAN FIORETTI	Manager, International Marketing Division
CHARLES V. SHEEHAN	Chief Finance Officer, Power Systems Sector
DAVID CROWLEY	Public Relations Manager, Power Systems Sector

COMBUSTION ENGINEERING, INC.

ARTHUR J. SANTRY, JR.	Chairman and Chief Executive Officer
WILLIAM J. CONNOLLY	Senior Executive Vice-President for Corporate and Investor Relations
JOHN WEST	Executive Vice-President, Nuclear Power Systems Division
EDWARD SCHERER	Director of Licensing, Nuclear Power Systems Division
R. F. VON HOLLEN	Sales Manager, Nuclear Power Systems Division
JOSEPH DIETRICH	Chief Physicist, Nuclear Power Systems Division
WILLIAM FLEMING	Director of Marketing, International Division
ROBERT KING	Chief Counsel, Nuclear Power Systems Division

BABCOCK & WILCOX CO.
(wholly owned subsidiary of McDermott, Inc.)

GEORGE ZIPF	Chairman, Executive Officer
JOHN MCMILLAN	Vice-President, Nuclear Power Generating Division
GEORGE STODDARD	Director, Corporate-Shareholder Relations, McDermott, Inc.
ALVIN KALMANSON	Counsel, Nuclear Power Generating Division
NELSON EMBREY	Manager, Marketing and Business Planning, Nuclear Power Generating Division
JAMES JONES	Assistant Counsel, Nuclear Power Generating Division
JAMES DEDDENS	Manager, Project Management Department
PAUL BERGSON	Manager, Legislative Affairs

II.   Architect-Engineering Firms

BECHTEL CORP.

W. KENNETH DAVIS	Vice-President for Nuclear Development
ASHTON O'DONNELL	Vice-President, Nuclear Fuel Operations Division

ROCKWELL INTERNATIONAL

WILLARD F. ROCKWELL, JR.   Former Chairman and Chief Executive Officer

III. Uranium Companies

PATHFINDER MINES
(wholly owned subsidiary of Utah International, Inc., a wholly owned subsidiary of General Electric Co.)

ROBERT MOYER   Manager of Marketing and Sales

HOMESTAKE MINING

RICHARD HOLWAY   Manager of Marketing and Sales

IV. Electric Utility Companies

COMMONWEALTH EDISON CO.

THOMAS AYRES   Chairman and Chief Executive Officer
JAMES O'CONNOR   President

DUKE POWER CO.

WILLIAM S. LEE   President

CAROLINA POWER & LIGHT CO.

SHERWOOD H. SMITH, JR.   Chairman and Chief Executive Officer

GENERAL PUBLIC UTILITIES CORP.

WILLIAM G. KUHNS   Chief Executive Officer

V. Wall Street Analysts

DREXEL BURNHAM

ALLAN BENASULI   Investment Analyst

L. F. ROTHSCHILD

HOWARD MAJOR   Investment Analyst

MOSELEY, HALLGARTEN & ESTABROOK

KEMP FULLER   Investment Analyst

BROWN BROTHERS HARRIMAN

MICHAEL D. LINSKY   Investment Analyst

VI. Public Relations Apparatus

ATOMIC INDUSTRIAL FORUM

PAUL TURNER   Vice-President for Public Affairs
CARL GOLDSTEIN   Assistant Vice-President for Public Affairs

EDISON ELECTRIC INSTITUTE

JACK YOUNG   Vice-President for Public Affairs

COMMITTEE FOR ENERGY AWARENESS

JACK BETTS
DON MACCAMMOND
WILLIAM PERKINS
ELLEN LEPPER

Appendix 2

CORPORATIONS OF THE NUCLEAR INDUSTRY

TABLE I. Reactor and Component Manufacturers

Name	1981 sales ($000)*	Nuclear Involvement	% Nuclear Dependent	Market Share	Other Activities
Westinghouse (Pittsburgh, Pa.)	$ 9,367,500	1. Reactor manufacturing	< 10%	35%	Military contracting; broadcasting; 7-Up bottling; leisure activity
		2. Reactor export	—	
		3. Breeder R&D		n.a.
		4. Uranium fuel fabrication		
		5. Uranium enrichment (attempted)		—
		6. Military contracting		—
General Electric (Stamford, Conn.) and subsidiary Utah International (San Francisco, Calif.)	$27,240,000	1. Reactor manufacturing	< 2%	30%	Electrical equipment manufacturing; commercial credit; jet engines; home appliances; broadcasting; robotics; minerals
		2. Reactor export	—	
		3. Breeder R&D		
		4. Uranium mining and milling		n.a.
		5. Uranium fuel fabrication		
		6. Uranium enrichment (attempted)		—
		7. Reprocessing (attempted)		
		8. Military contracting		—

Name	1981 sales ($000)*	Nuclear Involvement	% Nuclear Dependent	Market Share	Other Activities
Combustion Engineering (Stamford, Conn.)	$ 3,809,743	1. Reactor manufacturing 2. Reactor export 3. Breeder R&D 4. Uranium mining and milling (attempted) 5. Uranium fuel fabrication	< 10%	15% 0% — — n.a.	Electrical equipment manufacturing; pollution control; military contractor
McDermott, Inc. (New Orleans, La.) and subsidiary Babcock & Wilcox (Lynchburg, Va.)	$ 3,599,643	1. Reactor manufacturing 2. Breeder R&D 3. Uranium fuel fabrication 4. Naval submarines	< 10%	13% — n.a. —	Electric equipment manufacturing; oil drilling
Royal Dutch/Shell (Rotterdam, Holland) with Gulf Oil	$66,000,000	1. Reactor manufacturing 2. Military reactors 3. Reprocessing (attempted with Allied)	< 2%	n.a. —	petroleum
Rockwell International (Pittsburgh, Pa.)	$ 7,039,700	1. Breeder R&D 2. Waste management	< 2%	— —	Military contractor; automotive equipment; aviation equipment
Allis-Chalmers (Milwaukee, Wis.)	$ 2,041,844	1. Component manufacturing	< 2%	n.a.	Electrical equipment

Name	1981 sales ($000)*	Nuclear Involvement	% Nuclear Dependent	Market Share	Other Activities
		2. Reactor manufacturing (attempted)	—		manufacturing; military contractor

* 1981 sales figures from *Fortune* 500 listings, 1982.

TABLE II. Architect-Engineering Firms

Name	1981 sales ($000)*	Nuclear Involvement	% Nuclear Dependent	Market Share	Other Activities
Bechtel (San Francisco, Calif.)	$11,400,000	Design and construction of nuclear power plants	< 10%	40.3%	Built Alaska Pipeline; Washington, D.C. Metro; city of Jubail, Saudi Arabia
Stone & Webster (New York City)	$ 193,000†	"	< 5%	24.0%	Natural gas interests
Raytheon (Lexington, Mass.) and subsidiary	$ 5,636,184	"	< 2%	10.5%	Military contracting

Name	1981 sales ($000)*	Nuclear Involvement	% Nuclear Dependent	Market Share	Other Activities
United Engineers and Constructors					
Halliburton (Dallas, Tex.) and subsidiary Brown & Root	$ 8,508,133	"	< 2%	6.2%	Oil drilling; insurance
Fluor (Irvine, Calif.) and subsidiary Daniel International	$ 6,073,395	"	< 2%	6.2%	Oil drilling
Ensearch (Dallas, Tex.) and subsidiary Ebasco	$ 2,689,920	"	< 2%	8.9%	Natural gas, oil

* 1981 sales figures for architect-engineering from *Fortune* top 50 nonindustrial corporations, with the exception of Bechtel and Stone & Webster, which are privately held companies.
† 1979 Corporate Data Exchange.

TABLE III. Uranium Companies

Name	1981 sales ($000)	Nuclear Involvement	% Nuclear Dependent	Market Share*	Other Activities
Kerr-McGee (Oklahoma City, Okla.)	$ 3,826,420	1. Mining 2. Milling 3. Conversion	< 10%	21.0% 24.6% 60.0%	Oil and gas production
Exxon (New York, N.Y.)	$108,107,688	1. Mining 2. Milling 3. Enrichment (attempted) 4. Reprocessing (considered)	< 1%	2.5% 10.5% — —	Petroleum, gas, coal, solar energy; military contracting; office machinery
Gulf Oil (Pittsburgh, Pa.)	$ 28,252,000	1. Mining 2. Milling 3. Reactor manufacturing (with Royal Dutch/Shell) 4. Reprocessing (attempted with Royal Dutch/Shell, Allied)	< 1%	11.6%	Petroleum
Union Carbide (New York, N.Y.)	$ 10,168,000	1. Mining 2. Milling 3. Reactor manufacturing (attempted) 4. Enrichment 5. Operator, Oak Ridge National Laboratory	< 5%	1.0% 8.8% — n.a. —	Chemicals; electronics; plastics; agricultural products; metals; consumer products

Name	1981 sales ($000)*	Nuclear Involvement	% Nuclear Dependent	Market Share	Other Activities
Allied Corp. (formerly Allied Chemical) (Morristown, N.J.)	$ 6,407,000	1. Conversion 2. Reprocessing (attempted with Gulf, Royal Dutch/Shell)	< 5%	40.0% —	Chemicals, oil, natural gas
E. I. du Pont de Nemours (Wilmington, Del.) and subsidiary Conoco	$ 22,810,000	1. Reactor manufacturing (attempted) 2. Mining 3. Milling 4. Reprocessing 5. Waste management	< 5%	— 3.6% 6.2% n.a. n.a.	Chemicals; plastics; oil
Goodyear (Cleveland, Ohio)	$ 9,152,905	1. Enrichment	< 2%	—	Rubber; chemicals; plastics, metal products
Atlantic Richfield (Los Angeles, Calif.)	$ 27,797,436	1. Mining 2. Milling 3. Formerly, waste management	< 2%	2.2% 1.0% —	Petroleum, coal, natural gas, copper
Standard Oil of Ohio (Cleveland)	$ 13,457,091	1. Mining 2. Milling	< 1%	1.0%	Petroleum, coal; chemicals; plastics
Homestake Mining (San Francisco, Calif.)	$ 235,581	1. Mining 2. Milling	< 10%	n.a.	Gold, silver, minerals
UNC Resources (formerly United Nuclear Corp.) (Falls Church, Va.)	$ 259,428	1. Mining 2. Milling 3. Reactor manufacturing (attempted)	< 10%	5.8%	Minerals; machine tools

* Source for uranium market shares: June Taylor and Michael Yokell, *Yellowcake: The International Uranium Cartel* (New York: Pergamon Press, 1980). Data as of 1976.

Appendix 3

REACTOR ORDERS AND MARKET SHARES

	TABLE I. Profile of U.S. Market Growth		
		All zero to 1972	
	Annual Orders	*Cancellations*	*Cumulative Orders*
1953	1	0	1
1954	0		1
1955	3		4
1956	1		5
1957	2		7
1958	3		10
1959	3		13
1960	1		14
1961	0		14
1962	2		16
1963	4		20
1964	0		20
1965	7		27
1966	20		47
1967	39		86
1968	16		102
1969	7		109
1970	14		123
1971	22		145
1972	38	6	177
1973	41	0	218
1974	26	8	236
1975	4	11	229
1976	3	2	230
1977	4	9	225
1978	0	13	212
1979	0	8	204
1980	0	16	188
1981	0	6	182
1982	0	16 (year-end 1982)	166

Sources: Cancellations: Nuclear Information and Resource Service

TABLE II. U.S. Corporations' Domestic Market Shares

Year of Sale	General Electric			Westinghouse			Babcock & Wilcox			Combustion Engineering			Gulf General Atomic			Cum., total*
	A	B	C	A	B	C	A	B	C	A	B	C	A	B	C	
1953	—	—	—	1	100	100	—	—	—	—	—	—	—	—	—	1
1954	—	—	—	—	—	100	—	—	—	—	—	—	—	—	—	1
1955	1	33	25	—	—	25	1	33	25	—	—	—	—	—	—	4
1956	—	—	20	1	100	40	—	—	20	—	—	—	—	—	—	5
1957	—	—	14	—	—	28	—	—	—	—	—	—	—	—	—	7
1958	1	33	20	—	—	20	—	—	10	—	—	—	1	33	10	10
1959	1	33	23	1	33	23	—	—	8	—	—	—	—	—	8	13
1960	—	—	21	—	—	21	—	—	7	1	100	7	—	—	7	14
1961	—	—	21	—	—	21	—	—	7	—	—	7	—	—	7	14
1962	—	—	19	1	50	25	—	—	6	—	—	6	—	—	6	16
1963	3	75	30	1	25	25	—	—	5	—	—	5	—	—	5	20
1964	—	—	30	—	—	25	—	—	5	—	—	5	—	—	5	20
1965	3	43	33	3	43	30	—	—	4	—	—	4	1	14	7	27
1966	9	45	38	6	30	30	3	15	8	2	10	6	—	—	4	47
1967	9	29	35	12	39	33	5	16	11	5	16	10	—	—	2	78
1968	9	56	38	4	25	32	3	19	13	—	—	8	—	—	2	94
1969	3	43	39	3	43	33	—	—	12	1	14	9	—	—	2	101
1970	3	21	36	5	36	33	2	14	12	4	28	11	—	—	2	115
1971	5	23	34	10	45	35	3	14	12	—	—	9	4	18	4	137
1972	14	37	35	15	39	36	3	8	11	4	10	10	2	5	4	175
1973	8	19	32	16	39	36	6	15	12	11	27	13	—	—	4	216
1974	8	31	32	7	27	35	3	11	12	6	23	14	2	8	4	242
1975	—	—	31	4	100	36	—	—	12	—	—	14	—	—	4	246
1976	—	—	31	—	—	36	3	100	13	—	—	14	—	—	4	249
1977	—	—	30	—	—	35	—	—	13	4	100	15	—	—	4	253
1978	—	—	30	—	—	35	—	—	13	—	—	15	—	—	4	253
1979	—	—	30	—	—	35	—	—	13	—	—	15	—	—	4	253
1980	—	—	30	—	—	35	—	—	13	—	—	15	—	—	4	253
1981	—	—	30	—	—	35	—	—	13	—	—	15	—	—	4	253
1982	—	—	30	—	—	35	—	—	13	—	—	15	—	—	4	253
Total	77	—	30	90	—	35	32	—	13	38	—	15	10	—	4	253

LEGEND: A—number of reactors ordered. B—annual percentage of the domestic market. C—rolling cumulative percentage of the domestic market.

* A total of six reactors have been ordered from companies other than those listed above. They are: one reactor in 1955 from Power Reactor Development Co.; one reactor in 1957 and one in 1959 from Atomics International; and one in 1957, in 1958 and again in 1962 from Allis-Chalmers. This, together with the fact that the figures have been rounded off, causes percentages to add up imperfectly.

TABLE III.   Profile of U.S. Reactor Exports

	Annual U.S. Exports	Cumulative U.S. Exports	U.S. World Market Share, Annual*	U.S. World Market Share, Cumulative	U.S. Cumulative Share, Third World Market
pre-1960	4	4	28%	28%	—
1960	2	6	50%	33%	—
1961	0	6	0%	28%	—
1962	3	9	37%	30%	100%
1963	1	10	20%	30%	100%
1964	1	11	20%	28%	66%
1965	3	14	30%	28%	66%
1966	3	17	37%	29%	66%
1967	1	18	6%	25%	40%
1968	2	20	18%	25%	33%
1969	6	26	26%	25%	50%
1970	3	29	30%	25%	55%
1971	9	38	43%	28%	55%
1972	8	46	61%	32%	77%
1973	3	49	8%	27%	66%
1974	7	56	20%	26%	59%
1975	4	60	22%	26%	59%
1976	1	61	14%	25%	56%
1977	1	62	7%	24%	58%
1978	2	64	13%	23%	61%
1979	2	66	33%	23%	58%
1980	0	66	0%	23%	51%
1981	0	66	0%	22%	49%

SOURCES: General Electric Co., Center for Development Policy, Nuclear Engineering International, and Atomic Industrial Forum.
* "World market" is defined as all capitalist countries (i.e., United States, Canada, Western Europe, Japan, India, South America, Africa, Asia).

TABLE IV: U.S. Corporations' Export Market Shares

	Total U.S. Exports	Westing-house Annual Exports	GE Annual Exports	Westing-house Market Share	GE Market Share
pre-1960	4	2	2	14%	14%
1960	2	1	1	25%	25%
1961	0	0	0	0%	0%
1962	3	0	3	0%	37%
1963	1	0	1	0%	20%
1964	1	1	0	20%	0%
1965	3	1	2	10%	20%
1966	3	1	2	12%	25%
1967	1	0	1	0%	6%
1968	2	2	0	18%	0%
1969	6	4	2	17%	9%
1970	3	2	1	20%	10%
1971	9	6	3	28%	14%
1972	8	4	4	31%	31%
1973	3	1	2	3%	5%
1974	7	4	3	14%	9%
1975	4	2	2	11%	11%
1976	1	1	0	14%	0%
1977	1	0	1	0%	7%
1978	2	2	0	13%	0%
1979	2	2	0	33%	0%
1980	0	0	0	0%	0%
1981	0	0	0	0%	0%

SOURCES: General Electric Co., Center for Development Policy, Nuclear Engineering International, and Atomic Industrial Forum.

Appendix 4
THE NUCLEAR CORPORATIONS' FINANCIAL ASSOCIATES

1. J. P. Morgan & Co. (bank) 1981 total assets: $53,522,000,000
1981 profits: $347,000,000
Fortune ranking: 5

A. Stock Ownership in Nuclear Corporations

Name	Shares	% Control	Ranking†
Halliburton*	2,732,000	4.65	1
Combustion Engineering	1,190,400	3.64	2
Kerr-McGee	840,000	3.24	2
UNC Resources*	605,000	6.48	2
General Electric	2,310,000	1.02	4
Getty Oil	1,302,000	1.58	4
Rockwell International	639,000	0.85	4
Union Carbide	1,126,000	1.70	4
Du Pont	1,765,000	1.21	6
Allis-Chalmers	439,444	3.54	6
Exxon	4,314,000	0.95	7
Standard Oil of Ohio (Sohio)	1,577,000	0.66	8
McDermott	585,000	1.60	10
Gulf Oil	1,392,000	0.71	11

SOURCE: Corporate Data Exchange, *Stock Ownership Directory; Fortune 500* (New York, 1981). Figures are for year-end 1980.

B. Debt Relationship to Nuclear Corporations

Name	Loan Information
Allied Corp.	6-year, $125 million Eurodollar loan, due 1983 (Morgan is lead partner with 16 other banks)
	$250 million credit agreement (with Chase Manhattan, Citibank, 2 other banks)
Atlantic Richfield	$25 million bank loan (1973–?)
	8-year $200 million loan, 1/2 domestic, 1/2 Eurodollar, due 1985 (Morgan is agent/partner)

* 1979 figures from CDE *Stock Ownership Directory; Energy* (New York, 1980).
† Ranking in top 20 stockholders of corporation (CDE figures).

Name	Loan Information
Du Pont	$13 million outstanding debt at end of 1978
General Electric	$9 million outstanding debt at end of 1978
Goodyear	$30.8 million outstanding debt in 1978
Gulf Oil	7-year, $8 million note, due 1983
	6-year, $12 million note, due 1983 (Morgan Guaranty Trust, London)
Rockwell International	4-year, $200 million revenue credit agreement, due 1977 (canceled 1976) (with 11 other banks)
	6-year, $100 million Eurodollar loan, due 1980 (canceled 1976) (with 11 other banks)
Union Carbide	$8 million outstanding debt at end of 1978

SOURCE: Corporate Data Exchange *Debt Profile*, prepared for the author July 1979.

2. Bankers Trust   1981 total assets: $34,213,010,000
1981 profits: $187,980,000
Fortune ranking: 8

A. STOCK OWNERSHIP IN NUCLEAR CORPORATIONS

Name	Shares	% Control	Ranking
Allied Corp.	938,041	2.81	3
Homestake Mining*	48,798	0.42	7
Sohio	1,285,832	0.54	9
Union Carbide	714,448	1.08	7
General Electric	2,196,590	0.97	8
Fluor*	224,923	1.39	11
Raytheon	418,353	1.00	11
Goodyear	472,153	0.65	18
Combustion Engineering	232,800	0.71	19
Getty Oil	815,739	0.99	7
Conoco (now Du Pont subs.)	5,629,206	5.23	1

B. DEBT RELATIONSHIP TO NUCLEAR CORPORATIONS

Name	Loan Information
UNC Resources	6-year, $2 million term loan, due 1978
	$15 million credit agreement (partner with Chase Manhattan)

* 1979 figures. All other figures are for year-end 1980.

3. Chase Manhattan Bank 1981 total assets: $77,839,338,000
1981 profits: $412,150,000
Fortune ranking: 3

A. STOCK OWNERSHIP IN NUCLEAR CORPORATIONS

Name	Shares	% Control	Ranking
Stone & Webster*	462,181	11.22 (nonvoting)	2
Exxon	6,792,848	1.49	3
Getty Oil	1,256,124	1.52	5
Rockwell International	548,768	0.73	6
Gulf Oil	1,462,529	0.74	9
General Electric	1,432,603	0.63	15

B. DEBT RELATIONSHIP TO NUCLEAR CORPORATIONS

Name	Loan Information
Allied Corp.	5-year, $250 million credit agreement, due 1982 (partner with Citibank, Morgan, 5 other banks)
Allis-Chalmers	$80 million short-term loan, 1978, for merger of American Filter Co. (partner with Bank of America, Citibank, Manufacturers Hanover)
Atlantic Richfield	8-year, $25 million bank loan, due 1980
	$35 million of a 4-year revenue credit agreement (total $250 million), due 1978 (with 5 other banks)
General Electric	$6.8 million outstanding debt at end of 1978
Sohio	$600 million revenue credit agreement, term loan, 1974 (lent $90 million) (with 13 other banks)
	$62 million revenue credit agreement, 1978
Stone & Webster	$1.7 million letter of credit, 1976–77
Union Carbide	$73 million outstanding debt at end of 1978
UNC Resources	3-year, $12 million credit agreement, due 1975 (superseded by 1975 credit agreement)
	3-year, $15 million credit agreement, due 1977
	$15 million credit agreement, 1976 (partner with Banker's Trust) (loan to subsidiary guaranteed by parent)

* 1979 figures. All other figures in part A. are for 1980.

4. Manufacturers Hanover Trust Co. (bank) 1981 total assets:
$59,108,519,000
1981 profits: $252,117,000
Fortune ranking: 4

A. STOCK OWNERSHIP IN NUCLEAR CORPORATIONS

Name	Shares	% Control	Ranking
Union Carbide	2,177,824	3.30	1
Atlantic Richfield	4,063,515	1.72	3
Exxon	4,708,927	1.03	4
Du Pont	2,005,478	1.38	5
Conoco	1,512,616	1.40	5
(now Du Pont subs.)			
Westinghouse	726,00	0.85	6
McDermott	1,045,810	2.89	6
Fluor*	453,288	2.80	6
General Electric	2,260,206	0.99	7
Gulf Oil	1,784,977	0.91	7
Allied Corp.	487,130	1.46	11
Getty Oil	318,444	0.38	16
Raytheon	316,077	0.76	16
Halliburton*	538,484	0.91	17

B. DEBT RELATIONSHIP TO NUCLEAR CORPORATIONS

Name	Loan Information
Allis-Chalmers	$80 million short-term loan, 1978, for merger of American Filter Co. (partner with Bank of America, Citibank, Chase)
General Electric	$3.2 million outstanding debt in 1978
Goodyear	$152 million in promissory notes, 1966–92
	$105.6 million outstanding debt in 1978
Sohio	Revenue credit agreement (amount unknown), amended 1978
Stone & Webster	Lead bank (other information not available)
Union Carbide	$27 million of a $200 million revenue credit agreement, 1974, (with 22 other banks)
	$21 million outstanding debt in 1978

* 1979 figures. All others for year ending December 31, 1980.

5. Citicorp (bank) 1981 total assets: $119,232,000,000
                       1981 profits: $531,000,000
                       Fortune ranking: 1

A. STOCK OWNERSHIP IN NUCLEAR CORPORATIONS

Name	Shares	% Control	Ranking
Westinghouse	4,976,111	5.82	1
Atlantic Richfield	4,403,984	1.86	2
Sohio	3,322,814	1.40	3
Conoco	2,390,180	2.22	4
(now Du Pont subs.)			
Halliburton*	1,249,543	2.13	3
McDermott	1,190,328	3.25	4
Allis-Chalmers	488,400	3.94	5
Getty Oil	817,107	0.99	6
Kerr-McGee	352,845	1.36	8
Du Pont	1,447,951	1.00	8
Goodyear	1,043,544	1.45	8
General Electric	2,120,705	0.93	10
Exxon	2,530,395	0.55	15
Homestake*	25,300	0.21	16

B. DEBT RELATIONSHIP TO NUCLEAR CORPORATIONS

Name	Loan Information
Allied Corp.	6-year, $250 million credit agreement, (partner with Chase, Morgan, 5 other banks)
Allis-Chalmers	$80 million short-term loan, 1978, for merger of American Filter Co. (partner with Bank of America, Chase, Manufacturers Hanover)
Du Pont	$20 million outstanding debt in 1978
Fluor	$150 million short-term loan, 1977, for merger of Daniel International Corp. (lead bank/partner)
General Electric	$11.1 million outstanding debt in 1978
Gulf Oil	7-year, $8 million note (partner with Morgan) (Citicorp International Bank, London)

* 1979 figures. All other stock figures are for 1980. Debt information is as of July 1979.

6. Chemical Bank 1981 total assets: $44,916,933,000
1981 profits: $215,039,000
Fortune ranking: 7

A. Stock Ownership in Nuclear Corporations

Name	Shares	% Control	Ranking
Stone & Webster*	600,040	14.60	1 (nonvoting)
Ensearch*	570,761	1.94	3
Exxon	2,519,466	0.55	16
Combustion Engineering	250,438	0.76	16
Raytheon	294,742	0.71	17

B. Debt Relationship to Nuclear Corporations

Name	Loan Information
Du Pont	$8 million outstandiing debt in 1978
General Electric	$0.9 million outstanding debt in 1978

7. Prudential Life Insurance Co. 1981 total assets: $62,498,540,000
1981 profits: $3,744,666,000
(*investment income*)
Fortune ranking: 1†

A. Stock Ownership in Nuclear Corporations

Name	Shares	% Control	Ranking
Raytheon	1,479,600	3.56	1
Gulf Oil	3,579,200	1.83	3
Union Carbide	1,481,581	1.92	3
Atlantic Richfield	2,533,200	1.07	4
Du Pont	2,144,900	1.48	4
Fluor*	556,100	3.44	4
General Electric	2,263,100	0.99	6
Westinghouse	623,300	0.73	8
Halliburton*	980,300	1.67	8
Exxon	3,233,600	0.71	9
Combustion Engineering	233,600	0.71	18

* 1979 figures. All other stock figures are for 1980.
† Ranking of 50 largest insurance companies, 1981.

B. Debt Relationship to Nuclear Corporations

Name	Loan Information
Allis-Chalmers	$9 million outstanding debt in 1977
(Credit Corp.)	$72.3 million outstanding debt in 1977
Atlantic Richfield	$121.2 million outstanding debt in 1977
Combustion Engineering	$5 million outstanding debt in 1977
General Electric	$43 million outstanding debt in 1977 (Holdings of Utah International debt)
Goodyear	$166.6 million outstanding debt in 1978
Gulf Oil	$35 million outstanding debt in 1977
Halliburton	$9 million outstanding debt in 1977
Kerr-McGee	$48 million outstanding debt in 1977
McDermott	$67.4 million outstanding debt in 1977
(Babcock & Wilcox subs.)	$35 million outstanding debt in 1977
Sohio	$356.6 million outstanding debt in 1977 (for Sohio BP Trans-Alaska Pipeline) (consolidated)
Union Carbide	$156.5 million outstanding debt in 1977
Westinghouse Credit Corp. (not consolidated)	$75 million outstanding debt in 1977

8. Metropolitan Life Insurance Co. 1981 total assets: $51,757,845,000
1981 profits: $3,855,375,000
Fortune ranking*: 2

A. Stock Ownership in Nuclear Corporations

No holdings in top 20 shareholders

B. Debt Relationship to Nuclear Corporations

Name	Loan Information
Allis-Chalmers	$21.5 million outstanding debt in 1977
(Credit Corp.)	$50 million outstanding debt in 1977
Atlantic Richfield	$79.8 million outstanding debt in 1977

* Ranking of 50 largest insurance companies, 1981.

Name	Loan Information
Exxon	$193.6 million outstanding debt in 1977
GE Credit Corp.	$118 million outstanding debt in 1977
Goodyear	$101.1 million outstanding debt in 1978
Rockwell International	$12.2 million outstanding debt in 1977
Union Carbide	$245 million outstanding debt in 1978
Westinghouse Credit Corp.	$75 million outstanding debt in 1977

9. New York Life Insurance Co. 1981 total assets: $21,041,380,000
1981 profits: $1,503,589,000
Fortune ranking*: 5

A. STOCK OWNERSHIP IN NUCLEAR CORPORATIONS

No holdings in top 20 shareholders

B. DEBT RELATIONSHIP TO NUCLEAR CORPORATIONS

Name	Loan Information
Allis-Chalmers	$46.4 million outstanding debt in 1977
Atlantic Richfield	$34 million outstanding debt in 1977
GE Credit Corp.	$19.7 million outstanding debt in 1977
Kerr-McGee	$7 million outstanding debt in 1977
McDermott	$23.4 million outstanding debt in 1977
Raytheon	$5.5 million outstanding debt in 1977
Rockwell International	$9.2 million outstanding debt in 1977

10. Teachers Insurance & Annuity 1981 total assets: $11,439,344,000
1981 profits: $1,017,409,000
Fortune ranking: 10

A. STOCK OWNERSHIP IN NUCLEAR CORPORATIONS

No holdings in top 20 shareholders

* Ranking of 50 largest insurance companies, 1981.

B. Debt Relationship to Nuclear Corporations

Name	Loan Information
Sohio	$77 million outstanding debt in 1977 (for Sohio BP Trans-Alaska Pipeline)

11. Lord Abbett & Co. 1981 total assets: not available
1981 profits: not available
Fortune ranking: not available

A. Stock Ownership in Nuclear Corporations

Name	Shares	% Control	Ranking
Union Carbide	1,481,581	2.24	2
McDermott	1,262,500	3.45	3
Goodyear	1,358,705	1.89	5
Westinghouse	1,308,900	1.53	5
Allied Corp.	563,754	1.69	9
Conoco (now Du Pont subs.)	895,610	0.83	12
Kerr-McGee	260,200	1.00	13
Du Pont	939,990	0.64	14
Allis-Chalmers	103,600	0.83	16
Gulf Oil	870,300	0.44	16

B. Debt Relationship to Nuclear Corporations

No holdings in top 20 shareholders

Notes

CHAPTER 1 • Energy: The Struggle for Tomorrow

page 3   The James Madison quotation comes from a letter to W. T. Barry, August 4, 1822. Cited in Saul K. Padover, ed., *The Complete Madison: His Basic Writings* (New York: Harper & Row, 1971), p. 337.

page 4   "A chance to enter a new Eden": cited in Stephen Hilgartner, Richard C. Bell, and Rory O'Connor, *Nukespeak: The Selling of Nuclear Technology in America* (San Francisco: Sierra Club Books, 1982), p. 39.

page 6   "It's questionable whether we will ever be cumulatively profitable": interview with the author.

    The statements by John West, Philip Bray, and other nuclear executives were reported in *Nucleonics Week*, May 6, 1982.

    "I just don't understand this talk about nuclear being dead": interview with the author.

    "The public must be told that it will have to choose": "The Future of Nuclear Power," Remarks by Robert E. Kirby, Chairman, Westinghouse Electric Corporation, Atomic Industrial Forum Annual Conference, San Francisco, November 12, 1979.

    The plans and budget of the industry's Committee for Energy Awareness were reported in *Nucleonics Week*, May 13, 1982.

    The *CBS News* poll was reported in the *New York Times*, April 10, 1979.

page 7   For 1981 sales figures for the corporations of the nuclear industry, see appendix 2.

    For data regarding the nuclear corporations' financial associates, see chapter 5 and appendix 4.

    "A large percentage of the people involved": interview with the author.

page 9   "In much of their course interchangeable and independent": U.S., Department of State, *A Report on the International Control of Atomic Energy*, prepared by Dean Acheson and David E. Lilienthal (Washington, D.C.: Government Printing Office, March 16, 1946) (document no. 2498), p. 4.

CHAPTER 2 • The Birth of the Atomic Brotherhood

page 10   "We managed to build the bomb": interview with the author.

    The circumstances surrounding Thomas Edison's invention of the electric chair are described in Sheldon Novick, *The Electric War* (San Francisco: Sierra Club Books, 1967), chap. 24.

page 11   The original warning to Roosevelt about Germany's atomic plans
           came in a 1939 letter that Albert Einstein wrote on the advice
           of Leo Szilard, Eugene P. Wigner, and Edward Teller, three
           emigrant Hungarian physicists. In fact, the Germans were not
           preparing atomic bombs, perhaps because many of their best
           scientists had already left the country. After the war, Einstein
           mourned, "Had I known that that fear [of Hitler getting the
           Bomb first] was not justified, I, no more than Szilard, would
           have participated in opening this Pandora's box. For my distrust
           of governments was not limited to Germany." See Otto Nathan
           and Heinz Norden, eds., *Einstein on Peace* (New York: Simon
           & Schuster, 1960), p. 621.
               "The greatest single achievement of organized effort in his-
           tory": Stephanie Groueff, *Manhattan Project* (Boston: Little,
           Brown & Co., 1967) p. xi.
               Information on the bureaucratic decisions and arrangements
           that produced the Manhattan Project is provided in the defini-
           tive Roosevelt biography, James MacGregor Burns, *Roosevelt:
           The Soldier of Freedom, 1940–1945* (New York: Harcourt Brace
           Jovanovich, 1970) pp. 249–52, 456.
               Information on the Manhattan Project is drawn from Richard
           G. Hewlett and Oscar Anderson, Jr., *A History of the U.S.
           Atomic Energy Commission,* 2 vols. (University Park: Pennsyl-
           vania State University Press, 1962), vol. 1; Anthony Cave Brown
           and Charles B. MacDonald, eds., *The Secret History of the
           Atomic Bomb* (New York: Dial Press, 1977); and Leslie R.
           Groves, *Now It Can Be Told: The Story of the Manhattan Pro-
           ject* (New York: Harper & Brothers, 1962).

page 12   Szilard's complaint about how security procedures slowed work
           on the Project is noted in Bernard T. Feld and Gertrude Weiss
           Szilard, eds., *The Collected Works of Leo Szilard* (Cambridge,
           Mass.: MIT Press, 1972), p. 122.
               Brown and MacDonald, *Secret History of the Atomic Bomb,*
           especially chap. 7, lists the many corporations involved in the
           Manhattan Project and reveals that the Army occasionally had
           to exercise persuasion to get companies to work on the Project.
           For example, W. S. Carpenter, then president of the Du Pont
           Company, at first refused to construct the plant in Hanford,
           Washington, that would produce the bomb's plutonium. But
           being a long-time munitions and weaponry producer, Du Pont
           could not risk alienating the source of much of its business. The
           company finally assented to the Project, but only after the War
           Department assigned it "the highest priority." Besides the Han-
           ford plant, Du Pont worked on the gigantic gaseous diffusion
           plant at Oak Ridge, Tennessee, that would produce the enriched
           uranium for the bombs. This plant was built by the Kellex Cor-
           poration, then a new subsidiary of the M. W. Kellogg chemical
           construction company. Union Carbide, the giant chemical com-
           pany, was chosen to operate the plant, a job it continues today.

General Electric, Westinghouse, and Allis-Chalmers, three leading electrical equipment manufacturers that have since gone on to become leaders in the civilian nuclear industry, were each granted a portion of the contracts for the electromagnetic plant at Oak Ridge. Stone and Webster, today a leading builder of nuclear power plants, also got started in the nuclear business during the Manhattan Project by working on the Hanford plutonium plant. Hewlett and Anderson, *History of the AEC,* vol. 1, chap. 6, lists many of the universities that participated, including Chicago, Columbia, California Berkeley, California Technological Institute, Princeton, Johns Hopkins, and Wisconsin.

page 13 "During the war, the importance of the effort": interview with the author.

Information on the introduction of "cost-plus" contracts during the Manhattan Project comes from Hewlett and Anderson, *History of the AEC,* vol. 1, chap. 6.

page 14 Truman's ignorance of the Manhattan Project is reported in Peter Pringle and James J. Spigelman, *The Nuclear Barons* (New York: Holt, Rinehart & Winston, 1981), p. 35.

"Was one of noninterference": Groves, *Now It Can Be Told,* p. 265.

Regarding Japan's readiness to surrender, see Gar Alperovitz, *Atomic Diplomacy: Hiroshima and Potsdam, The Use of the Atomic Bomb and the American Confrontation with Soviet Power* (New York: Simon & Schuster, 1965), chaps. 7 and 8. President Truman always took full responsibility for the decision to drop the bombs and claimed he never felt guilty about his momentous decision. When Robert Oppenheimer told him after the war, "There's blood on my hands," Truman took aside Undersecretary of State Dean Acheson, who had accompanied Oppenheimer, and said, "Don't bring that man here again. After all, all he did was make the bomb. I'm the guy who fired it off." See Philip Stern, *The Oppenheimer Case: Security on Trial* (New York: Harper & Row, 1969), p. 90.

Byrnes's statement came during an interview with *U.S. News and World Report,* August 15, 1961.

The Blackett quotation comes from his *Military and Political Consequences of Atomic Energy* (London: Turnstile Press, 1948), chap. 10.

Clark Clifford's top secret memo was printed in the appendix to Arthur Krock, *Memoirs* (London: Cassell & Co., 1968).

page 15 The views of Truman and his top advisers, including Chester Barnard's "most deadly illusion" comment, are reported in Pringle and Spigelman, *Nuclear Barons,* chap. 3.

"A single demand of you, comrades": cited in ibid.

"Were rather apt to think they were the big boys": quoted in ibid.

The various attitudes of the main actors in the Manhattan Project are reported in Hewlett and Anderson, *History of the AEC,* 1:411–94.

page 16   Leo Szilard's dissident activities are related in his *Collected Works,* pp. 123–41.

"The discovery that had produced so terrible a weapon": David Lilienthal, *Change, Hope and the Bomb* (Princeton, N.J.: Princeton University Press, 1963), pp. 110–11.

The description of the legislative maneuvering that produced the 1946 Atomic Energy Act is drawn from Hewlett and Anderson, *History of the AEC,* 1: 411–530.

page 18   "That there was no firm line dividing": Ronald W. Clark, *The Greatest Power on Earth: The International Race for Nuclear Supremacy* (New York: Harper & Row, 1981), p. 248.

page 19   For more information on the AEC's first commissioners, see Hewlett and Anderson, *History of the AEC,* vol. 2, chap. 1.

"Changed from healthy adversaries into pals": H. Peter Metzger, *The Atomic Establishment* (New York: Simon & Schuster, 1972), p. 17.

page 20   "The language of military power": Krock, *Memoirs,* app. 1.

The Lilienthal-Truman meeting and subsequent atomic decisions are reported in Pringle and Spigelman, *Nuclear Barons,* chap. 6.

page 21   The January 1947 meeting is reported in Hewlett and Anderson, *History of the AEC,* 2: 29–32.

"Our perception of nuclear energy's commercial potential": interview with the author.

page 23   The details of the deal between Leslie Groves and General Electric are recorded in Hewlett and Anderson, *History of the AEC,* 1: 629, 634.

Zinn's complaint is reported in ibid., 2: 207.

page 24   "Because the military work was all secret": interview with the author.

For more information on the 1951 Industrial Participation Program, see Wendy Allen, *Nuclear Reactors for Generating Electricity: U.S. Development from 1946 to 1963* (Santa Monica, Calif.: RAND Corporation, 1977), pp. 20–24.

"The Congress and the AEC encouraged us": interview with the author.

The details of the Dow-Detroit Edison proposal are noted in Richard G. Hewlett and Francis Duncan, *Nuclear Navy, 1946 to 1962* (Chicago: University of Chicago Press, 1974), p. 226.

page 25   The AEC's decision to make civilian reactor development a top priority is recorded in ibid., p. 227.

"Once we become fully conscious of the possibility": quoted in the London *Times*, October 23, 1953.

page 26 The National Security Council's secret memo was unearthed by RAND researcher Wendy Allen and is quoted in her report, *Nuclear Reactors*, p. 30. Weinberg's testimony was given in U.S., Congress, Joint Committee on Atomic Energy, *Atomic Power Development and Private Enterprise*, 1953, p. 242.

Rickover's efforts to push for the nuclear-powered aircraft carrier also are detailed in ibid., p. 30.

page 27 Strauss's letter to Cole is also cited in ibid., p. 30.

page 28 "Staying number one is a struggle for permanent victory": Richard J. Barnet, *Roots of War* (New York: Penguin Books, 1973), p. 3.

page 29 "It is taking a Cold War to give motivation" U.S., Congress, Joint Committee on Atomic Energy, *Atomic Energy and Private Enterprise*, 1952, p. 281.

"This nation needs its best brains and skill": ibid., p. 322.

"What sweeter arrangement": ibid.

page 30 "For their part, executives in private industry": Lewis Strauss, *Men and Decisions* (New York: Doubleday & Co., 1962), p. 321.

page 31 The information regarding when the future Big Four reactor manufacturers set up their first nuclear departments was provided by the companies themselves.

For more information on the Power Reactor Demonstration Program, see Allen, *Nuclear Reactors*, chaps. 5–7.

Richard G. Hewlett, chief author of the official AEC history, provided the information on the infighting within the Atomic Brotherhood over the Power Reactor Demonstration Program, in an interview with the author.

page 32 "Strauss was obsessed with keeping nuclear power private": interview with the author.

page 33 For more information on the Price-Anderson Act, see the chapter by former Senator Mike Gravel in Environmental Action Foundation, *Accidents Will Happen* (New York: Harper & Row, 1979).

page 33 "We knew at that time that all questions weren't answered": interview with the author.

page 34 "Everybody was in there cutting each other's throats": interview with the author.

"A gap may occur": quoted in Lee C. Nehrt, *International Marketing of Nuclear Power Plants* (Bloomington: Indiana University Press, 1966), p. 77.

page 35   "If we try to do it, we will only dam our own influence": cited
           in Harold I.. Nieburg, *Nuclear Secrecy and Foreign Policy*
           (Washington, D.C.: Public Affairs Press, 1964), p. 75.
               The Atoms for Peace speech is reprinted, in part, in Eisen-
           hower's memoirs, *Mandate for Change* (New York: Doubleday
           & Co., 1963), pp. 313–16.
               "There is a growing tendency": U.S., Congress, Joint Com-
           mittee on Atomic Energy, *To Amend the Atomic Energy Act of
           1946*, 1954, pt. II, p. 685.

page 36   For background on America's bilateral agreements, see the re-
           port prepared by Warren Donnelly, senior expert at the Con-
           gressional Research Service, for the U.S. Senate's Committee
           on Government Operations, *United States Agreements for Co-
           operation in Atomic Energy*, doc. no. 64-626-0 (Washington,
           D.C.: Government Printing Office, 1976). See also Donnelly's
           report for the Subcommittee on National Security Policy and
           Scientific Developments of the Committee on Foreign Affairs
           of the U.S. House of Representatives, *Commercial Nuclear
           Power in Europe: The Interaction of American Diplomacy with
           a New Technology*, doc. no. 86-382-0 (Washington, D.C.: Gov-
           ernment Printing Office, 1972).
               "The U.S. does not immediately need atomic energy": state-
           ment made in Armand's June 23, 1958 speech to the European
           Parliament.
               The quotations from the Joint Committee, Senator Pastore,
           and Lewis Strauss are recorded in U.S., Congress, Joint Com-
           mittee on Atomic Energy, *EURATOM; Proposed Cooperative
           Program on Atomic Power Between U.S. and European Allies
           and Legislative Implementation of U.S. Participation*, July 22–
           August 13, 1958.

page 37   "A means of securing a good and early foothold": ibid.
               The facts of the Euratom deal are recorded in Henry Nau,
           *National Politics and International Technology: Nuclear Reac-
           tor Development in Western Europe* (Baltimore: Johns Hopkins
           University Press, 1974), chaps. 4 and 5.

page 38   "The Euratom program didn't really stimulate": interview with
           the author.

page 39   "You shouldn't pass up this chance": interview with the author.

CHAPTER 3 • The Corporate Nuclear War

page 40   "The enthusiasm for nuclear power grew a lot faster": interview
           with the author.
               "Civilian Nuclear Power: A Report to the President," 1962.
           Reprinted in U.S., Congress, Joint Committee on Atomic En-
           ergy, *Nuclear Power Economics—1962 Through 1967*, February
           1968, p. 134.

page 41   The $800 billion forecast appeared in *Business Week*, February 24, 1973.

page 42   "We had a problem like a lump of butter sitting in the sun": *Fortune*, October 1970.

page 43   "The turnkeys made the light water reactor a viable product": interview with the author.
           "The competition was rather desperate": interview with the author.
           "A financial disaster": interview with the author.
           The figure for GE's and Westinghouse's turnkey-plant losses is from Robert Perry, et al., *The Development and Commercialization of the Light Water Reactor* (Santa Monica, Calif.: RAND Corporation, 1977), p. 35.
           "Both GE and Westinghouse recognized the necessity": interview with the author.

page 44   For a complete record of U.S. and overseas reactor orders, by year and corporation, see appendix 3.
           Philip Sporn's "Great Bandwagon" phrase is reported in Irving C. Bupp and Jean-Claude Derian, *Light Water: How the Nuclear Dream Dissolved* (New York: Basic Books, 1979), p. 211, n. 12.
           One prediction that half of future U.S. power would be nuclear was noted in *Business Week*, March 11, 1967. See also the quotation from William Connolly of Combustion Engineering on page 45 of this chapter.
           The manufacturers' promises of eventually stable prices are reported in Bupp and Derian, *Light Water*, chap. 4.
           "On the average, the cost of all light water plants": ibid., p. 79.
           "Blurring the distinction": ibid., p. 47.

page 45   "You have to realize that GE and Westinghouse were actually integrating backwards": interview with the author.

page 46   Fitzgerald D. Acker's claim that the utilities urged Combustion to enter the nuclear reactor business was made in an interview with the author.
           "The turnkey era was a real threat to us": interview with the author.

page 46   "We went in at a time when the projections": interview with the author.
           "The shake-out period for the nuclear industry": interview with the author. Among the companies that wanted into the nuclear reactor business, according to Bertram Wolfe, were American Car and Foundry, AMF, United Nuclear (which did eventually enter the uranium business), Atomics International (later merged with Rockwell Corporation into Rockwell International, which is helping build the Clinch River Breeder Re-

actor), General Dynamics (which eventually sold its reactor division to Gulf, which in 1973 merged it with another of the Seven Sisters of the international oil industry, Royal Dutch/ Shell, under the name Gulf General Atomic), Dow Chemical, Union Carbide (which added uranium mining and milling to its previous operation of the uranium enrichment plant at Oak Ridge, Tennessee), and Du Pont (which was already operating the nuclear weapons production plant in Savannah River, South Carolina, a job it continues today).

page 47   The tripling of uranium industry production and the entrance of oil companies is reported in *Fortune*, March 1967.

GE's predictions about the nuclear fuel market are contained in Eric H. Smith, "Economics and Competitive Factors in the Nuclear Power Industry," *Financial Analysts Journal*, January– February 1966.

"It was like razors and razor blades": interview with the author.

page 48   GE's view of the future reactor market is contained in part 2 of Eric H. Smith, "Economics and Competitive Factors in the Nuclear Power Industry," *Financial Analysts Journal*, March–April 1966.

The names and activities of the companies interested in entering the nuclear reprocessing business are given in an article by AEC Commissioner James T. Ramey in *Harvard Business Review*, July–August 1968.

GE's $60 million investment and Schenectady expansion were reported in *Business Week*, March 11, 1967.

Combustion's and Babcock's actions were reported in *Business Week*, March 5, 1966.

Westinghouse's $285 million expansion was reported in *Chemical Week*, March 25, 1967. The additional $165 million was reported in *Forbes*, November 15, 1968.

Gulf Oil's 1967 entrance into the nuclear reactor industry is discussed in Pringle and Spigelman, *Nuclear Barons*, p. 336.

page 50   "With progress and profit in mind": Strauss, *Men and Decisions*, p. 321.

The AEC's licensing behavior is detailed in Elizabeth Rolph, *Regulation of Nuclear Power: The Case of the Light Water Reactor* (Santa Monica, Calif.: RAND Corporation, 1977). Rolph later published a longer work, *Nuclear Power and the Public Safety* (Lexington, Mass.: Lexington Books, D. C. Heath, 1979).

"Since the competitive margin": Rolph, *Case of the Light Water Reactor*, p. 28.

"Plants can now be designed": ibid., p. 23.

The nuclear industry's wish (granted) to draw up the very regulations it would have to obey is noted in ibid., chap. 4.

page 51   The industry's desire that the AEC spend its safety funds on commercially valuable design improvements is documented in ibid., p. 25.

The AEC's diversion of funds from safety research to fast breeder development is described in ibid., chaps. 4 and 5.

page 52   The AEC's attempt to keep the 1963 safety study secret is described in great detail in Daniel Ford, *The Cult of the Atom* (New York: Simon & Schuster, 1982), pt. 1.

The findings of AEC scientists Tamplin and Gofman are summarized in Ralph Nader and John Abbotts, *The Menace of Atomic Energy* (New York: W. W. Norton & Co., 1977), pp. 70–75.

The full title of the 1972 National Academy of Scientists/ National Research Council study: *The Effects on Populations of Exposure to Low Levels of Ionizing Radiation* (Washington, D.C., November 1972).

The David Burnham story appeared in the *New York Times* on November 10, 1974.

page 53   Willard Rockwell's statement about his company's annual nuclear investments was made in an interview with the author.

The activities of GE and Westinghouse in breeders are reported in *Fortune*, March 1967, in an article that also describes how the Big Two tried to influence government officials to delay breeder reactor development until the industry's two leading companies could fully recover their investments in light water reactors and thus be positioned to continue their dominance of the entire nuclear industry.

page 54   "The industry was relatively low-funded": interview with the author.

"By the time the bids were made": interview with the author.

page 55   "As reinforcing our number one position": *Business Week*, February 24, 1973.

The Clinch River Breeder Reactor cost estimate is by the U.S. government's General Accounting Office.

The Pacific Studies Center's study: *500-Mile Island; The Philippine Nuclear Reactor Deal* (Mountain View, Calif., June 1974).

page 56   That B&W had lost approximately $30 million was said in an interview with the author by a company official who declined to be publicly associated with the remark.

"We lost out to GE and Westinghouse in Europe": interview with the author, in which Mr. Fleming epitomized the diplomatic sensibility required for his post.

The 25 percent figure contrasts sharply with the accepted truth in nuclear circles. The history of the accepted truth is instructive. Beginning in the mid-1970s, when the convergence of a suddenly collapsed domestic market with unexpected competition and sales losses overseas from their upstart former stu-

dents, the Europeans, led Westinghouse and GE to start urgently
pressuring Washington for quick and strong support for nuclear
exports, lobbyists for the Big Two often made the impressive
but inaccurate claim that U.S. manufacturers (in other words,
they) had controlled fully 90 percent of the world export market
up until the early 1970s. Even if one wrenches the definition of
"world nuclear export market" to the point where it excludes
Western Europe, the world's second largest regional market after
the United States and one in which GE and Westinghouse had
been vigorously competing since the 1950s, the claim is exaggerated, as table IV in appendix 3 demonstrates. Yet the 90
percent figure was unquestioningly accepted and repeated by
antinuclear forces who, like their industry opponents that made
up the figure, cited it as proof of the industry's supposedly
imminent death.

page 57   "When we were planning our export markets in the 1960s":
interview with the author.
     The information regarding the Big Two's foreign licensing
deals was provided by company documents and interviews with
the author. The record of export sales dates is based on the
sources for table III in appendix 3.
     The $2 million figure is given in Pringle and Spigelman,
Nuclear Barons, p. 346.
     "The reason to establish a licensee agreement": interview
with the author.

page 58   "Westinghouse thinks in terms": *Dun's Review,* January 1972.

page 59   The $30 billion figure appeared in *Business Week*, December 5,
1970.
     GE's failures in Belgium and Sweden were analyzed in *Dun's
Review,* January 1972.
     The establishment of WENESE was reported in *Business
Week*, November 13, 1971.

page 60   The essentials of the negotiations between Westinghouse and
the French government were described by John Simpson, the
man in charge of Westinghouse's nuclear operations at the time,
in a subsequent interview with the author.
     Westinghouse's moves into Sweden and England were re-
ported in *Dun's Review,* January 1972.
     "I hope someday we'll build a plant": *Business Week*, Decem-
ber 5, 1970.
     Donald Burnham's 30 percent exports goal was reported in
Dun's Review, January 1972.
     GE's Rotterdam Nuclear subsidiary was reported in *Business
Week*, January 26, 1974.

page 61   President Nixon made his wish during his Project Independence
speech following the announcement of the oil boycott, reported
in the *New York Times*, November 8, 1973.

"As far as GE is concerned": *Business Week*, February 24, 1973.

The $800 billion figure appeared in ibid.

The $60 million figure for Westinghouse's annual nuclear investment appeared in ibid. The Power Systems Company's 1973 earnings are given in Westinghouse's 1973 annual report.

"Laid plans for expansion and consolidation": *Business Week*, February 24, 1973.

The figures on Westinghouse's and GE's exports are drawn from table IV in appendix 3.

page 62   Gulf's plans to spend $500 million on reactor development were reported in the *Wall Street Journal*, December 12, 1973.

The Shell official was quoted in *Business Week*, June 9, 1973.

For more information on the West Valley reprocessing plant, see Nader and Abbotts, *Menace of Atomic Energy*.

The inflation in nuclear reactor prices is described in Bupp and Derian, *Light Water*, pp. 78–79.

The RAND conclusions on delays in reactor licensing are found in Perry et al., *Development of Light Water Reactor*, Summary.

page 63   "A reactor vendor would come out with a new design": interview with the author.

page 64   "Go out on a technical limb": interview with the author.

"We're going to have some accidents": *Forbes*, November 15, 1968.

"It stopped the horsepower race": interview with the author.

"Nuclear power remains highly competitive": Bupp and Derian, *Light Water*, p. 82.

page 65   "Imposed a specific responsibility": Metzger, *Atomic Establishment*, pp. 269–70.

page 66   *Business Week*'s editorial appeared in the June 30, 1973 issue.

CHAPTER 4 • The Fall from Glory

page 68   Nixon's Project Independence speech was reprinted in the *New York Times*, November 8, 1973.

Jones's speech was reported in the *New York Times*, November 11, 1973.

The $40 billion annual European orders figure and the GE official's quote were reported in *Forbes*, May 1, 1974.

The OECD's pledge was reported in the *Wall Street Journal*, December 26, 1973.

Japan's nuclear plans were reported in the *New York Times*, February 6 and September 23, 1974.

page 69   Figures for annual coal-fired power plant orders come from the
           Edison Electric Institute.
               The 30 percent utility revenue rise was reported in *Business
           Week*'s May 29, 1979 cover story, "A Dark Future for Utilities."
               "When the AEC insists on a design change": *Industry Week,*
           February 25, 1974.

page 70   The 84 percent figure is cited in Nader and Abbotts, *Menace of
           Atomic Energy,* p. 278.
               Nader's Critical Mass '74 conference is described in Anna
           Gyorgy and friends, *NO NUKES: Everyone's Guide to Nuclear
           Power* (Boston: South End Press, 1977), p. 383, and by Gyorgy
           in conversation with the author.
               The scientists' petition is cited in Nader and Abbotts, *Menace
           of Atomic Energy,* p. 108.

page 71   The *New York Times'* story on the industry's public relations
           offensive appeared in the January 17, 1975 issue.

page 72   The AIF's move to Washington was reported in the *New York
           Times,* May 26, 1975.
               The industry's referenda spending is cited in Nader and Ab-
           botts, *Menace of Atomic Energy,* p. 348.
               The engineers' testimony appears in U.S., Congress, Joint
           Committee on Atomic Energy, *Investigation of Changes Relat-
           ing to Nuclear Reactor Safety,* March 2, 4, 1976.
               Two major books have been written about the Silkwood case:
           Howard Kohn, *Who Killed Karen Silkwood?* (New York: Summit
           Books, 1981), and Richard L. Rashke, *The Killing of Karen Silk-
           wood: The Story Behind the Kerr-McGee Plutonium Case* (Bos-
           ton: Houghton Mifflin Co., 1981).

page 73   The verdict against Kerr-McGee for $10.5 million was reported
           in the *New York Times,* May 19, 1979.
               The nuclear industry's sleuthing activities were reported in
           Environmental Action Foundation, *Accidents Will Happen,* pp.
           162–75.
               Lovejoy's exploits are documented in *Lovejoy's Nuclear War,*
           Green Mountain Post Films, 1976.
               "The [Wyhl] action": Gyorgy et al., *NO NUKES,* p. 386.

page 74   The growth of the antinuclear movement is related in ibid.

page 75   Information on GE's enrichment activities came from company
           officials.
               Vince Taylor's comprehensive studies, *The Coming Uranium
           Bust* and *The Myth of Uranium Scarcity* (Los Angeles, Calif.:
           Pan Heuristics, 1977), were the basis for much of my analysis
           of the Nixon administration's enrichment policies.

page 78   The Bechtel proposal was reported in the *New York Times,* June
           26, 1975.

page 81   "Brazil came with an order for six plants": interview with the
           author.
               The formation of the Uranium Enrichment Associates was
           reported in the *New York Times,* December 11, 1975.
               The nuclear export policy debate within the Ford administra-
           tion was reported in the *New York Times,* June 15, 1975.

page 82   The leak regarding the secret London conference was reported
           in ibid.
               The report on the close of the London meeting was in the
           New York Times, June 26, 1975. The report on the West Ger-
           man–Brazil deal appeared the following day.

page 83   The most reliable and comprehensive summary of the Westing-
           house uranium fiasco is June Taylor and Michael Yokell, *Yellow-
           cake: The International Uranium Cartel* (New York: Pergamon
           Press, 1980).
               "The reason Westinghouse sold so many reactors": interview
           with the author.
               "We realized what Westinghouse was doing": conversation
           with the author.

page 84   "Utilities really had no choice": interview with the author.
               "The most stupid performance in the history of American
           commercial life": Taylor and Yokell, *Yellowcake,* p. 206.
               "From whose bounty will flow legal fees": ibid.

page 85   The $100 million settlement was reported in the *New York
           Times,* January 30, 1981.
               Carter repeated the "only as a last resort" promise to a national
           television audience during the first Carter-Ford debate, Septem-
           ber 24, 1976.

page 86   The GE-Schlesinger meeting was reported in the *New York
           Times,* May 15, 1977. GE's views about the meeting's signifi-
           cance were offered by a high-level GE official in an interview
           with the author.
               "How many times can you take this horse and beat it?": *Nu-
           clear News,* March 24, 1977.

page 87   Commoner's analysis of the Carter energy program was con-
           tained in Barry Commoner, *The Politics of Energy* (New York:
           Alfred A. Knopf, 1980), chaps. 1 and 2.
               The Energy Department's assumption of nuclear waste stor-
           age responsibility is analyzed in Ronnie Lipschutz, *Radioactive
           Waste: Politics, Technology, and Risk* (Cambridge, Mass.: Bal-
           linger Publishing Co., 1980).
               Industry executives described in interviews with the author
           how later Carter aides would point to Carter's presiding at the
           White House union agreement meeting when trying to convince
           the industry men that the President actually supported nuclear
           power, a claim the executives found hard to believe.

page 88   The United States' persuasion of France and West Germany is
           recorded in Gordon Adams and Gloria Duffy, *Power Politics;
           The Nuclear Industry and Nuclear Exports*, (New York: Council
           on Economic Priorities, 1978), chap. 5.
               The passage of the Nuclear Non-Proliferation Act of 1978 is
           described in ibid., chap. 5.
               "Carter and the administration promised us": interview with
           the author.

page 89   "Slowly, very slowly, bleeding to death": *Nucleonics Week*, No-
           vember 13, 1977.
               "When the administration people talk to us": interview with
           the author.

page 94   Robert Hanfling's confirmation that he helped draft the state-
           ment was offered in an interview with the author that occurred
           too late to be incorporated into the *Mother Jones* story.

page 95   The NRC's disavowal of the Rasmussen Report was reported in
           the *New York Times*, January 20, 1979.
               The NRC's earthquake order was reported in the *New York
           Times*, March 14, 1979.

page 96   "We are operating almost totally in the blind": President's Com-
           mission on the Accident at Three Mile Island, *Report* (Washing-
           ton, D.C.: Government Printing Office, 1979), p. 337.
               The 98% figure was reported in the *Washington Post*, April
           15, 1979.
               The 66% figure was reported in the *New York Times*, April 5,
           1979.
               The 46% figure was reported in the *New York Times*, April
           10, 1979.

page 97   Secretary Schlesinger's recommendations to the Congress and
           the President of support for nuclear power were reported in the
           New York Times, March 31, 1979.
               Carter's statements at the Washington press conference April
           10 were reported in the *New York Times*, April 11, 1979.
               "Just as the nationwide Vietcong attack": *Washington Post*,
           March 28, 1980.

page 98   "We've been assured time and time again": cited in the *New
           York Times*, April 11, 1979.
               "Overwhelming support": quoted in the *New York Times*,
           May 10, 1979.
               "We're encouraged by this vote": quoted in the *Washington
           Post*, June 7, 1979.
               The defeat of the Markey amendment in the House was re-
           ported in the *New York Times*, November 30, 1979.
               "The appropriate lessons were learned": interview with the
           author.

page 99   "If the country wishes, for larger reasons": Commission on Three Mile Island, *Report,* Executive Summary.

The Kemeny Commission chairman's change in voting procedures was reported by Carolyn Lewis in "A Reporter Feels the Heat," *Columbia Journalism Review,* January–February 1980.

page 100   Udall's and Hart's reactions to the Kemeny Commission report were cited in the *New York Times,* November 4, 1979.

"Yet another unsettling element": Atomic Industrial Forum press release, November 1, 1979.

The full-page ads appeared in the *New York Times,* November 2, 1979.

"Yellow light": quoted in the *New York Times,* December 12, 1979.

page 101   "I just don't understand this talk about nuclear being dead": interview with the author.

page 102   The 60,00 figure for Pennsylvanians fleeing Three Mile Island is cited in *Newsweek,* April 16, 1979.

CHAPTER 5•A Sideline Business

page 103   "I think we could be profitable": interview with the author.

page 105   The percentage of dependence upon nuclear-related sales for the nuclear corporations was calculated by comparing figures on nuclear-related sales drawn from company annual reports, interviews, and estimates by financial analysts with the figures for total sales contained in the company annual reports.

The $600 million and $30 million figures for GE's nuclear sales and losses, respectively, were offered by leading Wall Street analysts in interviews with the author. GE officials broadly confirmed the $600 million figure, declined comment on the $30 million.

page 106   "Way out in the future": interview with the author.

"We had business plans from the beginning": interview with the author.

For a total listing of GE's nuclear sales, see appendix 2.

Wall Street's suspicion that four vendors were too many was relayed by William Connolly, a top Combustion Engineering financial officer, in an interview with the author.

page 107   Theodore Quinn's revelations about his former company General Electric are contained in Theodore Quinn, *Giant Businesses: Threat to Democracy; The Autobiography of an Insider* (New York: Citadel Press, 1962).

page 108   The definition of "cross-subsidization" is found in John Blair,

Economic Concentration; Structure, Behavior and Public Policy (New York: Harcourt Brace Jovanovich, 1972).

page 110　Nelson Embrey's plans regarding the B&W nuclear marketing offensive were outlined in an interview with the author.

"If firm A lowers its price": Paul Baran and Paul Sweezy, *Monopoly Capital* (New York: Monthly Review Press, 1966), chap. 3.

The definitive story of the international petroleum cartel is John Blair, *The Control of Oil* (New York: Pantheon Books, 1977).

page 111　The details of the international electrical equipment cartel are provided in *The Continuing Cartel: Report on the International Electrical Association* (December 1979), available from Horace J. De Podwin Associates, Inc., 350 Fifth Avenue, Suite 5707, New York, N.Y. 10118. The details of the verdict against Westinghouse and GE are given in Richard Austin Smith, "The Incredible Electric Conspiracy," *Fortune*, April 1961, pp. 132–218.

The definitive story of the international uranium cartel is Taylor and Yokell, *Yellowcake*, chaps. 6–13, especially 7, 11, and 13.

page 112　The rise of reactor prices during the 1970s, and the companies' explanations of it, were described in interviews with the author.

page 113　"The NSSS vendors were trying to get the price levels up": interview with the author.

"There will not be enough business": interview with the author.

"To tough it through this thin period": interview with the author.

The reactor vendors' statements at the April 1982 conference were reported in *Nucleonics Week*, May 6, 1982.

"The most confounding thing": interview with the author.

"It's questionable whether we will ever be cumulatively profitable": interview with the author.

page 114　"If you neglect our uranium difficulties": interview with the author.

"The one of maintaining adequate teams": Mans Lonnroth and William Walker, *The Viability of the Civilian Nuclear Industry* (New York/London: Rockefeller Foundation/Royal Institute of International Affairs, 1979), p. 79.

The figures on backlogs are based on data from the companies themselves, the Atomic Industrial Forum, and *Critical Mass Energy Journal*, October 1982.

Bertram Wolfe's statement that GE's nuclear equipment would be shipped by 1985–86 was made in an interview with the author.

Babcock & Wilcox's backlog situation was reported in *Nucleonics Week*, May 6, 1982.

Information on the closing and redirection of the Big Four's nuclear facilities was provided by the companies themselves.

"There's no level at which you go subcritical": *Nucleonics Week*, May 6, 1982.

"Are in much demand in the market place": Lonnroth and Walker, *Civilian Nuclear Industry*, p. 76.

page 115 "Some segments of the U.S. nuclear industry": *Nuclear News*, November 1981.

"Résumés were shooting out of the nuclear division": interview with the author by a source who declined to be identified.

"When the market bottomed out": interview with the author.

"Are all past history": interview with the author.

page 116 The company's statements regarding how many orders would be needed for profitable operation were made in various interviews with the author.

"I don't think we'll reduce": *Nucleonics Week*, May 6, 1982.

"We could operate very profitably": interview with the author.

"As an admission that GE isn't a high-technology ... company": interview with the author.

The dependence of the vendors on the electric utility business was calculated by dividing total sales by sales of the "Power Systems" divisions, as provided in annual reports.

"We can't cut our own throats": interview with the author.

"We've got thirty-five plants in our backlog": interview with the author.

page 117 The $8 billion figure for revenue from backlog plants was reached by multiplying the number of total backlog plants by $100 million, a rough estimate of the average cost of an individual reactor, including initial installation and maintenance.

That profits on refueling and servicing are one and one-half to two times the 10 to 12 percent margins on reactors was revealed by Babcock & Wilcox executive Nelson Embrey in an interview with the author.

page 118 "You don't have the normal day-to-day competitive pressures": interview with the author.

James Taylor's $1.5 billion projection was made in an interview with the author.

John West's $200 million projection was made in an interview with the author.

GE's 1980 sales of $200 million worth of nuclear fuel were reported in *Energy Daily*, December 9, 1980.

"One industry observer forecasts": Atomic Industrial Forum, "The Nuclear Industry in 1982," p. 4.

"Our naval nuclear work is very important": interview with the author.

page 119 The importance of exports to GE's and Westinghouse's overall nuclear sales is illustrated in the tables in appendix 3.

"The name of the game": cited in the *New York Times,* May 23, 1982.

"With today's unemployment": interview with the author.

Efforts by leaders of America's Atomic Brotherhood to win the crucial Mexico contracts were reported in the *New York Times,* May 23, 1982, and June 12, 1982, and in the *Wall Street Journal,* October 26, 1981.

page 120 "I think we could be profitable": interview with the author.

Thomas Vanderslice's message to Wall Street analysts was described by Charles Sheehan, a top GE financial officer, in an interview with the author.

GE Chairman John Welch's statement was reported in *Fortune,* January 25, 1982.

"To be in the business indefinitely": Bertram Wolfe, in an interview with the author.

Figures on the performance of GE's reactors were provided by the company.

"GE is a very introspective company": interview with the author.

page 121 "We still remain optimistic": interview with the author.

Westinghouse's uranium settlement with Gulf was reported in the *New York Times,* January 30, 1981.

The information on Westinghouse's sales and performance in 1981 comes from its annual report.

"Not a lot of capital": interview with the author.

The $1.5 billion investment projection was revealed by Gordon Hurlbert in an interview with the author.

page 122 In a 1979 interview with the author, top Bechtel nuclear fuels executive Ashton O'Donnell stated that his company had designed "all the chemical reprocessing plants. We built the Idaho plant, designed and built the West Valley plant, designed the Barnwell plant; and we're working on the design of the Exxon plant."

"Concerned over the present market hiatus": interview with the author.

"As a company we have no particular axe to grind": interview with the author.

"In good times, construction companies": *Business Week,* September 29, 1980.

page 123 Bechtel's sales and employment figures were reported in the *Washington Post,* June 26, 1982.

The information on Fluor, Halliburton, and Stone & Webster is provided in *Business Week,* September 29, 1980.

Raytheon's military work is documented by the Department of Defense's annual listing of top defense contractors.

Enserch's natural gas holdings are documented in the Corporate Data Exchange's *Energy Stock Ownership Directory* (New York, 1980).

Ebasco's entrance to the synfuels business was reported in *Business Week*, September 29, 1980.

"The front-end of the fuel cycle": Lonnroth and Walker, *Civilian Nuclear Industry*, p. 18.

page 124   "Electric utilities now account": interview with the author.

"If there is a moratorium": interview with the author.

The giant oil companies' entrance into the uranium business is documented in U.S., Congress, Joint Economic Committee, Subcommittee on Energy, *Horizontal Integration of the Energy Industry*, November 19, December 8, 1975, and in *Yellowcake*, chap. 5.

The American Petroleum Institute's 71.8 percent figure is cited in Michael Tanzer, *The Race for Resources: Continuing Struggles over Minerals and Fuels* (New York: Monthly Review Press, 1981), p. 120.

The brief history of the development of the uranium industry is drawn from Taylor and Yokell, *Yellowcake*, chap 3.

page 125   Robert Kerr's intervention with the AEC on behalf of his company is alluded to in Taylor and Yokell, *Yellowcake*, p. 31.

The uranium industry invasion was but one part of the giant oil companies' grand strategy to become total energy companies. Between 1965 and 1977, for example, oil giants bought up 27 coal companies. Today, oil conglomerates own 25 percent of all the coal in the U.S.; by 1985 they will likely produce 50 percent of American steam coal. Big oil has long had a hold on natural gas production, and in recent years has also managed to wrap its ever-groping fingers around solar energy and other alternative technologies. For documentation and more information, see *Horizontal Integration of the Energy Industry*, and Corporate Data Exchange, *Energy Stock Ownership Directory*.

Kerr-McGee's 60 percent conversion market share was reported in Norman Medvin, *The Energy Cartel* (New York: Vintage Books, 1974), p. 34. Kerr-McGee officials declined to confirm the figure, but other industry officials affirm it coincides with their own estimates.

page 126   Exxon's plans to enter the reprocessing business were revealed by Bechtel executive Ashton O'Donnell in an interview with the author.

The identities of nuclear waste contractors are given in Elaine Douglass, "The DOE's Hazardous Wastes," *The Nation*, December 27, 1980.

page 130   The power of Wall Street financiers in the half-century preceding World War II is described and analyzed in Paul Sweezy, "The Resurgence of Financial Control: Fact or Fancy?" in

Sweezy and Harry Magdoff, *Dynamics of U.S. Capitalism* (New York: Monthly Review Press, 1972).

page 131 The various relationships between the nuclear companies and Wall Street investment banks were researched by the Corporate Data Exchange and are detailed in appendix 4.

The paraphrase of Edward Herman regarding the relationship between banks and corporations is from "Kotz on Banker Control," *Monthly Review,* September 1979, pp. 46–56. See also Herman's *Corporate Ownership, Corporate Power* (Oxford: Oxford University Press, 1981).

page 132 "Permit an interchange of views": C. Wright Mills, *The Power Elite* (Oxford: Oxford University Press, 1956), p. 123.

The corporate interlocks referred to in the text existed as of year-end 1979. They were compiled by the Corporate Data Exchange and Joshua Klein by cross-referencing the boards of directors of the top nuclear companies and their major financial associates.

page 133 The Rockefellers' nuclear involvement is detailed in "The Rockefellers and Nuclear Power," unpublished paper.

page 134 The New Manhattan Project's charges are contained in *Up Against the Wall Street Journal,* a magazine compiled for the antinuclear action on Wall Street that occurred October 29, 1979, the fiftieth anniversary of the Great Crash, and available from The New Manhattan Project, Box 962, Seabrook, N.H. 03874.

CHAPTER 6 • Building America's Pyramids

page 136 "If you're a fifty-five-year-old chairman of the board": interview with the author.

The story of King Cheops and the pyramids is drawn from John A. Garraty and Peter Gay, *The Columbia History of the World* (New York: Harper & Row, 1972), pp. 72–74, and Kenneth Neill Cameron, *Humanity and Society: A World History* (New York: Monthly Review Press, 1973), pp. 59–61.

page 137 "The ultimate symbol of technocracy": Jean-Claude Poncelet, "A Taste of Things to Come: What To Expect From The Antis," Atomic Industrial Forum Conference, Boston, February 1980.

page 138 "Electricity is the most marvelous thing": interview with the author.

page 139 "Except in those cases where cities insisted": H. S. Raushenbush, "The Triumph of the Power Companies," *The Nation,* 1929, reprinted in Robert Engler, ed., *America's Energy* (New York: Pantheon Books, 1980). The history of the struggle over electricity supply in the United States is drawn primarily from various essays in this book.

"My idea would be not to try reason": "The Million Dollar Lobby," *The Nation* (editorial), 1928, reprinted in ibid.

page 140 The figures on the privately owned utilities' market share and assets are based on data from the industry's Edison Electric Institute.

"There was a substantial threat": interview with the author.

page 141 "We want atomic power": Atomic Industrial Forum, "The Meaning of the Congressional Hearings on Atomic Energy," 1954.

page 142 "We were concerned": interview with the author.

"Around 1953, we organized the 'Nuclear Power Group' ": interview with the author.

"Most people in the industry thought we were nuts": interview with the author.

page 143 "What has made nuclear energy competitive": *Forbes*, June 1966.

page 144 The concentration of the electric utility industry after World War II is cited in Metzger, *Atomic Establishment*, pp. 248–49.

"Alarming news for the U.S. coal industry": *Forbes*, June 1, 1966.

page 145 The advantage nuclear power gave utility executives over trade unions was noted in Eric H. Smith, "Economics and Competitive Factors in the Nuclear Power Industry," pt. 1, p. 121.

"The electric utility business is the most capital-intensive": interview with the author.

page 145 "We don't raise money for a specific plant": interview with the author.

"If I had a small company": interview with the author.

"Fifty percent of our stockholders": interview with the author.

page 147 "A Dark Future For Utilities," *Business Week*, May 29, 1979.

Komanoff's calculations are included in Charles Komanoff, *Power Plant Cost Escalation: Nuclear and Coal Capital Costs, Regulation and Economics* (New York: Van Nostrand Reinhold, 1982), p. 2 and pt. 3.

The figures on generic safety defects and additional post–Three Mile Island safety regulations are provided by the NRC.

page 148 The shutdown of U.S. nuclear plants one day out of eight was reported in the *New York Times*, October 4, 1981.

"Merrill Lynch and the investment community": testimony before the Oversight and Investigations Subcommittee of the House International and Insular Affairs Committee, October 23, 1981.

"Floating on an ocean of debt": *Wall Street Journal*, January 8, 1981.

page 149 "We cannot conserve ourselves into prosperity": John Emshwiller, "The Trouble With Utilities," *The Nation*, April 4, 1981.

The $365 billion figure is cited in ibid.

The utility industry's new financing techniques were reported in *Business Week*, February 15, 1982.

The industry's rate increases were reported in *Business Week*, August 3, 1981.

The information from Alden Meyer came in an interview with the author.

page 151 "Everybody has the same goal": interview with the author.

"After about three months"; "You ask the receptionist": interview with the author.

"Do you know we have to get permission": interview with the author.

page 152 "The construction-permit hearings": interview with the author.

"One of the industry's criticisms": interview with the author.

"The public should rely on the NRC": interview with the author.

page 153 "Sure, you've got cancellation privileges": interview with the author.

page 154 "Ever since the mid-1970s": interview with the author.

"For most U.S. companies": interview with the author.

The 87 percent figure was cited in Richard J. Barnet, *The Lean Years* (New York: Simon & Schuster, 1980), p. 93.

page 155 "Of the six thousand men": cited in Metzger, *Atomic Establishment*, p. 118.

page 156 "You can't afford to do that type of thing": interview with the author.

The MIT study was reported in *Nuclear News*, February 1981; the Department of Energy report, in *Engineering and Mining Journal*, January 1981.

"Taking a snapshot that accounts for how many reserves there are": interview with the author.

The *Wall Street Journal* reporting on U.S. uranium prices and production changes appeared November 3, 1981.

"At that point the material becomes the property of the utility": interview with the author.

page 157 The mystery centered on the Apollo plant was described in David Burnham, "The Case of the Missing Uranium," *The Atlantic*, April 1979.

David Comey's estimate was cited in Gyorgy et al., *NO NUKES*, p. 48.

page 158 The mishaps at Dresden were reported in Joseph R. Egan, "The Mischief Syndrome," *In These Times*, April 15–21, 1981.

"There was something comical": ibid.

The Associated Press story on Indian Point appeared in the *New York Times*, October 21, 1979.

page 159 Jeff Stein's infiltration of Indian Point was described in his article "Crashing Indian Point," *Village Voice*, September 10–16, 1980.

The raid on the government's Savannah River plant was reported in the *Washington Post*, September 17, 1982.

page 160 The Energy Department's prediction about 28 reactors running out of storage space was reported in the *Baltimore Sun*, June 6, 1982.

"Do we have the moral right": cited in *Not Man Apart*. October–November 1978.

page 161 The DOE's estimate of nuclear waste disposal costs was cited in Lipschutz, *Radioactive Waste*.

The $3.6 billion expenditures on nuclear waste disposal was cited in *Don't Waste America* (Fall 1982), available from the Nuclear Information and Resource Service, Connecticut Avenue NW, Washington, D.C. 20036.

page 162 "This legislative largesse": Atomic Industrial Forum year-end 1982 report.

Quotation from President Reagan can be found in the *Los Angeles Times*, January 1, 1983.

page 163 The struggle over military and commercial nuclear waste disposal, and NRC Commissioner Gillinsky's "camel's nose in the tent" quote, are described in Elaine Douglass, "The DOE's Hazardous Wastes."

"Antinuke types": interview with the author.

Chapter 7 • The Nuclear Imperative

page 165 "I'm counting on nuclear power": interview with the author.

page 166 "A large percentage of the people involved": interview with the author.

"People in this business wouldn't trade jobs": interview with the author.

"Just take a look at what happens": interview with the author.

"All of our forecasts indicate": interview with the author.

page 167 "We've got a population": interview with the author.

Chauncey Starr's congressional testimony, "The Utility Industry's Response to the Three Mile Island Accident," was delivered September 9, 1979.

Chauncey Starr's Business Council speech, "Energy Availability and Industrial Growth," was delivered October 13, 1979.

"You know, even if we killed hundreds of people": interview with the author.

page 168 "The Petro-Crash of the 1980s" appeared in *Business Week*, November 19, 1979.

page 169 Kissinger's threat to invade the Middle East was made during an interview *Business Week* printed January 1, 1975.

"The feeling in the company": interview with the author.

page 170 The Energy Department's March 1981 announcement was reported in *Critical Mass Energy Journal*, August 1981.

The 15.4 percent efficiency improvement was reported in *Business Week*, April 6, 1981.

"I think what we've seen in the last year": quoted in the *New York Times*, April 6, 1980.

The energy efficiency activities of the nuclear companies were reported in *Business Week*, April 6, 1981.

page 171 "If we are to keep making more and more stuff": interview with the author.

"There *is* no one solution": interview with the author.

page 172 "But when you come right down to it": quoted in "Sin And The Scientist," a review by David Joravsky of *Robert Oppenheimer: Letter and Recollections*, in the *New York Review of Books*, July 17, 1980.

"It's sort of philosophical": conversation with the author.

"We're in a time": interview with the author.

"By the end of the century": interview with the author.

"Will very probably force our descendants": Samuel McCracken, *Commentary*, September 1977.

page 174 "The nuclear controversy": Jean-Claude Poncelet, "A Taste of Things To Come: What To Expect From The Antis," Atomic Industrial Forum Conference, Boston, February 1980.

"Here's a throwaway product": interview with the author.

page 175 "The primary problem": Robert DuPont, "The Nuclear Phobia," Atomic Industrial Forum Conference, Boston, 1980.

page 176 "I have a vulgar analogy": interview with the author.

"It sounds weird, but the nice thing about nuclear waste": conversation with the author.

"Pretty innocuous . . . To me it's the craziest thing": interview with the author by a high-level industry executive who declined to be identified.

"Defense in depth": interview with the author.

"Finally you have to say": interview with the author.

"Just once I'd like to answer the phone": conversation with the author.

page 177 "The nuclear industry is not going to go away": interview with
the author.
    Weinberg's speech and the reception from industry faithful
are reported in Robert Jungk, *The New Tyranny: How Nuclear
Power Enslaves Us* (New York: Grosset & Dunlap, 1980), pp.
57–58.
    "That's a price you pay": interview with the author.

page 178 "An old ruling class": Daniel Singer, *The Road To Gdansk* (New
York: Monthly Review Press, 1981), p. 210.
    "They've been even more damaging": interview with the au-
thor.

page 179 "An anti-growth, sleeping-bag society"; "What are they about?"
"There are those who will tell you": interviews with the author.

page 180 "There's no compromising with the antinuclears'": interview
with the author.
    "But then the Sierra Club found out": interview with the
author.
    "They're against nuclear power": interview with the author.

page 182 "They're not really against nuclear power": interview with the
author.
    "Their plan is to strangle our society": H. Peter Metzger, "The
Coercive Utopians: Their Hidden Agenda," distributed by The
Atomic Industrial Forum.

page 183 "Americans are a pragmatic people": interview with the author.

Chapter 8 • The Great Comeback

page 184 "You know, President Coolidge once said": the author's notes
on a speech before the Atomic Industrial Forum Conference,
Boston, February 1980.

page 185 "The mood at this year's conference": conversation with the
author.
    "I think these guys are tired of being kicked around": ibid.
    The date and location of the EEI Board of Directors meeting
was provided by a Middle South Utilities Company employee.
    "Received input from all segments": drawn from a speech
Lee made before Wall Street investment analysts, "The Electric
Utility Industry Response to Three Mile Island: Toward A Safer
U.S. Nuclear Program," on November 6, 1979.
    "To ensure that appropriate lessons were learned": interview
with the author.
    NSAC and INPO were described in William Lee's Wall Street
speech cited in the note for page 185.

page 186 "In the kind of society we have": interview with the author.
    "We found it difficult": interview with the author.

"We were just astonished": interview with the author.

The formation of the Committee for Energy Awareness and the details of the May 30 meeting were reported in the Bechtel memo summarizing the meeting that was leaked to the *San Francisco Chronicle.*

page 187 The four essential messages of the CEA were also listed in the Bechtel memo.

page 188 The Blundell and Culbreath speech was entitled "Losing The Nuclear Energy Option: The Economic and National Security Implications."

That Blundell and Culbreath later made presentations in other cities was revealed by CEA director Jack Betts in a subsequent interview with the author.

Chauncey Starr's Business Council address was entitled "Energy Availability and Industrial Growth."

Membership of the Business Council is listed on the council's letterhead.

The author obtained a copy of the thank-you letter that council chairman Reginald Jones of GE wrote to Mr. Starr.

The keen interest of Wall Street analysts in Lee's speech was mentioned by CEA director Jack Betts in an interview with the author.

The details of the CEA's $700,000 ad campaign were revealed by Jack Betts in an interview with the author.

page 190 The AIF's jesting consideration of Khomeini was reported by *Philadelphia Inquirer* reporter Susan Stranahan to the author, on the basis of an interview with AIF president Carl Walske.

The CEA television commercials were viewed by the author at the AIF Boston conference in February 1980.

The name of the internal CEA document reporting on the success of the television campaign is "Electronic Advertising" (Spring 1980).

page 191 The CEA's offer to television stations of free legal counsel was noted in ibid.

page 192 Senator McClure's remarks, as quoted, are drawn from the author's notes on his speech.

Robert Kirby's speech was made available to the author by Westinghouse public relations officials.

page 194 "I've never heard the nuclear argument made any better": conversation with the author.

page 196 Copies of the speeches by Jonathan Carlson and Jean-Claude Poncelet were available at the conference.

page 200 The story of Nuclear Energy Education Day and Citizens for Adequate Energy was told by Thomas Saunders at the Boston conference.

page 202 The "Declaration of Energy Independence" was contained in the AEW's organizing brochure; that getting signatures on this petition was the primary goal of the AEW was stated by CEA director Jack Betts in an interview with the author.

The information on the NEED and the participation of other organizations in AEW are mentioned in the AEW organizing brochure, except for the facts regarding the New York City event, which were provided by a Consolidated Edison company public relations official in an interview with the author.

page 203 The circumstances that led to the spin-off of the AEW from the CEA were described by Jack Betts in an interview with the author, as were the financial and legal arrangements of the fledgling organization.

page 204 "We figured out which cities": interview with the author.

"We'd get a chief executive officer" interview with the author.

The information on the AEW's fund-raising lunches was provided by AEW executive vice-president Don McCammond in an interview with the author.

page 207 "Could perhaps 'supply' up to 40 percent": Robert Stobagh and Daniel Yergin, "The End of Easy Oil," in Stobagh and Yergin, eds., *Energy Future: Report of the Energy Project at the Harvard Business School* (New York: Random House, 1979), pp. 11–12.

"There is simply no reasonable possibility": Irvin C. Bupp, "The Nuclear Stalemate," in ibid., p. 135.

page 208 "There is no reason to be defensive about nuclear power": *Washington Post*, November 16, 1982.

The expansion of CEA's budget to between $25 and $40 million was reported in *Nucleonics Week*, May 13, 1982.

"A long-haul job": ibid.

CHAPTER 9 • Washington: Creator, Betrayer . . . Savior?

page 209 "You know, we Jeffersonian democrats": interview with the author.

"We are now bullish on nuclear power": *Business Week*, November 5, 1980.

"It's a helluva lot more pleasant": interview with the author.

The figures on Reagan's first budget were reported in the *New York Times*, August 2, 1981.

page 210 Reagan's nonproliferation policy was announced July 16, 1981.

Reagan's major nuclear power policy statement was delivered October 8, 1981.

page 211 The nuclear executives' reaction to the Reagan administration's initial positive-policy announcements was made in interviews with the author.

page 212 "Running the government is like running General Motors":
Washington Post, November 3, 1980.

The biographical background information on James Edwards
is drawn from Ronald Brownstein and Nina Easton, *Reagan's
Ruling Class,* published in 1982 by the Presidential Accountability Group, Box 19312, Washington, D.C. 20036.

page 213 "It isn't the traditional role": *Business Week,* November 16,
1981.

"Get rid of these strident voices": *Washington Post,* July 1,
1981.

The biographical information on W. Kenneth Davis was provided by Mr. Davis in an interview with the author.

page 214 "An obscene expression": *Rolling Stone,* September 2, 1982.

"If I'm not qualified": quoted in the *Washington Post,* July
16, 1982.

The information on Donald P. Hodel is taken from the *Washington Post,* October 26, 1982, and *Power Line,* published by
the Environmental Action Foundation, January 1983.

page 215 The background information on Nunzio Palladino is drawn from
his official biography, provided by the NRC Public Affairs Office, except for his tenure at Oak Ridge in 1946, which was
confirmed by Ronald Brownstein and Nina Easton in an interview with Mr. Palladino.

The information on Thomas Roberts and his former company
was reported in the *Washington Post,* June 30, 1981.

page 216 Mr. Reagan's services for General Electric are described in Patrick Owens, "The President From GE," *The Nation,* January 31,
1981.

Transcripts of Reagan's radio broadcasts concerning nuclear
energy during 1978 and 1979 were provided by the Sierra Club,
San Francisco, California.

page 218 The analysis of congressional nuclear voting records appears in
The Nuclear Congress, published 1982 by Critical Mass, Washington, D.C.

page 219 Criticism of the Clinch River breeder by *Time* and the *Wall
Street Journal* was cited in Ernie Beazley, "Senator Baker's
Costly Technological Turkey," *Reader's Digest,* August 1982.

"It just wasn't worth fighting": William Grieder, "The Education of David Stockman," *The Atlantic,* December 1981.

Howard Baker's efforts on behalf of the CRBR are reported in
the *Reader's Digest,* August 1982.

"It was good old-fashioned arm-twisting": cited in ibid.

The campaign contributions by CRBR-related companies
were researched by Congress Watch, a nonprofit Washington,
D.C. organization, and reported in the *Baltimore Sun,* August
10, 1982.

page 220 "Any president who wants to seek a prosperous country":
quoted in C. Wright Mills, *The Power Elite* (Oxford: Oxford
University Press, 1956), p. 169.
"Nuclear power is sinking": "Hard Times for Nuclear Power,"
New York Times Magazine, April 12, 1981.
"Any electric utility president": *Electrical World*, March 1981.

page 221 "No boon for commercial nuclear energy": AIF's *Press Info*,
February 1982.
The figures on solar and conservation spending were reported
in the Nuclear Information and Resource Service's *Ground-
swell*, January 1982.
Bowring's report, *Federal Subsidies to Nuclear Power: Reactor Design and the Fuel Cycle*, was completed for the Energy
Department's Energy Information Administration in March
1980. Several reporters obtained copies of the report and filed
stories in the *Washington Post* and the *Wall Street Journal*,
among others. Bowring's superiors repudiated his conclusions,
and delayed the official release until his work could be reana-
lyzed. The study as officially released in 1981 declared federal
subsidies to have been only approximately $12 billion, less than
a third of Bowring's estimate. See the *Washington Post*, April 8,
1981.

page 223 The $23 billion projection by the Energy Department was re-
ported in the *Congressional Quarterly Weekly Report*, March
18, 1978.

page 224 "For nuclear energy to grow": Alvin Weinberg, "Nuclear Power
After Three Mile Island," *Wilson Quarterly*, Spring 1980.
"There's a price to be paid": interview with the author.
"Finally and absolutely stop the era of uncertainty":
Kirby speech at AIF San Francisco conference, November
1979.

page 225 "We can no longer afford further iterations": Mr. Marcum made
a copy of his ANS speech available to the author.
"What is holding up the construction": *Washington Post*, September 7, 1981.

page 226 "A surprising lack of professionalism": Mr. Palladino's office
made a copy of his AIF speech available to the author.

page 227 For a report on the Israeli raid, see U.S., Congress, House,
Committee on Foreign Affairs, Subcommittee on International
Security and Scientific Affairs, *Israeli Attack on Iraqi Nuclear
Facilities*, June 17, 25, 1981; see also *Newsweek*, June 22, 1981.

page 228 "If we are to maintain our influence": Mr. Malone's office made
a copy of his London speech available to the author.

page 232 The White House's order regarding Taiwan was reported in
Business Week, December 28, 1981.

George Bush's meeting with Brazil was reported in the *Washington Post,* October 7, 1981.

The State Department meeting with South Africa was reported in the *Baltimore Sun,* October 22, 1981.

President Reagan's offer of enrichment technology to Australia was reported in the *New York Times,* November 20, 1981.

Edwards's approval of the Argentine export was reported in the *Washington Post,* July 19, 1982.

Davis's service on the Reagan transition team was reported in William Greider, "The Boys From Bechtel," *Rolling Stone,* September 2, 1982.

page 233 The communications between Bechtel's Harry Browne and the Energy Department were reported in ibid.

"In the insiders' jargon": *Washington Post,* July 20, 1981.

President Carter's charge was quoted in the *Washington Post,* December 18, 1981.

Reagan's "I just don't think it's any of our business" statement was made at a news conference in Jacksonville, Florida, January 31, 1980.

Two Washington, D.C. organizations specialize in monitoring U.S. nuclear exports in the global spread of nuclear weapons. The Center for Development Policy, located at 418 10th Street SE, Washington, D.C., 20003, produces a series of studies on the nuclear programs of specific foreign countries; and the Nuclear Control Institute (formerly the Nuclear Club) at 1000 Connecticut Avenue NW, Washington, D.C., 20036, organizes seminars and pressures Congress for tighter export restrictions.

page 235 The DOE memo concerning nuclear weapons work was obtained and reported upon on October 27, 1979, by Stephen Nordlinger of the *Baltimore Sun,* who also made a copy available to the author.

For information on the nuclear fuel cycle, see Howard Morland, *The Secret That Exploded* (New York: Random House, 1980).

Westinghouse's and Gulf General Atomics' efforts to sell a plutonium-production reactor to DOE were reported in the *Washington Post,* November 20, 1982. The reactor was estimated to cost $4 billion.

Information on the Department of Energy's proposed 1984 budget is taken from the *Washington Post,* January 14, 1983.

page 238 The $5 to $12 billion cost estimate for a new production reactor was provided by House Armed Services Committee senior staffer Seymour Schwiller in an interview with the author.

Much of the background information on the laser isotope separation program was provided by Thomas B. Cochran and Barbara A. Finamore of the Natural Resources Defense Council,

The Potential Use of American Commercial Spent Fuel to Produce Nuclear Weapons, House Committee for Interior and Insular Affairs, October 1, 1981.

page 240 "Nobody is going to buy Barnwell": interview with the author.
"Determine which regulatory barriers": *Washington Post,* June 29, 1982.

page 241 The DOE proposal regarding Barnwell sent to the President in the summer of 1982 was reported in the *Washington Post,* June 29, 1982.
"Talked to by DOE": interview with the author.
"Was paid for and instigated by Bechtel": interview with the author.
James Buckham's estimate was reported in the *Washington Post,* June 29, 1982.
"Would render the distinction between atoms": Cochran and Finamore, *Potential Use of American Commercial Spent Fuel,* p. 10.
"Implementation of this plan": U.S., Congress, Senate, *Congressional Record,* September 17, 1981, p. S9940.
"Would destroy whatever credibility": cited in Cochrane and Finamore, *Potential Use of American Commercial Spent Fuel,* p. 8.
Eklund's warning was reported in *Energy Daily,* September 28, 1981.
"Not just misguided but dangerous": *New York Times,* March 24, 1982.

page 242 "This could be a public relations disaster": *New York Times,* September 22, 1981.
"Give the marchers one more reason": interview with the author.
"You can certainly say the industry is not enthusiastic": interview with the author.

page 244 "I don't see how the plutonium knows": interview with the author.
The story concerning a 70% production increase appeared in the *Washington Post,* October 11, 1981.

page 245 "The stuff in Europe could catch fire": interview with the author.

CHAPTER 10 • **A Nuclear America?**

page 247 "Our new objective must be": David E. Lilienthal, *Atomic Energy: A New Start* (New York: Harper & Row, 1980), p 17.
"The great tragedy of our time": interview with the author.

page 248   Dixy Lee Ray's comment about 300 people choking to death
           every year was cited in "The Rise and Slump of Nuclear Power"
           (1978), unpublished article by John J. Berger, author of *Nuclear
           Power: The Unviable Option* (New York: Dell Publishing Co.,
           1976).

page 250   "Keep them confused": AEC Commissioner Gordon Dean's di-
           ary, May 27, 1953.

page 264   Report of the administration's "trigger-list" of weapons-related
           equipment is taken from the *Washington Post*, January 3, 1983.

page 265   Criticisms of the IAEA were reported in the *Washington Post*,
           June 23–24, 1981.

page 267   "What is holding up the construction of a waste site": *Washing-
           ton Post*, September 7, 1981.
               "May well prolong the high level of opposition": reported in
           the *Washington Post*, January 5, 1982.

page 269   "The basic philosophy of the Reagan administration": interview
           with the author.

page 272   "The nuclear industry does not have a product": reported in
           Energy Daily, June 8, 1982.

Index

About the Author

MARK HERTSGAARD grew up on a small farm in rural Maryland, graduated from Johns Hopkins University in economics, history, and international politics, and began a career at the Institute for Policy Studies in 1976, first under the direction of Orland Letelier and Michael Moffitt, and later under Howard Wachtel and Richard J. Barnet.

He has published articles in such journals as the *New York Times, Le Monde Diplomatique, The Nation,* the *Bulletin of the Atomic Scientists, Mother Jones,* and *The Progressive.* He has also contributed chapters to *Accidents Will Happen* (Harper & Row, 1979) and *America's Energy* (Pantheon Books, 1980). He lives in Washington, D.C.

LARRY McMURTRY

OH WHAT A SLAUGHTER

Massacres in the American West
1846-1890

Simon & Schuster

New York London Toronto Sydney

SIMON & SCHUSTER
Rockefeller Center
1230 Avenue of the Americas
New York, NY 10020

For information about special discounts for bulk purchases,
please contact Simon & Schuster Special Sales at
1-800-456-6798 or business@simonandschuster.com

Designed by Karolina Harris
Photography consultant: Kevin Kwan
Manufactured in the United States of America

10   9   8   7   6   5   4   3   2   1

Library of Congress Cataloging-in-Publication Data
McMurtry, Larry.
    Oh what a slaughter : massacres in the American West, 1846–1890 / Larry
McMurtry.
        p. cm.
    Includes bibliographical references and index.
        1. Indians of North America—Wars—West (U.S.) 2. Indians of North
America—West (U.S.)—History—19th century. 3. Massacres—West (U.S.)—
History—19th century. I. Title.

E78.W5M35 2005
978'.02—dc22   2005051849
ISBN-13: 978-0-7432-5077-1
ISBN:10:   0-7432-5077-X

Photo credits will be found on page 177.

Contents

Comes the most heartrending tale of all. As I have said Before
General Custer with five companies went below the village to
cut them off as he supposed but instead he was surrounded and
all of them killed to a man 14 officers and 250 men There the
bravest general of modder times met his death with his two
brothers, brotherinlaw and nephew not 5 yards apart, surrounded
by 42 men of E Company. Oh what a slaughter how many
homes made desolate by the sad disaster everyone of them were
scalped and otherwise mutilated but the General he lay with a
smile on his face.

PRIVATE THOMAS COLEMAN
I Buried Custer

OH WHAT A
SLAUGHTER

The Meat Shop

Of "massacre" (the noun) the *OED* suggests "shambles, butchery, general slaughter, carnage," a definition that would probably work for the great scout Kit Carson, who called the 1846 massacre of an undetermined number of California Indians, in which he took part, "a perfect butchery."

Of "massacre" (the verb) the same authority offers "to violently kill, mutilate, mangle," a fair description of what was done to the victims in the course of the various massacres I intend to consider in this book.

The Encyclopaedia Britannica, eleventh edition, allots the subject a hasty paragraph, concluding that—though the word is very obscure—the etymology suggests something like a meat shop: a very bloody place, a shambles, with discarded and undesirable pieces of meat scattered around.

The image of a meat shop seems apt to me, since what massacres usually do is reduce human beings to the condition of meat, though the bits of meat will be less tidily arranged than the cuts would normally be in a decent butcher shop.

If we know anything about man, it's that he's not pacific. The temptation to butcher anyone considered undesirable seems to be a common temptation, not always resisted. The twentieth century, just passed, more or less began with the million-plus massacre of the Armenians by the Turks, and ended with the terrible low-tech chopping up of some 800,000 Tutsis in Rwanda, an old-style massacre mostly accomplished with hoes and hatchets. When it ended a good deal of Rwanda resembled a meat shop.

What I want to do in this book is look at several massacres that occurred in the American West during the several decades when the native tribes of our plains and deserts were being displaced from their traditional territories by a vast influx of white immigrants. This process began in the 1830s, but accelerated sharply in the 1840s and 1850s: it was mostly completed, insofar as the native tribes were concerned, by 1890.

Judged by world-historical perspectives these massacres were tiny. The Custer defeat in 1876, a military encounter that, to the great surprise of the general who was soon to lie dead with a smile on his face, was the only one of these encounters to involve more than two hundred dead, a figure hardly to be counted among the world's huge cruelties. Though I describe here and there some tiny massacres, involving only a handful of people, I am mainly concerned with the famous massacres, with death tolls over one hundred people.

But it should be remembered that the body count in the six massacres I'm especially interested in still adds up to fewer than one thousand people, barely one-third of the number who died in New York and Washington on September 11, 2001.

But places and contexts differ: in the thinly populated West of the nineteenth century the violent extinction of more than one hundred people was no light thing, though a few of the assailants at first pretended that it was. Massacres are not like vast natural disasters: the Galveston Flood, the San Francisco Earthquake, the eruption of Krakatoa.

Massacres require human volition, and the extremes that result not infrequently produce trauma and, sometimes, guilt. Though in most cases the men who did the killings I describe escaped legal retribution, they did not escape the trauma that followed on the terror they inflicted.

Nephi Johnson, one of the participants in the Mountain Meadows Massacre, died crying "Blood, blood, blood!"

Nephi Johnson

Though more than a century has passed since Wounded Knee, the most recent of these massacres, bitterness has yet to leach out of the descendants of those massacred. Very probably one of the reasons The Church of Jesus Christ of Latter-day Saints (the Mormons) continues to deny complicity in the Mountain Meadows Massacre—although an abundance of evidence makes clear that they led it—is because there are in Arkansas and elsewhere descendants of the 121 people killed on that September day in

1857. Many of those descendants might not be averse to suing this now very prosperous church.

I have visited all but one of these famous massacre sites—the Sacramento River Massacre of 1846 is so forgotten that its site near the northern California village of Vina can only be approximated. It is no surprise to report that none of the sites are exactly pleasant places to be, though the Camp Grant site north of Tucson does have a pretty community college nearby. In general, the taint that followed the terror still lingers, and is still powerful enough to affect locals who happen to live in the area. None of the massacres was effectively covered up, though the Sacramento River Massacre was overlooked for a very long time.

But the lesson, if it is a lesson, is that blood—in time, and, often, not that much time—will out. In case after case the dead have managed to assert a surprising potency.

★ ★ ★

J. P. Dunn

In 1886 the historian and journalist J. P. Dunn published a pioneering study of Western massacres. He called his book *Massacres of the Mountains,* though few of the massacres he described actually took place in mountainous country; none of those that I am concerned with do.

The 1864 massacre at Sand Creek, in eastern Colorado, occurred in vast and still almost empty plains country. Dunn's book was a very popular account of the long and bloody war between whites and Indians (and, occasionally, Hispanics) during the long struggle for control of our Western lands. Dunn's title was catchy and his material vivid, to say the least.

Though overwritten and overlong, Dunn's book is a Black Book, of a sort that was only to become common after World War I. He had initially intended to stop his story in 1875, just before the Custer battle, but found that he could not resist following the Apache campaigns in the Southwest, which were still proceeding.

Nor, in the end, could he resist doing the Little Bighorn and the subsequent troubles with the Nez Percé and the Utes. Geronimo and his eighteen warriors didn't surrender to General Nelson Miles until 1886, the year Dunn's book was published.

The Ghost Dance troubles among the Dakota Sioux, Sitting Bull's controversial death, and the final tragic slaughter at Wounded Knee Creek were still four years ahead. After 1890 there continued to be plenty of white-Indian conflict—*The New York Times* as recently as October 29, 2002, reported that there was yet again trouble at the Pine Ridge Agency in South Dakota, not far from where the Wounded Knee Massacre took place. Plenty of troubles there have been, but no more massacres on the one-hundred-victim scale.

Massacres of the Mountains is still in print; it remains interesting today not merely for what J. P. Dunn reported—often in prose more than a little purple-tinted, as we shall see—but also for what he himself *felt* about these bloody troubles. He knew

well, and repeats over and over again, that the Indians were com-
monly the victims of massive and cruel injustices—systematic injustices at that. He knew and insists that the agency system,
which put the Indians on the public dole, was, time and time
again, used as a personal piggy bank by corrupt administrators.
The Great Sioux Uprising in Minnesota in 1862 would not have
occurred had the agents just given the starving Indians the food
that was both available and theirs by right.

J. P. Dunn knew that many of the Indian grievances were
just ones. By the time he wrote his book it was clear that the Indians were beaten—which is not to say that they were pacified.
The personal element that lends his graphic text its tension is
that J. P. Dunn was close enough to the frontier experience to
have felt, himself, some of the apprehension about Indian attack
that was, from the early seventeenth century until almost the end
of the nineteenth, a constant presence for pioneers as they strove
to expand the Western frontier.

Similarly, apprehension about what the well-armed whites
might do was something Indians in the line of advance seldom
felt free to ignore.

This deep, constant *apprehension,* which neither the pioneers
nor the Indians escaped, has, it seems to me, been too seldom fac-
tored in by historians of the settlement era, though certainly it
saturates the diary literature of the pioneers, particularly the diary
literature produced by frontier women, who were, of course, the
likeliest candidates for rapine and kidnapping.

In my opinion this grinding, long-sustained apprehension
played its part in the ultimate resort to massacre. President
George W. Bush has recently revived the doctrine of the preemptive strike, a doctrine far from new in military or quasi-military
practice. Most of the massacres I want to consider were thought
by their perpetrators to be preemptive strikes, justified by the
claim that the attacks were punishment for past harassments by
the native tribes.

* * *

It is as well to say at the outset of this inquiry that all the massacres I want to write about are subjects of controversy; in most
cases the only undisputed fact about a given massacre is the date
on which it occurred—almost everything else remains arguable,
including body counts. What I have to say, after having spent
some months with the books about these bloody events, is often
opinion, conjecture, or surmise—or just a best guess.

The Vulnerable Pioneer

My own grandparents were vulnerable pioneers, which is perhaps one reason I began this inquiry. They left violence-torn western Missouri in the 1870s, looking for a safer place in which to raise a family. In their first travels westward I suspect they felt the apprehension regarding Indian attack that I mentioned in the previous chapter. The power of the Comanches and the Kiowa had been broken by 1875; and yet my grandparents, like many pioneers, must have wondered in their first Texas years if these formidable people were really going to *stay* broken.

As luck would have it they found in Archer County a nice piece of prairie with a good flowing spring on it, and they settled—the family seat, as it happened, was only a few miles from where one of the last small massacres on the southern plains had taken place. This was the Warren Wagon Train Raid, in which some Kiowa, including two famous chiefs, Satank and Satanta, had drifted well south of their reservation—they fell on a luckless little convoy of teamsters hauling goods between two forts. A few teamsters escaped but seven were caught, hacked up, and burned in the traditional way. General William Tecumseh Sherman was in the area, on an inspection tour of some of the Texas forts, but the Kiowa managed to miss Sherman, who, in any case, was traveling with a well-armed escort.

Satanta

Satank

General Sherman had the good luck to be "missed" more than once by formidable Indians. In 1877, while visiting Yellowstone, he narrowly avoided riding into the path of the fleeing Nez Percé, who were mopping up on all and sundry as they made their dramatic dash for Canada.

Sherman, while at Fort Richardson, near the town of Jacksboro, heard about the attack and at once instigated a pursuit that in time resulted in the arrest of the principal participants.

My grandparents' homeplace was only about a dozen miles from the site of this massacre: they can scarcely have failed to have felt some apprehension. Even fifteen years after the event it was still possible for renegade Indians to drift off the Oklahoma reservations; some probably wouldn't have sniffed at the chance to chop up a few of the settlers, who had, after all, taken their country. Small attacks *did* occur all over the West in the transition

Norfolk, Nebraska

period between 1875 and the turn of the century. Had a few last diehards decided to drift south from Fort Sill my grandparents would have been their natural prey. Fear of attack was a worry shared by virtually every frontier family, and it was a worry slow to fade.

Complete safety has probably always been chimerical everywhere. As I was driving up the Nebraska-Colorado border, after visiting Sand Creek, three would-be bank robbers, on the other side of Nebraska, stormed into a bank in the small town of Norfolk just as the bank opened—probably before the cashiers had even gotten the money in their drawers. Perhaps the would-be robbers, who were Hispanic, didn't realize that in a small plains town it's apt to take an hour or so for the banks to get up-to-speed. These three men were only in the bank forty seconds, but that was time enough to kill five people stone dead. They effected a kind of small massacre of the sort that occurs frequently in America. At the same time, far to the east, two snipers were terrorizing the D.C. suburbs: they killed ten people and wounded three, a kind of mini-massacre of randomly chosen victims.

Just as arbitrarily, a few years back, a loner named George Hennard strolled into a packed cafeteria in Killeen, Texas, and quickly blew away twenty-four diners—a reminder, as was what happened on 9/11, 2001, that though we are no longer pioneers we're always vulnerable.

Still, while the arrival of homicidal violence may be impossible to predict, the ways in which it arrives differ from place to place and century to century. Fifty to one hundred (or more) armed men are not now likely to race onto an Indian reservation and shoot or hack down anyone and anything they see (for raiders sometimes killed Indian horses too). These sorts of doings were chapters in the long and successful effort at dispossession that went on in the American West through the second half of the nineteenth century.

Near the end of his life the tenacious Sioux chief Red Cloud remarked that while the whites had made his people many promises, more than he could remember, they had only kept one: "They said they would take our land and they took it."

The bloody work that taking it required is the subject of this book.

The Big Massacres
and Some Others

The massacres I want to look at closely in this inquiry are six:

The Sacramento River Massacre: Spring 1846
The Mountain Meadows Massacre: September 11, 1857
The Sand Creek Massacre: November 29, 1864
The Marias River Massacre: January 23, 1870
The Camp Grant Massacre: April 30, 1871
The Wounded Knee Massacre: December 29, 1890

In addition I want to consider two well-known and much studied military massacres, Fetterman and Custer, where something occurred that is rather rare in military history: the total wipeout, a battle in which one side succeeds in annihilating the other to the last man. This happened at Fort Phil Kearny in 1866 and at the Little Bighorn a decade later. (It also happened at the Alamo, which is outside my scope.)

These six massacres were dreadful events, leaving scar tissue that will always be a part of our history. But they were not without precedent. Patricia Nelson Limerick and others have reminded us forcefully that massacres of Indians did not start in the

West. The whole continent was strongly contested: the Indians yielded up none of it easily. But, first or last, East or West, the Indians were up against people with better equipment; as the whites continued to push westward, many massacres, large and small, occurred. The elimination of some seven hundred Pequots, many of them burned alive in a stockade, is one of the most frequently mentioned Eastern massacres.

Some years ago I wrote a screenplay about one interesting frontier encounter, a small massacre that occurred in what is now Indiana, in 1824. I was adapting a novel based on this massacre, Jessamyn West's *The Massacre at Fall Creek;* my adaption has yet to reach the screen, though it still might.

In the Fall Creek incident, records of which are scanty indeed, settlers on what was then the very edge of the advancing frontier made a preemptive strike against a small band of Indians who were foraging, fishing, picking berries. Nine Indians were killed in the attack—most of the bodies were thrown down a well. Like many such attackers, the settlers near Fall Creek considered that they had merely been taking protective measures; in this case, though, instead of reducing the threat to their families, they increased it. The powerful tribes to the north and to the west were outraged—suddenly the whole frontier came under threat. The Indians were thought to be planning a massive, coordinated attack.

Up to this point in time, according to Jessamyn West, it had not, as a matter of law, been a crime to kill Indians; but the government, headed by President James Monroe, became fearful of a widespread revolt. The hastily arrived at solution to the crisis was to make Indian-killing a crime retroactively. A show trial was rapidly convened: able attorneys were provided both for the prosecution and the defense. The Indians, in all their power and majesty, came to witness this strange instance of white man's justice. In the end three white men were hanged by their own neighbors; one boy was spared. The Indians stayed off the warpath for a time, though plenty of war was to follow.

The massacre at Fall Creek was a very obscure incident—how much of what Jessamyn West wrote was based on historical research and how much on her imagination is now difficult to say.

To me the most interesting aspect is that (if this hastily created "law" was actually put in place) it didn't work. Many more Indians were killed, by many more whites; it was to be a good long time in America before white men were judicially punished for killing Indians.

The Moral Taint

It is clear from the records that moral opprobrium did in time attach itself to many of the men who planned and executed the murders described in this book; but, in most cases, that was as far as matters went. The exception to this is John Doyle Lee, who—twenty years after the killing—was offered up

John Doyle Lee

by the Mormon church and made to take the blame for the
Mountain Meadows Massacre. He was justly outraged at this turn
of events, but the higher-ups in the Mormon church had decided
to give the public a sacrifice, in the hopes that then the whole
matter would be forgotten. (They were wrong about that; two
books about Mountain Meadows have been published within the
last year.)

John Doyle Lee, outraged or not, was duly executed.

The sharpest contradiction to my point about the moral
taint is surely John Milton Chivington, the fighting parson who
organized and led the attack at Sand Creek in 1864. Chivington

John Milton Chivington

neither relented nor repented; he weathered the controversy with his head unbowed. Though he resigned from the army, he was never charged or punished. There were critics, but, in general, Chivington remained a hero to his fellow Coloradans—to many he is a hero to this day. There is even a town named for him in southeastern Colorado, only a few miles from the massacre site—Chivington, Colorado, a kind of ghost hamlet, not far north of the Arkansas River.

Be as that may, there are yet those dead human beings—young, old, and in-between—who died in the massacres. They lost their lives, but not their moral potency. Hard as the men were who carried out these slaughters, conscience did, in time, stir in many of them. Long after the bodies had become merely bones, there were men who felt compelled to describe the horror they had participated in. Blame was imperfectly assessed, but guilt and outrage did make itself felt even in these small, vulnerable frontier communities. In most cases official inquiries were held, at the end of which the massacres were condemned. General Ulysses S. Grant himself called Sand Creek "murder," and he later said the same about the killings at Camp Grant. This may not seem like much but it was important: Grant was a well-respected man. Even now inquiries are going on about the more recent massacres in Bosnia and Rwanda. *Mass murder doesn't go unnoticed!* The repugnance decent people feel when faced with the slaughter of innocents eventually finds expression, though in many cases, no doubt, the worst killers, the really evil ones, entirely escape judicial reckoning. They probably sleep soundly and die unmolested in their beds. Only occasionally is an Eichmann or a Barbie brought to the bar.

During these massacres in the American West there were those who wished, as the killing went on and the blood spurted, that they had had the good sense not to saddle up that day. A

Ulysses S. Grant

good many of these eventually expressed rather dazed regrets;
they had failed to anticipate that the reduction of one hundred or
more human beings to the condition of meat in a meat shop
would be as terrible as it turned out to be.

These belated repentings didn't change the terrible killings,
but the fact that civilized human judgment finally rejects massacre is a hopeful sign.

Did Kit Regret?

Even the scout and Indian fighter Kit Carson, who had a strong stomach when it came to killing Indians, may have turned a little, conscience-wise, after taking part in the "perfect butchery" at the Sacramento River in 1846. This turn-

Kit Carson

ing, if it occurred, didn't prevent him from effecting the dreadful removal of the Navaho and the Mescalero Apache from their homelands in the 1860s. Kit invariably did what his superiors told him to do, whether he liked it or not; but, in these last instances, it is clear that he *didn't* like what he had been ordered to do. He was nearing the end of his life, and, by this time, knew as much about Indians as any Westerner—more, certainly, than any of his superiors knew. It may be that he finally came to understand what a tragic undertaking these removals were—in fact they were slow massacres, people dying and dying as they struggled to keep up in what the Navaho call the Long Walk.

Did Kit Carson wonder, at the end, if the whole enterprise of exploration and settlement, in which he had been perhaps the preeminent guide, or, at least, the guide who lasted the longest, had been worth it? Had it been, after all, a good thing? The right thing? What he felt we will never know. Except for a brief, dictated autobiography, Kit Carson, for forty years a scout in the dangerous West, kept his conclusions, if any, to himself.

John Chivington, long before he organized the attack at Sand Creek, had come to believe that he had an absolute right to kill Indians. He made it clear, when the time came to ride, that he didn't want to hear from anyone who harbored sympathy for the Cheyenne and the Arapaho. Reportedly he even told one volunteer that he longed to "wade in gore."

At the Sacramento River, Kit Carson actually did wade in gore—it doesn't seem that he enjoyed the experience.

John Milton Chivington never turned; he defended the action at Sand Creek to the very end of his life. Carson, who remained loyal to John Charles Frémont despite the Pathfinder's many moral lapses, expressed no fondness for Chivington. Kit Carson took part in many, many Indian fights. It's possible that, at the end, he would have welcomed peace.

John C. Frémont

★ ★ ★

A decent bibliography of the literature relating to these massacres
would run to at least sixty or seventy volumes: and that would
not include the hundreds of books that deal with Custer and the
Little Bighorn. And yet it was Kit Carson—an illiterate scout—
who produced the best phrase about the business of massacre
when he referred to "a perfect butchery."

All these massacres produced abundant butchery, fits of violence so extreme that they quite drove out reason. The few survivors and the many perpetrators alike were stunned by what had
occurred. They were stunned to such a degree that it makes it
difficult to judge the reliability of their comments, some of
which were not delivered until months or years after the event.
Some refused to speak of the massacre at all, while others, Ancient Mariner–like, seemed compelled to reveal the worst, and

reveal it over and over again. Others made stumbling, rambling efforts to make it all seem less bad than it had been.

Only the hardest cases, the true believers, display absolute conviction. Those less firm often try to construct self-exculpatory defenses. It is not always easy for the chronicler to decide what testimony, if any, can be relied upon, though, in my opinion, people who lie about the massacres have a value to the record too. The lies people make up about extreme actions may be as revelatory as the few truths they manage to cough up.

After several of these massacres, even the most hardened of the perpetrators gave vent to wild exaggerations, particularly where body counts were concerned. Chivington, after Sand Creek, at first reported that he had killed between five and six hundred Indians, or rather more than had been in the camp to begin with—the actual figure was around 140, the same number the historian Sally Denton gives for the Mountain Meadows dead, and very close to the count at Wounded Knee (146).

The most difficult thing for the historian of these massacres to judge is tone of voice. We may know what someone said, but how did he or she say it? Take Kit Carson's "perfect butchery" remark. He said it, but in what tone: happily, matter-of-factly, wearily, with an element of sadness or disgust in his tone? Did he sound resigned? Kit Carson had seen much Western death. He had killed Indians and scalped them, but most of his battles had been small-scale endeavors, a few Indians versus a few mountain men; they were bloody fights, to be sure, but still on a very different scale from what happened on the Sacramento River.

Chivington's tone we may guess at; he was almost always angry, even when he was not killing Indians. But what about Brigham Young's tone, or tones, during the years when he was trying to cover up Mountain Meadows? At the time the massacre occurred the U.S. Army was on its way to Utah, to curb Mormon excesses. As it happened, the army didn't get there until the following year, but at this juncture Brigham Young would have

Brigham Young

been careful not to say anything too inflammatory. But he was
thunderous and fiery when he demanded that the Mormons of
southern Utah hew to the official line, which was that the Paiute
Indians did the killing. Brigham Young was a politician as well as
a church leader; he had more than one oratorical instrument in
his orchestra and he shifted skillfully from one to another. Today
we'd see him on television and be able to judge for ourselves, but
as it is we have to base our judgment on letters, diary entries,
speeches, sermons, depositions, and records whose provenance is
not always well established.

    In the case of most of these massacres, the tones in the re-
ports seem to vary between jeremiad and lament—battle reports
through the ages often do much the same. Few observers of what
happened at Sand Creek or Wounded Knee were impartial. The

participants in the massacres were either trying to kill people, or trying to avoid being killed by people, a circumstance that doesn't enhance one's objectivity.

Everyone who has written about these massacres admits at some point that they are required to make judgments on the basis of very quivery evidence. The ground is rarely firm or the truth plain.

Nothing illustrates this better than the vexed question of body counts, which is where I'd like to begin my inquiry.

Counts

The very first thing one notices when sifting through these reports of massacres—whether personal, official, or journalistic—is that the body counts vary widely from report to report. As good an example as any are the body counts from Wounded Knee.

When I first began to rummage around in this literature I went first to *The New Encyclopedia of the American West,* published

Chief Big Foot

by Yale, an invaluable reference book that I use virtually every day. I looked up Wounded Knee first, where I found what I already knew: that the reason the U.S. Army decided, on that fateful day in 1890, to arrest Chief Big Foot and remove his people to a different, distant agency was part of a broad effort to suppress the Ghost Dance, a recently arrived religious phenomenon that—puzzlingly in my view—made both the military and civil authorities in South Dakota extremely nervous. (I will return to the matter of official anxiety before we are done.)

Before reading the whole of the long Wounded Knee entry, I flipped back to the Ghost Dance entry, where I read that "almost three hundred Indian men, women, and children were massacred by the 7th Cavalry."

That figure was higher than any I had previously seen for this massacre; other sources had put the dead at between two hundred and 230.

But when I flipped back again in my big reference book to the entry on Wounded Knee and read on through the article, the figure given there was 146 Indian dead; 146 also happens to be the figure given on the big historical marker at the site itself.

Time, and patient counting, had whittled down the figure given in the Ghost Dance entry by more than half.

It is well to remember that the Sioux, at Wounded Knee, though surprised and vastly outgunned, still managed to account for a good many soldiers, perhaps as many as thirty-one.

The widest and wildest swings in numbers of estimated dead at the other massacres are to be found in the histories of Sand Creek. Chivington's estimate of five to six hundred is the high figure, and seventy is the low figure. The number of troopers killed is usually put at fourteen, some of whom died off site.

Present-day thinking about Sand Creek, as I have said, is that about 140 Indians died. Only seven prisoners were taken, two women and five children, all of whom were soon left at nearby Fort Lyon.

* * *

Lieutenant James Bradley made the first body count of army dead after the Battle of the Little Bighorn, in 1876. At the battlefield itself he counted 197 bodies—probably a pretty accurate figure just for the men of Custer's command, though it left out Major Reno's casualty figures, which Lieutenant Bradley was still unaware of. Major Reno lost thirty-two men, with 152 wounded. How many of the wounded later died I don't know.

The Battle of the Little Bighorn was one of the most famous battles ever fought on American soil. There were soon to be recounts and recounts; in a sense the process continues to this day.

What of the Indian losses in that battle? First reports suggested two hundred Indians died, but, over time, this count has been whittled way down. More recent estimates put the number of Indian dead at forty-five. If you add to that the thirty-six warriors that Crazy Horse claimed had been killed at the Battle of the Rosebud, one week earlier, you get some eighty dead Indians, an enormous loss for a hunter-gatherer society; but, of course, these dead died in glorious triumphs—the numbers of the fallen did not dilute the triumph much.

It is well to remember that Fetterman, the Rosebud, and the Little Bighorn were the greatest victories the Plains Indians ever achieved.

Of these, of course, the Battle of the Little Bighorn was the greatest. It was also the last.

It should be remembered too that Fetterman, the Rosebud, and the Little Bighorn were *battles,* warrior against warrior, which sets them off from the massacres I'm considering here. In these massacres many more women and children were killed than fighting men.

At the Camp Grant Massacre, for example, except for one old man and a "well-grown boy," *no* warriors were killed, only

William Fetterman

women and children. Throughout the era of the massacres it was, overwhelmingly, women and children who were massacred.

In the Sacramento River Massacre, Kit Carson said frankly that he had no idea how many were killed, but two other participants in that slaughter tried to guess at the number. Thomas Martin thought the dead numbered between 175 and 250, whereas Thomas Breckenridge thought the dead numbered between 120 and 150.

Our confidence in these counts must be tempered somewhat by the wildly varying guesses these same three men made as to how many Indians were there in the first place. Thomas Martin thought there were between four and five *thousand*, Kit Carson estimated one thousand, and Thomas Breckenridge, whose guess was probably the most accurate, thought there might have been around four hundred, of which perhaps 150 were warriors and the rest women and children.

★ ★ ★

When one is heading into mortal, no-quarter-given combat, careful counting is the last thing most people would attempt. A more or less normal fear instinct would encourage participants to think they see more Indians than are actually there.

The frequent variation in post-massacre body counts is also explainable. Having just participated in the killing of more than one hundred human beings in an irrational spasm of violence, one would not be likely, while the blood of the living is cooling and the blood of the victims still soaking into the ground, to be able to wander through the meat shop and produce an accurate count.

In the Custer battle, incidentally, there was a good deal of decapitation as well as more routine mutilations. Quite a few limbs were also chopped off—it would not be hard, in such a context, for a counter such as Lieutenant James Bradley to overlook a corpse or two.

Massacres may be many things, but they are never neat—they might be considered the very antithesis of neatness. Not everyone died in a nice countable line; in fact, almost no one did. Some fled, some were chased; many were wounded, often mortally. Many of these last died at some distance from the center of the fight. A few might crawl away and live for days before dying. At Wounded Knee four Sioux babies and one or two women were found alive some days after the massacre, although a blizzard had passed through in the meantime. The resilience of babies, particularly, has been noticed in many such contexts.

It could be too that there are basic psychological reasons why body counts vary so greatly. Counting is a rational activity, requiring at least a little brainpower, whereas slaughtering people is a process during which reason is best negated. In indiscriminate killing reason gets pushed aside: the two modes, slaughtering and counting, are opposed. No one was carving notches while the bullets flew at Sand Creek or Wounded Knee.

★ ★ ★

Though body counts still meant something in the Vietnam War, most modern military conflicts have spread death on such a vast scale as to render counting irrelevant, and also impossible. In the firebombing of the German cities in World War II the intense heat of the fires left nothing countable, just globules of fat. How many *did* die in Dresden or Hiroshima? The count can only be approximate, as on a smaller scale, it still is for the victims of 9/11.

The massacres of the American West were intimate affairs compared to the vast impersonal slaughters that modern weaponry makes possible now.

The vocabulary of atrocity has always been rather limited. There are at most a couple of dozen ways in which deadly violence can be visited quickly on a human body, even a human community: these few are repeated endlessly, almost inescapably in every massacre. You can burn a body, hack it up, decapitate it, cut off—or out—its genitalia, smash its skull, tear fetuses out of pregnant women, shoot arrows or bullets into it, maybe rip out its heart or other organs; and, really, that is more or less the whole menu.

Usually most of the above can be accomplished by expert warriors in a very short time, as was proven at the Fetterman Massacre when eighty men were killed and thoroughly mutilated in only about half an hour.

What remained on that field was a meat shop, a deathscape out of Brueghel.

At the Little Bighorn the women of the Sioux and Cheyenne walked amid the pale white corpses and added a touch or two of their own—puncturing Custer's eardrums with awls, for example. He was not otherwise mutilated, but the women of the Sioux and Cheyenne did not want Long Hair (Custer) arriving in the spirit world fully intact.

In the grisly massacre at Sand Creek, where a battle of sorts raged for hours, scope was found for some inventiveness on the part of Chivington's more hardened Indian-haters. One hundred scalps were collected later to be exhibited in a Denver theater. The audience cheered wildly, and might have cheered even more wildly had there been two hundred scalps. At Sand Creek, mutilation of the dead was so common that it is commented on in virtually every account. Scrotums became tobacco pouches; the pudenda of the women were removed and used as hatbands or saddle horn covers.

And yet there does seem to be a human hunger for accuracy when it comes to keeping count of the dead. In almost all massacres there are, at first, conflicting sets of figures, a high and a low. Almost always patient investigation revises the figure downward: from six hundred to 140 at Sand Creek, from three hundred to 146 at Wounded Knee. People confronted with massacres at first want to know how many died—a little later some of them begin to want to know why.

Images, Heroes, Stars

When Paul Andrew Hutton produced his *Custer Reader* in 1992, he estimated that there existed at least 967 graphic representations—paintings, prints, drawings, sketches in newspapers—of Custer's Last Stand.

The two most famous representations of this event are paintings: John Mulvany's *Custer's Last Rally,* and Cassilly Adams's *Custer's Last Fight.* The latter, updated a bit by Otto Becker and published in a wide variety of formats—trays, calendars, handouts—by the Anheuser-Busch Company of St. Louis, was probably the one picture most Americans had seen. A copy of it hung in the barbershop in Archer City in my youth.

Custer's Last Fight, as Paul Andrew Hutton points out, is a wholly imaginary rendering of the famous encounter at the Little Bighorn. No white witness survived the battle. Many Indians—thousands—did survive it, and quite a few of them later had something to say about the deaths of Long Hair and his men; but it seems highly unlikely that either Mulvany or Adams attempted to reconcile their personal visions with those of actual witnesses to the battle.

Besides—as I point out in my short biography of Crazy Horse—the dust that would have been thrown up by those thousands of charging horses would have made any synoptic look at

Custer's Last Fight

AST FIGHT.
the Seventh Regiment U.S. Cavalry
EWING ASSOCIATION,

the battle quite impossible. Dust and horses and a glimpse now and then of a charging warrior or a weary doomed soldier are about as much as anyone could have seen.

Unquestionably, though, the two paintings helped shape a national myth, more or less as the many cheap pictures of Roland holding off the Saracens at the pass of Roncevaux have become part of the French national myth.

For Custer the stream of images continues to flow. Leonard Baskin's somber frontispiece to Evan Connell's *Son of the Morning Star* is a notable example—it catches something of the darkness that was in the man. Many films have featured Custer, one of the most notable being Arthur Penn's fine adaptation of Thomas Berger's *Little Big Man*.

Americans' lack of passion for history is well known. History may not quite be bunk, as Henry Ford suggested, but there's no denying that, as a people, we sustain a passionate concentration on the present and the future.

Backward is just not a natural direction for Americans to look—historical ignorance remains a national characteristic. When it comes to the Old West, subject of thousands of books and almost as many thousands of movies, most Americans now know only the broadest generalizations. They know that the settling of the West involved crossing vast plains and high mountains, sometimes in covered wagons. Most know that there was a gold rush or two; most know, also, that there were Indians there before us, most of whom did not want us taking their land—or land that they considered to be theirs. We, of course, considered that it ought to be ours, so we took it. There were many battles, and the Indians were defeated.

Now there are excellent histories covering almost every aspect of our successful conquest of the West—a complex often confusing process—but not many Americans read them. Their

knowledge of the winning of the West is mostly arrived at iconographically, from movies, and the movie images possess enormous
power. Regarded collectively, movie Westerns have done more to
determine our idea of the West than all the books ever written
about it, good or bad. If Custer's Last Stand could only have
taken place in Monument Valley, the single most powerful landscape could have framed the single most powerful story; and that,
so far as most people were concerned, would be quite enough to
know about the Old West, thank you.

The movies, by their nature, favor only a few stars, and only
a few real national heroes. Of the thousands of interesting characters who played a part in winning the West, only a bare handful have any real currency with the American public now.
Iconographically, even Lewis and Clark haven't really survived,
though Sacagawea has. With the possible exception of Kit Carson, none of the mountain men mean anything today. Kit
Carson's name vaguely suggests the Old West to many people,
but not one in a million of them will have any distinct idea as
to what Kit did.

The roster of still-recognizable Westerners probably boils
down to Custer, Buffalo Bill Cody, Billy the Kid, and perhaps
Wild Bill Hickok. Theodore Roosevelt, a Westerner manqué,
would once have made the list, but not today. Custer, Cody, and
Billy the Kid are clearly the top three, generating far more im-
agery than any of the other candidates.

Skimpy as the image bank is for white Westerners, it is even
skimpier for Indians. My guess would be that only Sacagawea,
Sitting Bull, and Geronimo still ring any bells with the general
public. Crazy Horse, who never allowed his image to be captured, is still important to Indians as a symbol of successful resistance, but less so to whites. Even a chief such as Red Cloud, so
renowned in his day that he went to New York and made a
speech at Cooper Union, is now only known to historians, history buffs, and a few Nebraskans.

REWARD

($5,000.00)

Reward for the capture, dead or alive, of one Wm. Wright, better known as

"BILLY THE KID"

Age, 18. Height, 5 feet, 3 inches. Weight, 125 lbs. Light hair, blue eyes and even features. He is the leader of the worst band of desperadoes the Territory has ever had to deal with. The above reward will be paid for his capture or positive proof of his death.

JIM DALTON, Sheriff.

DEAD OR A
"BILLY TH

Reward for
Billy the Kid

Billy the Kid

Wild Bill Hickok

Buffalo Bill Cody

At the broadest level, only the white stars Custer, Cody, and Billy the Kid, and two tough Indians, Sitting Bull and Geronimo, are the people the public thinks about when it thinks about the Old West.

Sitting Bull

Geronimo

Geronimo driving a car in Oklahoma, 1908

The Sacramento River Massacre, Spring 1846

I f my argument in the previous chapter is valid, then it should be no surprise that today the Sacramento River Massacre is, of these six tragic events, much the least known. From what I can find, the first historian to give it more than a paragraph or two is David Roberts, in his excellent study of Kit Carson and John Charles Frémont: the book is called *A Newer World*. Carson was Frémont's principal guide on the popular explorer's first three expeditions into the American West.

In 1846, when the massacre occurred, there were no particularly famous Indians. Tecumseh, plenty famous in his day, had been dead since 1813. California produced no famous Indians, then or later, with the exception of the martyred Captain Jack of the Modocs. The battle for the Great Plains hadn't yet started: we are well in advance of Crazy Horse, Red Cloud, Sitting Bull, and the rest.

The men who effected the massacre at the Sacramento River could probably not even have named the tribes their victims belonged to. David Roberts believes that the Indians dancing by the water were a mixture of Maidu, Wintu, and Yana, names that meant not much then and nothing now, except to very close students of Californian Indian life.

Most Indian tribes were largely unknown, except to the explorers or trappers who went among them, but, when it came to near total obscurity, the California Indians were in a class by themselves. To the whites who slaughtered them they were merely nameless savages, the quicker killed the better. When the Gold Rush started they were swept away in the thousands, with brutal efficiency.

John Charles Frémont, the Pathfinder as he was called (though he found no paths), was aware of the Paiute tribe, to the east of the Sierras, and of the Klamaths, to the north of where he was camped at that time; but it was unlikely that he had even heard the names of the tribes he allowed his men to slaughter. Maidu. Wintu? Yana? It's doubtful that these terms meant a thing to John Charles Frémont.

To this day, for that matter, the California Indians have contributed almost nothing to the popular iconography of the West. There is, as I said, the noble Captain Jack, hero and victim.

Then there was Willie Boy, a Morongo who, mad for love, kidnapped his beloved and led the posse that pursued them on an epic, almost five-hundred-mile chase across the desert. When the game was up he killed both the girl and himself—Robert Redford starred in a movie about him. Willie Boy made his run in 1909.

The movies were revving up by that time, but the movies didn't do that much with California Indian life, although both Mary Pickford and Dolores del Rio played Ramona, from Helen Hunt Jackson's novel of the same name, about a beautiful but ill-starred half-breed girl and her doomed Indian husband.

If David Roberts is right, then it's likely that a great many Maidu, Wintu, and Yana did gather on the banks of the Sacramento River in the spring of 1846, where their numbers and demeanor soon began to frighten the local whites. Possibly the Indians had merely come to the river to practice their own spring rituals.

The only force handy with sufficient strength to disperse

Willie Boy

the Indians was the group of men with Frémont, who was in California on his third exploring expedition. His first expedition, four years back, had made Frémont a national hero—he was easily America's most famous explorer, and fame had rather gone to his head.

In fact, by 1846 Frémont's principal achievements were already behind him, but neither Frémont nor anyone else suspected this at the time. Since the massacre is now mainly a footnote to Frémont's career, a word about this third expedition might be in order.

Frémont actually worked for the Army Corps of Topographical Engineers; he *was* a first-rate topographer. His orders on this occasion had been to survey rivers flowing *east* out of the Rockies, which, obviously, did not include the Sacramento, but Frémont, vain as a prince, at once delegated this tame assignment and made straight for California—he had been there once previously and suspected that the Mexican government, which was spread very thin, might soon collapse. If he could only manage to be in the right place at the right time, California—a major plum—might drop in his lap, in which case even more glory would be his. So he wandered up and down the state, more or less passively; when something *did* happen in the north—the Bear Flag Revolt—he postured a good deal but offered no real help.

Just before he headed north to the Sacramento River he decided, rather cavalierly, to challenge the Mexican authorities in Monterey. He and his men occupied a nearby hill—Gavilan Peak—threw up some breastworks, raised the American flag, and waited for the Mexicans to attack, which they declined to do. The flag fluttered in the breeze for three days; then the breeze became a gale and the flag blew down. The Pathfinder decided that honor had been satisfied, so he packed up his troop and went north. This strange retreat earned Frémont the undying contempt of the famous rather dandified mountain man Joseph Walker, who said Frémont was the worst coward, morally and physically, that he had ever known.

Frémont didn't know it, but his adventure in California was to end even less gloriously because of his refusal to recognize the authority of General Stephen Watts Kearny, who, after the Mexican defeat, took the Pathfinder back to Washington and court-martialed him.

Meanwhile, though, Frémont took his men far to the north, past Sutter's Fort, to bivouac for a time at the ranch of Peter Lassen, where the Sacramento River comes out of the mountains. Not long after Frémont's arrival, the Indians also arrived and the locals began to get nervous. They asked Frémont for protection. What happened next is related by Thomas Martin, in a memoir that surfaced in 1878:

> They asked Fremont to protect them. He replied that he had no right to fight Indians but he told us that those who wished to take part in the expedition against the Indians he would discharge and take us again afterward. . . . At the foot of the low hills where the Sacramento River comes out of the mountains . . . we found the Indians to the number of 4,000 to 5,000 on a tongue of land between the bends of the river, having a war dance preparatory to attacking the settlers. Our advance guard of 36 immediately charged and poured a volley into them killing 24. They then rushed them with sabres. The rest of the party came up and charged in among them and in less than 3 hours we had killed 175 of them. Most of the Indians escaped into the neighboring mountains.

His fellow writer Thomas Breckenridge, however, thought the war party, if it *was* a war party, consisted of "only 150 bucks and 250 women and children."

Kit Carson's brief commentary agreed with neither of the above as to the number of Indians awaiting them:

> During our stay at Lawson's [Lassen's] some Americans that were settled in the neighborhood came in stating that there were about 1,000 Indians in the vicinity making preparations to attack the settlements: requested assis-

tance of Fremont to drive them back. He and
party and some Americans that lived near
started for the Indians encampment, found
them in great numbers, and war started.

"He and party" seems to have convinced various biographers
that Frémont led the attack, an action that would have been,
for John Charles Frémont, entirely out of character. Unlike
Chivington, Frémont had no desire at all to wade in gore. He
rarely (if ever) fought, preferring, as his biographer Andrew
Rolle observed, to use Kit Carson as a hit man. Kit was a thorough hit man too.

Thomas Martin's account, if examined closely, seems rather star-
tling. If the advance guard of thirty-six men thought there were
four to five thousand waiting for them, then they were certainly
bold to launch an attack: as bold as Custer was, thirty years later.
    Even if the first volley killed twenty-four, that still left a lot
of Indians; many would have thought twice before attacking this
group with sabers. Even if we lower the count to Breckenridge's
four hundred, a saber attack was still bold. And if twenty-four fell
to a single volley, why would it take three hours to kill 175? Is it
not rather odd that Thomas Martin could count the victims of
the first volley when thousands of Indians were still ranged
against them? A mere twenty-four killed would not have made
much of a dent.
    Of course if Breckenridge was right and there were only
four hundred Indians there, twenty-four would have made a significant dent.
    That the men immediately waded in with sabers seems odd
too. If the first volley was so effective, why not keep shooting?
Hand-to-hand combat would have seemed far more dangerous.
Were the attackers in the grip of such a blood frenzy that they

couldn't stop, producing the "perfect butchery" that Kit Carson talks about?

The aloof John Charles Frémont, once the operation was seen to be a success, as usual makes it appear that he had been the prime mover, while getting no actual blood on his hands. The lesson administered, he says, "was rude but necessary, and had the desired effect."

David Roberts deserves much credit for addressing the Sacramento River Massacre in *A Newer World*. His own suspicion, backed up by what anthropological studies there are, was that the Indians had gathered to celebrate a spring ritual, possibly the Bear Dance, which the whites, unfamiliar with this ritual, mistook for a war dance.

The Maidu and Wintu were fairly settled, sedentary tribes, acorn-gatherers, salmon-fishers. Their numbers shrank so precipitously during the second half of the nineteenth century that by

Ishi

the time the anthropologists got there there were few left to
study.

The much publicized Ishi, last of the Yana tribe, *was* studied,
by the anthropologist Theodora Kroeber, but she knew nothing
of this massacre and did not try to determine if some trace of it
survived in Yana lore or memory.

In a sense the Sacramento River Massacre illustrates a problem that was to bedevil white-Indian relations from first to last:
the inability, on the part of whites, to distinguish between Indians
who were friendly and Indians who were hostile. Any big gathering of Indians, however well intentioned, made whites nervous—
to a degree it still does.

One of the continuing sources of disagreement about the
Sand Creek Massacre is that John Chivington led his troopers
into the camp of Black Kettle, probably the single best known

Black Kettle

Back row: Bosse, a Cheyenne; Left Hand, an Arapaho;
White Wolf, a Kiowa.
Front row: White Antelope, brother of Black Kettle; Black Kettle,
Cheyenne chief; Bull Bear, a Cheyenne; Neva, an Arapaho

peace Indian of that day. Black Kettle was so sure that he enjoyed
protection that he desperately waved an American flag even as
the Coloradans were mowing down his people.

From the first there were plenty of people in the West—indeed, in the country—who were frankly exterminationists. They
wanted all the Indians gone. It may be that a disproportionate
number of these genocidally minded settlers made their way to
California. The deaths at the Sacramento River were merely a
prelude to the rapid elimination of the California Indians.

For a good account of this grim slaughter the reader is directed to the "Far West" chapter of James Wilson's *The Earth Shall*

Weep. During the conflict with the Plains Indians, there were at least a few equal fights. In California, with the exception of the Modoc War, there were *no* equal fights. Men who believed that the only good Indian was a dead Indian overwhelmingly prevailed. During the Gold Rush particularly, exterminationists were thick on the ground. Indians were killed as casually as rabbits. I have reported elsewhere about a young vigilante who came to have qualms about killing Indian children with his rifle: the big bullets tore the small bodies so! The man was soon able to square his conscience by killing only adults with his rifle; the children he dispatched with his pistol.

It is only fair to say, though, that if one puts oneself in the position of an ill-trained and perhaps scrappily equipped young soldier, the distinction between friendly Indians and hostile Indians may seldom have been easy to make—or maintain—particularly in the frightening minutes just before a fight.

Similarly, most settlers, making their lonely way across the harsh distances of the West, might naturally have found all Indians a little frightening. By the end of the settlement period particularly, most settlers would have been well aware that the Indians had been pushed off their land. Why wouldn't they have been hostile?

Also, during the whole era of conquest and conflict, there was the constant problem of the young warriors—young men raised with a warrior ethic, in a warrior society. Raiding, for these boys, was not only a right: it was necessary training and, also, the source of self-esteem.

Many a well-planned Indian ambush was blown at the last minute by the impatient young warriors, who could not wait for the right moment to attack. The Fetterman Massacre in 1866 was one of the few ambushes in which the young warriors didn't spoil the plan.

Black Kettle himself, the most dedicated of peace Indians, had as much trouble with his young warriors as any other Indian, and he admitted it.

In the 1870s particularly, warring in the West extended over a vast border-to-border territory. In the Southwest were Cochise,

Quanah Parker

Red Cloud

Victorio, Geronimo, Quanah Parker. In the north were Sitting Bull, Crazy Horse, Red Cloud. In the vast middle were the southern Cheyenne, Arapaho, Kiowa, Comanche, Osage, Pawnee. All these tribes had constantly to watch their territory shrink: they had to watch the game on which they depended slaughtered. They were up against it and they knew it. They had no reason to hold back: they found their dignity in fighting.

To some extent, perhaps, it is human nature to think the worst about those who are not as we are. Tribalism was an instinct and an organizing principle for so long that it is planted deep in the human psyche. It can rarely be civilized out of us.

General Custer

It is easy to say that the army in the West should have been more particular about which bands of natives they attacked. Right now, in Iraq, we are finding out how difficult it is to hit only the bad guys when we make war. Even the best reconnaissance has its limits. Custer had excellent reconnaissance available to him on that fatal day at the Little Bighorn. He ignored it all. If someone had pointed out to Kit Carson that these Indians dancing by the Sacramento River were only doing their spring Bear Dance would he have let them be? It seems unlikely. The men were by then in a killing mood, and they killed.

Three hours of steady killing produced a well-stocked meat shop on that tongue of land. Only after it ended and tempers cooled did some of the men realize that *this* killing left a bad taste. No doubt they were excited at first, but three hours of steady killing may well have become an unpleasant chore. Some men may have become sated—walked away with their dripping sabers. Some may finally have been repulsed.

In fairness to Frémont's men, though, they were not many, and they were a long way from home. If the threat from these Indians was exaggerated by the panicky settlers, the *general* threat from Indians was real. Frémont always maintained that the only reason he attempted the nearly disastrous winter crossing of the Sierra Nevada in 1844 was because the Indians on the east side of the mountains—the Paiutes, particularly—were nibbling away at their horses and pack animals. His fear of being set afoot and having his men picked off one by one was not unreasonable.

In fact, only a few days after the Sacramento River Massacre, while camped farther north, in Klamath country, various of the party heard, during the night, a disquieting thud. Frémont got up to investigate, but found nothing. The next morning the party discovered that the thud had been the sound an axe made when it split the skull of Basil Lajeunesse, a popular man and one of Fré-

mont's special favorites. A punitive expedition was launched immediately. Many Klamaths were killed.

Ishi, last of the Yana, desperate, tired, and hungry, only allowed himself to be coaxed into the settlements in 1911, by
which time almost all the Maidu and Wintu were gone.

We are unlikely ever to know more about the massacre at
the Sacramento River than can be found in *A Newer World,*
whose author acknowledges many uncertainties. A bunch of Indians, gathered for what purpose we can only guess, frightened
the local whites, who called down death upon an unknown
number of them. Kit Carson and some of the men may have re-
gretted it; but they were soon back to killing Klamaths, in revenge for their young friend.

In 1862, Kit Carson, obeying the command of his superior,
Major James H. Carleton, reluctantly began to drive the
Mescalero Apache and then the Navaho from their homes. They
were marched to a prison camp on the Bosque Redondo, in eastern New Mexico. There they died in numbers that far exceeded
the death toll in any Western massacre. Their trek was called the
Long Walk, the Navaho Trail of Tears. All in all such removals
were more deadly than any single fight. The Indians understood
fighting, but no people easily accepts exile. Combatants can
sometimes reconcile, but unjust exile seems to burn forever.

Kit Carson may not have been as brilliant a pure explorer as
the prodigious Jedediah Smith—one of the few explorers who
sought geographical knowledge for its own sake—but, for dura-
bility, Carson had no equal. He first went to California with
Ewing Young in 1828: he beavered and he guided, and he was
still doing it thirty-five years later. He led Frémont on three expeditions; he led many others as well. When he was done he
could justly claim to have walked the whole West. The only guide
who may have been his equal was the Delaware scout Black

Beaver, who guided Captain Randolph Marcy on his explorations of the Red River country.

Saddened by the brutal business with the Apache and the Navaho, Kit Carson spent his last years with his beloved wife, Josefa, "Little Josie." In photographs he always looks melancholy. Josefa died, and, not long after, Kit died, sad at the end.

Josefa Carson

The Mountain Meadows Massacre, September 11, 1857

O n the very day, October 12, 2002, when I sat down to begin organizing my notes on the Mountain Meadows Massacre, there appeared in *The New York Times* a long piece by Emily Eakin about that long-ago event and the still continuing controversy it has engendered. Two new books have recently been published (Will Bagley's *Blood of the Prophets* and Sally Denton's *American Massacre*), and a third—which I understand will constitute a Mormon rebuttal—is now in the press.

Scarcely two weeks later the *New York Review of Books* carried a thoughtful essay by Caroline Fraser about this same, much studied massacre. The Mormon historians who are doing the rebuttal will argue, yet again, that Brigham Young, the Mormon leader, did not order this massacre.

Mountain Meadows was again very much in the news, reinforcing my point that massacres, once exposed, just won't go away. Of the six massacres I propose to study, Mountain Meadows is much the most complicated, and it is the only one in which there may have been a theocratic motive. Things just keep coming to light—2,605 bones and bone fragments accidentally uncovered at the monument site in 1999, for example—suggesting that we are probably still a long way from having heard the last word about Mountain Meadows.

Juanita Brooks

The cornerstone of Mountain Meadows studies is Juanita Brooks's classic—and, considering that she is a devout Mormon, heroic—book, *The Mountain Meadows Massacre,* first published by Stanford in 1950 and kept in print now by the University of Oklahoma. There is a lengthy shelf of related studies, some of them by Juanita Brooks herself—the most substantial of these are listed in my bibliography.

All these books attempt to describe what happened on that dreadful September day in 1857, when a large wagon train on its way from Arkansas to California was massacred by a force composed of local Mormons and Paiute Indians. (Even here body counts differ: I thought 121 people were killed, but Sally Denton puts the count at 140.)

These various studies also attempt to determine *why* the massacre happened, and—biggest and most intractable question—

who, if anyone, in the Mormon hierarchy ordered the killing. For nearly 150 years the finger of inquiry has been pointed at Brigham Young; it's an issue still very much in debate.

The final, comprehensive truth about Mountain Meadows may have remained elusive, but in fact we do know a great deal about this massacre, and evidence such as the 2,605 bone fragments just keeps appearing. (A lead scroll purporting to be John Doyle Lee's confession turned up as recently as 2002, but its authenticity seems questionable.) Talk about a massacre that won't go away.

The Church of Jesus Christ of Latter-Day Saints (the Mormons) has hoped from the first day to the present that if they just stuck together, hunkered down, and kept quiet, time would pass and people would forget.

Time did pass, but people have not even begun to forget.

When in 1999 the president of the Mormon Church, Gordon B. Hinckley, journeyed to southern Utah to dedicate the most recent of the various unsatisfactory monuments at the Mountain Meadows site, he not only declared that the truth about Mountain Meadows could never be known, but he also read a disclaimer from the church's legal team which affirmed that nothing said at the memorial service in any way implied Mormon complicity in these long-ago murders. (In less guarded moments President Hinckley has said that he suspected the local people did it.)

In suggesting that Mountain Meadows is an impenetrable mystery, President Hinckley has swung well wide of the truth. Juanita Brooks, a devout Mormon and fine historian, clearly and professionally penetrated many of these mysteries more than half a century ago, in *The Mountain Meadows Massacre,* a model of clarity. Will Bagley, Sally Denton, William Wise, and others have extended the valuable inquiry that she began.

* * *

Mountain Meadows would make a good opera. It is an American tragedy of blood. Billy the Kid's story has yielded a ballet; perhaps someday something operatic will emerge from this tragic story.

The uniqueness of Mountain Meadows for this study is that on this then grassy plain whites killed whites—or, to be more precise, whites with the help of Indians killed whites. Both Mormons and Paiutes have downplayed their part in the killing. It had long been supposed that the whites killed mostly men, and the Paiutes mainly women and children, but the bones in the mass grave uncovered in 1999 have complicated this picture—of which more later.

The immigrant train in question, the so-called Fancher party, was well armed and well equipped. There were some thirty wagons and they had made it all the way from Arkansas through dangerous territory. It is unlikely that the Paiutes alone could have overrun them. The Paiutes might have nibbled at them, as they nibbled at Frémont, but they were not temperamentally inclined to long sieges or lengthy battles.

Everyone who has written about Mountain Meadows has been at pains to point out that the massacre occurred at a moment of high tension in the Mormon capital of Salt Lake City. The tension was due to the fact that the United States Army was on its way to Utah, to address many reports of Mormon excesses. The U.S. government meant to subdue this unruly province once and for all. They also meant to replace Brigham Young, a full-fledged theocrat, with a civil governor. At that time Brigham Young was governor of Utah *and* the head of the Mormon church. President James Buchanan was fed up, both with the Mormons in general and Brigham Young in particular. He sent the army to forcefully put matters right.

Thus, in the summer of 1857, Brigham Young and Mormons throughout Utah were gearing up to defy both the president and the army. The Mormons had been pushed steadily westward, from New York state to Illinois, Missouri, and now Utah; they didn't intend to be pushed any farther, and they didn't want to be told how they might order their theocracy. They were no strangers to mob violence. Though forbidden by their creed to shed innocent blood—a moral prohibition that was to have large consequences later—they did subscribe to a doctrine of blood atonement, which instructed them to shed the blood of gentiles—that is, non-Mormons. The Fancher party consisted entirely of gentiles, and had, moreover, the added stigma of having come from Arkansas, where, very recently, the popular Mormon prophet Parley Pratt had been murdered.

The Fancher party was already on the road when Parley Pratt was killed—by an outraged husband whose wife the prophet coveted for his own purposes. This woman, Eleanor Mc-

Parley Pratt

Comb McLean Pratt, though in appearance an unlikely Helen of Troy, was soon recovered sufficiently from her grief to proclaim the evil of gentiles and appeal for vengeance. The Fancher party, though innocent, became the prime candidate for the enactment of the doctrine of blood atonement.

Thus there were two stressful elements in the Mormon communities in the late summer of 1857: the approach of the army and the outrage over the death of Prophet Parley. The Fancher party well knew that they were not popular. Though well financed, they were often refused supplies, and those they did manage to purchase were priced to the skies. Since it was a large party, with a herd of cattle numbering between six hundred and one thousand head; and since the country ahead was desert, both supplies and forage were important. When they got to Mountain Meadows it was the abundant forage that prompted them to stop. Mountain Meadows is no longer grassy, but in 1857 it was abundantly grassed, and the party paused—as any herds-men would—to allow the cattle to graze their fill before starting into more difficult country. Though they were close to being out of Utah, stopping was an eminently practical move for any group with hundreds of livestock to maintain.

The Paiutes and other desert Indians, who were subsisting on very little, not unnaturally wanted those cattle. A number of Mormon farmers and ranchers wanted them too. (These cattle were said to be longhorns, a breed not previously seen in Utah but abundantly available to the Arkansas party from the thousands that ran loose in nearby Texas at the time.)

Though the approach of the army was widely known and much talked about, the army, as it turned out, was having supply problems of its own. The command unit that was to march on Salt Lake City was still in far-off Laramie; the unit was not yet equipped to make the long journey across the plains with fall upon them—on those particular plains, especially what's called the Bridger Plateau, fall can be hard to tell from winter. Both can produce bitter cold.

By the time the Fancher party was attacked, on September 11—a date that might be said to favor massacres—Brigham Young had learned that he had nothing to fear from the U.S. Army that year. The supply problem was so severe that no troops would reach Salt Lake City in 1857. The big fight, if there was to be one, would not occur until the spring of the following year.

In fact, the Mormons never had to fight the army: the differences of opinion between the U.S. government and the Mormon authorities were mostly worked out in negotiations. The army did come on to Utah in 1858, but the Utah War, so called, was a big fizzle, an outcome only known long after the Fancher party had been reduced to the condition of a meat shop.

It was, though, the immigrants' misfortune to arrive in wild, lawless southwestern Utah just at a time when the Mormons were most highly stressed. It was only a day or two before the massacre that Brigham Young realized he would not soon be under attack.

Despite this element of relief, the Mormons remained stirred up. Even so, the Fancher party, had it just kept moving, might have passed through Mormon territory unmolested and gone on to the promised land of California, but for the temptation of that tall, waving grass. By stopping to let their cattle graze they made themselves an irresistible target, both to Indians and Mormons.

Six days after the massacre Brigham Young penned an entry in his diary about the likely behavior of the Indians:

> A spirit seems to be taking possession of the Indians to assist Israel [the Mormons]. I can hardly restrain them from exterminating the Americans.

In fact, he didn't restrain them, and yet the very day before the massacre Young claimed to have dispatched a letter by fast courier to Elder Isaac Haight, the leader of the southern Mormons. The letter read in part:

> We do not expect that any part of the Army will be able to reach here this fall . . . they are now at or near Laramie. . . . So you see that the Lord has answered our prayers, and again thwarted the blow which was aimed at our heads. In regard to the emigration trains passing through our settlements, we must not interfere with them *until they are first notified to keep away.* You must not meddle with them. The Indians we expect will do as they please, but you should try and preserve good feelings with them. There are no other trains going through that I know of. If those who are there will leave, let them go in peace.

That seems plain enough, and yet little in this history is exactly as it seems. The provenance of this letter, as Caroline Fraser has pointed out, is uncertain. In the best of circumstances it would have arrived in the south too late to save the Fancher party, but whether it was delivered at all is an open question. The Mormons are among the world's most efficient record-keepers, and yet the original of this letter is lost. Brigham Young admits this in a deposition given in 1875. A copy, sworn to and notarized by Nephi W. Clayton, turned up in a church letter book in 1884; but Hamilton Gray Park, one of Brigham Young's assistants, made a note claiming that the letter was in answer to a plea from the south for instructions as to what to do about the Fancher party.

The request for instruction and Brigham Young's answer were both entrusted to the courier James Haslem, who sped from the south to Salt Lake City and then back to the south, a distance said by some to be a round-trip of 496 miles, which he made in one hundred hours. Assuming that relays of horses were made available that does not seem especially fast to me, although Young had pleaded with the courier to ride night and day, insisting to Haslem that "that company [the Fancher party] must be protected from the Indians if it takes every LD Saint in Iron County to do it."

There are problems in regard to Brigham Young's letter and Hamilton Gray Park's memo about it that historians have so far not convincingly explained.

Was Brigham Young, relieved of the immediate threat of attack by the U.S. Army, sincere in his desire to save the Fancher party? Though the army was delayed, it was still coming; might it be that he wanted to be careful not to give them a new excuse to invade? However cynical he may have been about the immigrants themselves, he might not, at this juncture, have wanted to throw fuel on a smoldering fire.

Of course it's possible that this famous letter might not have been the only message he dispatched to the south. The nice letter may have been intended as cover in case things went wrong.

In an army report made by Major James H. Carleton (the same officer, who, just a few years later, commanded Kit Carson to go round up the Navaho), it was stated that the Paiute chiefs claimed that letters ordering the destruction of the emigrant train came from Brigham Young. The copious and meticulous Mormon archives are absent any such letters.

Where one stands on the several vexed questions having to do with the Mormon leader's involvement in the destruction of the Fancher party finally depends on what one believes about Brigham Young himself. The letter of September 10 instructing Elder Haight not to meddle with the immigrants could be shrewd political disinformation, something he could show to the army to prove his good intentions, if that became necessary. All his urgings to the fast rider, Haslem, could have sprung from the same motive. He wanted to appear to be doing his best to save the immigrants. Did he know that Haslem couldn't possibly get there in time?

On the other hand, once told of the massacre, not long after it happened, Brigham Young is said to have had the immediate and uncomfortable intuition that this massacre was something that would haunt the Mormon church forever—which, so far, it has.

He had this intuition, and then, for eighteen years, did his best to stonewall—and his best, considering his lofty position, was pretty good. Though he was told in some detail by Jacob Hamlin and John Doyle Lee what had happened at Mountain Meadows, he publicly insisted, for nearly two decades, that the Indians had done it, not the Mormons. It was only in 1875, in a deposition, that he finally admitted when he knew what he knew. It is clear that he used the power of his position as church leader to keep the truth from coming out, a practice that has been followed by many church leaders since.

Brigham Young had been aware of the Fancher party for some time. Had he wished, he would not have needed to wait until the last minute to instruct Elder Haight not to molest them.

The corresponding question that might be asked is whether Elder Haight and the Mormons of remote southern Utah would have executed all these travelers without the explicit approval of Brigham Young and the other Mormon authorities in Salt Lake City.

My own feeling about this is that the Iron County Mormons were raring to go for the immigrants. No doubt they would have welcomed a go-ahead from Brigham Young, but Salt Lake City was a long way off; the Iron County Mormons were in a mood to kill, and kill they did, on that plain with the seductive grass.

Doctrinally, in the eyes of the Mormon leaders, the majority of the immigrants—that is, the adults—were *not* innocents. They were, in Mormon terms, gentiles, enemies of the faith, perfect candidates for the enactment of blood atonement.

The council of elders held in southern Utah before the attack contained few if any moderate voices. What the elders seemed mainly to concern themselves with was rounding up enough Indian allies to help them at their bloody task. This proved not hard to accomplish—the sight of all those cattle was enough to tempt the Paiutes. Once the Fancher party paused to graze their herds, the stage was set; the Mormons and the Indians were ready.

Early on the morning of September 7, while the immigrants were at breakfast, the firing began.

Mountain Meadows (II)

————

The Fancher party, as I have said, was no pushover. Once bullets started whizzing into the breakfasting camp the wagons were immediately circled. Soon formidable breastworks were constructed. Had the party been camped a little closer to a nearby spring, so as to have an adequate water supply, they might have mounted a lengthy siege. The Paiutes did not like long battles, preferring to overcome their enemies in a wild rush or else pick them off one by one over a long stretch of time.

Though several immigrants were killed in the initial attack, the immigrants held off this first assault. They had not made it all the way from Arkansas to fold at the first sign of trouble. Also, they were not long in observing that a number of the "Indians" who were attacking them showed patches of white skin underneath their war paint. The attacking party probably numbered about 250 strong: two hundred Indians and perhaps fifty white people. They were not strong enough to overrun the barricade of wagons and breastworks. Butchering and booty-gathering were obviously going to take some time. Council had to be taken and taken quickly. The battle took place on an established trail. Other immigrants might show up, and, even if they didn't, the Paiutes might tire of the siege and drift off to other pursuits.

The immigrants, of course, soon recognized that they were

in a bad situation, in a remote and pitiless place. When night fell they sent scouts to the west, hoping that they might slip through to California quickly and bring help.

None of these scouts made it through. A statement the leaders had composed, describing the desperate situation, was lost with the scouts.

The Mormons were by then fully determined to eliminate the immigrants, but how? A long siege was out of the question; their allies the Paiutes would run off as many cattle as possible and then vamoose. Soldiers might show up along this much used route; soldiers, or merely other travelers.

After some praying and much discussion, the Mormons concluded that the best strategy would be to decoy the immigrants with a promise of safe passage. They would be told that if only they would disarm they would be allowed to proceed in peace. The arrangement would be for each male immigrant to hand over his weapons and then walk out with a Mormon escort. The women and children could walk ahead.

Here one has to step back and attempt to understand why the leaders of the Fancher party fell for this transparent ruse. They were not fools; they had come a long way through dangerous country. Why would they simply take the word of these white men, some of whom had been shooting at them over the course of three days? White men, moreover, who had taken the trouble to paint themselves up like Indians? That in itself should have registered as a bad sign; perhaps it did. The Fancher party had no reason at all to trust either the Indians or the Mormons. They knew quite well that the latter hated them, because of where they came from and because they were gentiles.

Were there not those in the party who questioned the wisdom of unilateral disarmament while surrounded by their foes? Did no one manage to foresee what was coming?

The question can't be answered—not with any certainty. Either the Mormon negotiators were exceptionally persuasive, or

the immigrants felt their position to be so hopeless that they
would grasp at any straw. Perhaps the members of the Fancher
party simply could not believe that white men would massacre
them and their women and children. Also, they may have had no
clear idea as to how large a force they were in conflict with.

Seventeen young children survived this massacre, but none
of the men who made the decision to disarm was spared. Any
opinion one might have about the decision-making would only
be guesswork; but, still, the ease and speed with which they accepted the Mormon offer seems inexplicable. The siege was only
in its fourth day. The fate of the scouts dispatched to California
was not yet known.

Perhaps crucially, they could not reach the nearby spring
without exposing themselves to rifle fire: perhaps it was thirst
that tipped the balance.

What we now know is that on the morning of September 11,
after a not especially prolonged parley, wagons were brought forward in one of which the armed immigrants were to stack their
weapons. This they meekly did. Then the menfolk of the Fancher
party were marched out, each man with an armed Mormon by
his side. The women and children were somewhat ahead of the
men, having marched out first. The Indians remained in hiding.

These women, having lived under conditions of terror for
four days, were likely not free of fears about what would happen
if the Indians were allowed to have their way. Perhaps, like the
men, they reposed their hopes in Mormon decency. The historian
J. P. Dunn suggests that they had even begun to perk up—it's not
clear to me how he could know this. He thought, from what reports I don't know, that the womenfolk had begun to regain their
confidence; if so, they didn't regain it for long.

Suddenly Major High Higbee, the military man who de-
vised the Mormon battle plan, appeared on a ridge ahead of

them. Major Higbee waved his arms and shouted something like Do-Your-Duty, whereupon the Mormon escorts immediately shot down the men they had been escorting. The few who failed to die immediately had their throats cut, so that, Dunn suggests, the atoning blood could flow more freely. (For whatever reason, a great many throats were cut during the massacre.)

According to Dunn, the Indians then fell on the women and children—they had been assigned the job of killing these tender ones, presumably to avoid the possibility of some Mormon shedding innocent blood. A baby had already been killed by the same bullet that cut down his father, who was carrying him at the time, a death that threw an instant taint over the whole gory enterprise.

The long-held view that the Indians took care of the women and kids received a severe challenge with the discovery of the mass grave at the massacre site in 1999. When those bones were uncovered the Mormon authorities must have felt at least briefly that the place was cursed. Thanks to the abundance of Native American remains in Utah, there were laws on the books protecting just such a discovery. With the help of the then governor, Mike Leavitt, a descendant of a massacre participant, and, of course, the Mormon hierarchy, these laws were eventually evaded, but not before a dedicated team of forensic scientists had had some time to work—and *did* they work, eighteen hours at a stretch; they were well aware that the powers that be would soon succeed in having those telltale bones reburied.

This, of course, is exactly what happened, but in fact the scientists still prevailed, assembling parts of twenty-eight individuals and piecing together eighteen skulls.

It was the skulls that cast most doubt on the old belief that the Indians had done most of the killing. Most of the males whose skulls were reassembled died of gunshots fired at very close range—the females, in most cases, had been bludgeoned. The close-range executions by pistol shot suggested white behavior rather than Paiute behavior. The Paiutes had long claimed the Mormons did the lion's share of the killing. Thus what had begun as an attempt to landscape the monument site had blown up in the Mormons' faces. The Paiutes were not entirely exonerated but the notion that they had more or less been slackers at this massacre gained currency again.

Whichever group, Mormons or Indians, accounted for the largest share of the dead did nothing to lessen the horror of what had occurred that September day. Terrible violence occurred, a terror in the desert. Many of the women were quickly dispatched but some children fled. Two young girls hid in some bushes, only to be spotted, dragged out, raped, and killed. One of them pled for her life but John Doyle Lee, the man eventually executed for his role in the massacre, cut her throat anyway. (Lee maintained that he killed no one, but various witnesses said otherwise.)

Seventeen children—innocents in Mormon terms, which meant that they were seven years old and under, were spared and, at first, divided among Mormon families. Most of them were eventually retrieved and sent back to Arkansas—twenty years later their testimony came back to haunt the perpetrators.

John Doyle Lee, Philip Klingensmith (a Mormon bishop), and Jacob Hamlin all insist that they reported the massacre to Brigham Young as soon as it was practicable to do so. The prophet seems much shocked by the killing of women and children, but he then made this remarkable statement about that grisly aspect of the affair:

> I have made that matter a subject of prayer. I went right to God with it, and asked him to take the horrid vision from my sight, if it was a righteous thing that my people have done in killing those people at Mountain Meadows.

> God answered me, and at once the vision was
> removed. I had evidence from God that he
> had over-ruled it all for good, and the action
> was a righteous one, and well intended.

Brigham Young evidently spoke those words to John Doyle Lee, and went on to say that he had heard from Mormons who took part in the killing with Lee, concluding that "we will look into that."

He certainly did look into it, firmly insisting for the next eighteen years that the Mormons had no part in the massacre; it was not until he gave his deposition in 1875 that he admitted to being an accessory after the fact. When he finaly got around to visiting southern Utah he even ordered the destruction of a cross that had been erected at the site of the killings. (The Mormons have had extremely bad luck with monuments on that site—if you count the first crude cross, the present monument is, I believe, the fourth to be erected; perhaps the reason for the bad luck is that—except for that cross—all have been dishonest, erring, always, by omission.)

The Mormon God was certainly a most forgiving deity to so easily cleanse the record of all those women and children, hacked and bashed to death in that remote meadow. Enough gentile blood soaked into the ground that day to atone for a hundred Parley Pratts.

Once the killing was done, the fun part—the looting and divvying up of the immigrants' considerable property—could begin. Six hundred cattle were a fine prize in themselves; John Lee may have gotten as many as two hundred of them. By Arkansas estimates the Fancher goods were worth $100,000; the Mormon reckoning was $70,000. John Lee, who seems to have been the treasurer of the local Mormon polity, actually charged the government $1,500 for property allotted to the Indians.

The bodies of the dead were quickly stripped and searched.

Ears were out off, that being the quickest way to get earrings. Fingers were lopped off and rings removed. According to Dunn, all the bloody clothing was for a time piled in the back room of an office in Cedar City, where it soon grew fragrant. It seems that the clothes were referred to locally as relics of "the Siege of Sevastapol," a somewhat surreal touch. Writing in 1886, Dunn suggested that some of the Fancher jewelry was still being worn by Mormon matrons.

As I have several times said, massacres will out, and this one did in spades. Brigham Young's efforts to contain the news did not succeed. The pile of naked, cut-up bodies—in effect a meat mountain—was soon discovered by a party of men passing through the same grassy meadow. Here is one account of what the travelers found, in testimony later given on the witness stand:

> Saw two piles of bodies, one composed of women and children, the other of men. The bodies were entirely nude, and seemed to have been thrown promiscuously together. They appeared to have been massacred. Should judge there were sixty or seventy bodies of women and children: saw one man on that pile; the children were from one and two months up to twelve years; the small children were almost destroyed by wolves and crows; the throats of some were cut, others stabbed with knives; had bullets through them. All the bodies were more or less torn to pieces, except one, the body of a woman, which lay apart, a little southwest of the pile. This showed no sign of decay and had not been touched by the wild animals. The countenance was placid and seemed to be asleep. The

work was not freshly done—suppose the bodies had been there fifteen or sixteen days.

The travelers who discovered the bodies gave testimony and
were believed. Soon, as J. P. Dunn reports, the news "flew on
wings of the wind" to every part of the country. The people of
California asked the president for support—the people of
Arkansas were forced to wonder if any of their loved ones were
alive. Outrage ran high, as it should have, prompting the Mormons to issue various lame statements—they are still issuing them
to this day, as witness President Hinckley's evasions at the dedica-
tions of the new monument.

The general thrust of these statements, for the first eighteen
years at least, was to put the blame squarely on the Indians.

The first lame line of defense was that the immigrants had
angered the Indians by giving them a poisoned cow; there was
the suggestion that the Mormons might also have poisoned the
spring. But when Dr. Forney, the superintendent of Utah, went
south to launch an investigation, the Paiutes themselves immediately gave the lie to these accusations. There was no poisoned
cow, and the spring ran as pure as ever. (Of course, with so many
animals, a cow might easily have eaten a poisonous weed: the
cow might have bloated and died; but the Paiutes, no fools,
would have been quick to note any such distemper. A bloated
cow is hard to miss.)

Dr. Forney had come south predisposed to believe the Mormons, but only a few days on the ground convinced him that the
Mormon story was seriously flawed. Kanosh, the leader of the
local Paiutes, flatly disputed all the stories of poisoning.

Meanwhile, in the court of public opinion, the fact that
the Mormons had let it be known that they intended to defy
the U.S. Army did not sit well. The Mormons were rapidly losing the public relations effort, as, in a sense, they still are.

Dr. Forney didn't press his investigation until the summer of

1859, but, though fooled at first, he soon realized that there was something wrong with the Mormon version of the killings. For one thing, the Mormon account and the Paiute account flatly contradicted each other.

The local Mormons, evidently thinking that Dr. Forney would believe any white man over any Indian, foolishly gathered together sixteen of the surviving children and tried to persuade Dr. Forney that they had been with the Indians all along. Both Kanosh and the children themselves denied it, which didn't stop the Mormons from presenting the superintendent with a bill for $1,700, which is what they claimed it cost them to buy the children back from the Paiutes. Somehow it didn't occur to the local Mormons that they wouldn't be believed.

Well, they weren't. Some of the children were now nine years old and quite able to confirm that they had been with Mormons, not Indians, for the past two years. Seven years of age

Kanosh

was, for Mormons, the cutoff point between innocence and knowledge. In this case it was the knowledge the children had that made them a threat to the Mormon story line. It was soon apparent that, in producing the children, the Mormons had merely produced so many witnesses against themselves. Several children pointed out that some of the killers were just painted white men. "White hell hounds," Dr. Forney called them; he went on to say that these men had "disgraced humanity."

In the spring of 1859, not long before Dr. Forney arrived, a company of dragoons and two companies of infantry were dispatched to Mountain Meadows to bury the bodies, which, by this time, were dispersed over a rather large area.

It was Major (later General) Carleton who ordered the rude cross erected at the site of the massacre. He felt he ought to do something to commemorate the victims.

It was this modest marker that disappeared during Brigham Young's visit to the south.

Fifteen of the seventeen children who survived were eventually sent east, first to Fort Leavenworth and then back to Arkansas; two boys who had been retained as witnesses were first taken to Washington and then returned to Arkansas as well. Eventually the U.S. government allotted each survivor 320 acres of land, but, so far as I know, the descendants of the victims have not gotten back any of the monies that the Mormons took from the dead. The descendants, of course, still might try to recover those losses, which is one reason the Mormons are so careful not to admit anything.

While Dr. Forney was pursuing his investigations, an attempt was made to hold a legal court of inquiry in southern Utah, but the attempt had to be abandoned when the U.S. Army refused to provide protection for the witnesses, who considered that they would be committing suicide to testify without such protection.

When Brigham Young finally came south with would-be judge John Cradlebaugh, Young is reported to have this to say about Mormons who don't support the official story:

> I am told that there are Brethren who are will-
> ing to swear against the Brethren who were en-
> gaged in this affair. I hope there is no truth to
> that report. . . . But if there is I will tell you my
> opinion of you and the fact so far as your fate is
> concerned. Unless you repent at once of that
> unholy intention, and will keep the secret of all
> you know, you will die a dog's death and be
> damned, and go to hell. I do not want to hear
> anymore treachery among my people.

Warrants had apparently been issued for some participants, but when the army declined to provide protection the warrants were set aside.

Some of the Mormons who had gotten away with being painted white men in the slaughter of the Fancher party soon tried it again on smaller groups of immigrants. There were at least four copy-cat attacks, involving rape, gougings, deaths of babies, in which painted white men were involved.

Soon, though, the dead of Mountain Meadows began to exercise their potency. Some of the participants wasted away; and the site itself, where grass had once grown belly-high to a cow, became sere and desolate, as it is today.

More than a decade passed after the first truncated attempt at an inquiry with little change. At this time, in Utah, the se-lection of jurors was still a prerogative of the Mormon church. Once Congress undid this, there was at least some hope of effective prosecution. John Doyle Lee was first brought to trial in 1875, in a proceeding that smacked of farce. Lee was sure that the church would protect him, and, for a time, it did, despite the fact that former bishop Philip Klingensmith, who had long since removed himself to California, came back, testified, and told the whole story. His testimony was corroborated by several witnesses, despite which a mostly Mormon jury promptly acquitted Lee.

Nevertheless, with this farce of a trial, the always shaky edifice of the Mormon cover-up began to crumble. Details of what happened at Mountain Meadows were soon known to the whole country—the media era had arrived. The testimony of Klingensmith and others fatally undermined the attempt to hold the Paiutes responsible for it all.

Somewhat to the surprise of the Mormon church, the national response to this coached verdict was immediate and severe. Suddenly nobody believed the Mormon story. The response, indeed, was so negative that the church did an abrupt about-turn and decided to sacrifice John Doyle Lee.

In their sudden panic the Mormons retreated to one self-defeating legal strategy after another; individual witnesses soon ensnared themselves ever and ever more tightly in the loops of their own previous falseshoods. Talk was one thing, but legal process something else: its coils began to tighten around many confused participants.

By this time Brigham Young himself had been deposed and had admitted that he was an accessory after the fact. Various witnesses who had remembered nothing at the first trial began to realize that they might unwittingly have implicated themselves. In desperate attempts to undo this damage, to free themselves from the coils of the court, they often contradicted themselves wildly; many soon lost track of what they knew and what they believed.

This time John Doyle Lee was speedily convicted and sentenced to death. He was allowed to choose the method of his own execution and he chose to be shot—in 1877, at the massacre site, he was killed by a firing squad.

John Doyle Lee spent his last days either cursing the Mormon church, or confessing, which he did four times, in wild spewings that contained many contradictions. Dunn dryly observes of the second trial that the jury that finally convicted Lee had no more right to sit in judgment of him than had the sultan of Turkey. He was killed by his own people, all of them hoping to save themselves.

Brigham Young, a man who kept many secrets, died peacefully a few weeks later.

J. P. Dunn ends his long account of the Mountain Meadows Massacre with this vivid splash of color:

> The Mormons were right in their superstition that a Nemesis stands, ever threatening them, on the mountains of southern Utah. She does stand there, and in her outstretched hands, for the ash branch and the scourge, she holds a curse over the doomed theocracy, while from her ghastly lips comes the murmur of those words which no prophet can still: "Vengeance is mine, I will repay," saith the Lord.

The theocracy was not doomed—it prospers today, but I would have to agree that Nemesis still broods over that massacre site, particularly in the area of the monument they can never get right. In attempting to pretty up the monument site a backhoe operator uncovered a mass grave, the very last thing the Mormons would have wanted to happen. But when it did happen they proceeded to remake laws in order to get the bones back into the ground before the forensic team could do its work, which only makes them seem the more guilty.

Nemesis may not depart, either, unless the Mormon church can somehow bring itself to be honest about Mountain Meadows, and that day has clearly not arrived.

Probably some of the Mormons who put on war paint and slaughtered immigrants did suffer agonies of remorse. Killing people is no light task. But if some few wasted away, quite a number seemed to live with the crime well enough, their discomfort level only increasing during the second trial of John Lee, when many of them had to abruptly change positions that they had been defending for twenty years.

John Doyle Lee had every right to be outraged at the church and the colleagues who sacrificed him. Yet he himself had wiped blood off his hands that day, helped himself to some of the cattle and some of the loot, and lived serenely as a prosperous farmer, for twenty years a well-respected man.

He took the massacre in stride, and so did many of his co-participants. Many of them felt genuinely indignant when they were finally linked to this crime they had committed so long ago. Some may have convinced themselves that they were off hoeing corn that day. A lie sustained for twenty years can come to seem like the truth.

Utah is a state with many fabulous beauty spots: Mountain Meadows is not one of them. It is a long way from anywhere. The monument—perhaps I should say the most recent monument, for who knows what Nemesis will yet wring out of the Mormons?—at least has the names of the victims on it. And yet this monument put up to honor the victims merely insults them yet again in its half-honesty. There are the names of the victims—where are the names of the killers? Unlike the fine memorial plaque at Wounded Knee, the Mountain Meadows monument leaves a bad taste in the mouth. In southern Utah dishonesty still rules; Nemesis is not yet satisfied. The simple cross that Major Carleton put up to begin with would have served mourners better than the present showy fraud.

The Mormons' final argument, once it had been proven by the testimony of Lee, Klingensmith, and others that they had participated in the massacre, was that the Indians made them do it. The authorities tried to argue that the Indians would have killed the Mormons had they not helped in the attack. This lacks even the semblance of probability: the Indians lacked the weaponry to do anything of the sort.

The authors of the most recent studies of this dread event offer different theories as to why the wagon train was attacked. Sally Denton thinks the principal motive was greed—no wagon train that rich had ever passed that way; the money to be made, the loot to be collected, drew the locals into action. Will Bagley argues that it was not greed but creed: the blood atonement creed.

The participants themselves may have remained defiant for twenty years, but many Mormons were so repelled by what they heard that they left the church. Neither Brigham Young nor anyone else could hold them, a fact that tells us much about the common horror at massive bloodletting.

If one contrasts the amount of commentary on the Sacramento River Massacre with the flood of commentary about Mountain Meadows, one might suspect a racial element in the accounting: whites killing whites attracted more attention than whites killing Indians. There are a dozen books and many historical commentaries on Mountain Meadows and yet I'm not sure that the racial point is valid. Probably the most written about massacre of the nineteenth century was Sand Creek, where, once again, whites were killing Indians. Mountain Meadows involved a theocracy that, due to a resort to terror, had been put on the defensive, whereas Sand Creek involved trade routes, settlement issues, and racial hatred. Mountain Meadows and Sand Creek both produced more than one official trial or inquiry. Like great battles, big massacres seem to demand repeated reassessments. Why the killing? How many died? Who was to blame? There is always much to be decided, but the way to a sound decision is never very clear.

Sand Creek, November 29, 1864

The Sand Creek Massacre site is now on land owned by a Colorado rancher named Bill Dawson—or at least it is unless he's recently sold his holdings. The site is just north of the hamlet of Chivington, Colorado: the town is named, of course, for John Milton Chivington, the man who planned and led the massacre.

The Arkansas River is a little distance to the south, flowing through expensive irrigated agricultural country. Not far upriver is the reconstructed Bent's Fort; it had been the first great trading post on the Santa Fe Trail, visited by everybody who traveled this famous trail. William Bent, who, with his brother Charles and the trader Ceran St. Vrain, built the original fort, which had initially been farther west, had a number of half-breed children by two Cheyenne sisters: first Owl Woman, who died, and then Yellow Woman.

At least four of William Bent's children were camped with their Cheyenne cousins on the day of the Sand Creek attack: Robert, George, Charles, and John. What happened that day turned one of these sons—Charles—into a half-crazed, white-hating Dog Soldier, a torturer and killer who at one point even went south meaning to kill his own father. Fortunately William Bent was away at the time.

William Bent

Bill Dawson, the rancher who owns the land where the massacre occurred, is, by all accounts, a reasonable and likable man who, while holding his own views on Sand Creek, has nonetheless been generous with Indian groups who want to hold prayer services there. In the 1990s he allowed Connie Buffalo, an Ojibwa woman who had come into possession of two scalps taken at Sand Creek to bury them at the site, with appropriate ceremonials. Connie Buffalo had been given the scalps by the owner of a small motel near the site. They had been in the man's family for years but the owner seemed to feel that Connie Buffalo had a better right to them: he offered them to her with tears in his eyes.

I mention this exchange because it suggests that the power of such an event as Sand Creek resonates through time as few other experiences do. Southeastern Colorado, like much of the Great Plains, is very thinly populated now. There are not many people there, but most of the farmers and ranchers who operate near the site had been in that place for a long time. Sand Creek, whether they like it or not, has always been in their lives. Some might still argue for Chivington's position, but few doubt that the tragedy marked their families and their region. Few, I imagine, see it as a simple case of white wrong. Though it *was* wrong, it had a context that few not of that region can appreciate now.

I would agree with the locals that Sand Creek wasn't simple. Perhaps the plainest thing about it was the character of John Chivington, who, though a longtime Free-Soiler, was also a racist Indian-hater. But Chivington was not the only man shooting Indians that day and Sand Creek was not an entirely spontaneous eruption of violence, in which some hotheads in Denver decided to attack a camp of one hundred percent peaceful Indians.

When I visited Sand Creek, the best I could do without bothering Mr. Dawson was to drive around it in a kind of box route, on dirt roads. From several rises I could see where the massacre took place. On much of my box route I was trailed by an SUV from Michigan—its occupants no doubt hoped I would lead them to this historic place. I couldn't, and they finally drove off down the road toward Kansas, which is not far away.

The country around the site is rolling prairie—very, very empty. From several modest elevations I could see the line of trees where the fighting took place. The plain is immense here; on a chill gray day the word "bleak" comes naturally to mind. "Pitiless" is another word that would apply. On a fine sunny day the plains country of eastern Colorado looks beautiful, but Sand Creek and Wounded Knee were winter massacres; the cold no doubt increased the sense of pitilessness. If you were at Sand Creek, being massacred and desiring to run, only the creek itself offered any hope. Otherwise, north, south, east, or west was only open country: totally open.

★ ★ ★

The first factor that might be noted in a discussion of Sand Creek is the date: 1864. The Civil War was in progress, a fact of some importance, as we will see.

More important, though, was that at this date the Plains Indians, from Kiowa and Comanche in the south, north through the lands of Arapaho, Pawnee, southern Cheyenne, and the seven branches of the Sioux, were unbroken and undefeated peoples. All were still able, and very determined, to wage a vigorous defense of their hunting grounds and their way of life. Up to this point what they mainly had to worry about in regard to the whites was their diseases, smallpox particularly. Though there had been, by this point, many skirmishes between red man and white, there had been only one or two serious battles.

The first major conflict occurred about a decade before Sand Creek, at Fort Laramie. The U.S. government called an enormous powwow, in which the various Indian tribes were to be granted annuities if they would agree not to molest the growing numbers of immigrants pouring west along the Platte—what we call the Oregon Trail. The natives called it the Holy Road.

The expectations the government nursed about this hopeful arrangement were wholly unrealistic—it involved a major misunderstanding of Native American leadership structures. No Indian leader had authority over even his own band such as a white executive might possess. No Indian leader was a boss in the sense that General Grant was a boss. And, all Indian leaders had trouble with their young warriors, who *would* run off and raid.

But few whites recognized these realities at the big gathering in 1854.

Shortly after this great powwow a foolish and arrogant young officer named Grattan took the part of a Mormon immigrant who claimed that a Sioux named High Forehead had killed one of his cows—a crippled cow, it may have been; it may even have been an ox.

High Forehead belonged to the Brulé Sioux, the branch

then led by a reasonable chief named Conquering Bear, who at once offered to make restitution for the cow. He may even have offered the Mormon a couple of horses; but Grattan insisted on High Forehead's arrest. Conquering Bear pointed out that High Forehead was a free Sioux: he himself had no authority to order an arrest.

At this point Grattan, determined not to lose face, shot off a small field piece, killing Conquering Bear, something even Grattan probably had not meant to do. The Sioux then immediately killed Grattan and thirty of his soldiers, including the fort's interpreter, who may have contributed to the disaster by exceptionally sloppy translation. The Sioux could probably have destroyed the Fort Laramie garrison at that point, but they chose, instead, to take their dying chief and melt away.

About a year later the army mounted a punitive expedition led by General William Harney, who went north and attacked a band led by Little Thunder, who had not been involved in the trouble at Fort Laramie. General Harney too had field pieces, and used them to slaughter many Sioux—about ninety, some say, an enormous loss for the Indians. This may have been the battle that showed these Western tribes the true killing power of the whites. Crazy Horse may have witnessed this slaughter and decided as a result to have nothing to do with white men, other than to kill them.

A second large-scale conflict prior to Sand Creek was the Great Sioux Uprising in Minnesota in 1862, a conflict that occurred because the Sioux in southeastern Minnesota were being systematically starved by corrupt Indian agents who refused to release food that they actually had in hand. The rebellion led by Little Crow was so fiercely fought and had so many victims on both sides that for a time it retarded emigration into that part of the country. The Indians were eventually defeated, but not before

Little Crow

they killed many whites and brought terror to the prairies. When it was over the whites prepared to hang three hundred Indians, but Abraham Lincoln took time out from his war duties to study the individual files, reducing the number hanged to about thirty.

If one considers the Plains Indians as they were in 1864—a mere twelve years before the Little Bighorn—they constituted a formidable group of warrior societies, all of them naturally more and more disturbed by the numbers of white people who surged across their territory, disrupting the hunting patterns upon which their subsistence depended.

In Colorado, where Sand Creek happened, emigration soared in the 1850s because of gold discoveries in the Colorado Rockies. This brought many thousands of people into the region in only a few years, and yet the Indians tolerated this great wave of whites pretty well at first. Denver was organized as a town in 1858; it was a rough community from the start, and its physical situation, at the very base of the Rockies, meant that it could only be reached from the east by crossing a vast plain; the natural terrain offered little protection. On that plain, in 1858, grazed millions of buffalo, the support of the nomadic warrior societies mentioned above. Soon freight routes across the prairie bisected the great herds and eventually more or less split them into northern and southern populations. The emigrants came in all sizes and shapes; there were large freight convoys bringing in much needed goods and equipment, but there were also single families traveling alone, struggling across the great emptiness in hopes of finding somewhere a bit of land where they could sustain themselves. If the 1850s were largely quiet, with neither the Indians nor the immigrants knowing quite what to make of each other, by the early 1860s Indian patience had begun to wear thin.

There began to be attacks, sometimes on a few soldiers, more often on the poorly defended immigrant families. From around 1862 on, immigrant parties that happened to run into Indians were apt to be roughly treated, the men killed and mutilated, the women kidnapped, raped, butchered. The meat shop attitude had clearly arrived on the Great Plains. The government built forts, here and there, but these the Indians could easily avoid. The forts offered little protection to the widely scattered immigrant parties.

Pioneering during this period was always a gamble, no matter which route one took across the plains. By the early 1860s all routes into Denver from the east were dangerous. Hundreds of miles of plain had to be crossed, with the immigrants vulnerable to attack all the way. But the westering force was irresistible in those years and the immigrants kept coming.

In Denver, every time a wagon train or immigrant family got wiped out, local temperatures rose. *Apprehension,* which I have earlier suggested as a factor in several massacres, became acute in Colorado during the first years of the 1860s. In the little towns and even in Denver women were oppressed by fears of kidnapping and rape. Every depredation got fulsomely reported. One captured woman, after a night of rape, managed to hang herself from a lodgepole; others survived to endure repeated assault and, in some cases, eventually escaped to report details of their ordeals.

John Milton Chivington was a Methodist preacher from Ohio. In New Mexico, at the Battle of Glorieta Pass, he became a Union hero by flanking a force of Confederates who had moved up from Texas; the Confederates lost most of their supplies and were forced into ignominious retreat. A major at the time, Chivington was made colonel and soon brought the authority of a military hero into the bitter struggle with the Plains Indians.

Some historians argue that the Confederates skillfully exploited the hatred of the plains tribes in order to increase pressure on Union troops. It is certainly true that in Oklahoma the Five Civilized Tribes, or such of them as had survived the Trail of Tears, fought mostly with the Confederates. The famous Cherokee general Stand Watie was, I believe, the last Confederate officer to surrender, which he did on June 23, 1865, well after Lee had had his talk with Grant.

No doubt there had been some deliberate provocation by the Confederates in Texas and New Mexico, but it's hard to believe that many of the Plains Indians much cared which side won this white man's war. What kept *them* stirred up was the whites' rapid invasion of their country.

In the decade following the Fort Laramie conference an ever-increasing number of smart Indian leaders saw very clearly the handwriting on the wall. Many of these had been taken to Washington and New York; they had seen with their own eyes the limitless numbers of the whites, and the extent of their military equipment. Many of these leaders came to favor peace, since the alternative was clearly going to be destruction. The problem was that even if Black Kettle—who led the band attacked at Sand Creek—strongly favored peace, that didn't mean he could then exercise full control of his warriors. Leadership among the plains tribes was collective but never coercive. Black Kettle and other leaders commanded a good deal of respect but it didn't gain them much control. Warrior societies, after all, encouraged aggressive, warlike action. Raiding, for the young men, was more than a sport: it was how they proved themselves.

In the late summer of 1864, some two months before Sand Creek, the army and the Colorado authorities organized a council in an attempt to arrive at some kind of peace policy that might work. If the various tribes could endorse such a plan, and if they kept their word, they would be promised protection from attack. The peace Indians could even be given some token—a medal, a certificate, even an American flag, which would enable soldiers to distinguish them from hostiles while on patrol.

This ill-formed policy only increased the confusion, and there had been plenty of confusion already. Many bands were eager to become peace Indians and get their medals, irrespective of whether they seriously intended to stop raiding.

At one time not long after the conference it was rumored that six thousand Indians were on their way to Fort Lyon to sign up for the new program. No doubt the figure was wildly inflated. Even six hundred Indians would have swamped Fort Lyon and exhausted the supply of medals, if there were any medals.

John Chivington attended this strange council, which he regarded, not unjustly, to be a fraud and a sham. Black Kettle and a number of other chiefs readily acknowledged that there was likely to be a problem with the young warriors, besides which there were the Dog Soldiers, renegades from many bands who saw themselves as defenders of the old ways—they intended to

Bull Bear

keep fighting no matter what. Bull Bear, a leading dissident, attended the council but was so disgusted by what he heard that he stormed out, vowing to fight on—he fought on, and died at Sand Creek.

Of all the leaders of the southern Cheyenne, Black Kettle seemed the most sincere in his determination to live in peace with the whites. In fact he was sincere to the point of naïveté. He had been given an American flag in 1861 and had acquired a white flag as well, both of which he waved frantically to no effect as Chivington and his men rode down on the camp.

In the weeks before Sand Creek, the routes into Denver came under increasing pressure from roving bands of Indians, and every attack or small conflict merely strengthened Chivington's hand. Soon enough, with Governor John Evans's consent, a

Silas Soule

poster was printed asking for volunteers to fight the Indians. The volunteers were to serve for one hundred days—Chivington easily raised a sizable force, but, in casting his net wide, he took with him a number of men, such as young Captain Silas Soule, who were not convinced of the necessity of the proceedings. Several such men were opposed to massacre as a method of control. Some of the men, particularly those under Silas Soule, refused to fire when the time came: some, including Soule, testified against Chivington in the rather unhelpful inquiries following the massacre.

Even so, Chivington had plenty of firepower and an abundance of converts. He was six foot four and his towering presence easily cowed such waverers as dared to question the operation. Chivington was no coward. Twice in his career as a fire-breathing minister he had faced down formidable opposition, sometimes preaching with a loaded revolver on both sides of his pulpit. The congregation's objection was probably to his Free-Soil, anti-slavery belief, convictions that are to his credit and which he never abandoned.

Just as intensely as he longed to free the slaves, Chivington also longed to exterminate the Indians, even unto the women and children. Well before Sand Creek he had been quoted as saying "Nits breed lice." General Sherman, for a time at least, shared this view. And in fact no effort was made to spare the women and children at Sand Creek, at least not by the troops operating directly under Chivington's command.

General William Tecumseh Sherman

As with all massacres, there are puzzling lacunae in the many narratives of the survivors. How far from Sand Creek was Fort Lyon, from which the expedition set out at 8:00 P.M. on the evening of

November 28? Some thought it was forty miles, some thought thirty, and others said merely "a few."

The vast company troop, somewhere between seven hundred and one thousand men, left the fort under cover of darkness, so that their movements would not be detected. Of course, had there been any Indians in the vicinity who were not stone-deaf they would not have needed to see much to know that a large body of men was on the move. The troops were traveling with artillery, which by itself would have made a good deal of clatter. The fact that, however far they came, they were in position above Black Kettle's camp at dawn on the 29th suggests that they pressed on at a good clip through the night.

Controversy lingers about the scouts that led Chivington and his men across that darkling plain. One was the half-breed scout Jack Smith, who so ran afoul of Chivington that he was executed after the battle. Another was the old mountain man Jim

Jim Beckwourth

Beckwourth, who lived to testify against Chivington at the inquiry; whether he witnessed the whole battle is disputed. And
there was Robert Bent, son of William, who, some think, was
forced to lead Chivington to the camp. If so Robert Bent must
have been quite uncomfortable with what was happening, since
he knew that various of his siblings were likely to be in the camp.
All the Bents survived, though George received an ugly wound
in the hip.

In the first predawn moments when the troops began
thundering toward the camp, some of the Cheyenne women
thought a buffalo herd must be nearby. They soon learned better.
Chivington and the troopers always maintained that a Cheyenne
fired first; if so, it was a lonely effort. About two-thirds of the
Cheyenne in camp were women and children—there were perhaps fifty or sixty warriors. What saved the survivors were the
steep creek banks, in which the fighters among the Cheyenne at
once began to dig shallow rifle pits. The steepness of the banks
enabled some to flee southeastward without exposing themselves
to a fusillade from the troops. That the surprised Cheyenne managed to put up any resistance at all is a testament to their fighting spirit. Not for nothing did George Bird Grinell call them
the "fighting Cheyenne."

Young Captain Silas Soule immediately infuriated Chivington by refusing to order his men to fire; he even briefly inter-
posed his troops between the Indians and the volunteers. Some
say the ensuing battle lasted from dawn until mid-afternoon; others say the mopping-up operation continued all day. The few
warriors who survived the first assault dug their rifle pits deeper
and fought bravely to cover the retreat of those who fled beneath
the creek banks. Black Kettle's wife was shot nine times, and yet,
when darkness fell, he carried her to Fort Lyon, where the doc-
tors saved her.

Various stories from this battle exist in so many versions that
they have become tropes. One involved a little Indian boy who

stood watching the soldiers. One volunteer shot at him but missed; a second volunteer announced that he would "hit the little son-of-a-bitch," but he too missed. A third took up the challenge: he didn't miss.

Another often-told story involved a wounded Indian woman who held up her arms beseechingly, hoping to be spared; but, like the old, bloody-eyed woman in the Odessa Steps sequence of *Battleship Potemkin,* she was hacked down.

The Cheyenne fought gallantly, well into the afternoon—a few of the warriors managed to slip away. When the firing tapered off, the looting began. As at Mountain Meadows, fingers and ears were lopped off, to be stripped of rings and ornaments. Almost every corpse was scalped and many were sexually mutilated. A kind of speciality of Sand Creek was the cutting out of female pudenda, to be dried and used as hatbands.

Chivington and his men returned to Denver, to celebrity and wild acclaim. The scalps—one hundred in number—were exhibited in a Denver theater. Chivington, very much the hero of the hour, claimed to have wiped out the camp.

In fact, though, quite a few Cheyenne and Arapaho survived Sand Creek, including all of William Bent's sons. The Indians hurried off to tell the story to other tribes, while the one-hundred-day volunteers celebrated.

Chivington's most fervent admirer, Colonel George Shoop, confidently announced that Sand Creek had taken care of the Indian problem on the Great Plains—his comment was the prairie equivalent of Neville Chamberlain's famous "peace in our time" speech, after Hitler had outpointed him at Munich. Shoop was every bit as wrong as Chamberlain. Sand Creek, far from persuading the Indians that they should behave, immediately set the prairies ablaze.

It sparked the outrage among the Indian people that led in-

evitably to Fetterman and the Little Bighorn. The Indians immediately launched an attack against the big freighting station at
Julesburg, in northeastern Colorado. But for another blown ambush by the young braves, they might have wiped out the station.
As it was, they killed about forty men. The trails into Denver that
had been dangerous enough before Sand Greek became hugely
more dangerous.

In the twelve years between Sand Creek and the Little
Bighorn there were many pitched battles. Some, like Custer's attack on the Washita in 1868, in which Black Kettle and his tough
wife were finally killed, went to the whites; others, such as Fetterman or the Battle of the Rosebud, went to the Indians. All up
and down the prairies, from the Adobe Walls fight in Texas to
Platte Bridge in Wyoming, a real war was now in progress.
Charles Bent became one of the most feared of all Dog Soldiers,
killing and torturing any whites he could catch.

In Denver, Chivington's account of the raid did not go long un-
challenged. In this case the power of the dead began to make itself felt almost at once. Stories soon seeped out about the terrible
mutilations of women and children. People who had fully approved the attack—people tired of apprehension, of being afraid
even to venture out of town for a picnic, were nonetheless troubled by some of the horrors they heard about. Stories about mutilated children—despite the "nits breed lice" doctrine—did not
play as well as they had at first.

Reports that the Indians hadn't wanted to fight were
shouted down by the Chivington mob, but they kept leaking
out. The carnage began to sit heavily on certain consciences, as
it usually does after massacres. There had been a few soldiers, like
Silas Soule, who refused to shoot down helpless Indian women
or their children; in time some of them expressed their disgust
at the proceedings. Chivington's supporters were well in the ma-

jority, but there *was* a substantial minority opinion and it did get expressed.

Even as the battle began there had been doubters who informed Chivington that the Indians were trying to surrender; but he brushed this aside. He did not want to hear from Indian sympathizers and was not pleased by the least equivocation on the part of his militia. He had gone on a mission of vengeance and he made no bones about that fact. He frequently reminded the soldiers of what had been done to white women in the recent raids, and he succeeded well enough in keeping most of his troops stirred up.

But even Chivington, forceful as he was, did not succeed in banishing all doubt, all regret. The field of battle was one thing; a formal court of inquiry quite another. The formality inherent in even such a crude judicial procedure is about as far as civilized man gets from the dust, smoke, noise, and blood of a battlefield.

The inquiry was ordered by Congress. Once it got underway, Chivington objected to almost every question that was asked. With his towering presence and his power of denunciation he could intimidate many witnesses, but not all witnesses. Silas Soule held his ground and yielded nothing to Chivington's bluster; the preacher made little headway with old Jim Beckwourth either. In the East the greatly respected General Grant gave it as his opinion that what happened at Sand Creek had been nothing more than murder. (He was equally blunt about what happened at the Little Bighorn twelve years later, declaring at once that the tragedy was Custer's fault, a judgment that cannot have pleased the grieving Libbie Custer.)

Despite Chivington's resistance, the commission of inquiry made it clear that what happened at Sand Creek was an out-and-out massacre. Joseph Holt, the army's judge advocate, called it "cowardly and cold blooded slaughter, sufficient to cover its perpetrators with indelible infamy and the face of every American with shame and indignation."

In this the judge advocate clearly went too far, because there were plenty of American faces in Denver who expressed neither shame nor indignation. Neither Chivington nor Shoop was charged with anything; to have charged them at that moment in Denver would have led to civil insurrection.

In April 1865, three weeks after he had married, Silas Soule, the officer whose testimony had done Chivington the most harm, was assassinated while taking a stroll on a pleasant evening. His murderer was most likely a man named Squiers, who promptly fled to New Mexico. The army sent Lieutenant James Cannon to apprehend him, which Cannon accomplished without undue difficulty. Squiers was returned to Denver but escaped again and headed west. This time Lieutenant Cannon could not pursue him because Lieutenant Cannon had been found dead in his hotel room, probably poisoned. Squiers was never brought to trial.

The carnage and ambuscade on the prairies east of Denver did not stop. Julesburg was attacked a second time. Then the Civil War ended, a cessation that forced the military authorities to notice that there was a full-scale Indian revolt going on in the West, conducted by a goodly number of highly mobile and also highly motivated warriors who were, at this juncture, fully determined to prevent the whites from taking their land.

Through the long winding, up and down, of the Indian wars, John Chivington remained popular in Colorado. To the end of his life he defied his critics, declaring, over and over again, that he stood by Sand Creek. He was to have his trials and sorrows. His son drowned and his wife died, after which he quickly married his son's young widow, who soon took herself home. There were allegations of abuse. Chivington moved to San Diego, but soon returned to Denver, where he became an undertaker and, eventually, the county coroner. He died in 1894, about thirty years after the attack that made him famous, or infamous.

* * *

More than one Western historian has defended Chivington, one being J. P. Dunn, he of *Massacres of the Mountains,* who makes quite a spirited defense of the fighting preacher and his one-hundred-day volunteers. Dunn calls Chivington "a colossal martyr to misrepresentation." In his polemic Dunn points out, correctly enough, that there was a life-or-death struggle taking place on the western prairies in the early 1860s. The conflict *was* brutal; many immigrants did lose their lives.

It could hardly have been otherwise. The Indians were rapidly being squeezed out of the country that supported them—country they held dear. The tactical problem that the first Denver council tried to address, how to tell a peaceful Indian from a hostile Indian, was never solved. A fighter such as Roman Nose, a war Indian for sure, might nonetheless visit a peace Indian such as Black Kettle. Plains Indians moved around, visiting for a time with this band or that. The hostile and the peaceful were never to be easily separated out.

After the Fetterman Massacre in 1866, General Sherman made a blunt exterminationist remark. According to H. L. Mencken, it was Sherman, not General Philip Sheridan, who, when approached by an Indian beggar at a railroad depot with the claim that he was a good Indian, replied that the only good Indian *he* had ever seen was a dead Indian.

Sherman was not happy, two years later, at the end of what has been called Red Cloud's War, when the government was forced into its only public retreat in the whole era of this conflict: it agreed to abandon three forts that had foolishly been thrown up along the Bozeman Trail. They had been supposed to protect miners and other travelers to Montana but happened to have been erected right in the heart of Sioux country. With what meager manpower the army had at the time they could not be defended.

The army had, for once, truly overreached—it had underestimated the power of the tribes. Custer was to make the same
mistake at the Little Bighorn.

Once the forts were abandoned, the Indians burned them.

Part of J. P. Dunn's admiration for Chivington stems from the fact
that the fighting parson never gave ground. He never tried to
shift the blame for Sand Creek to anyone else, or to pretend that
he had intended to do anything other than what he did do: kill as
many Indians as possible. Dunn's argument is that at this stage of
the fighting nothing but merciless cruelty would impress the Indians. He even argued that the mutilations had the same purpose:
to convince the Indians that white men could deal in terror as effectively as they themselves could. He felt that the Indians did
not respect gentle treatment, though he himself knew that they
did respect *fair* treatment.

Dunn ends his defense with one of those purple perorations
of which he was so fond:

> Was it right for the English to shoot back the
> Sepoy ambassador from their cannon? Was it
> right for the North to refuse to exchange
> prisoners while our boys were dying in Libby
> and Andersonville? I do not undertake to an-
> swer these questions, but I do say that Sand
> Creek is far from being the "climax" of Amer-
> ican outrages to the Indian, as it has been
> called. Lay not that unflattering unction on
> your souls, people of the East, while the
> names of Pequod and Conestoga Indians exist
> in your books; nor you of the Mississippi Val-
> ley while the blood of Logan's family and the
> Moravian Indians of the Muskingum stain

your records; nor you of the South, while a
Cherokee or a Seminole remains to tell the
wrongs of his fathers; nor yet you of the Pacific Slope while the murdered family of
Spencer or the victims of Bloody Point and
Nome Cult have a place in the memory of
men—your ancestors and predecessors were
guilty of worse things than the Sand Creek
massacre.

That summary is hard to dispute. The burned-alive Pequots
probably did have it worse. The reason Sand Creek gets high-
lighted is because some of those killed were prominent peace Indians. Black Kettle's peaceful position had been well known for
many years, but Chivington didn't care. He attacked the largest
encampment he could find—the more militant bands would not
have been so easily found, and it's doubtful that they could have
been surprised. Black Kettle's band was easy pickings precisely
because they believed they were safe. To some extent Black Kettle
compounded this lapse when he was attacked and killed on the
Washita.

Arthur Penn's rendering of Thomas Berger's *Little Big Man* contains at least three massacres. The first might loosely represent
Sand Creek, the second the Washita, and the third the Little
Bighorn. If Americans—or even Westerners—remember anything
about Sand Creek it is that Black Kettle was frantically waving
his American flag as the troopers charged in. Some say his com-
panion White Antelope was holding up a peace certificate when
he was shot dead; it is more probable that he was merely making
some gesture of surrender. From the point of view of poorly
trained or wholly untrained cavalry, that there were a lot of peace
Indians in this camp might not have been obvious. Most of the

attackers were probably more frightened than enraged, though rage or at least adrenaline arrived quickly enough once the shooting started.

The mutilations the victors performed were horrible, though not nearly as encyclopedic as those the Sioux and Cheyenne managed to visit on Fetterman's men two years later, in a battle that barely lasted half an hour. Here is what the troops found when they went out to bring in the bodies after the Fetterman wipeout: the words are those of Henry Carrington, at that time commander of Fort Phil Kearny, whose military career was destroyed by this disaster:

> Eyes were torn out and laid on rocks; noses cut off; ears cut off; chins hewn off; teeth chopped out; joints of fingers; brains taken out and placed on rocks with other members of the body; entrails taken out and exposed; hands cut off; feet cut off; arms taken out of sockets; private parts cut off and independently placed on the person; eyes, ears, mouth, and arms penetrated with spearheads, sticks or arrows; ribs slashed to separation with knives; skulls severed in every form, from chin to crown; muscles in calves, thighs, stomach, breast, back, arms, and cheeks taken out. Punctures upon every sensitive part of the body, even the soles of the feet and the palms of the hand.

Considering the short duration of the Fetterman Massacre, as opposed to the nearly all-day struggle at Sand Creek, the Sioux and Cheyenne made Chivington's men seem like amateurs of massacre, which indeed they were.

The same catalogue could be restated for the Little Bighorn, with the addition of decapitation and a few other refinements. Chivington's hundred-day volunteers were for the most part Sunday soldiers, content with pouches made from scrotums and the like. When it came to making a meat shop they possessed only the crudest skills.

I am not sure that Sand Creek admits of any conclusions. Two peoples with widely differing cultures were rubbing against each other, constantly and insistently. The Indians were trying to defend their cherished way of life, the whites to make that way of life vanish so they could go on with their settling, farming, town-building, etc.

On a world scale countless massacres have been perpetrated over those and similar issues. Land is frequently a principal element in these disputes. Is it my land or your land, our land or their land? Time after time, in the Balkans, India, Pakistan, Kashmir, the Middle East, large parts of Africa, the same concerns develop. Peoples don't seem to be good at sharing land, even when there's a lot of it to share. Where land is in dispute massacres are just waiting to happen—it's only a question of time, and usually not much time at that.

The Marias River Massacre, January 23, 1870

The massacre of Piegan Blackfeet in their winter camp on the Marias River, in what is now Montana, in January of 1870 is unique among the massacres considered in this book.

Why? Because this large band of Blackfeet were dying anyway: of smallpox, at the rate of six or seven per day.

It is not likely that Colonel E. M. Baker, who lead the assault on the Blackfeet camp, knew that the tribe was infected when he set out to eliminate them as a raiding force, but he found out soon enough and went right on with the killing; at the end of the day the army claimed to have killed 173 Indians, a big total.

What was odd about it—apart from the circumstance that the army chose to kill Indians who were dying already—is that the army claimed to have killed 120 warriors, a proportion of warriors to women and children not seen in any other massacre. J. P. Dunn throws up many statistics in order to suggest that the army's count couldn't have been right. There were *always,* in his view, more women and and children to be found in a camp than men.

Well, if they don't have smallpox, maybe. The 120 warriors might well have been in camp because they were too sick to be anywhere else.

But if they were that sick, why bother to kill them?

Because they were Blackfeet—probably the most feared of all Western tribes—that's why.

When Captains Meriwether Lewis and William Clark made their great trek across America and back in 1804–1806 they encountered many Indians, some of them ill-disposed toward the Corps of Discovery; but they got all the way to the Western Ocean without killing a single native, a high tribute to the care they took to get on with the local tribes.

On the return journey they were not quite so lucky. While Captain Lewis and some of the Corps were exploring the Marias River country, not too far from where the 1870 massacre would occur, they traveled for a while with some Piegan Blackfeet, although the Piegans were well known to be brazen thieves.

Sure enough, one morning, a Piegan boldly seized a rifle and attempted to make off with it. The attempt didn't work and, in the struggle over the gun, the Piegan was stabbed to death. Another Piegan fired at Captain Lewis, who shot back, wounding him. Whether he died is debated. The Corps proceeded home; there was no more trouble with Indians—the stabbed Piegan was the only sure kill on the whole amazing journey.

The Blackfeet country is in northwestern Montana and some of Idaho. No group of Indians was more determined to keep whites out of their lands. As early as 1731, when the great Canadian explorer La Verendrye tried to cross from what is now South Dakota to the Western Ocean it was most probably the Blackfeet who turned him back. Travel in the Blackfeet country, from the Yellowstone over to the Columbia, was just not safe.

Indeed, one of the famous episodes in the history of the American fur trade involved the militant Blackfeet. On their way back down the Missouri in 1806 the captains met two intrepid traders who were resolutely setting out to trap in the High West.

This intrigued young John Colter, a member of the Corps. He was given permission by the captains to go back upriver and try to keep his hair while he sought his fortune.

John Colter *did* keep his hair, but, upon encountering some Blackfeet, two of his companions were not so lucky. They were killed, but the Blackfeet must have been feeling sporting, because they gave Colter a chance. He was stripped naked and told to run. The Blackfeet allowed him a decent start and then set out in pursuit.

John Colter *could* run. With his life on the line he ran so hard that blood gushed out of his nose. Even so, one fast-running warrior was closing in on him, spear at the ready. Colter whirled suddenly, taking the warrior by surprise. He wrested the warrior's spear away and killed him with it.

Then he ran some more, finally eluding his captor pursuers by slipping into an icy pond and hiding under a beaver dam.

The annoyed Blackfeet finally gave up.

Naked, Colter walked out, through a land of geysers. The likelihood is that he discovered Yellowstone.

The Blackfeet were a handsome people. The first painters who managed to get upriver, to Fort Union or Fort McKenzie, loved to do their portraits and have left us some fine ones.

The painters were the American George Catlin and the Swiss Karl Bodmer. Some of the portraits they did on the upper Missouri between 1832 and 1834 are among the finest examples of Western art.

The relevance of all this to the massacre of the dying Piegans in 1870 is that the militancy of the Blackfeet was well known and widely respected. That particular part of Montana is thinly populated even today, in part because of Blackfeet resistance.

Thus when Colonel Baker arrived at the Blackfeet encampment that morning he killed the raiders he had come to kill. Many of them no doubt would have died, but Colonel Baker was not disposed to leave it to chance, his reasoning perhaps being that those who managed to recover would soon be able to be troublesome again.

When Blackfeet were involved, the U.S. Army would rather be safe than sorry. They had come to kill, and they killed.

Kiäsax, Piegan Blackfeet Man
Karl Bodmer (Swiss, 1809–1893)
Watercolor on paper

The Camp Grant Massacre, April 30, 1871

With the exception of the Sacramento River Massacre, Camp Grant seems to have been the least studied of these Western slaughters, though it is certainly remembered in Arizona by all the peoples involved: Apache, Mexican, Papago, and white. Sometimes it's called the Aravaipa Massacre, for the creek north of Tucson where it took place. What distinguishes it from the other killings is that in this case *all* the people killed—excepting one old man and a "well-grown" boy—were women and children. At the Marias River all the victims were sick; at Camp Grant they were either female or young.

The fighting men were not at home.

The Aravaipa band of western Apache were as much feared as the other, more militant, bands, such as those that had been led at various times by Cochise, Victorio, or Geronimo. Though the Aravaipa leader, Eskiminzin, was a capable raider, the Apaches who eventually settled near Camp Grant were largely semi-agricultural. The commander at Camp Grant at the time, Lieutenant Royal E. Whitman, allowed them to camp near the post but kept them under tight control, counting them every other day and attempting to keep track of their goings and comings. Urged by his superiors, he made some effort to get them to go to the White Mountain Reservation, but they didn't like the White Mountains and refused to go. Some of them became friendly with the local ranchers and helped them cut hay and do other chores.

When the number of these unreservationed Indians swelled to around five hundred, Lieutenant Whitman decided he had better seek counsel from his superiors as to whether he was allowed to grant such a number of Indians de facto asylum. At this juncture a little military surrealism enters the story: Lieutenant Whitman's request for instruction was returned unread because he had failed to summarize his message on the outside of the envelope, a nicety the military code seemed to require.

This rejection came in early March 1871. In recent months there had been a number of small-scale attacks well south of Tucson, a good distance from the Aravaipa but close enough to alarm the citizenry of Tucson—white, Mexican, and Papago—to take up arms. The Apache and the Papago were bitter enemies; likewise the Apache and the Mexican.

On the 28th of April Captain Penn at Fort Lowell sent Lieutenant Whitman a message saying that a large and mixed group of men were said to be heading north out of Tucson, in the direction of Camp Grant. The messenger bringing this news arrived at the camp in the early morning of April 30.

Lieutenant Whitman immediately sent some men to the Apache camp to urge the Apaches to come closer to the fort, but when the men reached the encampment they discovered that they were too late. The men from Tucson—six whites, forty-eight Mexicans, and ninety-four Papago—had already done the work they came to do. More than one hundred Apaches were dead—all had been killed with knives, hatchets, or clubs. The Papago, particularly, favored clubs.

A puzzlement to me, at least, is that the raiders could slip in and destroy a camp this size with no one at the nearby fort suspecting anything. Dunn says the fort was only half a mile from the camp—perhaps it was farther away; otherwise it seems strange that no one or no thing at the fort heard anything. Surely the horses would have been alarmed, or the dogs, or the sentries. Even though the raiders didn't use guns it seems odd that a hundred people could be put to death without breaking the early morning silence. Did no one scream, or no babies cry, or no dogs bark? Lieutenant Whitman had deliberately kept the Indians close so he could monitor their comings and goings.

Besides this, the camp was set afire—did no one smell the smoke and wonder what was going on with the Apaches?

Perhaps Dunn was wrong—the bulk of the Apache camp may have been farther away than he thought; otherwise it's hard to believe that such deadly work produced no outcry at all.

When, later in the day, a doctor was sent from Camp Grant to bring in the wounded, he found very few wounded to attend. The raiders with their knives and clubs had done a very thorough job—though they missed Eskiminzin, the man they wanted most. In fact, they missed all the men. A few women were able to take advantage of the half-darkness to flee; but those who didn't were treated with the usual severity.

Twenty-nine Apache children were taken in this raid; most were sold into slavery in Mexico, a source of great bitterness to the survivors. J. P. Dunn called this massacre "pure assassination," and the succinct President Grant called it "murder, purely."

Grant eventually sent an able investigator, Mr. Vincent Colyer, to Arizona with the legal power to bring the culprits to justice. Once again murder had outed, quickly in this case, but Mr. Colyer soon found the citizens of Tucson to be even more stridently defiant than the Mormons had been after Mountain Meadows or the citizens of Denver in regard to Sand Creek. The Arizona press was flamboyantly pro-massacre. The papers were so violently biased in favor of the killers that J. P. Dunn was moved to speak harshly about them.

But the uproar in the East was just as passionate, and did not subside. To the great outrage of the citizens of Tucson a trial was finally held and 148 raiders were indicted.

The legal proceedings, conducted in circumstances of high tension, were as farcical as the first trial of John Doyle Lee. The jury took only nineteen minutes to acquit the defendants, surely one of the shortest jury deliberations in the annals of jurisprudence.

But, at least, the light of the law had been shone on the massacre. The atrocities were aired in open court.

Practically speaking, this massacre, like Sand Creek, backfired, intensifying the combat between the Apaches and everyone else. Cochise, the Chiricahua leader who had been living peaceably, went back to his stronghold in the mountains. Fifteen more years of raiding and killing followed.

The Bureau of Indian Affairs, always several steps behind the action, attempted to stabilize the situation by shifting small groups of Indians from here to there, but these efforts mostly stirred the Indians up, rather than calming them down. The situation soon became so volatile that the army was forced to send one of its very best men, General George Crook, to sort things out.

By the time Crook arrived in Arizona the situation with the Apaches was beyond the power of any one administrator to fully correct, but Crook took his time, did his best, and effected some real improvements.

George Crook's career as an Indian fighter and administrator contradicts perhaps more clearly than any other J. P. Dunn's assertion that the Indians only respected merciless behavior. Crook was no softie, of course, but he did try to be fair, and the Indians recognized as much and respected him for it. Custer might have flair, but Crook was solid. His assistant John Gregory

Bourke's *On the Border with Crook* continues to be one of the most readable books about this period. Bourke would be the first to admit that Crook was not easy to work with; but his ability was never in doubt.

Unlike most military administrators, Crook took the time to try to understand the differences between the nine branches of the Apache people, from the Mescalero, far to the east between the Rio Grande and the Pecos, all the way west, to the Apaches who lived near the Gila. It was Crook who recognized the folly of cramming disparate and incompatible bands onto the same reservation. He made real progress. Even Geronimo, a particularly hard sell, developed some respect for General George Crook.

Unfortunately for peace in Arizona, Crook's skills and authority soon came to be in even more urgent demand elsewhere: that is, on the northern plains, where Red Cloud and his allies were still proving to be a little too strong for the U.S. Army to subdue. Crook was called north and given a sizable command, perhaps too sizable, because it slowed his power of maneuver. In the main he was less effective in the north than he had been in Arizona. His all-day battle on the Rosebud, a week before the Little Bighorn, was no army triumph; but for the bravery of his Crow and Shoshoni scouts it might have been a very bloody defeat.

In Arizona, absent Crook's calming hand, the situation failed to improve. The army and the Bureau of Indian Affairs muddled and then muddled some more. Eventually, well after his inconclusive pursuit of the victors at the Little Bighorn, Crook was sent a second time to the Apacheria, his main task being to catch Geronimo, though Geronimo was by no means his only problem. By 1882, when George Crook returned to the Southwest, many Apaches were off the reservation, doing as they pleased. Crook had to do some hard campaigning, in very inhospitable places;

but he did eventually get many of the Apache bands back on more or less suitable reservations.

At one point Crook almost reeled in Geronimo, but that slippery fellow developed second thoughts: he went out one last time. Crook had done most of the work, but it was General Nelson Miles who eventually took Geronimo's surrender.

It had been Miles, also, who accepted the famous surrender of Chief Joseph of the Nez Percé, in the Bearpaw Mountains, not far from Canada, to which the Indians were headed in their long and dramatic flight.

Miles would have dearly loved to take Crazy Horse's surrender too—that would have given him an enviable triple—but this was not to be.

It is nearly impossible to calculate, at this distance, how many deaths occurred in the Apacheria between the Camp Grant Massacre and Geronimo's surrender. Camp Grant turned out to be a particularly pointless massacre, in which the least threatening Indians in the region were killed. Like most massacres, it proved to be counterproductive. The outrage it spawned just led to more fights. Papago-Apache strife was not new—it had been going on ever since the two people had begun to inhabit the same country; and, likewise, the strife between Apaches and Mexicans. Old hatreds were involved—to some degree they still are.

As in Colorado, the influx of white people into arid southern Arizona was partly due to rich mining possibilities. The geologist Raphael Pumpelly, who came to Arizona because of the mines, has some excellent descriptions of white-Apache conflict in his travel book *Across America and Asia*.

According to Pumpelly, the Apaches found the Americans laughably bad as fighters. In the north the Sioux and Cheyenne held the same opinion. Some of Major Reno's men, at the Little Bighorn, were so obviously terrified that the Sioux and Cheyenne youth split their sides laughing as they chased them down. According to Pumpelly the western Apache found the white man's attempts at warfare so laughable that they let them live, so as to have a good laugh another day. Geronimo, who did not appear to have much of a sense of humor, probably would have killed them.

The issue of the twenty-nine children taken in the Camp Grant raid rankled for years. Once they were across the border, it was virtually impossible to recover stolen children.

Though much vilified in the Arizona press, which claimed that he debauched with native women, Lieutenant Whitman was a decent young officer who had done his best to help the local Apaches, whom he had come to like. Some of the ranchers in the area had begun to soften toward the Apaches too, employing them when they could. What was lost as a result of the massacre was the small, fragile measure of trust that the two peoples were beginning to develop for each other. This trust had only been possible because of Whitman, a calm, sensitive administrator.

In time a good many Apaches came to trust Crook, who fought them hard when he fought but who had never been an exterminationist. Once he had subdued a given group of Indians, he did his best to secure decent treatment for them.

The Aravaipa leader Eskiminzin lost two wives and five children at Camp Grant. He fled into the mountains and did not come back. He also may have taken revenge when an opportunity presented itself. J. P. Dunn, who liked statistics, reckoned that there were fifty-four attacks by Apaches on whites following Camp Grant, which is more or less what happened after Sand Creek.

When Crook returned to fix what could be fixed, Dunn had this to say about the difficulties he faced:

> It must be remembered that he had left to
> him a legacy of hatred of three centuries be-
> tween the people he had to pacify; that a large
> proportion of the white population were as
> barbarous in their modes of warfare as the
> Apaches themselves; that Arizona was still a
> refuge for the criminal and lawless men of
> other states; that war and pillage had been
> bred into the Apache, until they were the
> most savage and intractable Indians in the
> country; that large bands of their nation in-
> fested northern Mexico, and had almost im-
> penetrable strongholds there; that Mexico still
> pursued war in the old way and still paid
> bounty for Apache scalps, no matter where
> procured; that slaving still existed in Mexico,
> and it was next to impossible to recover Indi-
> ans once carried over the line.

All true. The president's man, Mr. Colyer, did a conscien-
tious job of trying to sort things out, but the local white power
structure was wholly hostile to him; for a long time the situation
remained unsatisfactory and unsettled. Apaches, like most people,
naturally have a strong preference for their own particular kind of
country, whether desert, mountain, or plain. Shuffling them
around from one poor reservation to another seldom improved
anybody's mood; and yet remnants of that system are evident in
Arizona today.

Red Cloud's old remark about the white man promising to
take their land and then taking it is everywhere evident in Arizona. As soon as a given bunch of Apaches, attempting to make

the best of a bad situation, began to adapt to one reservation, likely as not they would be shifted to another.

If the Apaches succeeded in making a given location cultivatable, then the whites would inevitably want it.

Neither General Crook nor his successor, Colonel Kautz, liked this way of doing things; but they were soldiers, not bureaucrats; and by this time management of Native American affairs came more and more to be the domain of bureaucrats. In the end the Indians always lost. What applied to Red Cloud, Spotted Tail, Sitting Bull, Quanah Parker, or Crazy Horse turned out to apply, as well, to Cochise, Victorio, Geronimo, and the rest.

In the Southwest this pattern has been established as far back as 1863, when some soldiers captured the Apache leader Mangus Coloradas, killed him, and cut off his head. That the struggle then continued for more than twenty years was mainly because Geronimo—the last of the desert Apache leaders—was far from easy to catch or kill.

In the end, though, as was to be the case from sea to shining sea, the whites had better equipment, and always prevailed.

The Broken Hoop: 1871–1890

The two decades between the Camp Grant Massacre in 1871 and the final carnage at Wounded Knee Creek at the very end of 1890, were years in which the Indians of the West, from southern Arizona and northern Texas all the way north to Canada and west from the Missouri River to the lava beds of northern California, where the Modocs mounted their final, futile resistance, slowly lost their freedom, their land, and their way of life.

Though there were brilliant victories—Fetterman, the Rosebud, the Little Bighorn—the contest was always unequal and its end inevitable.

The whites—the people with the better equipment—won. Most of the fighting Indians whose names have survived in popular memory—Captain Jack of the Modocs, Chief Joseph of the Nez Percé, Quanah Parker of the Comanches, Red Cloud and Crazy Horse of the Oglala Sioux, Sitting Bull of the Hunkpapa, Spotted Tail of the Brulé, Cochise and Geronimo of the Apaches, fought, died, or surrendered during this period.

Captain Jack was hanged in 1873.

Chief Joseph, after declaring that from where the sun stood then he would fight no more, forever spent the rest of his days in places he did not want to be.

Crazy Horse, the most inspired of all the Sioux warriors, was killed at Fort Robinson, Nebraska, a victim in the main of his own people's jealousy. Without quite realizing it, he had become too big a star.

Sitting Bull of the Hunkpapa took his people to Canada for a few years, but received no help and finally came back and surrendered. He was killed by native policemen on the Standing Rock Reservation while resisting arrest. His death occurred about two weeks before the massacre at Wounded Knee.

Quanah Parker of the Quahadi (Antelope) Comanche surrendered in 1875 and became an effective leader of his people during the painful years of transition from free life to reservation life.

Red Cloud, the Sioux's most able negotiator, lived until 1909 and died in his bed, a wise but not a happy man.

Spotted Tail, cautious leader of the Brule Sioux (and Crazy Horse's uncle) was also killed by one of his own people.

Geronimo, the Apache warrior who held out the longest, surrendered in 1886 and died at Fort Sill, Oklahoma, also in 1909.

Quanah Parker died in 1911, also at Fort Sill.

A number of distinguished military men had their careers defined by the efforts they made in the West to bring the Indian wars to a close.

The most famous of these of course was George Armstrong Custer, who died at the Little Bighorn, his great folly, with a smile on his face.

George Crook did honest service, both against the northern tribes and the desert Apache. He died in 1890, without having to witness the shame of Wounded Knee. His old adversary Red Cloud remarked, almost fondly, of Crook: "He never lied to us. His words gave the people hope."

One of the most able Indian fighters of all was Ranald Slidell Mackenzie. He fought far out on the Staked Plains, where few officers dared to go. In 1875 he broke the power of the Comanches and was sent north to help out with the northern tribes. On the day when he was supposed to be married, Ranald Slidell Mackenzie went permanently insane.

A fourth able leader was General Nelson Miles, who fought in Texas in the Red River War and then went north with Mackenzie. Miles chased both Sitting Bull and Crazy Horse with mixed success, but he survived and, as I said, took the surrender of both Chief Joseph and Geronimo—although, in both cases, he did little of the chasing.

The three chiefs who more or less mastered the diplomatic skills necessary to deal with the white officials and their bureaus were Red Cloud, Spotted Tail, and Quanah Parker; the latter was the half-white son of Cynthia Ann Parker, the most famous of the Comanche captives.

Sitting Bull, who hated the whites from first to last, was surly, impatient, and never a particularly good negotiator. The only white he unstintingly admired was Annie Oakley, his "little sure-shot." Sitting Bull also came to have some respect for Buffalo Bill Cody, in whose show he appeared for a season. Cody, the great showman, in one of his rare understatements, called Sitting Bull "peevish."

In fact the great Hunkpapa was a good deal more than peevish. Even at the very end of his life he still so frightened the whites that, when the Ghost Dancers began to dance and he refused to stop them, the authorities sent the Indian police and some cavalry as well to bring him in.

Though the time between the Camp Grant Massacre and Wounded Knee was almost twenty years, it only took about a half-dozen of those to essentially defeat the Plains Indians.

Geronimo was a special case, protected by a harsh but helpful environment.

The government made treaties and broke them constantly. Most of the Indians knew how little chance they had; they knew, if from nothing more than the rapid disappearance of the buffalo, that their way of life was gone. The gathering at the Little Bighorn was their greatest conclave, and their last. They wiped out the arrogant Long Hair and then just melted away, into the vast spaces of the West. With the possible exception of the Fort Laramie council in 1854 they had never gathered in such numbers and they never would again.

After Custer the whites made a great outcry for vengeance, but it was not easy to find Indians to wreak vengeance on. Buffalo Bill, by then a showman, rushed back west and took what he claimed was the first scalp for Custer, that of the Cheyenne warrior Hay-o-wei, or Yellow Hair. Whether or not Cody actually killed Hay-o-wei is not absolutely clear, but he *did* take the man's scalp, which he sent to his estranged wife as a trophy, hoping it would somehow mollify her. Understanding of the ways of the female heart was not one of Cody's strengths.

General Crook, the gray fox, with a huge contingent of some four thousand men, lumbered around the northern prairies for a while, finding no one to fight. General Miles chased Sitting Bull to Canada but had to let him go. In the dreadful winter of 1876–1877 Crook did hit a Cheyenne village, on a night so cold that eleven babies froze to death.

General Miles switched his attention to Crazy Horse and harassed him into the depths of the winter, but didn't catch him. In the spring Crazy Horse concluded that, for a time at least, the game was up. He came in, with nine hundred people and a lot of horses.

Not long after the army disarmed Crazy Horse, the Nez Percé roared out of Idaho into Montana and made for Canada, mopping up everyone who got in their way. The army, horrified by this unexpected outbreak, seems to have briefly concluded that Crazy Horse might be the only man who could stop them. Bizarrely, as it must have seemed to him, they offered to arm him again if he would go fight the Nez Percé. The offer must have confused him—if he understood it. Puzzled, perhaps, he may have said okay, he would go fight the fugitives until every last Nez Percé was killed. The interpreter at this council, Frank Grouard, who knew Crazy Horse and may have been jealous of him, apparently told the white officers that Crazy Horse had intended to fight until every last white man was dead. Some of the listeners who understood Sioux were horrified; they tried to persuade the officers that Crazy Horse hadn't said anything of the sort, but a dark doubt had been planted in the officers' minds, the fruit of which was the decision made by General Crook to arrest Crazy Horse at once and have him shipped to the Dry Tortugas, to the dreadful prison for incorrigibles.

As is well known, when an effort was made to arrest him, Crazy Horse resisted and was bayoneted by a white soldier, while Little Big Man—once his friend, now an Indian policeman—held his arms.

Crazy Horse died in 1877. The years between his death and 1890 were sad and unheroic times for the native peoples. As it was in Arizona, so it was in Wyoming, Nebraska, and the Dakotas. The government was constantly trying to position these defeated, demoralized people in places where they would do the least harm; this meant, in most cases, allocating them the worst land—even though what at first seemed the worst land soon enough turned out to be land that the whites thought they might just have a use for after all. Few places in the whole West turned out to be so bleak that the whites wouldn't eventually want it.

There was little happiness among these reservationed peoples. There were a few decent, honest Indian agents, but there were many more who were corrupt, interested only in greasing their own palms at their wards' expense. J. P. Dunn rightly excoriated this all too numerous breed.

Then, in the 1880s, out of the desert places, there arose a prophet, a messiah of sorts, who soon began to attract a following; he preached a message of Renewal and Return, to be achieved through a dance ritual that came to be known as the Ghost Dance, since one of its purposes was to have the dead rise up.

This prophet was a short, stocky Paiute named Wovoka—though when he lived with a white family, as he often did, he introduced himself as Jack Wilson. Wovoka, or Jack Wilson, lived into the 1930s—he may even have appeared in a silent movie.

The doctrine he preached—mildly, it should be said—the doctrine of a Return, common to many preachers of various faiths, nonetheless set the stage for the final conflict at Wounded Knee Creek.

Why it should have been thus is a complicated story.

Wounded Knee,
December 29, 1890

The anthropologist James Mooney, the author of what is still the classic monograph on the Ghost Dance, happened to be on the southern plains when the massacre at Wounded Knee occurred. Mooney was a pupil of John Wesley Powell at the newly formed Bureau of American Ethnology, one of Powell's personal fiefdoms.

James Mooney had come west specifically to investigate the ritual dance that caused the problem at Wounded Knee. When the first rumbles from the north occurred, he heard them. Mooney had chosen to begin his investigations into the origin and nature of the Ghost Dance in what is now Oklahoma, where he talked with Arapaho, Kiowa, Comanche, Apache, Caddo, Wichita, and other people, all of whom could be met with easily on the southern plains.

I doubt that Mooney was surprised to hear that the Sioux had taken up the Ghost Dance, though I doubt that he supposed such a spasm of violence would result.

When violence flared, James Mooney found himself drawn into an ambitious, multitribal study of the Ghost Dance, soon producing a study called *The Ghost Dance Religion and the Great Sioux Outbreak of 1890,* which appeared as Part II of the Fourteenth Annual Report of the Bureau of Ethnology.

Very fortunately, for students and historians, James Mooney happened to be in the right place at the right time, *and with the right training*—training enough, at least, to allow him to make some sense of what happened on the northern plains in the second half of 1890. In the course of a century or more, his work has often been criticized, but Mooney is still where one must start in attempting to understand how these troubles started, and why.

Mooney's analysis was more than an attempt to explain the government's catastrophic reaction to the Ghost Dance as practiced at the end of the 1880s by the Sioux. He wanted, first of all, to set the Ghost Dance in a universal context, for notions of a return to a time of happiness and plenty hardly just belonged to Wovoka. Many peoples dream of a return to a time when life was good rather than bad.

In the course of his study Mooney provides a fairly full account of millennial beliefs among native people in all parts of North America. He starts his survey with the preachings of a Delaware prophet in the 1760s, but other scholars have since gone further back. James Wilson, in *The Earth Shall Weep,* an excellent one-volume history of Native American life, claims that the Pamunkey leader Nemattanew was preaching a millennialism not unlike the Ghost Dance as early as 1618, by which date the more astute native leaders had already figured out that these pale-faces were a problem not likely to go away. Visions of Eden, as Mooney notes, are woven into the religion of many peoples.

My aim here is to describe how a massacre came to occur, not to write an essay in comparative religion. What is relevant is the power of the desire to return to happier times, a longed-for event often brought about through the appearance of a messiah. Tecumseh's brother, Handsome Lake, preached some such doctrine, and—nearer in time to Wounded Knee, so did the Apache prophet Noch-ay-del-klin, who lived near Cibecue Creek in

Arizona, where he was killed, along with a number of his follow-ers, by soldiers who thought his preachings were stirring up the natives they wanted to settle and subdue. Noch-ay-del-klin was only one of many preachers to get in trouble with the civil au-thorities. Mooney finds elements common to the Ghost Dance in a number of nineteenth-century faiths: Beckmanites, Jumpers, Shakers, Ranters, etc.

I find it broadly interesting that in the last quarter of the nineteenth century, natives in at least four parts of the world kicked out their white invaders in a final surge of native powers. All had intense dancing as a means of preparation; all felt that if they danced fer-vently enough they would become invulnerable to bullets. (This belief still surfaces occasionally.) The four groups were:

The Boxers in China.
The Mahdists in the Sudan.
The Zulus in South Africa.
The Sioux and other tribes in North America.

The Boxers were convinced of their invulnerability as they marched on the trapped legations; the Zulus believed it as they prepared their triumphant ambush at Islandwanda; the Mahdists believed it as they faced Kitchener's guns at Omdurman; and the Sioux believed in it in South Dakota—some wore Ghost Shirts that were to keep the bullets from finding them.

Though himself never a disciple of Wovoka—he was much too hardheaded (as was Geronimo)—it is worth remembering that just before the Battle of the Little Bighorn, Sitting Bull stared at the sun and danced until he fainted. When he was revived he at once reported a vision of soldiers falling upside down into camp;

and soon enough Custer and his men *did* fall into camp, after which the victorious warriors could sing "Long Hair [Custer] returns no more."

All these native victories were to be *last* victories; none of the four groups were ever to triumph on such a scale again. By the time Wounded Knee occurred—fourteen years after the Little Bighorn—the likelihood of the Sioux mounting any really serious resistance to the U.S. military was small indeed. But the soldiers and the Indian agents had not yet managed to rid themselves of *apprehension* should a given group of Indians stir at all: the old habit of always fearing attack had not yet died out.

Wovoka began to export his Ghost Dance principles to various delegations from tribes that wanted to know about it; but he was, after all, only one prophet, and he was exporting only his version of this hopeful creed. Other prophets, over in Oklahoma or down in Arizona, might be practicing variations, and these Wovoka saw no reason to oppose. Some of these he may never have known about, but he doesn't seem to have considered that he had the only answer.

What remains, for me, the biggest question is why this dancing scared the authorities, particularly the military authorities, so much. The Sioux were poor and weak—what could a little dancing hurt?

Wovoka wrote a number of messiah letters—Mooney reprints three, none in any way militant. The three differ only in syntax. Here is one in which Wovoka, signing himself Jack Wilson, speaks in his own name:

> When you get home make a dance to continue five days.
> Dance four successive nights. On the last night keep up

the dancing until the morning of the fifth day, when you must bathe in the river and disperse to your homes. You must all do in the same way.

I, Jack Wilson, love you all and my heart is full of gladness for the gifts you have brought me. When you get home I will give you a good cloud [rain] which will make you feel good. I give you a good spirit and give you all good paint. I will want you to come again in three months, some from each tribe there [Indian territory], there will be a good deal of snow and some rain. In the fall there will be such a rain as I have never given you before.

Grandfather [a universal title of reverence among Indians and here meaning the messiah] says when your friends die you must not cry. You must not hurt anybody or do harm to anyone. Do right always. It will give you satisfaction in life. The young man had a good father and mother [possibly he refers to Casper Edras, the young Arapaho who wrote down the message of Wovoka for these delegates].

Do not tell the white people about this. Jesus is now upon the earth. He appears like a cloud. The dead are all alive again. I do not know when they will be here, maybe in the fall or in the spring. When the time comes there will be no more sickness and everybody will be young again.

Do not refuse to work for the whites and do not make any trouble when you leave here. When the earth shakes [at the coming of the new year] do not be afraid. It will not hurt you.

I want you to dance every six weeks. Make a feast at the dance and have food that everyone may eat. Then bathe in the water—that is all. You will receive good words again from me sometime. Do not tell lies.

Jack Wilson

That would seem to be very mild preaching, and preaching, moreover, that contains a number of Christian elements. There are other Wovoka/Jack Wilson prophecies in which he speaks of a great flood that will drown all the whites and just leave Indians to people the earth—a rather Noah-like prophecy. Dee Brown, in *Bury My Heart at Wounded Knee,* quotes him as saying that Indians who don't dance will "grow little, just about a foot high, and stay that way." After all, Wovoka was a preacher and few preachers deliver the same sermon time after time, with no variation. In none of the sermons I've seen does Wovoka suggest that the Indians take up arms. He himself was very attached to the Wilson family and didn't seek trouble; he suggests that the whites will all be taken care of by the Great Spirit, after the Return.

Why did the instructions of this mild prophet, one who only asks for good behavior, make the whites in Dakota so deeply apprehensive?

At first, in fact, they *weren't* apprehensive. Two experienced agents, Valentine McGillycuddy and James McLaughlin, both told the military, at first, that the Sioux were behaving well: these expert opinions were simply overruled. General Miles also, at one point, thought the situation was well under control. But, despite this opinion, the army kept bringing in troops, which can have only alarmed the Sioux, who had shown no tendency to fight for about ten years. They were weak and poorly fed. Why did this doctrine out of the desert provoke such a terrible massacre?

A part of the answer, I think, was the government's fitful, inconsistent policy of moving Indians from one reservation to another at the least sign of trouble. In virtually every move the Indians lost a little—or a lot—more of the land they held so dear. In 1876–1877 they lost the Powder River country and the Black Hills—the latter their sacred place. As one result of Red Cloud's war the Black Hills had been granted to the Sioux people in per-

petuity in 1868; but very soon afterward General Custer discovered gold there. Perpetuity turned out to be a matter of some
four years.

The government debated endlessly and schemed and chis-
eled dishonestly time and again, as they came up with ever more
ingenious ways to get this suddenly valuable land away from the
Sioux. (In Oklahoma, a few decades later, much the same thing
went on when black gold—oil—was discovered in vast quantities
on Indian land.)

When waves of immigrants began to sweep into the Dakotas in the 1880s it became necessary once again to find land for
them, which usually meant whittling down what the Indians had
been allotted. This constant revision of land rights reached all the
way down to Indian territory, in what is now Oklahoma, where
the Five Civilized Tribes, having already been dispossessed of
their Eastern lands, soon found themselves being dispossessed a
second time of some of the good land they had traveled to along
the Trail of Tears.

In 1877 the northern Cheyenne under Little Wolf and Dull
Knife found that they could no longer endure the low, muggy
Oklahoma reservation they had been exiled to for whatever role
they played in the defeat of Custer. They announced their intention to return to their homeland in Montana, and they went,
making the epic march described by Mari Sandoz in *Cheyenne
Autumn,* a story later filmed by John Ford. Only half of them
made it back, still a remarkable effort, considering that most of
the soldiers in the West were chasing them. The Cheyenne version of this epic march was related to me by a tribal elder, Mrs.
Elk Shoulders, in Lame Deer, Montana, in the early 1980s, about
a century after the Cheyenne made their great march.

Throughout the 1880s particularly, the Indians were frequently pushed into lands they didn't like, onto reservations they

came to hate, in order that incoming white pioneers would have places to settle. In the Dakotas the Great Sioux Reservation at first extended to the 104th meridian; eventually the boundary was moved back to the 103rd.

All this occurred while the authorities were still trying to coax Sitting Bull back from Canada. The old man by this time was practiced in resistance, but finally he did come south, and was soon hired by Buffalo Bill to appear in his Wild West Show. Sitting Bull lasted only one season.

Of the Indian leaders still active at this time Sitting Bull was the one the white authorities feared most. He was able, and his dislike of whites—excepting only Annie Oakley and Buffalo Bill—was as evident as it had always been. (Another exception was the Brooklyn philanthropist Catherine Weldon, who seems to have fallen in love with Sitting Bull. At least she lived with him for a time. The nature of this union kept everyone wondering. Agent James McLaughlin, who was in charge of Sitting Bull, insisted that the relationship "wasn't criminal," but the historian Robert Utley has mentioned that there is evidence that suggests otherwise. Mrs. Weldon's young son died of lockjaw while she was ministering to the Sioux.)

Wounded Knee (II)

Once Sitting Bull established himself on the Standing Rock Reservation, the same agent, James McLaughlin, got along with him about as well as any white official could expect to. There had been a long, complicated debate about whether the Sioux should sell the now much coveted Black Hills. When asked to mediate, General Crook gave the Sioux some blunt advice: the Indians might as well take the money, because the whites were certainly going to take the Black Hills, holy or not.

As the fall of 1890 edged into winter on the northern plains, a general apprehension seemed to grow, both in Indians and whites. It is hard to say why. The Ghost Dance might have some kind of millennial implications, but it was just a dance held by some poor Indians—and Indians, like the whites themselves, had always danced. Despite these dances the Sioux were still a very subdued people. The two agents, McGillycuddy and McLaughlin, as well as General Miles, continued to insist that there was no cause for alarm, athough McLaughlin did allow as to how the dancing kept the Indians a little "stirred up," the very condition the military authorities found to be the most frightening. More troops were readied, to put down this nonexistent revolt.

Though apprehensive about the troops, the Ghost Dancers kept dancing. The Sioux Short Bull went into the Badlands, where he intended, in private, to dance as much as he pleased. Quite a few tribesmen decided to go with him.

When feeling even slightly nervous about conditions at Standing Rock, agent McLaughlin had a tendency to put the blame on Sitting Bull. In the fall of 1890 the increased presence of soldiers was naturally nervous-making for the Indians. The Indians got the sense that they were going to be punished yet again, though no one knew why and no one wanted to be punished. More and more Sioux adopted Short Bull's tactic and drifted off to the Badlands or the hills.

It took almost no movement on the part of the Sioux to frighten the settlers.

Agent McGillycuddy, who, as a doctor at Fort Robinson, had treated Crazy Horse's wife, was not a man easily panicked. Apropos the Ghost Dance, he made the reasonable point that even the Seventh-day Adventists put on strange robes and performed strange rituals in *their* wait for the coming of the Messiah. Why shouldn't the Sioux be granted the same license?

Agent McGillycuddy's reasonable opinion did not prevail. The army was alarmed, and so a plan was made to arrest the usual suspect, Sitting Bull. General Miles reasoned that if a bunch of white soldiers rode in to arrest Sitting Bull there would very likely be a violent protest, perhaps even a revolt. Miles's first notion was to summon Buffalo Bill Cody, whose show was then in Chicago, in hopes that Cody could coax Sitting Bull to join him for a special performance of some kind. If Sitting Bull agreed, then he could be arrested somewhere off the reservation and sent to a military prison.

It doesn't seem likely that Cody had been informed about this plan; after all, he employed more than one hundred Indians in his show. If he had assisted in the arrest of their most renowned chief it is doubtful that the Wild West Indians would

have approved. They might even have revolted themselves, perhaps killing a few of the cowboys and stagecoach drivers that
they routinely chased in the show.

Cody may have sensed, or found out, what the real plan
was. On his own he made his way to Standing Rock; but then
agent McGillycuddy objected to allowing Sitting Bull and
Cody—in his view two slippery characters—to get together.
Cody was told there could be no meeting, after all; in a huff the
great showman went away without ever seeing his old star.

Sitting Bull had last talked to Crook in 1889. Since then he had
been living quietly. McLaughlin knew that arresting him would
be tricky: it would require great care. He thought it might be accomplished through the use of Indian policemen, of which by
this time there were a goodly number. The young men of the
Sioux may have regarded their policeman jobs as status symbols.

When the day of the arrest came no fewer than forty native
policemen went to Standing Rock to arrest the old man. They
were under the command of a Lieutenant Bullhead. As an extra
precaution a detachment of cavalry went with them.

The native policemen arrived early, perhaps hoping to
whisk the prisoner out before the camp was really awake. Sitting
Bull himself was still asleep. Once awake, though grumpy, he finally agreed to go to the agency—it was not the first time he had
been so summoned. The arresting officers were Lieutenant Bullhead and Sergeant Red Tomahawk.

By the time Sitting Bull got dressed and stepped outside, a big
crowd of Ghost Dancers had gathered. Seeing that he had crowd
support, Sitting Bull suddenly balked. He appeared to change his
mind. The old show horse that Buffalo Bill had given him was
waiting, but Sitting Bull suddenly dug in his heels, forcing the policemen to push him toward his horse. Angered by this treatment of
their leader, a Sioux named Catch-the-Bear whipped out a rifle

Red Tomahawk

Bullhead

and shot Lieutenant Bullhead, who shot back, hitting Sitting Bull. Red Tomahawk also fired, hitting Sitting Bull in the head. Sitting Bull fell, dead. At this juncture fierce fighting broke out between the Ghost Dancers and the native policemen. The nearby cavalry, hearing sounds of battle, came rushing in and managed to save most of the native policemen, who otherwise would probably have been slaughtered to the last man.

The old show horse, some say, took the shooting as his cue and went through his repertoire of tricks while the battle raged.

Dee Brown and others have argued that it was only the power of belief in the Ghost Dance, with its promise of a Return, that kept a general revolt from flaring up. Some Sioux may have hesitated on that score, but, with Sitting Bull dead right before their eyes, many merely felt leaderless and fearful. Sioux by the hundreds soon fled the Standing Rock Reservation and made their way to the camp of the strongest surviving chief, in this case Red Cloud, who was at the Pine Ridge Agency.

Other frightened Sioux fled to the Badlands, where Short Bull still was. Others went to the mountains. Still others flocked to the other Ghost Dance sites.

Not many seemed to want to stay in the place where Sitting Bull had been killed, a place where worse might follow.

Perhaps as many as one hundred Standing Rock Sioux made their way to the camp of Big Foot, a well-respected Minniconjou chief.

Big Foot was then camped east of Pine Ridge, near Cherry Creek.

Wounded Knee (III)

Two days after Sitting Bull's death, the army issued a warrant for the arrest of Big Foot himself. The old chief had done nothing hostile at all; he was merely on the arrest list, with many others, as a possible fomenter of trouble. In the eyes of the military he was an enemy combatant, much like the unfortunate Afghans who are being held in Cuba today.

What made this arrest order particularly inconvenient was that Big Foot was seriously ill. He had pneumonia, and was hardly able to stand, yet he was traveling in an open wagon, in wintertime. He was spitting blood; his shirt was stained with it.

On December 28 he saw some cavalry approaching and immediately ran up a white flag. The commanding officer of this troop, Major Samuel Whiteside, insisted that Big Foot and his band come with him to the large cavalry encampment on Wounded Knee Creek. The major wanted to disarm the Indians then and there, but a half-breed scout named John Shangneau persuaded him to wait until the Indians were safely in camp.

Once in the camp the Indians were carefully counted: 120 men and 230 women and children. Major Whiteside had by this time realized that Big Foot was seriously ill; he had a heated tent prepared for him and sent an army doctor to attend him.

Sometime after dark more soldiers arrived. Colonel James

Forsyth took over the command, with orders to take Big Foot and his followers to a military camp near Omaha, a goodly distance from Wounded Knee Creek.

By morning Big Foot was very sick indeed; he was barely able to breathe. His people, now entirely surrounded by soldiers, were naturally very fearful.

The next morning Colonel Forsyth ordered all the Sioux to assemble, so the process of disarming them could begin. Though not happy with his order, the Sioux began, rather tentatively, to comply.

(From this point on, it is only fair to say, there are many versions of what happened, all made by participants.)

The army, with its propensity for taking things too far, too fast, began to search the tents and the baggage in them, confiscating knives and hatchets as they went. Not many rifles were surrendered, and most of the ones handed over were defective in varying degrees. One of the few good rifles belonged to a Sioux named Black Coyote (or Fox), who brandished his gun above his head and informed the crowd that he had paid good money for it, an indication of his reluctance to part with it.

In the opinion of a witness named Dewey Brand, Black Coyote did intend to turn in his gun and was just having a little fun, but opinions as to Black Coyote's intentions are numerous. One Sioux thought Black Coyote to be a man of bad character. The soldiers were hustling Black Coyote away when his rifle evidently went off—perhaps an accident. Some think no one was hurt, others think an officer was either killed or wounded.

Whatever the truth of that, the well-primed soldiers—most of them members of the 7th Cavalry—began to fire indiscriminately into the mass of Indians. Big Foot, the sick chief, was killed by the first volley. The Sioux then began to fight with what little they had to fight with—knives, clubs, etc. Some of the soldiers who had been carrying out the disarming fell in hand-to-hand fighting.

Next, a Hotchkiss gun opened fire. This fire would seem to be as dangerous to the soldiers as to the Indians on the flats and, indeed, some of the soldiers were in danger from friendly fire. The marker at Wounded Knee says that 146 Indians were killed: the death toll for soldiers is usually thought to be between twenty-five and thirty-one. The Indians began to flee—many were cut down. A blizzard was on the way. When the firing finally stopped most of the wounded Indians were gathered up and taken to the Pine Ridge Agency, where they were housed in the mission.

James Mooney believes that when the sun rose that morning neither the soldiers nor the Indians were expecting trouble. This seems hard to believe. The Sioux were surrounded by soldiers. A machine gun was trained on the camp.

There were more than one hundred warriors with Big Foot. Mooney says a Ghost Dancer named Yellow Bird blew on an eagle-bone whistle and may have danced a few steps. In Mooney's account the Sioux at first relinquished only two rifles, prompting the provocative search of tents and baggage. Mooney thinks Yellow Bird may have told the Sioux that if they were wearing their Ghost Shirts the bullets would not find them. Mooney isn't sure what may have gone on between Yellow Bird and Black Coyote. No one is sure whether the latter fired accidentally or on purpose, or whether he wounded an officer or what.

Once the soldiers began to fire into the crowd, a frenzy developed that was not much different from the killing frenzies at the other massacres. Fear, nervousness, blind rage all contributed to a force that was soon unstoppable. The Sioux either fought or fled, and were hunted down in either case. Some got as far as two miles from the point of eruption before they fell. Mooney thinks Yellow Bird may have egged Black Coyote on, but did he? The point, if there is one, is that in situations of high tension it takes only one vague, perhaps accidental, action to start a violent spasm of killing.

All the ingredients for catastrophe were there: the armed and jittery soldiers, a group of frightened, nervous, much harassed Indians. Perhaps Black Coyote meant to fire his gun, but then perhaps not. He was being shoved around—the shot *might* have been accidental.

At the other massacres—Sacramento River, Mountain Meadows, Sand Creek, Marias River, Camp Grant—massacre was the whole point of the engagement. But at Wounded Knee it seems that it really could have gone differently. A peaceful surrender might have been carried out. But a gun went off, and then many guns went off in response, and, before long, dead human beings littered the plain.

As with Sand Creek and Camp Grant, the ferocious violence at Wounded Knee bred violence elsewhere; for a short time there *was* a revolt among the Sioux, a great many of which were camped near Pine Ridge. Some immediately went into fighting mode; there were a number of ambushes and small attacks. Colonel Forsyth and his troops came under strong assault and might have fared badly had not reinforcements arrived. For some three days after Wounded Knee confusion reigned—confusion mixed with terror. There was plenty of trouble in the south, and yet, at the same time, Indians who had not yet heard of Wounded Knee were trickling into Pine Ridge.

On New Year's Day 1891, a party of soldiers was sent to the battlefield, charged with burying the dead and bringing in such wounded as had survived the battle and the subsequent blizzard. Mostly the soldiers found dead bodies, and yet four babies were found alive, and also a woman named Blue Whirlwind and her children. The dead bodies were stripped and thrown into an open pit. "It was a thing to melt the heart of a man, if turned to stone . . . to see those little bodies shot to pieces," one witness reported.

A little girl was found wearing a cap with a beadwork American flag on it. She lived.

A cowboy named Henry Miller seems to have been killed in the first battle. Why he was there in the first place is not stated.

For Red Cloud it was a particularly anxious time—he was afraid his own hotheads might go out, undoing all he had accomplished in his years of diplomacy.

A Negro private, W. H. Prather, of the 9th Cavalry, wrote a lengthy poem about the battle:

> The redskins left their agency, the soldiers left
> their post
> All on the strength of an Indian tale about
> Messiah's ghost
> Got up by savage chieftains to lead their tribes
> astray,
> But Uncle Sam wouldn't have it, for he ain't
> built that way.

Private Prather was only outdone in eloquence by Black Elk, the Oglala sage:

> I did not know then how much was ended.
> When I look back now from the high hill of
> my age I can still see the butchered women
> and children lying heaped and scattered along
> the crooked gulch as plain as when I saw
> them with eyes still young. And can see that
> something else died there in the bloody mud
> and was buried in the blizzard.
> A people's dream died there. It was a

Black Elk

beautiful dream . . . the nation's hoop is broken. There is no center anymore and the sacred tree is dead.

James Mooney's book contains pictures of the children
who survived: Marguarite Zitkala-noni, Jennie Sword, Herbert
Zitkalazi, and the children of Blue Whirlwind. Captain Colby
of the Nebraska State Militia adopted one little girl; Lost Bird,
she was called. George Sword, the captain of the Indian police,
adopted another little girl, who was called Jennie Sword. One
boy, Herbert Zitkalazi, was adopted by Lucy Arnold, a teacher
at the agency. Herbert was the son of the medicine man Yellow
Bird, he of the eagle-bone whistle.

★ ★ ★

Confusing claims circulated and still do. The many descendants of the dead tell the stories they heard, and the stories differ.

Spotted Horse claims that Black Coyote did fire the first shot and that it killed an officer. Others insist that the shot missed.

American Horse, who had been at the Fetterman massacre and even claimed to have cut Fetterman's throat, said that he had seen a mother shot down while nursing a baby. "And that especially was a sad sight," said American Horse.

The influential leader Young Man Afraid of His Horses—which means the *enemy* was afraid of his horses—had been away at the time of the massacre; when he returned he used his considerable influence to quiet things down. He did his best to stop the raiding and skirmishing and, to a degree, succeeded. General Miles, in his turn, made conciliatory sounds; slowly things returned to normal, if anything about reservation life can be said to be normal.

By the middle of January 1891, the Wounded Knee uprising was over. Many Sioux later claimed that it was men of the 7th Cavalary—Custer's old troop—who started the ferocious firing. They thought the attack was revenge for Custer, who had been defeated and killed fifteen years earlier; many of the descendants of the massacred, as reported in William Coleman's *Voices of Wounded Knee,* certainly believed the 7th was out for revenge that day.

If so, the 7th in this case probably exceeded their mandate. Miles and the other military men could hardly have wanted a massacre—they were well aware that there were thousands of Sioux near Pine Ridge who might go out again and have to be expensively rounded up and subdued.

Meanwhile the power of apprehension did its work. The citizens of communities far away in Nebraska and Iowa fled from what they feared would be the return of terror. Some of these communities were at least 150 miles from the nearest Indian. Mooney considered these panics to be entirely ridiculous.

Not long after the Wounded Knee outbreak a man named Albert Hopkins, who wore a blanket and claimed to be the Messiah, appeared at Pine Ridge. He claimed the Indians were expecting his arrival, that he acted under what he called "the Pansy Banner of Peace." Besides being the Messiah he was also president of the Pansy Society of America. Red Cloud ridiculed him and had him put off the reservation, but he later surfaced in Washington. He said the Indians would all be waiting for his appearance in the spring, but then he vanished and was heard from no more.

The Waning Moon

———

Though the big historical marker at Wounded Knee claims that the Ghost Dance ended there, in fact it didn't. It was taken up by the Cheyenne, the Arapaho, and other tribes then living in Oklahoma. A second Sitting Bull appeared, this one an Arapaho. A Ghost Dance was held by the Canadian River, near the present-day town of Darlington, Oklahoma: a thousand or more Indians were said to have danced. The Arapaho Sitting Bull instructed all comers: Caddos, Wichitas, and other southern tribes. The local whites were alarmed at first, but the soldiers who came in contact with *this* Sitting Bull found him to be likable and free of humbug—free also of threat.

The dances continued under various leaders—many delegations traveled west to visit Wovoka and receive his instruction—but, in time, most of the tribes who practiced the Ghost Dance lost faith in it. This is not surprising, since none of the things predicted ever came to pass. No new earth formed, no flood swept away the whites. The Paiutes, who had the easiest access to Wovoka, kept dancing longest. There may have been isolated Ghost Dances in northern Arizona as late as 1912; but the failure of the dance to achieve the desired results caused it to be abandoned by most Indians.

★ ★ ★

Why the Ghost Dance frightened the white authorities so much is still puzzling, and yet it clearly scared them. The fact that Sitting Bull—the Sioux—was doing nothing remotely aggressive didn't save him from death. He failed to stop the Ghost Dance at the whites' request, which he rightly judged to be hypocritical. The whites had *their* dances: why shouldn't Indians have the same right?

Perhaps some whites feared the Ghost Dance because subconsciously they thought it might actually work, at least to the extent of reawakening the warrior instinct in the Sioux. This did happen, but only briefly; wiser heads, such as Young Man Afraid of His Horses, were quick to soothe the situation and prevent more killing.

Long before 1890 the Sioux leaders were well aware that they stood no chance in a shooting war with the American army. Their great victories were a decade and a half behind them. Red Cloud in the north and Quanah Parker in the south did everything they could to ease the difficulties their people felt during this time of transition. Scattered acts of renegadism did occur, but nothing large-scale was ever attempted again.

For a time, though, almost any gathering of Indians, of any size, continued to awaken old fears. When the northern Cheyenne broke out in 1877 the whole of the population of the Great Plains went into a panic. The old apprehension was waiting there in the yeast of pioneer memory; it easily swelled up. In situations such as occurred at Wounded Knee, one shot, accidental or not, was enough to set off one more unnecessary slaughter.

The Great Plains of the American West is a huge space, and yet there proved to be not enough room in it for two races, two ideas of community identity to coexist. Both races, it seemed, needed all the land there in order to survive in their traditional ways. Wounded Knee was a final spasm in the long agony of dispossession.

Black Elk said that he didn't realize at first how much had been lost on that snowy battlefield. In fact, by the time of Wounded Knee, a whole continent had been lost to the native peoples. A process begun in the seventeenth century on the shores of Virginia and Massachusetts got finished on that bleak plain in South Dakota at the ending of the year.

Wounded Knee was not the last conflict between the white government and the native people, but after Wounded Knee the scale changed, and also the methods of dispossession. The latter, since then, has mainly been accomplished through the Congress and the law courts. Chiseling turned out to work as well as shooting. The Five Civilized Tribes in Oklahoma suffered a second dispossession when they were made American citizens—merely a clever ruse to end their system of communal ownership of land. They ceased to be sovereign nations—as brand-new American citizens they were easily cheated.

The white man's appetite for land and profit never slackened: the Indians repeatedly found themselves left with the short end of the stick. Within the last year revelations of large-scale misuse of Indian trust funds have come to light, an indication that this pattern hasn't changed. Large gatherings of Indians are still viewed with suspicion by police, even when Indians are the police. The general attitude seems to be that it cannot be good for too many Indians to assemble, even if they are only getting together for celebration and meditation.

Despite all these losses the native tribes of America still exhibit a good deal of resilience. Some have prospered running casinos—others have managed significant wins in court.

Just over the hill from the Wounded Knee battlefield is Wounded Knee village, a rather cheerful, somewhat suburban community. Someone has taken the trouble to line the highway with vividly painted Drive-Slow signs, urging drivers to remember that there are children at play. The signs insist on responsible driving, and this in a place where most people don't like to drive slow. Wounded Knee, the battlefield, is, like most of the other massacre sites, a somber place; but you only have to go over the hill a few hundred yards to realize that the Sioux are still here and still lively.

History, both ancient and modern, reminds us that the impulse to turn whole groups of people into meat shops is not likely to be extinguished. Wounded Knee may have been an impulsive massacre, but the others I have considered were not. What happened in Rwanda was not impulsive, either: nor was Saddam's gassing of the Kurds.

Long ago, when I was a young cowboy, I witnessed a herd reaction in a real herd—about one hundred cattle that some cowboys and I were moving from one pasture to another along a small asphalt farm-to-market road. It was mid-afternoon in mid-summer. Men, horses, and cattle were all drowsy, the herd just barely plodding along, until one cow happened to drag her hoof on the rough asphalt, making a loud rasping sound. In an instant that sleepy herd was in full flight, and our horses too. A single sound on a summer afternoon produced a short but violent stampede. The cattle and horses ran full-out for perhaps one hundred yards. It was the only stampede I was ever in, and a dragging hoof caused it.

So it may have been at Wounded Knee. But for Black Coyote's perhaps unintentional shot the old sick chief and his people might merely have grumbled a bit about the disarming and then trundled harmlessly off to Nebraska. But when that shot sounded, the soldiers on the ridge went off like my cows, and, once more, slaughter was unleashed.

★ ★ ★

A final point about these homely little massacres and the even more terrible ones that keep occurring throughout the world: women and children are almost never exempted. A small anthology could be assembled just of quotations about the desirability of killing the women and children while one is killing undesirables. There one would find John Chivington's "nits breed lice" remarks, and General Sherman's famous grim one-liner.

A star item certainly would be Heinrich Himmler's famous speech delivered in Posen in October of 1943, in which he informed the Nazi hierarchy of the program to exterminate the Jewish people; Himmler himself raises the question of women and children and concludes, after only the briefest pause, that they had better be killed too.

And they were.

This is an old conclusion, many times restated by those inclined to massacre. The earliest statement I have been able to find comes from the prophet Ezekiel, who wrote about 600 B.C.:

> Go yet after him through the city and smite:
> let not your eye spare, neither have ye pity:
> slaughter old and young, both maids and little
> children.
>
> Ezekiel 9:5–6

Time and time across history, Ezekiel's advice has been followed to the letter. The making of meat shops seemingly has no end.

Bibliographical Note

The literature on the massacres of the American West is not really vast, though it certainly might swell in size if one included all the memoirs in which one or another of the massacres is mentioned. This would include the often homespun recollections of pioneers, travelers, soldiers, administrators, local historians, newspapermen, (and women), miners, ministers, railroad men, cowboys, and the like.

Virtually any of the memoirs might contain a line or two that throws new light on some aspect of some massacre: perhaps only a memory, probably inaccurate, passed down to them from parent or grandparent.

The genius of Evan Connell's great book on Custer, *Son of the Morning Star,* is that he mined just such memoir literature brilliantly, constructing around Custer's defeat a kind of mosaic of local memory, white, Native American, military, journalistic, and so forth. William Coleman, in *Voices of Wounded Knee,* has done something of the same thing for that encounter.

There is nothing so comprehensive about any of the other massacres in this book. The one study that attempted comprehensiveness, J. P. Dunn's *Massacres of the Mountains,* was published too soon to include Wounded Knee.

The most solid facts about any of these massacres are the

dates on which they occurred. All other statements need to be regarded with caution. Will Bagley cheerfully restates this principle in *Blood of the Prophets,* his recent book about Mountain Meadows. The principal fact, in each case, is that a lot of people turned up dead.

How many exactly, and why, is, in almost every case, still disputed.

These are the books I've worked from:

Backus, Anna Jean. *Mountain Meadows Witness: The Life and Times of Bishop Philip Klingensmith.* Arthur H. Clark, 1996.

Bagley, Will. *Blood of the Prophets: Brigham Young and the Massacre at Mountain Meadows.* University of Oklahoma Press, 2002.

Brooks, Juanita. *The Mountain Meadows Massacre.* University of Oklahoma Press, 1962. The classic account.

Brown, Dee. *Bury My Heart at Wounded Knee.* Holt, Rinehart & Winston, 1970.

Coleman, William. *Voices of Wounded Knee.* University of Nebraska Press, 2000.

Connell, Evan S. *Son of the Morning Star.* Promontory Press, 1993. The illustrated edition.

Cutler, Bruce. *The Massacre at Sand Creek.* University of Oklahoma Press, 1995.

Denton, Sally. *American Massacre: The Tragedy at Mountain Meadows, September 1857.* Knopf, 2003.

Dunn, J. P. *Massacres of the Mountains.* Archer House, 1965.

Hoig, Stan. *The Sand Creek Massacre.* University of Oklahoma Press, 1961.

Jackson, Helen Hunt. *A Century of Dishonor.* Boston, 1881.

Lamar, Howard (ed). *The New Yale Encyclopedia of the American West.* Yale University Press, 1998.

Mendoza, Patrick. *Song of Sorrow: Massacre at Sand Creek.* Willow Wind, 1993.

Mooney, James. *The Ghost-Dance Religion and the Sioux Outbreak of 1890.* Bureau of American Ethnology, Fourteenth Annual Report, Part II, Washington D.C., 1896.

Roberts, David. *A Newer World: Kit Carson, John Charles Frémont, and the Claiming of the American West.* Simon & Schuster, 2000.

Schellie, Don. *Vast Domain of Blood.* Westernlore, 1968.

Scott, Bob. *Blood at Sand Creek.* Caxton, 1994.

Wilson, James. *The Earth Shall Weep.* Atlantic Monthly Press, 1999.

Wise, William. *Massacre at Mountain Meadows: An American Legend and a Monumental Crime.* Crowell, 1976.

Index

Page numbers in *italics* refer to illustrations.

Photo Credits

The author gratefully acknowledges permission from the following sources to reproduce pictures in their control.

54   Black Kettle: Colorado Historical Society, Neg # F4911.

55   Group Portrait with Black Kettle & Bull Bear: Colorado Historical Society, Neg # F3469.

57   Quanah Parker (top) and Red Cloud (bottom): both Corbis.

58   General Custer: Culver Pictures.

61   Josefa Carson: Taos Historic Museums.

64   Juanita Brooks: Utah State Historical Society, all rights reserved.

67   Parley Pratt: Utah State Historical Society, all rights reserved.

83   Kanosh: Utah State Historical Society, all rights reserved.

92   William Bent: Colorado Historical Society, Neg # F2.

96   Little Crow: Hulton/Archive/Getty Images.

100   Bull Bear: Colorado Historical Society, Neg # F2772.

101   Silas Soule: Denver Public Library, Western History Collection, X-22202.

102   General William Tecumseh Sherman: Culver Pictures.

103   Jim Beckwourth: Culver Pictures.

118   Kiäsax: Joslyn Art Museum, Omaha, Nebraska, Gift of the Enron Art Foundation, 1986, (JAM1986.49.395).

146   Red Tomahawk (top): Denver Public Library, Western History Collection, Photo by Frank Bennett Fiske, X-31690. Bullhead (bottom): Denver Public Library, Western History Collection, Photo by D. F. Barry, B-511.

154   Black Elk: Denver Public Library, Western History Collection, Photo by Joseph G. Masters, X-33351.